Markus Krah
American Jewry and the Re-Invention of the East European Jewish Past

New Perspectives on Modern Jewish History

Edited by Cornelia Wilhelm

Volume 9

Markus Krah

American Jewry and the Re-Invention of the East European Jewish Past

—

ISBN 978-3-11-065584-1
e-ISBN (PDF) 978-3-11-049943-8
e-ISBN (EPUB) 978-3-11-049714-4

Library of Congress Cataloging-in-Publication Data
A CIP catalog record for this book has been applied for at the Library of Congress.

Bibliographic information published by the Deutsche Nationalbibliothek
The Deutsche Nationalbibliothek lists this publication in the Deutsche Nationalbibliografie;
detailed bibliographic data are available on the Internet at http://dnb.dnb.de.

© 2019 Walter de Gruyter GmbH, Berlin/Boston
This volume is text- and page-identical with the hardback published in 2018.
Typesetting: Integra Software Services Pvt. Ltd.
Printing and binding: CPI books GmbH, Leck
Cover illustration: Hasidic Jews in a shtetl near Stanislawow (Poland), ca. 1928, photograph by
Marian Jerzy Sitarski (Courtesy of United States Holocaust Memorial Museum, photograph #07087).

♾ Printed on acid-free paper
Printed in Germany

www.degruyter.com

Contents

Illustrations —— VIII
Acknowledgments —— XI

        Introduction —— 1
           Obsessively Engaged: Postwar American Jewry and the East European Past —— 3
           A Community Coming of Age – by Trying on a Usable Past —— 5
           Jews in Postwar America: a Not-So-Golden Era? —— 7
           State of the Field —— 10
           From Yiddish to English: a Multiplicity of Sources —— 12
           Methodology and Discipline: Discourse Analysis and Cultural History —— 14
           Chapter Overview —— 16
           Larger Patterns: Memory in American and Jewish Contexts —— 18

1   The Search for New Modes of Jewishness in Postwar America —— 21
           Interwar Years: *Yiddishkayt* in the Urban Ghetto – Doomed to Decline —— 22
           Mourning the World of East European Jewry – Claiming American Legitimacy —— 25
           American Crisis and Jewish Inclusion —— 30
           Suburbia as Uncharted Territory – Synagogues Marking Jewishness —— 34
           Jewishness Redux – the Wounded Jewish Soul and the East European Medicine —— 42

2   Launching a Discourse: YIVO's Bridge From the Old World to the New —— 47
           Weinreich Puts Adolescent American Jewry on Freud's Couch —— 53
           YIVO: Research Institute, Myth, or Instrument of Self-Expression? —— 60
           Forging an American Jewishness – on Yiddish Terms —— 65

3   New (York) Jewish Intellectuals: The Past as Culture —— 71
           New York Jewish Intellectuals: Refashioning Their Jewishness Out of the Past —— 75
           Bridging the Gap Between the Intellectuals and the Community —— 80

Dialectics of Jewish Pastness and American Presentness —— 86
Accepting Ambivalence – Vis-à-Vis Eastern Europe
and America —— 89
Translating the East European Past for the American Jewish
Present —— 93

4 Religious Culture as an Antidote to Liberal Judaism and Secular Jewishness —— 96
Judaism: Eastern Europe as a Resource for a Broader Concept
of Judaism —— 97
Heschel's Apotheosis of Ashkenazic Jewish Life —— 103
Soloveitchik: Bringing "Halakhic Man" from Lithuania
to America —— 110

5 Spiritual Needs, the Past, and the Denominational Landscape —— 119
Reform: Taking a New Look at a Distant Past —— 119
Conservative Judaism: East European Jewishness as *ersatz
Yiddishkayt* —— 126
Orthodoxy: Silencing, Historicizing, Idolizing the Recent East
European Past —— 132
Renewing American Judaism on Religious Terms Found
in the Past —— 143

6 From East European Radicalism to Postwar American Progressivism —— 144
Journalistic Infighting Over Communism and Jewishness —— 147
American Jews: Mindlessly Assimilating, or Forming a New Spiritual
Center? —— 151
East European Folk Culture as Part of Jewish Leftists' Political
Project —— 154
Memory as Content, From a Means to an End —— 158
Preserving the Heritage – Sacred Duty in the Service
of Continuity —— 163

7 Presenting a Rich Jewish Culture: *The Eternal Light* and *Life Is with People* —— 167
The Eternal Light: East European Spiritual Jewishness Made
Audible —— 169
Aestheticizing Judaism – On a "High Church" Note —— 176

Life Is with People: Ethnography Presents a Rich East European Jewish Culture —— 179

"Sex, Taboo, and Superstition:" Attracting American Jewish Interest in the *Shtetl* —— 184

8   Making Jewishness Meaningful: In School and in Hasidism —— 189

Textbook Cases: Spiritual Culture as a Source of Fortitude in the Face of Persecution —— 194

Hasidism: Everyone's Third Way —— 200

Hasidic Wholeness, Antinomianism, Ethical Judaism, and Proto-Socialism —— 205

9   Tevye in Kasrilevke, the *Fiddler* in America: East European Jewishness in Literature —— 212

Maurice Samuel Applies Sholem Aleichem to America —— 212

Affirmation or Alienation: The Jewishness of Cultural Translators —— 217

Isaac Rosenfeld: From Alienation to the Affirmation of a Cultural Jewishness —— 219

A Sacred Treasure: Anthologizing East European *Yiddishkayt* for American Jews —— 224

The Postwar *Shtetl:* Re-Invention of "the Greatest Invention of Yiddish Literature" —— 227

Isaac Bashevis Singer and the Subversive Spirituality of East European Judaism —— 230

Final Curtain: *Fiddler on the Roof* —— 234

10   Conclusion: Re-Inventing Jewishness Out of Memory —— 241

A New Idea Out of Many Failing Ones —— 246

Community of Memory —— 249

Re-Inventing the Past to Re-Invent Jewish Ethnicity —— 254

Epilogue —— 258

Bibliography —— 261
Index —— 285

Illustrations

Fig. 1 Front page Yiddish *Forverts*, March 20, 1940

Fig. 2 Hasidic Jews in a *shtetl* near Stanislawow (Poland), ca. 1928 (Photograph by Marian Jerzy Sitarski. Courtesy of United States Holocaust Memorial Museum, photograph #07087)

Fig. 3 Rosh Hashanah service at military Camp Blanding, St. Augustine, FL, 1945 (Courtesy of The Jacob Rader Marcus Center of the American Jewish Archives, Cincinnati, Ohio at americanjewisharchives.org)

Fig. 4 Scholars at 1947 Conference on Science, Philosophy, and Religion, Philadelphia (Courtesy of The Library of The Jewish Theological Seminary, image #1964)

Fig. 5 Congregation Beth Sholom, Elkins Park, suburban Philadelphia, September 1959 (Courtesy of Congregation Beth Sholom)

Fig. 6 Exhibit commemorating American Jewish "Tercentenary," Cincinnati, 1954 (Courtesy of The Jacob Rader Marcus Center of the American JewishArchives, Cincinnati, Ohio at americanjewisharchives.org)

Fig. 7 YIVO's New York headquarters, 1048 Fifth Avenue, not dated (Courtesy of The Jacob Rader Marcus Center of the American Jewish Archives, Cincinnati, Ohio at americanjewisharchives.org)

Fig. 8 Three Jewish youth share a daily Yiddish newspaper, Lithuania 1939-41 (Courtesy of United States Holocaust Memorial Museum, photograph #21314)

Fig. 9 Max Weinreich teaching Yiddish at City College New York, not dated (Courtesy of the Archives of the YIVO Institute for Jewish Research, RG 121)

Fig. 10 Irving Howe, not dated (Courtesy of Robert D. Farber Archives & Special Collections Department, Brandeis University)

Fig. 11 Martin Buber, 1957 (Courtesy of Robert D. Farber Archives & Special Collections Department, Brandeis University)

Fig. 12 Abraham Joshua Heschel, 1972 (Courtesy of the Library of The Jewish Theological Seminary, image #68)

Fig. 13 Joseph B. Soloveitchik, not dated (Courtesy of The Jacob Rader Marcus Center of the American Jewish Archives, Cincinnati, Ohio at americanjewisharchives.org)

Fig. 14 Orthodox journal *Jewish Life*, 1951

Fig. 15 Telegram from head of Brooklyn-based Mir Yeshivah to a student of the prewar yeshivah, 1946 (Courtesy of United States Holocaust Memorial Museum, photograph #67028)

Fig. 16 Members of the Socialist *Bund* march in a May Day parade in Bialystok (Poland), 1934 (Courtesy of United States Holocaust Memorial Museum, photograph # 63632)

Fig. 17 Morris Schappes, not dated (Courtesy of The Jacob Rader Marcus Center of the American Jewish Archives, Cincinnati, Ohio at americanjewisharchives.org)

Fig. 18 Protagonists of *The Eternal Light* radio program at the 1950 ceremony of the Annual Brotherhood Award (Courtesy of The Library of The Jewish Theological Seminary, image #1065)

Fig. 19 Congregation Emanu-El B'ne Jeshurun, Milwaukee, WI, 1952-53 (Courtesy of The Jacob Rader Marcus Center of the American Jewish Archives, Cincinnati, Ohio at americanjewisharchives.org)

Fig. 20 The (seventh) Lubavitcher Rebbe, Menahem Mendel Shneerson and a group of Hasidism, not dated (Courtesy of The Jacob Rader Marcus Center of the American Jewish Archives, Cincinnati, Ohio at americanjewisharchives.org)

Fig. 21 Sholem Aleichem with prominent members of the Jewish community of the Polish *shtetl* of Bedzin, 1905-13 (Courtesy of United States Holocaust Memorial Museum, photograph #17966)

Fig. 22 Postcard by the Y. L. Peretz Library, commemorating Yiddish writer Mendele Mokher Sforim, 1936 (Courtesy of United States Holocaust Memorial Museum, photograph #39492)

Fig. 23 Isaac Bashevis Singer, not dated (Courtesy of The Jacob Rader Marcus Center of the American Jewish Archives, Cincinnati, Ohio at americanjewisharchives.org)

Acknowledgments

This book has been inspired, guided, and shaped by many scholars, mentors, and colleagues who have advised and helped me in different ways. It is a great pleasure to express, however insufficiently, my gratitude and acknowledge their contributions. All the help and advice I received notwithstanding, I bear the sole responsibility for whatever faults and idiosyncrasies remained in this work.

The book is a revised version of the doctoral dissertation I wrote at the Graduate School of the Jewish Theological Seminary (JTS) in New York. It bears the imprint of my advisor, Jack Wertheimer. His knowledge, sensitivity, curiosity, and passion for the subject matter are on every page, as are his respect for my approach to it and his patient support for my particular perspective. I could not have asked for a better advisor.

I thank the other members of my committee who in different roles guided the dissertation and helped me turn it into a book. David Fishman (JTS) introduced me to East European Jewish history and kindled my fascination, which led me to integrate it into my passion for the American Jewish experience. Ismar Schorsch, former Chancellor of JTS, has been model of a mentor and scholar in his commitment to the discipline of history and its value, and a *mentsh*. This book would not be what it has become without his advice. Alan Mittleman bears large responsibility for my coming to JTS, so it is fitting that he saw me out with a dissertation that, while not in his field of Jewish Thought, reflects many ideas and perspectives he shared with me over the years.

Hasia Diner, of New York University, took an interest in my project early on and supported me in many ways. Though I have never been an academic orphan, I am grateful that she adopted me and invested so much time and energy into advising me. David Roskies (JTS) has inspired me by his passionate engagement with the scholarly subject of East European Jewish culture ever since I met him before coming to JTS.

I received advice on my research from many outstanding scholars at my alma mater, JTS: Aryeh Davidson, Arnold Eisen, Benjamin Gampel, Stephen Garfinkel, Shira Kohn, Alan Mintz z"l, Bruce Nielsen, and Shuly Rubin Schwartz. Other scholars from various institutions shared their insights with me in individual meetings, at conferences and workshops, and in other ways. I thank each of them and ask for understanding that I merely list them in alphabetical order and without their academic affiliations: Jonathan Brent, Gennady Estraikh, Jeffrey Gurock, Samuel Heilman, Edward Kaplan, Eli Lederhendler, Julian Levinson, Michael Meyer, Thomas Meyer, Tony Michels, Deborah Dash Moore, Jonathan

Sarna, Mel Scult, Eugene Sheppard, Nancy Sinkoff, Daniel Soyer, Beth Wenger, Stephen Whitfield, and Steven Zipperstein.

Several fellow doctoral students commented on my work at various conferences, workshops, or in other ways, greatly expanding my horizon and providing peer encouragement. Among them are Allan Amanik, Rachel Deblinger, Josh Furman, Rachel Rothstein, Jason Schulman, and Brian Smollett. Two fellow JTS students in particular accompanied me in many ways through graduate school and beyond: Zach Mann provided intellectual companionship, advice, and friendship from start to end. Sonia Isard, close companion and friend from day one at JTS, read and edited every sentence of the dissertation, out of which this book grew.

My understanding of the New York intellectual scene in the 1940s to '60s was greatly improved by conversations with Neal Kozodoy and Norman Podhoretz, both former editors of *Commentary*. On the other end of the ideological spectrum, David Twersky z"l, then Washington correspondent of the *Jewish Daily Forward* was the first to introduce me to the fascinating world of American Jewry.

Researching this study was made smooth and pleasurable by a number of professionals in libraries and archives who generously gave of their time and expertise in support of my project. Among them are Sarah Diamant, Hector Guzman, and Jerry Schwarzbard at JTS; Fruma Mohrer and Leo Greenbaum at the YIVO Archives; Zachary Loeb of the American Jewish Historical Society; Dana Herman, Kevin Proffitt, and Gary P. Zola of the American Jewish Archives in Cincinnati. I am grateful to several archives and their (photo) archivist for providing the images that illustrate this book: Sharon Liberman Mintz of the Library of The Jewish Theological Seminary; Chloe Morse-Harding of the Robert D. Farber University Archives & Special Collections at Brandeis University; Joe Weber of the American Jewish Archives; and Vital Zajka of the Archives and Library of YIVO. Special thanks to Congregation Beth Sholom in Elkins Park, PA, for a historical image of their synagogue. I am particularly thankful to the United States Holocaust Memorial Museum for allowing me to use a photo from its collection for the book cover and several other ones to illustrate the text.

My graduate work and this dissertation were funded by several institutions, which generously awarded me fellowships and grants, or invited me to workshops and conferences. JTS awarded me a Revson Fellowship and other forms of funding throughout my graduate work. YIVO named me their Rose and Isidore Drench and Dora and Mayer Tandler Fellow in American Jewish History. I received an International Dissertation Fellowship from the Memorial Foundation for Jewish Culture. The Herbert R. Bloch Jr. Memorial Fellowship allowed me to do research in the American Jewish Archives. Additional support came from Targum Shlishi and the American Academy for Jewish Research. I also benefited from the invitation by Martin Treml to spend time as a fellow at the Center for Literary and Cultural Research in Berlin.

The Potsdam School of Jewish Theology, where I have been teaching since its founding in 2013, generously supported the publication of this book by defraying costs for the use of images; I am very grateful for this and the other ways in which it has supported my scholarship. I also thank the Potsdam Graduate School (PoGS) for its support.

I thank my colleagues at the School of Jewish Theology at Potsdam University for having my back in the final stages of the writing process. And I am grateful for the continuing mentorship and friendship of Berndt Ostendorf, my M.A. advisor and emeritus in American Studies at Ludwig-Maximilians-University Munich where I first pursued my interest in American Jewish history. I thank Cornelia Wilhelm for accepting my book into her series at de Gruyter, and to Julia Brauch, my editor there, and the entire team for smoothly turning my original text into this book. My indefatigable copy editor, Anne Popiel, improved the text of this book in innumerable ways.

Closer to home, more people kept me company during various important stages of my life prior to, during, and since my time in New York. My parents, Gisela and Willi Krah, stayed remarkably calm, when they learned that their son would give up a permanent job as a journalist to go to graduate school to get a Ph.D. in Modern Jewish Studies, and they supported me throughout in every way they could. Only Ulrike Fleischer herself knows how much she contributed to this project and the present book resulting from it. I am indebted to her beyond words. My former boss in journalism, Andreas Krieger, learned more about American Jewry over countless dinners than he ever would and kept me sane and straight in many ways.

Mirjam Thulin has come to play an ever greater role in this book project and, more importantly, my life beyond it. I dedicate this book to her.

Introduction

On March 19, 1940, a new actor entered the American Jewish intellectual scene. As reported by the Yiddish *Forverts* on the following day, Max Weinreich, the leading scholar of the previously Vilna-based YIVO research institute, arrived in New York aboard a Swedish ship.[1] Even though the article suggested that Weinreich was just visiting, his arrival did mark the institute's permanent relocation to New York. YIVO's settling in the New World symbolically marked a new chapter in the drama of how American Jews related to the Old. Dedicated to the preservation of the East European Jewish heritage, it provided a bridge to a heritage for a community that was as uncertain about its past as it was about its future, amidst a world dramatically changing before its eyes.

In a portentous coincidence captured in two stories on the same *Forverts* cover, along with Weinreich another prominent figure of East European Jewry stepped off the boat in New York: the (sixth) Hasidic Lubavitcher Rebbe Yosef Yitshak Shneerson fled Europe, bringing with him his own heavy Old World baggage.[2] Furthermore, two days later, on March 21, Abraham Joshua Heschel, who would become one of the most vocal guardians of East European heritage in the US, arrived in New York, too.[3]

All three intellectuals had traveled long and winding routes, physically, culturally, and emotionally, from Eastern Europe to the US. Weinreich (1894–1969) was stranded with his family in Copenhagen, where he had traveled in 1939 to attend a scholarly conference, just before World War II broke out. He and his son Uriel, who would later become a highly influential Yiddish scholar, barely escaped from Denmark before it was occupied by Nazi Germany. When Heschel (1907–1972) arrived in New York, he had both a traditional *smikhah* and a liberal rabbinic ordination, which he had received in Berlin, and had also succeeded Martin Buber at the *Jüdisches Lehrhaus*. Before escaping to the US, he had been deported to Poland in 1938 and lived in London for eight months. Shneerson (1880–1950) was also rescued in Poland, where he had fled (via Latvia) from the Soviet Union. The anti-religious campaigns of its Communist

---

1 "Dr. M. Weinreich Has Arrived in America" [Yiddish], *Forverts*, March 20, 1940, 1, see following page. (I thank Prof. Gennady Estraikh for this reference). All translations are mine, unless otherwise indicated. YIVO had had an American section ("Amopteyl") in New York since its founding in 1925; cf. Cecile Esther Kuznitz, "YIVO," in *YIVO Encyclopedia of Jews in Eastern Europe [vol. 2]*, ed. Gershon D. Hundert (New Haven: Yale University Press, 2008), 2091.
2 "Masses of Hasidim and Rabbis Meet Lubavitcher Rebbe on His Arrival" [Yiddish], *Forverts*, March 20, 1940, 1.
3 Edward K. Kaplan and Samuel Dresner, *Abraham Joshua Heschel: Prophetic Witness* (New Haven: Yale University Press, 1998), 302.

DOI 10.1515/9783110499438-001

Figure 1: On March 20, 1940, the Yiddish daily *Forverts* reported on the front page the arrival in New York of Lubavitcher Rebbe Yosef Yitshak Shneerson (left side of page, under the portrait) and of leading YIVO scholar Max Weinreich (bottom, second story from right)

regime had put increasing pressure on him, as he had become one of the most influential leaders of Russian Jewry in the interwar years.

All three men fled from a world that was going up in flames, which would consume most of its inhabitants and their culture, and came to America at a time when Jewry there faced an uncertain future.

Obsessively Engaged: Postwar American Jewry and the East European Past

Whether or not Weinreich, Heschel, and Shneerson had any premonition of it in March of 1940, Yiddish-based East European Jewish culture, Ashkenazic spirituality, and Hasidism in particular would become important factors when over the coming years, American Jews unpacked and re-assembled what they had brought from their East European origins. The mid-decades of the twentieth century witnessed an unprecedented, almost obsessive occupation of American Jews with the East European past. It was evoked, retold, romanticized, written up and written off in works of fiction and memoirs, sermons and political pamphlets, dramas and exhibitions, and in countless articles in journals of different stripes. The sheer number of essays produced by highbrow authors, ideologues, secular and religious thinkers, labor leaders, and popular writers about the East European Jewish past during the immediate postwar decades is undeniable. A torrent of reflections on this experience burst forth, presenting a wide range of colorful and contradictory images of this past. Eastern Europe was depicted as a dark place of poverty and parochialism, from which the Jews had been lucky to escape to America. Still, it could also be the locus of an ideal, holistically Jewish spiritual life led in the blissful tranquility of a *shtetl*. The depictions included many narratives in between these two and of a very different kind, lived in the *shtetl* or in a city, centered around a Hasidic court, a literary café, or a revolutionary circle.

One might explain this outpouring by noting that the children of East European immigrants were coming to grips with their family histories. They were trying to make sense of the lives lived by their forebears. The diversity of images might merely reflect the diversity of the Jewish experience in Eastern Europe. Upon closer inspection, though, it becomes clear that this is an insufficient explanation. Something else was drawing them to reflect on the East European Jewish past: the set of challenges and opportunities facing them in postwar America. When postwar American Jews talked about Eastern Europe, what they really meant was the American present. And when they debated their parents' past, they were actually debating their children's future.

With the American Jewish present, many observers from within found much to worry about: low levels of observance, little Jewish pride, materialism at the cost of intellectual interests, spiritual uncertainty in the face of new challenges and opportunities. Most thinkers agreed that American Jewry could be – had to be – moved forward to a more stable understanding of its own role in order to sustain itself and the future of world Jewry. But, there was little agreement on the direction of the way forward.

In some cases, advocates of opposing agendas laid open how the past, real or imagined, was re-constructed in different ways to be usable for different purposes. In 1952, the Conservative rabbi Herbert Parzen, writing in *Commentary* magazine, launched a broadside against an influential school of thought in the debate about the American Jewish present and the East European past. He dismantled the legend of the pious East European Jew untouched by modernity, a legend created in response to "the disintegration and emptiness of present-day American Jewish life," which makes many "thinking Jews [...] homesick for a home they never knew." Polish-born Parzen accused "spiritual leaders of what is the largest section of American Jewry" of falsely claiming that America with its modernist-materialist force destroyed traditional Judaism.[4]

The unnamed target of the essay was Heschel, by then a professor at Conservative Judaism's flagship Jewish Theological Seminary and one of the most visible Jewish religious intellectuals. In his scholarship and as a spiritual leader, this scion of a Hasidic dynasty tirelessly championed the East European Jewish tradition as the essence of Judaism: folk-oriented, self-reliantly particularist, deeply spiritual and holistic, with Yiddish as its medium. In Heschel's view, articulated in 1948 also in *Commentary,* this tradition should "shape a cultural pattern for American Jewish life," but was sadly underappreciated by American Jewry.[5]

Parzen and Heschel were two of many voices that formed the broad discourse in which vastly different images, narratives, and lessons of the East European past competed for hegemony over the American Jewish communal consciousness. The diversity of images of this past mirrored the wide range of concerns and ideas about the nature and meaning of being Jewish in America: secular, religious, cultural, political, liberal, radical, and many combinations thereof, expressed in English or in Yiddish.

The analysis of the many voices suggests that the discourse about the East European past for the sake of the American present was particularly open in the mid-decades of the twentieth century. YIVO's arrival in 1940 represented the

---

4 Herbert Parzen, "When Secularism Came to Russian Jewry," *Commentary* 13 (April 1952): 355.
5 Abraham Joshua Heschel, "The Two Great Traditions: The Sephardim and the Ashkenazim," *Commentary* 5 (May 1948): 416–22.

beginning of a more conscious, social science-driven way to relate to the East European heritage than ever before. It inspired other intellectuals to translate this past, literally and culturally, into a new, American idiom, in order to further their respective agendas. This discourse remained quite open for the length of a generation, until in 1964 one set of images won the competition by popular vote. From its Broadway premiere in that year onward, the musical *Fiddler on the Roof* lodged a certain imagery of *the* East European Jewish past in the collective memory of American Jewry, which affirmed both their Americanness and their Jewishness in the new cultural and social climate of the 1960s.

The twenty-five years in between were characterized by greater fluidity and ambivalence regarding the ways of understanding and expressing Jewishness in America. The discourse about the East European past marked a critical point in the American Jewish community's development. Second- and third-generation Jews appropriated this past as they responded to a crisis of postwar American Jewish life that was born out of a complex constellation of developments and events. The shock over the destruction of East European Jewry and its culture in the Holocaust coincided with far-reaching changes in the American context. The makeup of American Jewry had just shifted from an immigrant majority with a living memory of the *alte heym* to their native-born children and grandchildren, who made America their home and related to their East European origins in new ways. Moreover, the inclusion of American Jews as a religious group in the (white) mainstream of American society called for a redefinition of Jewishness and Judaism. New ways had to be found to express Jewish distinctiveness, which had to find its place in the continuum of Jewish history or derive Jewish legitimacy out of itself. American Jews struggled with fundamental questions: inclusion or separateness, at-homeness or ambivalence vis-à-vis America, continuity or discontinuity with traditional forms of Judaism.

A Community Coming of Age – by Trying on a Usable Past

By answering these questions, American Jews engaged with even larger issues of Jewish modernity, or rather: modernization. Over the first postwar decades, the framework and categories in which group distinctiveness was negotiated shifted in profound ways. As Jewish distinctiveness was at first largely limited to religious expressions, other group characteristics were expected to assimilate to majority norms. More and more, however, this reduction of Jewishness to Judaism was questioned from within, as this study will show. Different groups within American Jewry pushed for different expressions of a broader Jewish distinctiveness. As ethnic traits became increasingly legitimate expressions of group distinctiveness, the nature of Jewish ethnicity emerged as a major point of debate. It pitted different models of Jewishness against each other, which advocated different ways to re-fashion traditional religious impulses, ideas, texts, and behaviors. The East European experience served as a resource or a foil for these different propositions, as its memory emerged as a major force that united the competing ideas about the future of the American Jewish community.

This memory was formed out of the diverse narratives of the East European Jewish past. The intense engagement with this past, its reconstruction in history and memory, and its integration into group consciousness are therefore significant, but under-analyzed elements of how American Jews conceived of themselves as a distinct group in the American body social and politic, and within the continuum of Jewish history. This process happened first at a time when the majority of American Jews were immigrants. As sociologist Ewa Morawska has shown, "changing images of the Old Country constitute an important component in the development of ethnic group consciousness among immigrants." What her analysis demonstrated for first-generation immigrant Jews may well also be true for the community increasingly made up of their children and grandchildren: "Within the group, these metaphors provide both a sense of collective historical continuity in a drastically altered sociocultural environment and a foil against which the immigrants define themselves and their new situations."[6]

The postwar American social, cultural, political, religious, and economic environment pushed both the immigrants and the next generations into rapid processes of modernization. These included a new self-conceptualization as a group within society at large, a task that fell in particular to the native-born children and grandchildren. Like them, American Jewry came of age and into its own at mid-twentieth century, defining itself in relation to America and the Jewish world. Like an adolescent facing the end of childhood and the beginning of adulthood, American Jewry fashioned a new personality out of various elements. As they turned to the past, American Jews pondered what were precious gifts to keep of the heritage, and what were second-hand items to be discarded, outgrown over time to be replaced by new ones. The underlying attitudes fell on a spectrum from filiopietistic to patricidal.

This group identity formation played out in different ways among the second and third generations after immigration. Contemporary observers used a scholarly approach premised on the generation model to analyze how different

---

6 Ewa Morawska, "Changing Images of the Old Country in the Development of Ethnic Identity among East European Immigrants, 1880–1930s: A Comparison of Jewish and Slavic Representations," *YIVO Annual of Jewish Social Science* 21 (1993): 273.

generations related to the pre-immigrant past. "Hansen's Law," named for the Swedish scholar Marcus Lee Hansen, postulates that the second generation is so keen on integrating in the new setting that it sheds what seems burdensome of the old country heritage, whereas the third generation feels secure enough to rediscover it: "[what] the son wishes to forget the grandson wishes to remember." Postwar American Jewish intellectuals re-discovered this approach and, in a 1952 *Commentary* article and other writings, used it to explain the community's engagement with the East European past.[7] According to this model, the third generation of American Jews turned to their collective East European grandfathers in search of a Jewishness that could offer meaning to their fragmented lives as modern Jews. Many were attracted by the quality often called "Yiddishkayt," a vague concept denoting an emotional sensitivity, cultural taste, ethnic identification, and/or group loyalty that they associated with the East European Jewish experience, precisely because the term did not break up this experience in distinct categories such as religion. For those in search of such a holistic sense of Jewishness, the East European Jewish past was far more than a subject of nostalgia and a walk down memory lane. Echoing Franz Rosenzweig's perspective a generation earlier and a continent away, this experience was seen as redemptive for the wounded Jewish soul that craved wholeness and authenticity. The East European past was a potential source of renewal. It was seen by this generation as a way forward, not merely a backward glance.

Jews in Postwar America: a Not-So-Golden Era?

This narrative of postwar ambivalence and ferment in American Jewish life, which was driven to an obsessive occupation with the past, engages with important historiographical debates and theoretical frameworks. It contributes to the nuancing of the previously popular historiographical narrative of the so-called

---

[7] Marcus Lee Hansen, "The Third Generation in America," *Commentary* 14 (November 1952): 495. Swedish scholar Hansen's analysis of generational differences in relationship to the pre-immigrant past had originally been published in 1938 as a brochure, *The Problem of the Third Generation Immigrant* (Rock Island, Ill.: Augustana Historical Society Publications). It informed sociological works such as Will Herberg's *Protestant – Catholic – Jew: An Essay in American Religious Sociology* (Chicago: University of Chicago Press, 1983; orig. publ. 1955). For a critical discussion of "Hansen's Law," cf. Peter Kivisto and Dag Blanck, eds. *American Immigrants and Their Generations: Studies and Commentaries on the Hansen Thesis after Fifty Years* (Urbana/Chicago: University of Illinois Press, 1990).

"golden era," which described the two postwar decades as a period of relative consensus among American Jews on fundamental questions of Jewishness in America.[8] Symptomatic of this dominant narrative has been Arthur Goren's optimistic description of the years from 1945 to 1955 as "a golden decade for American Jews."[9] Other historians have extended this period into the mid-1960s.[10] According to Goren's analysis, American Jewry enjoyed a broad consensus based on the "doctrinal core" identification of Jewishness as a religious category; the supposed congruence of Jewishness and Judaism made for a stable communal identity.[11]

This popular narrative has been undermined by new perspectives suggesting that American Jews in the postwar decades struggled with profound questions about their identity. In her history of the American Jewish experience, Hasia Diner added an illuminating question mark to the phrase "golden era."[12] Placing the Jewish experience in the larger perspective of the "politics of consensus," literary historian Wendy Wall points out that the broad agreement on values associated with the "American way" was actually created as a political project that responded to ethnic and other tensions characterizing the interwar years.[13] Along with Phillip

---

[8] This revision of the narrative of the Jewish experience in mid-century America corresponds to a tendency toward a more nuanced view of American society at large during this period. Cf. Mary Caputi, *A Kinder, Gentler America: Melancholia and the Mythical 1950s* (Minneapolis: University of Minnesota Press, 2005); Grace Elizabeth Hale, *A Nation of Outsiders: How the White Middle Class Fell in Love with Rebellion in Postwar America* (New York: Oxford University Press, 2011).

[9] Arthur Goren, "A Golden Decade for American Jews: 1945–1955," in *A New Jewry? America since the Second World War [Studies in Contemporary Jewry VIII]*, ed. Peter Y. Medding (New York: Oxford University Press, 1997), 3–20. For an example of a narrative that emphasizes the positive dimensions of choice and success, see Pamela S. Nadell, "Jews and Judaism in the United States," in *The Cambridge Guide to Jewish History, Religion, and Culture*, ed. Judith R. Baskin and Kenneth Seeskin (Cambridge and New York: Cambridge University Press, 2010), 208–32.

[10] Cf. Leonard Dinnerstein, *Antisemitism in America* (New York: Oxford University Press, 1994), 178. The term "golden era" has been used to capture the supposedly untroubled identification of Jews with America, their social and economic ascent, and their communal harmony. This stretches Goren's thesis beyond its original, narrower scope.

[11] Goren, "Golden Decade," 8. Albert Gordon also presented a largely positive and optimistic picture of Jewish life in the suburbs, which contributed to the overall narrative that, for American Jews, the positive developments in their postwar lives far outweighed any negative ones: *Jews in Suburbia* (Boston: Beacon Press, 1959), particularly the concluding chapter.

[12] Hasia Diner, *The Jews of the United States, 1654 to 2000* (Berkeley: University of California Press, 2004), 259. This revision includes recognition of a greater role of the Holocaust in more American Jewish discourses before 1967; cf. Diner, *We Remember with Reverence and Love: American Jews and the Myth of Silence after the Holocaust, 1945–1962* (New York: New York University Press, 2009).

[13] Wendy Wall, *Inventing the "American Way:" The Politics of Consensus from the New Deal to the Civil Rights Movement* (Oxford: Oxford University Press, 2008).

Roth, we may understand the postwar decades as the period in which "America discovered itself as America."[14] In parallel, new types of Jewishness emerged amidst severe birth pangs. Riv-Ellen Prell argues that "[How] Jews emerged from the devastations of World War II in the 1940s to enter a utopian moment in 1967, which led to a reshaping of American Jewish life, is a more complex story than most scholars have assumed."[15] Prell sees these decades as a period of broad and deep transformation, characterized by questions, tensions and mixed feelings, particularly around the issue of Jewishness. "The postwar period, then, is best understood as a dynamic moment when the fundamental definitions of what it meant to be an American Jew were worked out in the new synagogues, living rooms, organizations, and political debates of the time."[16] Historian Lila Corwin Berman has suggested that much of the ambivalence of American Jews toward their new position within the American mainstream stemmed specifically from concerns about their new middle-class status, which seemed to undermine both their communal boundaries and the content meaning of Jewishness.[17] Historian Michael Staub has undermined the idea that postwar American Jewry rested stably on a liberal political consensus.[18] More broadly, historian Susan Glenn replaces the "golden era" image with the concept of a "Jewish Cold War" that was waged in the postwar years. Its eponymous global counterpart impacted Jewish life much more disruptively than previously acknowledged, as it "triggered a complex debate about postwar pressures for Jewish group loyalty and conformity."[19]

---

[14] Quoted in Claudia Roth Pierpont, "The Book of Laughter: Philip Roth and His Friends," *New Yorker*, October 7, 2013, 35.

[15] Riv-Ellen Prell, "Triumph, Accommodation, and Resistance: American Jewish Life from the End of World War II to the Six-Day War," in *The Columbia History of Jews and Judaism in America*, ed. Marc Lee Raphael (New York: Columbia University Press, 2008), 115. See also Prell, "Community and the Discourse of Elegy: The Postwar Suburban Debate," in *Imagining the American Jewish Community*, ed. Jack Wertheimer (Waltham: Brandeis University Press/Hanover: University Press of New England, 2007), 67–90. For another revisionist study, see Lila Corwin Berman, "American Jews and the Ambivalence of Middle-Classness," *American Jewish History* 93 (2007): 409–34.

[16] Prell, "Triumph, Accommodation, and Resistance," 115.

[17] Berman, "Ambivalence of Middle-Classness," 432–34. Examples of contemporary texts recording such uncertainty and doubt include Clement Greenberg, "Self-Hatred and Jewish Chauvinism: Some Reflections on 'Positive Jewishness,'" *Commentary* 10 (November 1950): 426–33; Adolph Held, "Jewish Culture and the American Jewish Community," *Workmen's Circle Call* 28 (1959): 2–3; J. Alvin Kugelmass, "Name-Changing – And What It Gets You: Twenty-five Who Did It," *Commentary* 14 (August 1952): 145–50.

[18] Michael Staub, *Torn at the Roots: The Crisis of Jewish Liberalism in Postwar America* (New York: Columbia University Press, 2002).

[19] Susan A. Glenn, *The Jewish Cold War: Anxiety and Identity in the Aftermath of the Holocaust* (Ann Arbor: Frankel Center for Judaic Studies, University of Michigan, 2015), 10.

Contemporary observations can illustrate this notion. Harry Gersh, a Jewish professional writing for *Commentary*, summed up these uncertainties in his reflection on his postwar experience: "For the first time, I found myself nagged for specific answers to an old question: 'What am I if I am a Jew?'"[20] This uncertainty about Jewish identity and authenticity kept American Jews from wholeheartedly embracing the new social, cultural, and ideological developments that were changing their lives. Instead, it led many of them to turn to the East European past for guidance.

State of the Field

There is no broadly-based study that relates postwar American Jewry's engagement with this past to its ambivalent Jewishness in the context of a changing American society. However, the meaning and function of the (East European) Jewish past to other and later Jewries is by no means uncharted territory, particularly as it was mediated through cultural products. In *The Jewish Search for a Usable Past,* cultural historian David Roskies offers a comprehensive picture of the diverse ways Jews related to their past since the nineteenth century and of attempts to discover a "usable past" as the key to defining the highly contested Jewish future.[21] He asserts that the image of the *shtetl* as the most important symbol of the East European past was fixed in the American Jewish imagination already during the interwar years; the present study of the postwar image of the *shtetl* follows up on his findings. The sociological findings by Ewa Morawska also relate to a period ending in the interwar years. Her study of "old country" relations of Jewish and Slavic immigrants from 1880 into the 1930s found that, for Jews, the contrast between the perceived "pastness" of Eastern Europe and the presentness of America grew further during the interwar period; the second generation built ethnic ties on American bases and saw East European Jewry as backward and in need of financial help. Yet, the *alte heym* was also depicted in nostalgic ways, as American Jews differentiated between the positive images of East European Jewish life and its hostile, oppressive gentile environment.[22] Historian Daniel Soyer has highlighted the mutual (transnational)

---

[20] Harry Gersh, "The New Suburbanites of the 50's: Jewish Division," *Commentary* 17 (March 1954): 214. Gersh was introduced as director of community relations for the Jewish Family Service of New York and as coming from a labor background.

[21] David G. Roskies, *The Jewish Search for a Usable Past* (Bloomington: Indiana University Press, 1999).

[22] Morawska uses the German terms "Vaterland" and "Heimat" to contrast the civic and emotional attachments to the United States and East European places of origin, respectively.

interaction between American and East European Jewries in the interwar period, particularly through journeys and subsequent travelogues by American Jews to the Soviet Union.[23]

American studies scholar Matthew Frye Jacobson has compared the "diasporic imagination" of Irish, Polish, and Jewish immigrants in the US.[24] He emphasizes the "exile" dimension of grief and loss in the immigrants' experience that shapes how they relate to their "old" nation. In the case of the Jews, he points to the transnational sense of Jewish peoplehood prevalent among immigrants to the US, focusing on Zionism, not identification with East European Jewish life, as its concrete expression.

Historian Steven Zipperstein, in *Imagining Russian Jewry*, has analyzed how the situation and cultural needs of American Jews in the second half of the twentieth century shaped their perception and imagination of Eastern Europe. He traces a development in the image of Eastern Europe: first essentialized as the locus of pogroms, it took on a new role after 1945 as a resource of pedigree, spirituality, wholeness, and community, expressed in the iconic image of the *shtetl*. Zipperstein points out that the East European past was used to claim the continuity of American Jewish life with tradition, and both affirm and critique the impact of America on their Jewishness. His analysis of key cultural products, such as *Fiddler on the Roof*, Philip Roth's novel "Eli the Fanatic," writings of the "New York Jewish Intellectuals," the reception of Yiddish authors, and the anthropological study *Life is with People* prefigures the notion of competing narratives.[25] Cultural scholar Barbara Kirshenblatt-Gimblett has also pointed to a popular, communal, and historiographical shift in the second half of the twentieth century toward a greater appreciation of Jewishness as positive and particular. The growing popularity of this ahistorical image of a dematerialized, spiritualized *shtetl* culminated, she suggests, in *Fiddler on the Roof*.[26]

The emotional attachment is to a specifically Jewish home, which exists in tension with the surrounding non-Jewish society (Morawska, "Changing Images," 276).

23 Daniel Soyer, "Transnationalism and Mutual Influence: American and East European Jewries in the 1920s and 1930s," in *Rethinking European Jewish History*, ed. Jeremy Cohen and Moshe Rosman (Oxford and Portland: Littman, 2009), 201–20.

24 Matthew Frye Jacobson, *Special Sorrows: The Diasporic Imagination of Irish, Polish, and Jewish Immigrants in the United States* (Cambridge: Harvard University Press, 1995).

25 Steven J. Zipperstein, *Imagining Russian Jewry: Memory, History, Identity* (Seattle: University of Washington Press, 1999). Cf. also Ben Cion Pinchuk, "Jewish Discourse and the Shtetl," *Jewish History* 15 (2001): 169–79.

26 Barbara Kirshenblatt-Gimblett, "Introduction," in *Life is with People: The Culture of the Shtetl*, 2nd ed., ed. Mark Zborowski and Elizabeth Herzog (New York: Schocken, 1995), ix–xlviii.

Historian Hasia Diner, in *Lower East Side Memories*, has made a similar argument for the emergence of the old immigrant quarter as the imaginary place for the founding myth which American Jews needed particularly from the 1960s onward.She traces its roots to earlier decades, as American Jews, both in light of the Holocaust and of their successful integration in America, needed a physical reference point of their origin and of their (lost) Jewish authenticity.[27] Historian Eli Lederhendler has woven many of the cultural phenomena engaging the East European past into a rather pessimistic reading of ethnic cohesion among post-1945 New York Jews. His study aims to correct Deborah Dash Moore's portrait of interwar Jewish identity as stable and transmittable to the following generations.[28]

From Yiddish to English: a Multiplicity of Sources

Complementing these studies, the present work offers a discourse analysis drawing from a broad array of sources, by which it illuminates a critical piece of American Jewish cultural history. Much of this elite discourse about the East European Jewish past took place in journals of various ideological camps within American Jewry. These journals, along with other publications of these groups, form the most important source basis of this study. These groups used different reconstructions of the past as they competed to shape the present and future. The analysis of this discourse is therefore structured around the voices of key sets of participants: immigrant intellectuals, American-born secular thinkers, religious thinkers and leaders, and the Jewish left. In a second step, it explores more popular cultural products that present specific images of the East European past to broader audiences.

Following a large-scale trajectory from an immigrant community to an American one, this is a story that starts with Yiddish and ends with American pop culture. Along the way, it traces the translation of the East European past into a new, American idiom. For that reason, the analysis is mostly based on

---

[27] Hasia R. Diner, *Lower East Side Memories: A Jewish Place in America* (Princeton: Princeton University Press, 2000).

[28] Eli Lederhendler, *New York Jews and the Decline of Urban Ethnicity, 1950–1970* (Syracuse: Syracuse University Press, 2001); Deborah Dash Moore, *At Home in America: Second Generation New York Jews* (New York: Columbia University Press, 1981). Moore rejected Lederhendler's arguments; cf. Moore, "At Home in America? Revisiting the Second Generation," *Journal of American Ethnic History* 25 (2006): 156–68.

English-language sources, except in the sections on Orthodoxy and textbooks. Of course, there was a sizable Yiddish-speaking sub-community within American Jewry at mid-twentieth century; or rather, a bilingual community of immigrants and their second-generation offspring who used both languages, to different degrees and functionally differentiated. This community engaged with the past in its own, distinct ways. Crucially, for example, Yiddish speakers engaged with the destruction of (East) European Jewry earlier and in more direct ways than English speakers, even though by now we know that the latter also dealt with the Holocaust earlier than the "myth of silence" prior to the 1961 Eichmann trial implied. The Yiddish-speaking community's complex post-1945 relationship to the recent and not so recent past in the *alte heym* deserves a study of its own, complementing and complicating this study, as it tells the story of linguistic and cultural translation of the East European past into American terms.

The narratives of a group's past and its identity are shaped in important ways by elites who produce cultural products, largely texts that express how a group sees itself and is seen by others. These elite-driven processes interact with how other, larger parts of the community see themselves and relate to the past. Rank-and-file American Jews read *The World of Sholom Aleichem*, went to see an exhibition of Roman Vishniac's photographs, heard talks at YIVO, attended meetings of their local chapter of the *Workmen's Circle* or a lecture on Hasidism at their synagogue, and listened to an *Eternal Light* radio show on Eastern Europe. The discourse on the past was a broad phenomenon that transcended divisions in an increasingly differentiated community made up of immigrants, American-born offspring, and their children.

The choice of a variegated set of data for this study reflects the plurality and openness of the discourse in the mid-decades of the century. Taking a page from New Historicism, the study is based on the premise that all kinds of sources, including literary texts, form "mutually intelligible networks of signs," or a cultural formation.[29] A feature characteristic of the "new historicist" approach is the conviction that the observer of a culture distant in time (and, potentially, space) can uncover "meaning" in cultural expressions which their producers did not consciously invest or express through them. Treating all sources as potentially meaningful, in the sense of pointing to the "meaning" that a culture generates and expresses, implicitly weakens the boundaries between different genres of texts, first and foremost literary and non-literary ones.[30]

---

[29] Catherine Gallagher and Stephen Greenblatt, *Practicing New Historicism* (Chicago: University of Chicago Press, 2000), 7–8.

[30] Cf. Clifford Geertz's concept of culture as a source of "meaning". Clifford Geertz, "Thick Description: Toward an Interpretive Theory of Culture," in *The Interpretation of Cultures: Selected Essays* (New York: Basic Books, 1973), 213–31.

Methodology and Discipline: Discourse Analysis and Cultural History

This study in cultural history uses discourse analysis as its main method, arguing that American Jews *discursively* constructed a usable East European Jewish past for their present needs. Underlying this analysis is a strong argument for the dynamic role of discourse in the creation of social reality. Discourses create ways of understanding the world, they do not mirror reality; they do not reveal some hidden, pre-constituted reality, but rather provide concepts, objects, and subject positions which actors use to fashion a social world.[31] Accordingly, this study combines discourse analysis and interpretive content analysis as its methods.

"Eastern Europe" and the "East European Jewish experience" are themselves discursive constructs that became solidified concepts in the process analyzed in this study. Jews from politically, culturally, socially, and in other ways different backgrounds in Poland, Russia, later the Soviet Union, and other countries in the Eastern parts of Europe often related to local places of origin more than to larger regions, countries, or "Eastern Europe." The latter gradually became the overarching framework of reference, as external observers and officials did not differentiate between the various immigrant groups, and as subsequent, American-born generations related less and less to specific places of their families' origins. Crucially, in the period under consideration here, "Eastern Europe" became a trope in the context of the Cold War, which also made for a strong presentist perspective with a tendency to elide the periods before the geopolitical confrontation.[32] This study reflects therefore, an a-historic usage of the term "Eastern Europe" that referred to regions that were at or became at mid-century part of the "East bloc."

As the process of constructing a usable East European past is related to the fashioning of the social world of the American Jewish present, it involves issues of power and competition. The analysis therefore explores how various actors struggled to establish an understanding of this past conducive to their goals

---

31 Cf. Nelson Phillips and Cynthia Hardy, *Discourse Analysis: Investigating Processes of Social Construction* (Thousand Oaks: Sage Publications, 2002); Ruth Wodak, R. de Cillia, M. Reisigl and K. Liebhart, *The Discursive Construction of National Identity* (Edinburgh: Edinburgh University Press, 1999). They build on Michel Foucault's by now classic conceptualization of discourse; cf. *Archeology of Knowledge* (New York: Routledge, 2002).
32 For an analysis of the "ethnicization" of immigrant Jews into "East European Jews," cf. Jonathan D. Sarna, "From Immigrants to Ethnics: Toward a New Theory of 'Ethnicization,'" *Ethnicity* 5 (1978): 370–78. For the larger context of the construction of "Eastern Europe" by the "West," cf. Larry Wolf, *Inventing Eastern Europe: The Map of Civilization on the Mind of the Enlightenment* (Stanford: Stanford University Press, 1994).

and interests. Given that American Jewry operates within an entirely voluntaristic framework, power is wielded not coercively, but by means of persuasion and in competition for power among aspirants. For example, the postwar American social norm of defining Jewishness in religious terms granted greater influence to religious institutions, actors, texts, and ideas, such as synagogues, rabbis, and the Bible. Conversely, secular forms faced less externally ascribed legitimacy and less power. The analysis shows that the refashioning of Jewishness in postwar America was to a considerable degree an act of challenging and transforming traditional and religious understandings and concepts of Jewishness in light of new realities. Thus, there are still important questions of authority at stake.

The underlying claim of the analysis is that in the period between 1940 and 1965, the discourse about the East European past was particularly open, thereby reflecting the unsettled question of the authority to define the nature of Jewishness in the American present. In the larger process of the modernization of American Jewry, the period was characterized by increasing differentiation. While the American Jewish community at mid-century was not a single, unified hermeneutic community, the various actors in the discourse responded to a shared set of texts and events, motifs and motivations. They formed an "intellectual field," in Pierre Bourdieu's conceptualization.[33]

A community's collective understanding of its past, present, and future can be established and expressed through shared narratives. Seen not as a linguistic text type, but as a particularly structured discourse, narratives allow for dynamic identities and their temporality, incorporating divergent parts of complex identities in their change over time, striving to give them coherence, such as in shared myths of origin. The narrative approach, besides reflecting the constructed nature of identities, also emphasizes the agency and assertion of control by the subjects, even if they may not act consciously in the creation of such narratives and even if these narratives counter externally ascribed narratives and identities.[34]

Narratives play an important role in the construction of communal memory; rituals and other practices are other cultural factors in how a community establishes, expresses, and preserves a collective memory. As Morawska and others have argued, a collective past, present, and future, and a common culture, are,

---

33 Pierre Bourdieu, *The Field of Cultural Production: Essays on Art and Literature* (New York: Columbia University Press, 1993), 30.
34 Phillips and Hardy, *Discourse Analysis*, 32. Cf. also Peter Burke, *What is Cultural History?* (Cambridge: Polity, 2008), chap. 6 ("Narrative in Cultural History").

in turn, core areas of the discursive constitution of (national or communal) identity.³⁵ Collective memory of the past is embedded in a community's culture and is generated by an interplay of many factors, among them history, literature, politics, and other spheres. The re-negotiation of its collective memory was one aspect in the processes by which American Jews refashioned Jewishness in cultural terms as source of meaning.³⁶ These processes of group identity formation have been understood as the "Americanization" of an immigrant community and as its "ethnicization," itself a distinctly American concept.³⁷

Chapter Overview

The present study traces these processes from the symbolic beginning of the new discourse about the East European past with YIVO's relocation to America in 1940 to the success of *Fiddler on the Roof* in 1964.

Chapter 1 sets the stage on which different writers and actors presented their version of the past. YIVO intellectuals like Weinreich in 1940 brought their ideas from Eastern Europe to America, but came to realize that their focus on Yiddish did not score well with the new audience (Chapter 2). Intellectuals around *Commentary* translated its message into an American idiom. They mined the East European Jewish culture in a public search for a meaningful Jewishness, for themselves and the community (Chapter 3). These secular thinkers competed with religious thinkers, who emphasized the deeply and broadly spiritual nature of East European Jewishness as a model for American Jews, as analyzed in Chapter 4. The different denominations latched onto very different reconstructions of East European Judaism, as they, too, struggled with the limitations that the postwar American scene placed on a comprehensive sense of Jewishness (Chapter 5). The Jewish

---

35 Ewa Morawska, "Polish-Jewish Relations in America, 1880–1940," in *Polin [vol. 19]: Polish-Jewish Relations in North America*, ed. Miecyzslaw B. Biskupski and Antony Polonsky (Oxford: Littman, 2007), 71–86; Yael Zerubavel, *Recovered Roots: Collective Memory and the Making of Israeli National Tradition* (Chicago: University of Chicago Press, 1995). Cf. also in this context Yosef Hayim Yerushalmi, *Zakhor: Jewish History and Jewish Memory* (New York: Schocken, 1989; orig. publ. 1982); Amos Funkenstein, "Collective Memory and Historical Consciousness," *History & Memory* 1 (1989): 5–26; Allan Megill, "History, Memory, and Identity," *History and the Human Sciences* 11 (1998): 37–62; Oren Baruch Stier, "Memory Matters: Reading Collective Memory in Contemporary Jewish Culture," *Prooftexts* 18 (1998): 67–82.
36 Cf. Geertz, "Thick Description."
37 "Ethnicization" engages traditional categories of Jewish modernization, such as "assimilation," "confessionalization," and others, derived from the analysis of other Jewries' experiences.

Socialists and Communists offered a secular-cultural and politically radical alternative that was out of step with the *zeitgeist*; it had to exit stage left (Chapter 6).

A broader American Jewish public encountered the East European past in more popular products, some of which are analyzed in the following section for their imagery and appeal to their audiences. The popular radio show *The Eternal Light* drew on East European Jewish motifs to present Judaism as a resource of spiritual guidance for its listeners. The anthropological study *Life is with People* (also analyzed in Chapter 7) created a generic, timeless *shtetl* that felt subversive enough to be attractive for a new generation of American Jews in search of an identity. Textbooks used in schools were charged with socializing young Jews with a conscious understanding of their place in history; their depiction of the East European past, explored in Chapter 8, is therefore an overt attempt to make this past usable. Many of the texts making up the American Jewish discourse displayed a strong fascination with Hasidism. Tracing the attitudes of various groups to this movement, the chapter leads from popular depictions back to the secular intellectuals of *Commentary* and their particular fascination with the aesthetics and antinomianism of Hasidism. These literary-minded thinkers engaged the past largely through literature: works of fiction, criticism, anthologies, and translations. Chapter 9 shows how they fastened onto the transformative creativity and spiritual dynamic they found in this past, in order to craft a culturally elevated American Jewishness.

The drama ends with the final curtain that came down on this vision and on the openness of the discourse, symbolically marked by *Fiddler on the Roof*. In the twenty-five years before, American Jewry had explored and rejected a number of self-understandings that various thinkers had advocated. With the competition over, a new paradigm of Jewishness emerged from the discourse, wrested from the East European past. American Jewry became a "community of memory," deriving a positive affirmation of Jewishness out of its sacred relatedness to a past that was imaginatively reconstructed and vicariously realized as a source of meaning.[38] The concluding chapter places these developments into larger historical and scholarly contexts: the formation of ethnic identities, the role of history and memory in the American Jewish experiences, and the function of religion in modern societies, as they challenge traditional categories of Jewish modernization. These developments did not end when the *Fiddler* took center stage, but rather enjoyed many encores and re-runs up to the present.

---

[38] Nathan Abrams, "'America Is Home' *Commentary* Magazine and the Refocusing of the Community of Memory, 1945–1960," in *Commentary in American Life*, ed. Murray Friedman (Philadelphia: Temple University Press, 2005), 9–37.

Larger Patterns: Memory in American and Jewish Contexts

Postwar American Jewry's attempt to assure itself of the past in order to face the future is a story set in two contexts, American and Jewish. The processes of American Jews reconstructing a past out of memory for political reasons and as a response to traumatic experiences and new opportunities, reflect, shape, or catch up with larger developments in American society and culture, as Michael Kammen described them in his magisterial work *Mystic Chords of Memory: The Transformation of Tradition in American Culture*. He traces a (civil) religious function of memory already to the late nineteenth century. In the 1940–1960s, Americans in general responded to their shock over World War II and anxieties associated with the Cold War, the transformation of US society, and other factors with a sense of nostalgia for the past.[39]

The Jewish context requires a wider lens, as postwar American Jewry's engagement with the East European past fits an even larger pattern. In post-biblical history, Jews have repeatedly been dislocated from previously stable settings. The loss of such physical, social, and cultural homes – along with the religious imperative to remember a historical origin – has made imaginative relationships to times past a constant feature of Jewish religion and culture. This has been particularly prominent in the wake of expulsions and other traumatic ruptures.

Developments following the expulsion of the Jews from the Iberian peninsula in the late fifteenth century present an illuminating incidence of the pattern and an intriguing parallel to the events in the New World that was "discovered" at the same time. In both cases, the Jews and their new surroundings used different categories over time to understand them(-selves) as a religious or ethnic/national group. As is most likely true for any group that had an emotional attachment to the "old" country, memory, origin stories, and myths became important factors in how Jews expelled from Spain and Portugal, or who immigrated from Eastern Europe to the US, defined themselves on various levels: vis-à-vis other Jews, within Jewish history, and in relation to non-Jews. Like sixteenth-century expellees in Amsterdam, many Jews of East European background in twentieth century America identified with the culture of the old country, either with a particularistically East European Jewishness, or with the larger culture. Even intra-Jewish differences between Sephardim and Ashkenazic Jews fleeing Central

---

39 Michael Kammen, *Mystic Chords of Memory: The Transformation of Tradition in American Culture* (New York: Knopf, 1991), 194–227, 533–36.

Europe during the Thirty Years' War mirror to some extent the confrontation between "German" and East European Jews in nineteenth- and twentieth-century America.

Like the *conversos,* crypto-Jews, and re-Judaized refugees from Iberia in early modern Amsterdam, American Jews several centuries later faced the need to build a community after changes that had undermined previous pillars of communal life. In both cases, they transferred, modified, or re-invented institutions and less formal social ties and expressed their old-world identities by taking an interest in other communities of expellees/immigrants, but also gradually adapted, acculturated, and assimilated to the new cultural environment. The shift from Portuguese to Dutch for Iberian Jews in Amsterdam was mirrored in the transition from Yiddish to English in the United States.[40]

Figure 2: A group of Hasidic Jews in the market square of a small town near Stanislawow, Poland, ca. 1928. (Photograph by Marian Jerzy Sitarski. United States Holocaust Memorial Museum)

Some 450 years after the expulsions from Iberia, when Weinreich, Heschel, and the Lubavitcher Rebbe arrived in America, this transition entered a new stage. American Jews tried to make sense of the East European past, of which they

---

[40] Cf. Miriam Bodian, *Hebrews of the Portuguese Nation: Conversos and Community in Early Modern Amsterdam* (Bloomington: Indiana University Press, 1999), 10, 85–86, 153–61.

encountered highly ambiguous images open to widely divergent interpretations. The cover photo of this book, showing a group of Hasidic Jews in a *shtetl* in interwar Poland, is an example. Taken ca. 1928 by a photographer named Marian Jerzy Sitarski and preserved in the United States Holocaust Memorial Museum, it can be read as an illustration of the complexity of the East European past: The Hasidim share what seems to be a market place with other inhabitants, who are dressed in more modern style. Culturally closer to a postwar American viewer, the latter are not identifiable as Jews by any visible attributes, but only by inference from the context. Whereas the Hasidism in the center most likely conversed in Yiddish, did the man in the background call the child to the left in the same language, or in Polish? The unnamed small town seems to occupy a middle position on the spectrum between traditional and modern, poor and developing. But, any development and the lives of the people in the picture may well have been cut short little more than a decade later, during the war and in the Holocaust. Or did some of the Hasidic Jews find refuge with their rebbe in the US?

Beginning in the 1940s, American Jews asked these questions with an urgency that drove a generation-long quest to make sense of the East European past and the American present.

1 The Search for New Modes of Jewishness in Postwar America

> We've gone through all the motions of belonging, but we still do not feel we really belong. We're in it, still not of it. [...] No denying it, though, suburbia has caught up with us, and we're not sure we like it.[1]

In these hesitating words, Evelyn Rossman, a pseudonymous writer for *Commentary*, summed up a key aspect of her Jewish experience in postwar America: the ambivalence of belonging and not-belonging that played out in suburban settings. Suburbia was the backdrop of this ambivalence, which was fed by a complex constellation of factors that drove the American Jewish impulse to retrieve the East European experience: the Holocaust and the founding of the State of Israel, the Cold War and a mid-century sense of crisis, the categorization of Jewishness in religious terms, and the dialectic of inclusion and separateness of being Jewish in postwar American society.

As Americans, Jews were affected by the large-scale phenomena that characterized postwar society at large: suburbanization, social conformity, religious goodwill, liberal consensus, and economic prosperity. As Jews, however, they encountered these developments in distinct ways, which reflected their unique status as a group of recent immigrants with an ethno-religious identity. American Jewry was politically and culturally further Americanized and found increasing social acceptance. The immigrant generation and culture gave way to a native-born majority that answered the offer of inclusion with greater ease. Economic inclusion and a rapid rise to middle-class status, expressed in the move to Jewishly unmarked suburbia, made for greater interaction with non-Jews in the workplace and led more Jews to embrace middle-class values. The concomitant shift from class-based politics to a liberal individualism also questioned previous forms of expressing Jewishness. As religion was increasingly validated, Judaism became the most accepted form of expressing Jewishness, but in turn reduced Jewishness to a narrower category than before. The result was a fragmentation of any broader sense of Jewishness, which was, at least for external consumption, deprived of previously constitutive aspects, such as ethnic loyalty and cultural (as opposed to merely religious) distinctiveness. Thus, greater choice and

---

[1] Evelyn N. Rossman [pseud.], "The Community and I: Belonging: Its Satisfactions and Dissatisfactions," *Commentary* 18 (November 1954): 399. In a follow-up article two years later, the same author stated that she now felt at home in her suburb, but still recorded ambivalence about Jewish life in this setting: Rossman, "The Community and I: Two Years Later – The Wine, or the Blessing?" *Commentary* 21 (March 1956): 230–38.

DOI 10.1515/9783110499438-002

new questions about the forms and limits of Jewish distinctiveness resulted in the need for more conscious decisions than in the past. These developments resulted in a profound sense of uncertainty and ambivalence among American Jews about their place in society and the nature and meaning of their Jewishness. With more and different choices now before them, including the choice of how – and even whether – to realize their Jewishness, "Jews [were] re-examining their faith and their obligations and responsibilities to their group and their institutions," sociologist and rabbi Albert Gordon wrote in his 1959 study, *Jews in Suburbia*.²

In the postwar decades, American Jews realized that they were free – and hence obligated – to redefine what Jewishness, Judaism, and Jewish life in America meant. Previous assumptions, obstacles, outside ascriptions, and internal certainties no longer constricted or determined the meaning of being Jewish in America. In this constellation of newness and choice, ambivalence and uncertainty, engaging with the Jewish past was a common move. Jews defined themselves and their place in the American present by rejecting and affirming pasts both real and imagined, constructing meaningful continuities and discontinuities. The ferment that defined postwar American Jewry as a community in transition and drove their engagement with the East European past derived to a large extent from the changes they experienced in interwar America.

Interwar Years: *Yiddishkayt* in the Urban Ghetto – Doomed to Decline

Even though World War I and the restrictive legislation of 1924 had largely ended immigration from Eastern Europe, and even though by the 1930s a majority of American Jews were native-born, in the interwar years they were still widely perceived as an immigrant group, or even as a distinct race.³ Well into the early 1940s, Jews were excluded from important facets of majority society, from housing to higher education. For some, anti-Semitism and exclusion suggested continuities with the East European past and shaped how some immigrant Jews related to their non-Jewish neighbors. Harry Gersh, a Jewish professional writing for *Commentary*, recalled both his mother's attitudes and how his generation reworked this legacy under new conditions:

---

2 Albert I. Gordon, *Jews in Suburbia* (Boston: Beacon Press, 1959), 166.
3 Leonard Dinnerstein, *Antisemitism in America* (New York: Oxford University Press, 1994), chap. 5–7; Beth Wenger, *New York Jews and the Great Depression: Uncertain Promise* (New Haven: Yale University Press, 1996).

We knew her stories of pogroms. [...] We understood these stories as episodes from another world. [...] But we knew these things had happened because we were Jews. [...] But the storied *goy* was never identified with anyone we knew.... [The] "enemy-*goy*" had to be more than a non-Jewish individual. He had to be the landlord, the people who owned the "interests" and the trusts, the rich men who controlled the police and, sometimes, Pop's job. These were the *goyim* that were our enemies. But they were Luig's and Mick's enemies, too. Later we identified them as the class enemy.[4]

Combined with the traditional Jewish self-perception as a separate group, these factors resulted in the emergence of an "anxious subculture."[5] Intent on becoming Americans and remaining distinctly Jewish, American Jews created structures and institutions paralleling those in the mainstream society from which they were excluded. They were, in historian Oscar Handlin's words, "Jews in America, at home there and in their own way contriving a style of life out of the practical necessities about them."[6] The physical, social, cultural, and economic bases of this subculture were Jewish neighborhoods.[7] These "areas of second settlement" were, in many cases, more homogeneously Jewish than immigrant quarters like the Lower East Side, where Jews interacted more with other recent immigrant groups.[8] "We thought of them as Jewish neighborhoods, still ghettos, but not slums," Gersh recalled of his life in the East Bronx.[9] The interwar-period experience of attending public schools where a majority of students and teachers were Jewish, shopping with mostly Jewish local businesses, working in heavily Jewish, increasingly white-collar professions, and spending leisure time in Jewish contexts, too, resulted in a thick Jewishness that was more ethnic and secular than religious, transmitted osmotically rather than through formal Jewish education, comprehensive but often unself-conscious.[10] This Jewishness was a social fact met with the ambivalent acceptance generated by situations that seemed natural and inescapable. "Things Jewish were ingrained in our lives and not resented," Gersh

---

4 Harry Gersh, "The New Suburbanites of the 50's: Jewish Division," *Commentary* 17 (March 1954): 211. Luig and Mick reference (generic) Italian and Irish immigrant neighborhood boys.
5 Jonathan D. Sarna, *American Judaism: A History* (New Haven: Yale University Press, 2004), 208.
6 Oscar Handlin, "The American Jewish Pattern, after 300 Years: The Recent Decades – the Prospect Ahead," *Commentary* 18 (October 1954): 302.
7 Deborah Dash Moore, *At Home in America: Second Generation New York Jews* (New York: Columbia University Press, 1981), 233–36.
8 Hasia Diner, *The Jews of the United States, 1654 to 2000* (Berkeley: University of California Press, 2004), 225–26.
9 Gersh, "New Suburbanites," 210.
10 As such, the neighborhood-based Jewishness invited (ex-post-) analogies with pre-modern East European Jewish communities; cf. Eli Lederhendler, *New York Jews and the Decline of Urban Ethnicity, 1950–1970* (Syracuse: Syracuse University Press, 2001): 28.

recalled. "Jewishness [...] was taken for granted, accepted; it was unquestioned, it was not tortured and examined this way and that way." At least in retrospect, life in the 1930s and 1940s seemed less complicated than later life in suburbia, despite the dark sides of the urban Jewish experience: "Paradoxically, looking backward, those days of depression, of bread-hunger and job-hunger, of Hitler and Franco, of Popular Front and Father Coughlin, were simpler than the books say, indeed simpler than the later periods. The answers were evident and concrete. We knew where we were and where we wanted to go."[11]

For many Jews in the interwar years, the way to go was left. In their commitment to leftist causes, they could see themselves continuing an East European heritage of radicalism that for many became synonymous with Jewishness, a secular alternative to traditional or later religious expressions. Secularism as an ideology was politically and culturally respectable in the 1930s; it corresponded to the broad decline in religious knowledge, practice, and education that characterized large parts of American Jewry during the "religious depression" of the 1930s, which only at the end of the decade gave way to a religious renaissance. In the interwar period of "Jewishness without Judaism," religion was seen as a source of tensions and not the medium of choice to feel and express one's belonging to a group.[12] Membership in synagogues and enrollment in religious schools were low; Jewish identity was shaped not by a "logic of affiliation" but by a "logic of space."[13]

This thick Jewishness owed its binding strength also to ties that connected American Jews to their East European past, as seen from the perspective of the American present. The social lives of immigrant and second-generation American Jews reflected old-world social relations and practices that could be maintained within a geographically and culturally tight-knit urban community. Gersh recalled constant visits with *landsleyt* in the neighborhood. "When it was our turn to serve the tea and cake, we served them to families that lived next door in the old country. The New World friendships were made in the Workmen's Circle, the union local (Yiddish-speaking), the *landsmanshaft*."[14] Yiddish language and culture were the most immediate legacies of East European Jewishness. There was still a large

---

[11] Gersh, "New Suburbanites," 210.
[12] Sarna, *American Judaism*, 223–27; Martin E. Marty, *Modern American Religion [vol. II]: The Noise of Conflict, 1919–1941* (Chicago: University of Chicago Press, 1991), 2–5; Jeffrey S. Gurock, "American Judaism Between the Two World Wars," in *The Columbia History of Jews and Judaism in America*, ed. Marc Lee Raphael (New York: Columbia University Press, 2008), 95–96.
[13] Riv-Ellen Prell, "Community and the Discourse of Elegy: The Postwar Suburban Debate," in *Imagining the American Jewish Community*, ed. Jack Wertheimer (Waltham: Brandeis University Press/Hanover: University Press of New England, 2007), 70–76.
[14] Gersh, "New Suburbanites," 211.

Yiddish-speaking community within American Jewry well into the postwar period, with a rich cultural production in journals, theater, and literature. Still, when YIVO had to relocate its headquarters from Vilna to New York in 1940, the Yiddish-speaking community in America was already in decline. Cut off from the East European sources of its parent culture and rapidly Americanizing, it was not replenished through immigration.[15] The *landsmanshaftn,* the most important organizational structure for Yiddish-speaking Jews in America, aged and declined, as the organizational and symbolic world they had created did not speak to their members' American-born children. The Workmen's Circle, YIVO, and the Communist organization *Morning Freiheit* in the 1930s and 1940s started publishing English-language newsletters to supplement their Yiddish publications. In 1945, the closing of the famous "Café Royale" on New York's Second Avenue symbolically marked the decline of the Yiddish theater.[16] Yiddish culture seemed to fade out in America, just as its bearers, the Jews of Eastern Europe, were killed and the places that had shaped the culture were destroyed.

Mourning the World of East European Jewry – Claiming American Legitimacy

More than other factors, the Holocaust shaped how American Jews related to the now "vanished world" of their real and mythical ancestors. Approximately one generation after the end of major immigration from Eastern Europe, the murder of six million Jews had more immediate and intimate effects than what the abstracting term "Holocaust" and its immeasurable historical and moral implications convey today. For many American Jews in the 1940s, it meant the loss of close relatives. The destruction of Jewish towns meant the disappearance of the emotional reference points for personal and communal histories, the *shtetl* of a grandparent's telling, or the origin of an entire *landsmanshaft.* Prior to the war,

---

15 The Yiddish-speaking, ultra-Orthodox courts that transplanted themselves to America in the 1940s were too separatist in ideology and practice to provide a cultural infusion for the thoroughly secular Yiddish mainstream culture. Cf. Solomon Poll, "The Role of Yiddish in American Ultra-Orthodox and Hassidic Communities," *YIVO Annual of Jewish Social Science* 13 (1955): 125–52.
16 Daniel Soyer, *Jewish Immigrant Associations and American Identity in New York, 1880–1939* (Cambridge: Harvard University Press, 1997), 190; A. Leyeles, "To Thee America," *Workmen's Circle Call* 14 (1944), 8–9; Diner, *Jews of the United States,* 241–43; Ruth R. Wisse, "Ups and Downs of Yiddish in America," in *Yiddish in America: Essays on Yiddish Culture in the Golden Land*, ed. Edward S. Shapiro (Scranton: University of Scranton Press, 2008), 18.

"Eastern Europe" was not an abstraction shaped by geopolitical conflict or nostalgic reconstruction, but a more direct, often personal concern. Even though the number of American Jews who actually traveled to Eastern Europe in the 1930s and 1940s was small – mostly community leaders on relief missions or ardent leftists exploring the motherland of Communism – their first-hand impressions were magnified by media coverage and fundraising campaigns for East European Jewish communities left in poverty by accelerated modernization. *Landsmanshaftn* and the press played a key role for their members and readers in the preservation of links to real East European Jewish places and in the creation of images thereof – as well as to real Jews still living there.[17] The immigration of Jewish refugees in the 1930s and 1940s was numerically relatively small, but because of the heightened attention to refugees from Nazi Germany, Holocaust survivors, and the fate of European Jewry, their arrival had a strong impact on the American Jewish perception of East European Jewry. This was particularly true for high-profile immigrants, like Abraham Joshua Heschel, Orthodox rabbi Aharon Kotler, and the Lubavitcher Rebbe Yosef Yitshak Schneerson, who continued as important religious leaders in America.[18] Even as these encounters spoke to an American Jewish sense of difference and distance from the East Europeans, the shock of the Holocaust made it difficult for American Jews to continue to base their role in Jewish history upon a sense of discontinuity with the European past.

The geopolitical developments of the postwar period, in contrast, heightened the sense of difference, distance, and discontinuity. As the Cold War intensified in the 1940s and 1950s, personal forms of relating to concrete Jewish communities in Eastern Europe were gradually replaced by more abstract perceptions of "the persecuted Jews behind the Iron Curtain." "Eastern Europe" was reconstructed as a political space in the ideological and military confrontation between the two blocs.[19] The same confrontation made traveling and other avenues of

---

[17] Daniel Soyer, "Back to the Future: American Jews Visit the Soviet Union in the 1920s and 1930s," *Jewish Social Studies* 6 (2000): 124–59; for the larger context, cf. Paul Hollander, *Political Pilgrims: Travels of Western Intellectuals to the Soviet Union, China, and Cuba, 1928–1978* (New York: Oxford University Press, 1981); on fundraising-related contacts by *landsmanshaftn* and the Joint, see Samuel D. Kassow, "The Shtetl in Interwar Poland," in *The Shtetl: New Evaluations*, ed. Steven T. Katz (New York: New York University Press, 2006), 132–33; Rebecca Kobrin, *Jewish Bialystok and Its Diaspora* (Bloomington: Indiana University Press, 2010). For a contemporary account of a visit, see Gerold Frank, "Visit to the Old Country: The Lodz That Was," *Commentary* 14 (October 1952): 345–51.
[18] Diner, *Jews of the United States*, 245.
[19] Soyer (in "Back to the Future") points out that the dissonant perceptions of Russia as the "old" *shtetl*-related Jewish homeland and as the "new Russia" associated with Moscow and industry already shaped visitors' relations to the country before the war; for an example of the Cold War narrative, cf. S. Adhil Fineberg, "Religion behind the Iron Curtain," *CCAR Journal*, June 1962: 12–16, 37.

personal contact difficult, which, in turn, enhanced the interest in the few firsthand accounts as well as expert analyses of the fate of Jews in Poland or Russia, now threatened by Communist suppression of religious life and anti-Semitic campaigns.[20] It also resulted in a focus on the present and the political, which competed with the American Jewish interest in pre-1917 or pre-Holocaust Jewish life in Eastern Europe. A series of events within a condensed period in the early 1950s illustrated the co-existence of these different perspectives on Eastern Europe, past and present, political and historical. In 1951, in a domestic climate of witch hunts, blacklists, and McCarthyism, Julius Rosenberg, son of immigrants, and his wife Ethel went on trial for spying for the Soviet Union. The case led many American Jews to emphasize their distance from the East European Communism with which they felt they were collectively associated. In the following year, the anthropological study *Life is with People* about *shtetl* life in pre-Soviet Russia suggested very different images and connections between Jews and Eastern Europe in a vicarious and nostalgic identification with a pre-modern Jewish culture. In the same year, 1952, the creation of the first chair in Yiddish at an American university signaled the validation of their cultural heritage by the American academy, while simultaneously this heritage was brutally suppressed in the Soviet present. Uriel Weinreich, who accepted the chair at Columbia University, started teaching the language and literature of authors like Peretz Markish and Dovid Bergelson, who were executed in July of the same year, about a year before the Rosenbergs.[21]

The destruction of Jewish life during the Holocaust and the suppression of its remnants in postwar Communist Europe highlighted for American Jews their own safety, freedom, and prosperity; after all, the 1950s were also when color TV was introduced and *Playboy* magazine debuted with Marilyn Monroe on the cover. The American and Jewish parts of their identity meant engaging with radically different developments. Elvis Presley emerged as a star in 1956, the same year Anne Frank's *Diary* won the Pulitzer Prize. Such seemingly contradictory experiences raised the questions of what cultural references defined American Jews. As much as they took part in American culture, many were aware that, as Jews, they had been depending on cultural and spiritual centers that had been

---

20 A small selection of such reports includes: Gottfried Neuburger, "My Visit to Moscow: A Layman's Report on Jewish Life in Soviet Russia Today," [Orthodox] *Jewish Life* 23 (1956): 7; Samuel Sillen, "A Visit With Polish Jewry," *Jewish Life [Morning Freiheit Association]* 4 (1950): 21–24; Gerold Engel, "An Appraisal of the Rabbis' Visit to Moscow," *Jewish Forum* 40 (1957): 162–63; [An Expert on Soviet Affairs], "Anti-Semitism in the Soviet Union," *CCAR Journal*, October 1956: 28–39, 54; Maius Bergman, "Return to Poland: Pages from a Diary," *Commentary* 27 (May 1959): 395–404.
21 Mark Zborowski and Elizabeth Herzog, *Life is with People: The Jewish Little-Town of Eastern Europe* (New York: International Universities Press, 1952).

wiped out. Abraham Joshua Heschel's eulogy for the lost world of Ashkenaz had its counterpart in his disdain for the spiritual shallowness he found among American Jews.[22] Some American writers presented the ultra-Orthodox refugees, who transplanted their way of life and institutions to the New World, as urgently needed role models of an authentic Jewishness.[23] Many writers and thinkers discussing the state of American Jewry in the middle decades of the twentieth century started from a diagnosis of cultural and spiritual deficiency and religious laxity; they differed not in kind, but in degree.

This perception was all the more painful and poignant in light of the new responsibilities that American Jewry faced in the post-Holocaust era of Jewish history. Conservative rabbi Robert Gordis in early 1945 pointed to the imbalance: "It is a commonplace that the destruction of the great centers of cultural and religious vitality in Europe has catapulted American Jewry into a position of leadership and responsibility undreamt of twenty-five years ago, for which, incidentally, we are far from adequately prepared."[24] Even after the founding of the State of Israel, American Jewry remained the politically and financially strongest community in the Jewish world. This situation at first glance seemed to validate the rhetoric of America as the new "promised land" for the Jews and as heralding a new chapter in the history of mankind. But, patriotic narratives that defined America through its "break" with Europe could now seem obscene, like a "We told you so" in the face of the millions of innocent victims. Shame, reverence, respect, and sorrow over the loss of beloved individuals, real or mythical places of origin, and of an entire culture would in time induce a greater appreciation of the East European past among American Jews, as they faced questions of Jewish legitimacy in America and, particularly with the founding of the State of Israel, in the Jewish world.

American Jews' attitudes toward the new Jewish state have been the subject of historiographical revisions. Recently, the popular narrative has been challenged according to which most American Jews did not ardently identify with Israel prior to the Six Day War in 1967. A more nuanced account suggests that the fate of the fledgling community in Palestine, which became the destination of many Holocaust survivors, did occupy American Jews in political, philanthropic, and emotional ways and strengthened their Jewishness, but did not

---

22 Abraham Joshua Heschel, *The Earth is the Lord's: The Inner World of the Jew in Eastern Europe* (Woodstock, VT: Jewish Lights, 1995; orig. publ. 1949; republ. as paperback 1963).
23 Charles Raddock, "Hasidism – and They Mean It!" *Jewish Forum* 33 (1950): 232–34.
24 Robert Gordis, "The Task before Us: A Preface to Our Journal," *Conservative Judaism* 1 (1945): 1.

determine Jewish identity as it would in later times.[25] At a time when a recently Americanized immigrant community feared questions about their political loyalty, the existence of a state demanding Jewish political and financial support could not feel like an unmixed blessing. The "exchange of views" between Israeli prime minister David Ben Gurion and the leader of the American Jewish Committee, Jacob Blaustein, in 1950, which sought to lay to rest doubts about American Jews' loyalty, in turn illustrated the perceived need for such overt reassurances. It was directed at an American audience whose new readiness to accept the Jews should not be jeopardized by the demands of the ideology underlying the new Jewish state.[26]

These ideological demands complicated not only American Jews' standing within their American context, but also intra-Jewishly challenged their legitimacy as a diaspora community. American Jews' increasing engagement and subsequent identification with the East European past can be read as a response to this challenge. They linked themselves into the authentically Jewish historical tradition in order to extend its legitimacy to their American Jewish present. The debate about competing guarantors of Jewish authenticity – Zionist vs. diasporic – was expressed in the postwar argument about the pronunciation of liturgical Hebrew in American synagogues. Efforts to shift from the Ashkenazic pronunciation (associated with Yiddish and Eastern Europe) to the Sephardic one associated with Israel had been underway since the 1930s, but the Holocaust and the founding of Israel added powerful layers of meaning to it. A 1962 article in the Reform *CCAR Journal* pointed out that a significant group of American Jews "saw *Ashkenazic* Hebrew as being a still vibrant and meaningful tool in maintaining our contact with historic *European* Jewish traditions." The writer quoted Rabbi Solomon B. Freehof as arguing that "American Jews should express their solidarity with Israel in other ways. [...] As for our *RELIGIOUS* life, based upon our own traditions, this should remain *OURS*."[27]

As became clear over the postwar decades, the battle ground on which American Jews fought to protect their own Jewish legitimacy was not so much the political sphere. Israeli leaders realized that mass-immigration from across the Atlantic was unlikely, and American Jews found other, albeit sometimes difficult,

---

25 Diner, *Jews of the United States*, 227–28.
26 The issues of dual loyalty underlying the Ben Gurion-Blaustein agreement of 1950 were caused by the Zionist claim to represent all Jewry, which in turn was expected to physically join the new polity; cf. Charles Liebman, "Diaspora Influence on Israel: The Ben Gurion-Blaustein 'Exchange' and Its Aftermath," *Jewish Social Studies* 36 (1974): 271–80.
27 Harold Silver, "'An Oy for an Eye or an Eye for an Eye': Some Reactions Towards the Trend Away from Ashkenazic Pronunciation," *CCAR Journal*, June 1962: 48–49, emphasis in the original.

ways to integrate or balance political loyalty to the US with political and financial support for Israel. Much as American Jews came to define their Jewishness in cultural terms, it was the realm of culture and aesthetics in which hegemony over authentic Jewishness was contested and defined. Was it represented by Israeli aesthetics of the *chalutz*, soldier, and *sabra*, or by images of traditional Jews, radical revolutionaries, and Yiddish poets of the East European diaspora? In the early 1960s, American Jews could choose whether authentic Jewishness in the post-Holocaust world was best embodied by Ari Ben Canaan, the protagonist of Leon Uris's novel *Exodus*, played by Paul Newman in the eponymous 1960 movie, or by Sholem Aleichem's Tevye, played by Zero Mostel in the 1964 Broadway production. In contrast to the original stories, the Tevye of the musical leaves Eastern Europe not for Eretz Israel but for America. Each work presented its own version of the "exodus" from the old home and competing founding myths for a new home of authentic Jewishness.[28] In contrast to Israel's political, financial, and ideological demands, the "old home" Eastern Europe made no such claims. It was tragically and safely part of the past, whose meaning for the present and future of Jewishness could be reconstructed to fit the needs of American Jews searching for meaning in their Jewishness amid a disorienting American present.

American Crisis and Jewish Inclusion

Jews in postwar America also struggled as Americans with a larger sense of crisis. The experience of worldwide war ending in Hiroshima and Nagasaki, the threat of Communism on the world stage and at home, the pernicious effects of mass society on individuals and communities, and racial tensions seemed to undermine social and political stability, while the atomic bomb and the Cold War posed a threat to physical survival. Journals and other publications of the time overflowed with diagnoses of individual instability and social malaise, adding up to a mid-century sense of *fin de siècle*. Many felt that they lived in "the age of the Broken Atom and the Displaced Person," Conservative rabbi Wilfred Shuchat said in a sermon published in 1956.[29] More than a decade after the war's end, he mave been referring to psychological dislocations more than postwar refugees, but the term had a special resonance with his Jewish listeners. For them, the murder of

---

28 Seth Wolitz, "The Americanization of Tevye or Boarding the Jewish 'Mayflower,'" *American Quarterly* 40 (1988): 514–36.
29 Wilfred Shuchat, "How to Face a New Age," in *Best Jewish Sermons of 5715–5716*, ed. Saul I. Teplitz (New York: Jonathan David, 1956), 177.

six million Jews was an additional reason to doubt promises of moral and technological progress that had emerged from Enlightenment beliefs in the perfectibility of man. Literally closer to home, the perception that the city was in crisis called into question a Jewish utopia of urban cosmopolitanism and questioned the paradigm of Jewishness based in urban settings. The Jewish move to the suburbs was both an exodus *to* a promising land and *from* an environment increasingly seen as problematic, on Jewish and more general terms.

The American sense of crisis and restlessness was reflected in the unprecedented boom of therapeutic and self-help literature, which often pulled together psychology and religion as complementary modern and traditional sources of orientation. Norman Vincent Peale, the most prominent preacher in 1940s and 1950s America, pioneered the trend in a 1940 book co-authored with psychoanalyst Smiley Blanton: *Faith Is the Answer: A Psychiatrist and a Pastor Discuss Your Problems.*[30] In 1946, Rabbi Joshua Loth Liebman published *Peace of Mind,* which argued that "religion and psychology were twin angels" that could collaboratively heal the soul of the crisis-stricken American.[31] It was a pioneering attempt to reconcile Freudian psychology with religion from a specifically Jewish perspective. Liebman was the first rabbi to break into the mass market of spiritual self-help books. Written from a distinctly Jewish perspective, *Peace of Mind* was the first book to confront an American mass audience with a Jewish message on questions of spiritual well-being. With more than one million copies sold within the first three years, Liebman's bestseller was one of the most influential nonfiction books of the 1940s.[32] It was also a symbol of Judaism being presented and accepted as a source of meaning for America at large, a new perspective for a community that had long perceived themselves as outsiders to America. Postwar inclusion and acceptance of Judaism and Jews became tangible and visible in the same areas that had been characterized by exclusion and separation in the 1930s. Restrictions in the housing markets and admission quotas in higher education subsided, as prosperity and a new political climate reduced the impact of anti-Semitism. Nazism, defined as the moral opposite of Americanism, had thoroughly discredited anti-Jewish ideology and the underlying concepts of race,

---

30 Smiley Blanton and Norman Vincent Peale, *Faith Is the Answer: A Psychiatrist and a Pastor Discuss Your Problems* (New York: Abingdon-Cokebury, 1940). Later editions put Peale's name first.
31 Joshua Loth Liebman, *Peace of Mind* (New York: Simon & Schuster, 1946).
32 Andrew R. Heinze, "*Peace of Mind* (1946): Judaism and the Therapeutic Polemics of Postwar America," in *Key Texts in American Jewish Culture*, ed. Jack Kugelmass (New Brunswick: Rutgers University Press, 2003), 226; Heinze, *Jews and the American Soul: Human Nature in the Twentieth Century* (Princeton: Princeton University Press, 2004), 195.

which in parallel were undermined by the social-scientific turn toward cultural concepts of group identities. The success of the 1947 movie *Gentleman's Agreement*, a powerful indictment of anti-Semitism, directed by Elia Kazan and starring Gregory Peck, which won an Academy Award in 1948, was another sign of the change in the cultural climate.[33]

In the political reality of the mid-decades, however, the effect of the discrediting of race was largely limited to giving it up as a category of difference among white people. It did not eliminate, and may even have sharpened, the line between "whites," now including Jews, and others, particularly black people in America. For reasons of their own, Jews responded with ambivalence to the inclusion under the new label as "whites." Symbolic acts proving this measure of inclusion were recognized and celebrated as meaningful in their own time, but did not dispel the lingering sense of ambivalence.[34] "Miss New York," Bess Myerson, who in 1945 was the first Jewish woman to win the "Miss America" pageant, was a source of great joy and satisfaction for American Jews. If the competition for this most visible position defining America in terms of an aesthetic and moral ideal could be won by a member of the Hebrew race, then race was no longer a category and "America" had accepted them as their own. Meanwhile, and in the same sphere of aesthetic approximation, every nose operation performed on a Jewish woman in these years, every name change, and every effort to shed Yiddish accents, indicated that Jews were not necessarily at home in America and that their acceptance felt incomplete. Eight years after Myerson's victory, Saul Bellow let his protagonist Augie March claim Jewish Americanness for a fact, by opening the eponymous novel with the statement, "I am an American, Chicago-born."[35] Still, the stir it caused suggests that the assertion was not self-evident.

In the postwar climate, class, like race, increasingly lost ground as a category through which to understand individual and social roles. Or rather, the economic boom of the 1940s and 1950s, as well as developments longer in the making, transported many Americans into a middle class that regarded

---

33 Donald Weber, "The Limits of Empathy: Hollywood's Imaging of Jews circa 1947," in *Key Texts in American Jewish Culture*, ed. Jack Kugelmass (New Brunswick: Rutgers University Press, 2003), 91–104. The movie *Crossfire* (1947) was another important case of cinematic engagement with anti-Semitism.
34 Matthew Frye Jacobson, "Hyphen Nation: Ethnicity in American Intellectual and Political Life," in *A Companion to Post-1945 America*, ed. Jean-Christophe Agnew and Roy Rosenzweig (Malden: Blackwell, 2006), 175–91; Eric L. Goldstein, *The Price of Whiteness: Jews, Race, and American Identity* (Princeton: Princeton University Press, 2006).
35 Saul Bellow, *The Adventures of Augie March* (New York: Viking, 1953).

class-based politics with disdain. For Jews of East European background, who had been economically ascendant well before World War II, the rise into the middle class meant transcending earlier associations of Jewishness with lower-class immigrant characteristics. If Michael Gold's novel *Jews Without Money* (1930) sounded the theme of the class-conscious 1930s, one generation later Herman Wouk's *Marjorie Morningstar* (1955) illustrated the new middle-classness and the conflicts between immigrant parents and thoroughly American children.[36] Jacob Zukerman, head of the *Workmen's Circle*, summarized the shift in terms of occupation: "Second generation and third generation American Jews are found less in shops and factories and more at desks. What Jewish family doesn't boast of a doctor, a lawyer, a teacher, an accountant, a businessman (not necessarily a tycoon, but more than a candy-store owner)?"[37] In these professions, East European Jews joined their "German" brethren, who had become middle class earlier on. Even though Marshall Sklare and Joseph Greenblum in 1957–1958 still found significant socioeconomic and cultural differences between the two subgroups, the trend pointed clearly to greater homogenization.[38] Jews were self-conscious of their rapid socioeconomic ascent and wary of its effects on their Jewishness, as a few examples may illustrate. The repeated re-issuing of Abraham Cahan's classic *The Rise of David Levinsky* (in 1951 and 1960) can be read as an indicator of such ambivalence. The protagonist's conclusion from his life experience is that material success is punishable by emotional and spiritual emptiness. The intellectual, spiritual, and ultimately moral hollowness of middle-class Jewish life was the underlying theme of much of Philip Roth's work of these decades, particularly in *Goodbye Columbus*.[39] Like him, many intellectuals were turned off by what they saw as the uncultured materialism of the self-righteous allrightniks in the community.

Looking at American Jewry at large, observers and communal leaders warned that the broad liberal consensus of the time and the social pressure to conform in the suburbs would give additional pull to some Jews' tendency to adapt and assimilate and thereby abandon what made Jews and Judaism distinct

---

36 Michael Gold, *Jews Without Money* (New York: H. Liveright, 1930); Herman Wouk, *Marjorie Morningstar* (London: Hodder, 2008; orig. publ. 1955).
37 Jacob T. Zukerman, "What's on the Horizon for our Arbeter Ring?" *Workmen's Circle Call* 26 (1957): 4.
38 Marshall Sklare and Joseph Greenblum, *Jewish Identity on the Suburban Frontier: A Study of Group Survival in the Open Society,* 2nd ed. (Chicago: University of Chicago Press, 1979; orig. publ. 1967), 32–41.
39 Philip Roth, *Goodbye, Columbus, and Five Short Stories* (Cleveland: World Pub., 1963).

and different.[40] Worried, secular intellectuals, religious thinkers, labor organizers, and, prominently, social scientists began to explore and articulate "new modes of Jewishness" that would be in sync with the new sensitivities and interests of American Jews, their middle-classness (and attendant ambivalence) key among them.[41] Their search was driven by the fear that, unless such new modes could be found, the new inclusion of Jews would result in the large-scale dissolution of the boundaries and communal identity of American Jewry. Princeton sociologist Melvin Tumin phrased this sense of crisis dramatically in an article that described American Jews as utterly lacking any definable center, of meanings, intentions, or identity: "[Never] before has any group of Jews had such an indeterminate identity, such amorphous boundaries, at the same time that there exists such an extraordinary opportunity to create for themselves virtually any identity they desire."[42]

Suburbia as Uncharted Territory – Synagogues Marking Jewishness

Whatever identity American Jews may have desired and crafted, suburbia was the stage on which to perform it. From the 1940s to the 1960s, millions of Jews left their urban neighborhoods and moved to suburban developments, accelerating and intensifying demographic processes already in motion. Even in its own time, this change was seen as the single most important factor to shape the contours of American Jewish economic, educational, and religious life in the postwar decades. In Handlin's words, it "altered long-established patterns of thought and behavior."[43] If American Jewry was in transition, not yet formed and under-defined, so was suburbia for them. The title of Sklare's and Greenblum's study, *Jewish Identity on the Suburban Frontier*,

---

[40] Cf. for example, Joseph R. Fiszman, "One Benefit Above All," *Workmen's Circle Call* 23 (1954): 6, 16.
[41] Lila Corwin Berman, "American Jews and the Ambivalence of Middle-Classness" *American Jewish History* 93 (2007): 426. A key argument of Berman's study is that one consideration of the search for these new forms was the need to explain Jewish (economic) power to suspicious non-Jews. For the efforts of social scientists, see Berman, *Speaking of Jews: Rabbis, Intellectuals, and the Creation of an American Public Identity* (Berkeley: University of California, 2009).
[42] Melvin M. Tumin, "Conservative Trends in American Jewish Life," *Judaism* 13 (1964), 131–42.
[43] Oscar Handlin, "Foreword," in Albert I. Gordon, *Jews in Suburbia* (Boston: Beacon Press, 1959), ix.

was suggestive. The suburbs were beyond the Jewish comfort zone, a new territory that needed to be explored, tamed, cultivated, and regulated. Rights of symbolic ownership needed to be negotiated by religious and other groups before they could be expressed by buildings and other forms that marked belonging. Like the earlier American frontier, the suburbs represented opportunity and newness, the chance of a fresh start, the freedom to re-invent oneself, and the risk of the unknown. The editors of *Commentary* went so far as to compare the move to a suburb to the immigration from the Old World to the New.[44] "We came to the land with a full-blown insecurity that shows itself in constant comparison and seeking for advice," Gersh remembered.[45]

Once they settled in, suburban Jews were quick to create Jewish structures. Yet, those who came to suburbia early faced a geographical and cultural space empty of any Jewish institutions and traditions that would have catered to their practical needs and to their need to feel and express their Jewishness. If in the Jewish neighborhood of the 1930s the presence of kosher butchers and delicatessens, Jewish school teachers and rabbis, yeshivas and *landsmanshaftn*, relatives and friends, had sustained an unself-conscious, day-to-day Jewishness, their absence in the suburbs made Jews realize that they lacked the suppliers of the basic material and communal services that held their Jewishness together. Sol Gittleman's quip that "You could take the Jew out of the *shtetl*, but, it so happened, you could not take the *shtetl* out of the Jew" sounds apt, as American Jews grappled with a new psychological situation as they moved from the *shtetl* or "ghetto" into the suburban American mainstream.[46] While in the old neighborhoods they found it unnecessary to consciously think of themselves as Jews, in suburbia Jews had to make conscious decisions, individually and communally, as to whether, to what degree, and how they would define and express their belonging to something that for many was as uncharted as their suburb itself.

The patterns of suburbanization made for paradoxical minority-majority constellations of Jews and non-Jews. For practical reasons and out of social need, many Jews voluntarily clustered in certain suburbs, making for disproportionate shares of the inhabitants, but they still acutely perceived themselves as a minority in suburbia at large. The need for (Jewish) companionship competed

---

[44] "In this tercentenary year of Jewish settlement, we are increasingly aware that there has been underway a migration almost as massive as any of the earlier waves of immigration that shaped the American Jewish story." (Editorial note introducing Rossman, "The Community and I, 1954," 393)

[45] Gersh, "New Suburbanites," 216, 210.

[46] Sol Gittleman, *From Shtetl to Suburbia: The Family in Jewish Literary Imagination* (Boston: Beacon Press, 1978), 148.

with the middle-class values of privacy and the focus on the nuclear family. The re-fashioned balance between privacy and sociability and the mixture of Jewish dispersion and concentration shaped how Jewishness was conceived in the suburbs. The result was a rich and sometimes paradoxical texture of experiences, captured in Gersh's words: "[In] seeking a less 'Jewish' existence, no matter how subtly expressed, we find in Suburbia, a more 'Jewish' existence."[47] On the other hand, Rossman was left dissatisfied by the socializing among Jews for its own sake. This socializing was promoted even by her rabbi, whom she quoted as saying that "It was better for Jews to get together and play bridge or basketball than not to get together at all." To Rossman, this smacked of a blind desire to be distinct, despite the absence of anything that would give the distinctiveness real meaning, an absence that nobody else in her circle seemed to find problematic.[48] The *American Jewish Year Book* had already in 1949 noted that "the search for 'Jewish content' was not a simple one."[49] Yet, even with little content, Jewish apartness was seen as a positive value. Gersh sensed that most suburbanizing Jews did not flee Jewishness as such, but rather that its previous definition had limited them and had not allowed them to choose for themselves what Jewishness meant. "In moving from city to suburb we had, if only subconsciously, a vision of a less 'Jewish' existence. Though the accusation has been made by various kinds of ideological and institutional zealots, this is not a running away from *Yiddishkeit*. But it is a running away from the ghetto [...] from life within a bloc – political, social, cultural."[50] In these settings, it seemed, the challenge was how to express a Jewishness that was in sync with the value of personal choice, was serious but not tribal, communitarian but with "content" and "meaning." One expression presented itself as part of the *zeitgeist* of postwar America: religion.

The resurgence of religion as a positive force, and one that paved the way for the acceptance not only of Judaism but also of Jews, had been in the making since the early 1940s and particularly in World War II. The war experience has been called "the great watershed" for American Jews. More than half a million Jews served in the US Armed Forces during the war – more than ten percent of American Jewry – with many more affected as family members and friends of those serving.[51]

---

47 Gersh, "New Suburbanites," 218.
48 Rossman, "The Community and I" (1954), 398, 403. This sentiment, of course, touches on a long and ongoing scholarly debate about positive Jewishness resting on "content" (e.g. religion) or on "structural" factors, such as socializing for its own sake.
49 Sholom J. Kahn, "Cultural Activities," in *American Jewish Year Book 1948–1949*, ed. Harry Schneiderman and Morris Fine (New York: American Jewish Committee, 1949), 178–210.
50 Gersh, "New Suburbanites," 218.
51 Edward S. Shapiro, "World War II and American Jewish Identity," *Modern Judaism* 10 (1990): 65; Sarna, *American Judaism*, 264–65.

For many Jews, the military provided a first intensive encounter with non-Jews, and vice versa, as the separation of Jewish subcultures had previously limited such interactions. It is impossible to prove to what degree these personal experiences contributed to the decrease, over the 1940s and beyond, of the anti-Semitism that had been prevalent in 1930s society. Whether or not this was true for every military unit, the war had a strong homogenizing effect on American society. Christian and Jewish organizations went to great lengths to advocate for understanding and goodwill among the religious and ethnic groups in the military and in society at large. Political and propaganda activities promoting patriotic identification with America against the enemy, Nazi Germany, had deep resonance for American Jews, who, since 1942, gradually learned about the fate of their European brethren. The horror about the unfolding Holocaust had its counterpart in a renewed appreciation for the relatively beneficial conditions of Jewish life in America. American Jews found their particular group interests to be consonant with the larger American ones, spurring them to embrace and support the war effort wholeheartedly. This placed them in opposition to xenophobic populists like the Catholic priest Father Charles Coughlin and celebrity aviator Charles Lindbergh, who opposed American involvement in the war. Recognizing the popular appeal of the mixture of anti-Semitism and anti-war rhetoric, American Jewish leaders were careful not to contribute to the suspicion that America under President Franklin D. Roosevelt, denigrated as Jewish and thus called "Rosenfeld" by anti-Semites, or under the influence of Jewish supporters and advisers, fought the war "for the Jews."

Figure 3: Rosh Hashanah service at military Camp Blanding, St. Augustine, FL, 1945. (American Jewish Archives)

The war experience, the propagandistic need for unifying patriotic themes, the Jewish search for politically safe forms of expressing distinctiveness, and the overall sense of distress about the mass killing and dying in Europe resulted in two key developments: a new appreciation of religion in American society in general and a renewed identification among American Jews with their Jewishness, and particularly with Judaism, as meaningful attributes. The ensuing postwar expression of Jewishness through Judaism grew out of an increased identification with Jewishness more broadly that had begun before the war. This renewal was visible in a growing interest in Jewish education and other types of formal affiliation, with religious expressions becoming increasingly dominant. Leaders of American Jewry furthered religious articulations of Jewishness by joining with the larger patriotic discourse that defined "religion" as an American value in contrast to the Godlessness of the Nazis (and later of the Communist Soviet Union in the Cold War). Religious and civic values were closely intertwined in the patriotic rhetoric of the war years and the decade that followed. The rise of fascism and Communism was seen as proof that the tensions inherent in ethnic and cultural diversity were explosive, as the interwar years had suggested, unless they were contained and managed by the unifying effect of religion, which regulated the differences it limited and allowed.[52] American Jewish organizations and institutions tried to make use of this development in different ways, as they sought to position Judaism and the Jews as belonging to the social mainstream. Secular organizations, such as the umbrella National Community Relations Advisory Council (NCRAC), and its constituent entities like the American Jewish Committee, defined anti-Semitism and discrimination as instances of universal conflicts in "group relations." Thereby, they aimed to preserve the notion of Jews as a distinct group within society, but at the same time defined the problem in universal terms; its solution would therefore be in the interest of America in general. While some groups, such as the American Jewish Congress, retained their focus on *ethnic* Jewish distinctiveness within a *culturally* pluralist society, the religion-minded cultural climate favored religion as the category of distinctiveness. From the congregational to the national level, Jewish organizations engaged in interfaith dialogue in order to carve out a legitimate and safe space for Jews and Judaism in a religiously pluralistic society.[53]

---

[52] Wendy Wall, *Inventing the "American Way:" The Politics of Consensus from the New Deal to the Civil Rights Movement* (Oxford: Oxford University Press, 2008), 6–9; Michael Kammen, *Mystic Chords of Memory: The Transformation of Tradition in American Culture* (New York: Knopf, 1991), 571–72; Marty, *Noise of Conflict, 1919–1941*, 2–5; Marty, *Modern American Religion [vol. III]: Under God Indivisible, 1941–1960* (Chicago: University of Chicago Press, 1996), 54–64, 115–29.

[53] Stuart Svonkin, *Jews Against Prejudice: American Jews and the Fight for Civil Liberties* (New York: Columbia University Press, 1997), 2–6; Naomi W. Cohen, *Not Free to Desist: The American Jewish Committee 1906–1966* (Philadelphia: Jewish Publication Society, 1972), 333–37.

Figure 4: Interfaith scholarly meeting, Conference on Science, Philosophy, and Religion, Philadelphia, September 1947; from left: Alain Locke, architect of the African American "Harlem Renaissance" and of Baha'i faith; Louis Finkelstein, chancellor of the Jewish Theological Seminary; Robert M. MacIver, sociologist; John Courtney Murray, Jesuit theologian; Swami Akhilananda, Hindu scholar. (The Library of The Jewish Theological Seminary)

The challenge was to align this objective with the need for Jews to find meaningful expressions of Jewishness in the strange new environment of suburbia. The single greatest attempt to integrate both societal expectations and Jewish needs was to be found in the suburban synagogue. Among American Jews, the 1950s' "religious boom" manifested itself visibly in the construction of new synagogues in suburbia, a Jewishly uncharted territory where Jews had to define for themselves and for the outside world how they would realize and express their Jewishness. In Gersh's assessment, "The synagogue symbolizes the most important change in the move to Suburbia – a change in our concept of ourselves as Jews."[54] As physical spaces and chartered entities, synagogues came to replace the web of institutions and relationships of the urban neighborhood and of Yiddish culture. They provided

---

54 Gersh, "New Suburbanites," 217.

American Jews with alternative, tangible support structures for their persistent, yet largely undirected subjective Jewishness. In practical terms, synagogues offered a space where Jews could realize their Jewishness together in various forms. They encompassed Hadassah and Men's Club activities, Hebrew schools and adult education, fundraising for Israel and social action. They did so under an umbrella – religion – that was intelligible and acceptable to their non-Jewish fellow suburbanites. In a cultural climate that eschewed ethnicity as a category of difference and identity, synagogues were a socially viable way to put Jews and Judaism on the suburban map and to assert a measure of legitimate distinctiveness. As a result, the synagogue came to be seen, by Jews and non-Jews alike, as *the* representation not just of Judaism, but also of Jews and Jewishness in suburban America. "In Suburbia, there is no question about who speaks for us," Gersh stated. "The closest thing to a Jewish community in the United States is the suburban synagogue. [...] The Jew is perforce a member of his religious community. Even if he refuses to accept formal membership, he does not openly dispute the synagogue's right to speak for him."[55]

Suburban Jews subjected their expression of Jewishness to a new logic that was in line with broader societal development: "affiliation" became the category by which social identities were organized. In contrast to the earlier neighborhood-based and unself-conscious Jewishness, affiliation also implied individual, conscious choice. In this behavior, American Jews followed larger societal norms. "The logic of affiliation implied 'American' values," Prell argues, which in the postwar decades meant the valorization of religion and the concomitant depreciation of secularism as an ideology.[56] Among the various groups and institutions Jews could join, synagogue affiliation, which reached unprecedented rates, was therefore of particular import.[57] Contemporary accounts illustrate that, besides larger societal trends, decisions to join and attend synagogue were the result of complex personal decision-making processes that considered factors such as external expectations, friendship ties, and spiritual needs. "[Out] here it's the path of least resistance to join," Gersh admitted. "If we don't go [to synagogue] the occasions for seeing our new friends are limited."[58] Religious needs were rarely mentioned among the primary motivations to join a synagogue. Attendance at services remained lower among Jews than among other groups experiencing the "religious revival" of the 1950s, and religious observance beyond the synagogue was low, too.

---

55 Gersh, "New Suburbanites," 217.
56 Prell, "Discourse of Elegy," 75.
57 *American Jewish Year Book* 1958 ed. Morris Fine (Philadelphia: Jewish Publication Society, 1958), 117; Jack Wertheimer, *A People Divided: Judaism in Contemporary America* (New York: Basic, 1993), 5–6.
58 Gersh, "New Suburbanites," 219–20.

Figure 5: Procession bringing the Torah scrolls into the newly completed Main Sanctuary of Beth Sholom Congregation, Elkins Park, PA, September 1959. The synagogue, designed by famous architect Frank Lloyd Wright, is located in a suburb of Philadelphia. (Congregation Beth Sholom)

Jews joined synagogues or other groups out of a need for community: immediate community realized in social relations and more abstract community as a ground for identification. Sklare and Greenblum found that Jews in postwar suburbia sought out other Jews as friends and companions sharing a perspective born out of common experience. Forty-two percent of their respondents said that all their close friends were Jews; 89 per cent reported that "most" (60 per cent or more) of their close friends were, a slight increase compared to their parent generation's number (87 per cent, with 30 per cent reporting exclusively Jewish friendship circles).[59] These

---

[59] Sklare and Greenblum, *Suburban Frontier*, 272; cf. also Rossman, "Community and I" (1956), 236. Eisen sees the almost exclusive choice of other Jews as friends as "gestures of separation" out of a feeling of being ill at ease with gentiles. A sense of superiority was expressed only in the in-group, but suppressed on the outside; cf. Arnold M. Eisen, *The Chosen People in America: A Study in Jewish Religious Ideology* (Bloomington: Indiana University Press, 1983), 143–46.

data underlay Sklare's assessment that synagogues served as "ethnic churches:" religious institutions providing a socially acceptable façade for communities based de-facto on ethnic cohesion.[60] Communal leaders, even rabbis, at the time recognized the need for a broader sense of Jewishness. The question whether postwar America would accept ethnic or cultural pluralism was a major fault line among Jewish leaders and thinkers at the time.

Beyond providing community in the here and now, synagogue affiliation allowed suburban Jews to identify with the larger, historical Jewish community in a way that was in line with how American society organized differences and identities. The Workmen's Circle's Zukerman registered "an increased interest in Jewishness, often reflected in the growth of the synagogue centers, appearing to be not necessarily a return to religion but rather an expression of the desire for Jewish identification."[61] In the social logic of the time, identification in religious categories fulfilled the need for both assimilation *and* separation. Will Herberg analyzed the seeming paradox of inclusion and distinctiveness on a larger scale. His seminal study of 1955, *Protestant – Catholic – Jew,* even in its very title conveys the fact that Judaism, the religion of some three percent of the U.S. population, had come to be accepted on equal footing with the two largest Christian traditions. Together they formed the "triple melting-pot" whose dividing lines seemed relatively stable (measured by low rates of intermarriage) and allowed for distinctiveness within the larger commonality of the Judeo-Christian tradition.[62]

Jewishness Redux – the Wounded Jewish Soul and the East European Medicine

Inclusion came with a price tag. Judaism, like Protestantism and Catholicism in Herberg's analysis, were little more than taxonomic labels for the structure of society and religious ideologies in the service of a set of unifying national values.

---

[60] Marshall Sklare, *Conservative Judaism: An American Religious Movement* (Glencoe, Ill., 1955), 35, cf. also ch. 2; Charles S. Liebman, *The Ambivalent American Jew: Politics, Religion, and Family in American Jewish Life* (Philadelphia: Jewish Publication Society, 1973), 42–45, 68–73; Gordon, *Jews in Suburbia*, 153; Bernard J. Bamberger, "Charting the Future of Reform Judaism," *CCAR Journal*, January 1958: 15; William Stern, "What are the Positive Factors for Jewish Survival in America?" *Workmen's Circle Call* 27 (1958), 5–6.
[61] Zukerman, "What's on the Horizon," 4.
[62] Will Herberg, *Protestant – Catholic – Jew: An Essay in American Religious Sociology* (Chicago: University of Chicago Press, 1983; orig. publ. 1955), 32–34, 256–57.

"America today may be conceived, as it is indeed conceived by most Americans, as one great community divided into three big sub-communities religiously defined, all equally American in their identification with the 'American Way of Life,'" wrote Herberg.[63] Contemporary and later observers, Herberg himself among them, registered that this functional and reductive conception of Judaism did not satisfy the needs of American Jews for meaningful Jewishness. Even though many second-generation Jews had been distant from traditional Jewish practices and ideas, plenty of signs spoke to genuine spiritual needs left unfulfilled by the suburban synagogue. Since it represented liberal American Judaism, it was the primary form for expressing Jewishness and therefore the first target of critics, whose alternative ideas reflected vastly divergent agendas for American Jewry. Some stayed within a broadly defined category of religion. The "new Jewish theology" emerging in the 1950s sought to save existential Judaism from its liberal reduction.[64] Others rejected religion in general as a category of meaningful Jewishness. Zionist Ben Halpern forcefully argued that, by defining themselves as a religious rather than national community, American Jews had subjected their tradition to Christian concepts of religion, which emphasized individual, subjective, and private categories of belonging (faith) over communal, objective, behavioral, and public forms, such as text study, ritual observance, and *kashrut*. They had thereby reduced Jewishness and deprived American Jewry of the fullest expressions of their heritage.[65] Yet, other observers faulted the bland construct that historian Lila Corwin Berman has called "sociological Jewishness." The attempt to present Jews in universal terms as a social group with a distinct religious value to American society failed as a basis on which to build and sustain a vital, creative community.[66] The combined, frustrating sum total of these different efforts was, in Herberg's analysis, that "among some American Jews there was perplexity and restlessness. Was this all there was to Judaism after all? Had it no higher purpose or destiny? What was it, in the last analysis that made the Jew a Jew, and kept him a Jew?"[67]

---

[63] Herberg, *Protestant – Catholic – Jew*, 38.
[64] Robert G. Goldy, *The Emergence of Jewish Theology in America* (Bloomington: Indiana University Press, 1990).
[65] This is the core argument of Ben Halpern, *The American Jew: A Zionist Analysis* (New York: Theodor Herzl Foundation, 1956); cf. also Richard L. Rubenstein, "The Intellectual and Contemporary Jewish Life," *Conservative Judaism* 14 (1960): 40–46.
[66] Berman, *Speaking of Jews*: 2–4, 120–22.
[67] Herberg, *Protestant – Catholic – Jew*, 198. In his incarnation as one of the "new theologians," Herberg advocated an existentialist alternative to Halpern's national solution. Cf. Herberg, *Judaism and Modern Man: An Interpretation of Jewish Religion* (Philadelphia: Jewish Publication Society, 1951).

Contemporary observers traced this restlessness to a sense of loss and fragmentation that left Jewishness incomplete and that none of the different approaches to making Jewishness meaningful could address. Gersh articulated this feeling in relation to the promise of meaning and community which Judaism as a religion made but failed to keep: "There's a consciousness of loss that cannot be exactly pinned down," he mused. "Many of us turn [inward] for satisfying answers to our many questions. [...] It is important to integrate the inner and outer man [...] with the Jew. This is a private process, and a longer story – of which we have so far seen only the beginning."[68] As Prell has pointed out, the downside of the suburban logic of affiliation was often criticized in the language of the divided self, schizophrenia, and emptiness: Jews searched for ways to navigate the public space that was no longer unproblematically Jewish, while the synagogue and their homes were the private spaces in which their Jewishness was now performed.

Authenticity and identity became key concerns for those worried about the health of the community and the individual.[69] The psychological approach was on the one hand distinctly American, as in Liebman's *Peace of Mind*, but on the other hand echoed a discourse from across the Atlantic reaching back twenty-five years. The rhetoric of the wounded Jewish soul in need of healing and the critique of liberal forms of religion as shallow and fragmentary present a telling parallel to the interwar Central European discourse, out of which emerged new concepts of Judaism that responded to the crisis of liberal theology.[70]

Aware of these fragmentations and inner tensions, some observers of American Jewry pointed to the need to come to terms with the specific issue of American Jewry's collective East European past. Rabbi Wilfred Shuchat suggested in his sermon that his listeners could find consolation in the beauty of traditional *shtetl* life as depicted in *Life is with People*.[71] Freudian notions of the

---

[68] Gersh, "New Suburbanites," 220–21.
[69] Prell, "Discourse of Elegy," 78–79; Prell, "Triumph, Accommodation, and Resistance: American Jewish Life from the End of World War II to the Six-Day War," in *The Columbia History of Jews and Judaism in America*, ed. Marc Lee Raphael (New York: Columbia University Press, 2008), 120.
[70] Cf. Peter Eli Gordon, "Franz Rosenzweig and the Philosophy of Jewish Existence," in *The Cambridge Companion to Modern Jewish Philosophy*, ed. Michael L. Morgan and Peter Eli Gordon (Cambridge: Cambridge University Press, 2007), 122–46. For an underexplored parallel with developments in interwar Germany, cf. Steven E. Aschheim, *Brothers and Strangers: The East European Jew in German and German Jewish Consciousness, 1800–1923* (Madison: University of Wisconsin Press, 1982); Michael Brenner, *The Renaissance of Jewish Culture in Weimar Germany* (New Haven: Yale University Press, 1996).
[71] Shuchat, "How to Face a New Age," 179–81.

healing effect of bringing unconscious longings and experiences from the past to consciousness informed many therapeutic ideas for American Jews who felt rootless, disoriented, and overwhelmed by the new choices.[72]

Figure 6: Exhibit commemorating the 300th anniversary of Jewish settlement on the North American continent; 1st National Bank Building, Cincinnati, November 1954. The "Tercentenary" was an occasion for American Jews to take stock of their place in America and in Jewish history. (American Jewish Archives)

Having trained their eyes on the present and future, they now found themselves missing something. "Sometimes, perhaps, the Jews wondered whether something valuable was not lost in the accommodation. Now that few remnants of the

---

[72] Examples of Freud-inspired approaches include Jakob J. Petuchowski, "The Grip of the Past: A Study in the Dynamics of Religion," *Judaism* 8 (1959), 132–41; E. Steindletz, "Hasidism and Psychoanalysis," *Judaism* 9 (1960), 222–28; Max Weinreich, "Jewish Culture in America – To-Day and To-Morrow [Speech at Commencement of Baltimore Hebrew College]," June 10, 1945, typescript, YIVO Archive, Weinreich Collection, RG 584.9.

immigrant culture remained, the idealized image of the ghetto was strangely fascinating," Handlin wrote in 1954, on the occasion of the Tercentenary.[73] After three centuries as an immigrant community, American Jewry came into its own in the New World by training its eyes on the Old World, probing connections and bridges that related them to the East European past.

---

[73] Handlin, "American Jewish Pattern, after 300 Years," 306.

2 Launching a Discourse: YIVO's Bridge From the Old World to the New

When YIVO arrived in New York in 1940, it brought to the New World the same objective for which it had been founded in 1925. It aimed "to collect and preserve materials pertaining to Jewish life, past and present, all over the world [and] to study past and present Jewish life with the methods of modern social science," as the mission statement on the front page of its very first English-Yiddish newsletter published in the US declared in 1943.[1] Beyond the practical purposes of documentation, this program was the concrete formulation of the larger agenda that YIVO pursued: encouraging Jewish self-reflection and self-expression, so that Jews could acquire self-knowledge, particularly of their heritage as embodied in the East European Jewish experience. This would be the force behind the creation of a community and of a positive Jewish identity under new circumstances at a time when the very continuity of Jewish life was at stake. The 1943 mission statement called YIVO's work "a means of giving the Jew the opportunity to acquire self-knowledge and of providing him with new implements in the intellectual struggle for survival."[2] This conviction determined YIVO's distinctive approach to the past. Of course, American Jews had been engaging with their East European past in the six decades between the beginning of mass immigration and the arrival of the institute in New York. But, Weinreich and YIVO supplied a new program for the conscious appropriation of this heritage. To support a positive sense of Jewishness, this heritage would be defined in broad cultural terms. That, in turn, would be the key to continuity under modernizing circumstances.

The program was based on two constitutive assumptions: a firm belief in social science as a universal tool to safeguard a Jewish future in a modern environment, and the expectation that this very future of Jewry would be decided in America. Weinreich pronounced explicitly that self-knowledge was an antidote not just for the challenges facing East European Jewry in the early twentieth century, but at least as much for

---

[1] "[Mission Statement]," *YIVO Newsletter* 1 (September 1943): 1*. The bilingual newsletter, which over time also appeared as *News of the YIVO*, distinguishes its English-language pages by an asterisk (*) from the Yiddish ones; articles were not signed. Examples of the larger agenda included a plan to create a "Museum of the Jewish Homes of the Past," cf. *Newsletter* 5 (November 1944): 4*; the acquisition of documents and material relating to the Jewish past, among them Theodore Herzl's diary, cf. "Three Outstanding Diaries in YIVO's Archives: The Legacy of Vilna to New York," *Newletter* 22 (September 1947): 1*–2*, 8*; and "YIVO Receives Important Materials on History of Jewish Labor Movement," *Newsletter* 29 (November 1948): 3*.
[2] YIVO mission statement (1943), 1*.

American Jewry at mid-century. In his diagnosis of a community coming of age and in search of itself, Dr. Weinreich spoke for many observers who found American Jewry to be an ill patient in need of intellectual, religious, political, or cultural help with pronounced identity problems. For Weinreich and others, it was a matter of group identity. Speaking in 1948 at a *Commentary* conference, where some 30 intellectuals discussed the state of American Jewry, he lamented the Jews' "superficial Americanization" and the false prediction that adaptation to the new environment would solve their problems.[3] Weinreich's diagnosis echoed his background in psychology: "[Personality] problems have remained for almost every Jew. Only part of the Jewish community share in the joys that being a Jew can offer whereas all Jews share in the disabilities of being a Jew. This makes for very strong personality problems."[4] The Yiddish doctor-psychologist-social scientist prescribed a therapy of scientifically guided reflection on how American Jewry understood itself, which would lead to the self-consciousness needed to respond to the changes affecting them. Individual and group self-knowledge would be the key to the stable and positive sense of Jewishness required for group distinctiveness and continuity.[5]

At the time that Weinreich came to New York, the murderous policies of the Nazis and the war in Europe were progressing and gave tragic urgency to YIVO's concerns: the meaning of Jewishness in the face of the Holocaust, the preservation of the East European Jewish culture being destroyed, and the role of American Jewry after the murder of much of European Jewry. In light of these fundamental changes, YIVO adjusted its mission.[6] In November of 1944, it reported on a project "to gather and preserve *all* materials which depict

---

[3] Participants of the May 22–23 conference included Hannah Arendt, Daniel Bell, Moshe Davis, Nathan Goldberg (American Jewish Congress), Solomon Grayzel (Jewish Publication Society), Hyman B. Grinstein (Yeshiva College), Sidney Hook, Guido Kisch, Bertram Korn, Irving Kristol, Harry L. Lurie (Council of Jewish Federations), Jacob R. Marcus, Charles Reznikoff, Arthur M. Schlesinger, Leo Srole (Columbia University), (Rabbi) Joshua Trachtenberg (Temple Covenant of Peace, Easton, Pa.), Weinreich, and Louis Wirth. "Proceedings" were circulated among participants in September 1950 ("Report on a Conference on the Jewish Experience in America (sponsored by *Commentary*)," May 1948, typescript, YIVO Archives, Max Weinreich Collection, RG 584, folder 225A).

[4] Weinreich, in "Report on a Conference on the Jewish Experience in America," 63–64.

[5] Max Weinreich, "[Jewish Scholarship Today; speech at 1941 Annual YIVO Conference, Yiddish]," typescript, YIVO Archives, Max Weinreich Collection, RG 584.4, 11; Weinreich in "Report on a Conference," 65.

[6] On the rhetorical trope of a "vanished world" and the implied comprehensiveness and separateness of East European Jewish life (and the metaphysical value implied by the term), cf.

the life of the Jews in various countries of Europe and thus to build a monument to those ways and institutions that have been destroyed by the war and also to bring before the Jewish youth of America a rich and colorful exhibit which shows how their parents and grandparents lived in their old homes." An exhibition which opened at YIVO in January 1944, "Pictures of Jewish Life in Pre-War Poland" by Roman Vishniac, served that purpose, as did the plan to publish a cultural history of Jewish life in Eastern Europe for American readers.[7] The declaration adopted at the annual conference in January 1945 showed how YIVO hoped to draw on the East European past to shore up American Jewry, the best hope for the future of world Jewry:

> We know the responsibility incumbent upon each of us for the future of the whole Jewish people, for the fate of American Jewry. In the hope that the greatness of the historic mission will give us greater strength, the 19th Annual Conference of the Yivo proclaims: [...] We will do all in our power, through recording and collection, research and study, publication and dissemination, to preserve for the generations to come the creative spirit of European Jewry. We will do all in our power to enrich Jewish life in America with the life-giving spirit of Jewish creativity, that the splendor of the Divine Presence which revealed itself in the ghettos shall not be dimmed, but with ever growing brilliance [sic] glow in us, our children, and children's children.[8]

This statement, occasioned by the Holocaust and YIVO's move to a new world, articulated what became the institute's primary tenet: that the "creative spirit" of this culture could – and should – be preserved for its own sake and for that of a Jewry existing under fundamentally different circumstances. Speaking in 1964 at the 38th annual YIVO conference, union leader and YIVO activist Israel Breslow solemnly summed up the institute's mission, now mostly for American Jewry: "A man who has lost his memory ceases to be an individual [...] A people that has lost its yesterday has no tomorrow," Breslow said, quoting historian Shimon Dubnow. "Ever since its

---

Jeffrey Shandler, *Shtetl: A Vernacular Intellectual History* (New Brunswick: Rutgers University Press, 2013), 74.
7 "Museum of the Jewish Homes of the Past," *Newsletter of the YIVO* 5 (November 1944): 4*, emphasis in the original; "Exhibition of Art Photographs," *Newsletter* 2 (February 1944): 5*; "The Contribution of Eastern European Jewry to Jewish Culture," *Newsletter* 8 (April 1945): 4*.
8 "Declaration of the 19th Annual Conference of the Yiddish Scientific Institute – YIVO," *YIVO Newsletter* 7 (February 1945): 3*. The institution referred to itself as "Yivo" into the 1950s before it changed to "YIVO;" in its own publications of the time, it often used the definite article when referring to itself.

establishment in Vilna, the YIVO has been the memory of the Jewish people. [...] The YIVO has preserved our yesterday, helping thereby in the shaping of our tomorrow."[9]

From the time of its relocation to New York, YIVO made great efforts to pursue this mission in a new environment and to insert its perspective into the Jewish conversation in the US, realizing early on that this was an uphill struggle. "The American soil is stony," Weinreich admitted as early as 1941.[10] As it tried to strike roots in America, YIVO adapted its scholarly program and the means of communicating its scholarship to a new audience. Besides the bilingual newsletter and bilingual edition of the works of Yitzhak Leib Peretz, it published the first English-language *YIVO Annual* in 1946, a series which often contained translations of earlier Yiddish texts, such as Heschel's eulogy for Ashkenazic Jewry and research on Eastern Europe and the United States. It invited the public to "Friday Evening Teas" and public lectures to discuss topics such as "the future of the Jews in America," as well as to an oral history project on Jewish life in the US and an autobiography contest among recent immigrants in 1942; it also offered a course on Jewish history for public school teachers.[11] Exhibitions were another instrument for transmitting knowledge gained through historical and social-scientific research. YIVO presented, first on 123rd Street and later on Fifth Avenue, exhibits on Jewish life during the Holocaust (1946), Jewish children in Europe after World War II (1948), Peretz (1952), the *shtetl* (1958), Vilna (1960), Shimon Dubnow

---

[9] "Variety of Scholarly Topics Discussed at the 38th YIVO Conference," *News of the YIVO* 89 (February 1964): 2*.

[10] Weinreich, "Jewish Scholarship Today," 11.

[11] For reports on the results, see "The YIVO Contest for the Best Autobiographies of Jewish Immigrants to America," *YIVO Newsletter* 1 (September 1943): 4*, and Moses Kligsberg, "The Golden Land: The Jewish Immigrant in America: Self-Portrait," *Commentary* 5 (May 1948): 467–72. In "Socio-Psychological Problems Reflected in the YIVO Autobiography Contest" *(YIVO Annual of Jewish Social Science* 1 (1946), 241–49), Kligsberg reports on the extensive correspondence between YIVO and contestants. Bernard Weinryb, "Yivo Annual" [review], *Jewish Quarterly Review* 42 (1952): 326–28; Abraham Joshua Heschel, "The Eastern European Era in Jewish History," *YIVO Annual of Jewish Social Science* 1 (1946): 86–105; "The YIVO Bilingual Edition of Peretz," *News of the YIVO* 21 (June 1947): 1*; "Friday Evening Teas at the Yivo," *Newsletter* 1 (1943), 2*: "Oral American Jewish History," *Newsletter* 86 (1963): 5*; "YIVO Course for Public School Teachers," *Newsletter* 95 (1965): 1*. Cf. also Deborah Dash Moore, "Preface," in *East European Jews in Two Worlds: Studies from the YIVO Annual,* ed. Moore (Evanston, IL: Northwestern University Press, 1990), vii.

(1961), and the Warsaw Ghetto Uprising (1963).[12] With the exception of the Holocaust- and war-related exhibitions, the Yiddish and English texts accompanying the visual images and artifacts largely struck a sober tone, avoiding overt political-ideological positions.

Figure 7: YIVO headquarters at 1048 Fifth Avenue in New York, not dated. From 1955 to 1994, the institute was located in the former Vanderbilt mansion. (American Jewish Archives)

As in the case of YIVO's scholarship in general, the selection of the topics and time periods and the omission of others, like Zionism, implied a commitment to

---

12 Cf. exhibition catalogs in the collection of the YIVO archive (some unprocessed), *Jewish Children After World War II [Yiddish]* (New York, 1948); *The Shtetl, 1910–1939* (New York: YIVO, 1959); *Vilna: A Jewish Community in Times of Glory and in Time of Destruction* (New York: YIVO, 1960); *Life, Struggle and Uprising in the Warsaw Ghetto* (New York: YIVO, 1963); "Exhibition of Art Photographs," *YIVO Newsletter* 2 (February 1944): 5*; "Y. L. Peretz Exhibition at YIVO," *News of the YIVO* 44 (1952): 5*; " YIVO Arranges Exhibition About the *Shtetl*," *News of the YIVO* 69 (1958): 4*; "Opening of the Dubnow Exhibition at Yivo," *News of the YIVO* 78 (April 1961): 5*; "The Exhibition Commemorating the Warsaw Ghetto Uprising," *News of the YIVO* 86 (1963): 1*–2*, 8*.

non-partisanship and pluralism, but also to diaspora Jewish life.[13] This "big tent approach included Marxists like historian Raphael Mahler and religious thinkers like Heschel, and was based on the potent common denominator of Yiddishism: the belief that Jewishness is centered in a Yiddish-based culture – the shared reference of YIVO's 'engaged scholarship.'"[14] Both pluralism and engagement were important as YIVO aspired to become a central address for the scholarly and intellectual life of American Jewry, a think tank where social science would transcend the many religious and ideological divisions that kept American Jewry from finding common solutions to shared problems.[15] Particularly in the 1940s to 1960s, YIVO gained recognition for its efforts to fulfill this function for the community at large, as it received funding from a wide range of sources. Both the Conservative Rabbinical Assembly and the Reform Central Conference of American Rabbis (CCAR) financially supported it. Many individuals and institutions turned over their papers and records to YIVO, which in 1950 announced the establishment of the "Central Archives on Jews in America." In 1955, it came an important step closer to attaining this ambitious goal when the organizers of the American Jewish Tercentenary Committee decided to deposit its records at YIVO, thanks to the offices of Horace Kallen, who played leading roles in both institutions.[16]

---

[13] Cf. Lucjan Dobroszycki, "YIVO in Interwar Poland: Work in the Historical Sciences," in *The Jews of Poland Between Two World Wars*, ed. Yisrael Gutman, Ezra Mendelsohn, Jehuda Reinharz and Chone Shmeruk (Waltham: Brandeis University Press/Hanover: University Press of New England, 1989), 507.

[14] Cecile Esther Kuznitz, "YIVO," in *YIVO Encyclopedia of Jews in Eastern Europe*, ed. Gershon D. Hundert (New Haven: Yale University Press, 2008), 2093–94. There were many personal, biographical, thematic, and ideological relations to the left, such as the presence of Workmen's Circle president Nathan Chanin on the YIVO board, the research on continuities of the Jewish labor movement in Eastern Europe and the US, and Weinreich's and others' Bundist past. According to his biographer, Heschel had been familiar with YIVO from his youth in Warsaw, and on its board in America was "perhaps its only religiously committed member;" cf. Edward K. Kaplan, *Spiritual Radical: Abraham Joshua Heschel in America, 1940–1972* (New Haven: Yale University Press, 2007), 16.

[15] In its 1943 mission statement, YIVO laid claim to this role. "The Yivo has become the meeting place for those Jewish intellectuals who have preferred to seek knowledge through research rather than to accept preconceived ideas at their face value." (YIVO mission statement (1943), 1*)

[16] "CCAR in Support of YIVO," *News of the YIVO* 20 (April 1947): 8*; "The Rabbinical Assembly of America in Support of Yivo," *News of the YIVO* 24 (December 1947): 5*; "YIVO to Establish Central Archives on Jews in America," *News of the YIVO* 38 (September 1950): 1*–2*; "Archive of the American Jewish Tercentenary Committee at YIVO," *News of the YIVO* 58 (September 1955): 4*; Kallen letter to YIVO's Nathan Reich, dated May 20, 1955, typescript, American Jewish Archives (henceforth AJA), MS-1 (Horace Kallen papers), box 37, folder 4. Cf. also the glowing assessment of YIVO in 1950 by the Library of Congress (Anon. [Lawrence Marwick?], "[Untitled Report of Library of Congress on YIVO Library and Archives]," 1950, typescript, YIVO Archives, Max Weinreich Collection, RG 584.153; Marwick was the head of the Hebraic section of the Library of Congress.

Thus, YIVO was well-positioned to provide a forum for the American Jewish conversation about the East European past. Such an exchange would allow American Jews to gain the self-knowledge that would in turn form the basis of their individual and communal identities. Based on this ideological perspective, YIVO formed a network of individuals and institutions concerned with the current and future state of American Jewry. Even though other players sometimes dominated the conversation, YIVO could claim a central role in organizing it.

Weinreich Puts Adolescent American Jewry on Freud's Couch

Weinreich was a key figure in these processes, foreshadowing the broad, cultural concept of an integrated Jewishness many other observers would reconstruct from the East European past for the sake of the American Jewish present. He provided a comprehensive rationale for the American Jewish self-reflection that he and YIVO advocated, based on a mixture of Freudian and social psychology as well as sociology and anthropology. Weinreich had translated some of Freud's work into Yiddish, and applied key concepts from psychoanalysis to his observation of American Jewry. His outlook on the modern challenges to (American) Jewish identity was shaped by his experience as a fellow at Yale in the early 1930s. The seminar he taught there in 1932–1933, titled "The Impact of Culture on Personality," dealt with the relationships among individuals, families, and larger social units and their interrelations with processes of acculturation. Its perspective would later inform how he guided YIVO in America.[17] This intellectual background and

---

17 Barbara Kirshenblatt-Gimblett, "Coming of Age in the Thirties: Max Weinreich, Eduard Sapir, and Jewish Social Science," in *YIVO Annual of Jewish Social Science* 23, ed. Deborah Dash Moore (New York: YIVO, 1996), 1–103; Daniel Soyer, "Documenting Immigrant Lives at an Immigrant Institution: The YIVO Autobiographical Contest of 1942," *Jewish Social Studies* 5 (1999): 219–23. In his public comments, Weinreich articulated positions that were far more coherent and ideological than what YIVO as an avowedly non-political, pluralist institution dedicated to scholarship could and would entertain, yet they were extensions of the foundational values and principles in which YIVO as an institution was grounded since its founding in 1925 Vilna. On the historical and ideological background of YIVO's early years, see Kuznitz, "YIVO," 2090–96; Paul Glasser, "Max Weinreich," in *YIVO Encyclopedia of Jews in Eastern Europe*, ed. Gershon D. Hundert (New Haven: Yale University Press, 2008), 2014–16; David H. Weinberg, *Between Tradition and Modernity: Haim Zhitlovsky, Simon Dubnow, Ahad Ha'am, and the Shaping of Modern Jewish Identity* (New York: Holmes & Meier, 1996); Emanuel S. Goldsmith, *Architects of Yiddishism at the Beginning of the Twentieth Century: A Study in Jewish Cultural History* (Rutherford, NJ: Farleigh Dickinson University Press, 1976).

YIVO's role as a newcomer from the outside (an "imported institution," in his words) led Weinreich to claim for himself and for YIVO a perspective as insider-outsider observers of American Jewry, which uniquely positioned them to assess the real state of the community.[18] "Up to the time of the Yivo there was no one who could look at Jewish life in America from the inside, to see its local specificness and at the same time its roots in Jewish tradition," Weinreich said in a speech in 1944, adding that the institute "seeks to aid American Jewry in understanding the Jewish situation," as nobody else could.[19]

What Weinreich saw from his vantage point as a scientific observer embedded in the community of his study was an adolescent American Jewry: not yet formed, beginning to define itself in relation to its ancestry, in need of conscious reflection on its characteristics and its relation to others, and all this with enormous potential to become a strong, vital, creative personality, self-confidently at ease with itself and its distinctive character. "Jewish life in America does not yet hold its own," he said at the 1941 annual YIVO conference," suggesting that it would, if properly guided.[20] Despite this optimism, he couched his assessment of American Jewry in terms of diagnosis and social therapy, echoing the psychological language of many other thinkers who were observing the community at the time. This language gave his voice additional resonance as he joined the conversation with others who more critically challenged American Jews' self-conception as a strong and stable community. This image had been reinforced by the decades-long material support for an East European Jewry under economic and political pressure, and ultimately the threat of extinction. Weinreich presented a very different picture. As previously outlined, his starting point was the wide-spread absence of a positive, unapologetic identification with Jewishness, particularly among younger American Jews. As a result, this generation lacked the tools and strategies to cope with external negative judgments of Jewishness and suffered from inner tensions due to their futile efforts to suppress their subjective Jewishness.[21] Weinreich, following the approach of his Yale seminar, attributed this individual lack of positive Jewishness to the absence of a culturally constituted

---

18 Max Weinreich, in "Report on a Conference," 32.
19 Max Weinreich, "Highlights of the Paper Read by Dr. Max Weinreich at the Conference on 'The Place of the Yivo in Jewish Life,'" *Newsletter of the YIVO* 2 (February 1944): 2*; "YIVO Conference Outlines Broad Program," *Newsletter* 7 (February 1945): 1*.
20 Weinreich, "Jewish Scholarship Today," 8.
21 "They don't know anything of *Yiddishkayt*, don't have any of the pleasures and consolations which not just the traditional Jew had but even we have. But all carry the burden of being Jewish," he asserted at the 1941 conference (Weinreich, "Jewish Scholarship Today," 12).

communal Jewish identity that could provide a reference point for identification; he explained this reasoning in a graduation speech at Baltimore Hebrew College in 1945:

> In order to keep his personality intact and vigorous, the Jewish individual needs acceptable and sufficiently flexible psychic defenses. These defenses cannot be provided in the present state of atomization of Jewish life in this country. A healthy individual life evidently presupposes a healthy group life. [...] Hasn't American social psychology taught us that culture and personality are but different aspects of one whole, such as army and soldiers, or students and class?[22]

In the same speech, Weinreich spelled out a key element of his program: "the existence of a forceful Jewish group life, in other words the perpetuation of a meaningful, potent Jewish culture, is indispensable." On its twentieth anniversary, YIVO declared the notion of "Jewry as a cultural entity" as the first of its basic principles.[23] Culture was the concept that would integrate a pluralistic Jewish life into a whole and thereby constitute the group. It formed the core of the distinctly modern concept of Jewishness that Weinreich (and YIVO) advocated, in which a Yiddish-based culture surpassed traditional religion as the main source of Jewish identity.[24]

In Weinreich's view, culture also formed the link – or rather, the missing link – between the East European past and its meaning for the American present. As historian Daniel Soyer has pointed out, for Weinreich, East European and American Jewry both represented communities that were socio-psychologically destabilized by the processes of modernization. American Jewry, however, faced the problem in an even more difficult situation: "Unmoored from traditional sources of emotional and spiritual strength, American Jews inevitably suffered psychologically from social discrimination and feelings of inferiority, despite their comparative material well-being. The American Jewish community [...] could not provide the positive emotional reinforcement its members needed."[25] The financial support it had provided for East European Jewry over recent decades and its collective

---

[22] Max Weinreich, "Jewish Culture in America – To-Day and To-Morrow [Speech at Commencement of Baltimore Hebrew College]," June 10, 1945, typescript, YIVO Archives, Max Weinreich Collection, RG 584.9: 7–8.
[23] Weinreich, "Jewish Culture in America," 6; "Twentieth Anniversary of the YIVO," *Newsletter of the YIVO* 8 (April 1945): 2*.
[24] Cf. Milton R. Konvitz, "Yivo Comes to Morningside," *Commentary* 3 (January 1947): 49.
[25] Soyer, "Documenting Immigrant Lives," 222.

success in establishing itself economically in the United States could not make up for what was missing. After the disruption of immigration and under the radically new conditions in the new country, the newcomers and their children had focused on material challenges, but had neglected the psychological dimension of the change. East European Jews had adjusted admirably to the US compared to other immigrant groups, Weinreich acknowledged. However, the adjustment had not made up for the emotional stability that had been lost as they left the *alte heym*. "[In] terms of personality integration [...] we have not succeeded in building up new psychic defenses," he said, as "far too little has been done to make our younger generation take in and assimilate Jewish culture as a buttress to Jewish personality."[26]

What was needed, from Weinreich's and YIVO's perspective, was scientifically guided reflection on the Jewish past and present that would make American Jews – both individuals and the adolescent community at large – conscious of the cultural heritage that informed their personality and defined their place in history. Social science and history would be the twin angels presiding over the growth of a mature community. Whereas other American Jewish institutions had not acted on this insight, YIVO, Weinreich argued, was committed to and equipped for this program.

For proof, Weinreich pointed to the institute's 1942 contest for immigrant autobiographical essays.[27] This event illustrated a key aspect of YIVO's presentation of the East European Jewish past in relation to the American present: the notions of unity and continuity linked the two and suggested an ideal of Jewishness comprehensive and rich enough to constitute group distinctiveness and meaning derived from belonging.[28] The American contest followed on earlier ones held in 1934 and 1938–1939 in Poland; YIVO scholar Moses Kligsberg was in charge of all three of them. In 1942, some 250 first-generation American Jews submitted essays to the prompt, "Why I left the Old Country and what I have achieved in America." The question allowed participants to create narratives that integrated their pre-immigration life in Eastern Europe with their experience in the US into a positive, meaningful whole. According to Kligsberg, almost all of them expressed satisfaction with their decision to emigrate and with their experience

---

26 Weinreich, "Jewish Culture in America," 5.
27 Weinreich, in "Report on *Commentary* conference," 35.
28 Cf. Daniel Soyer, "Yiddish Scholars Meet the Yiddish-Speaking Masses: Language, the Americanization of YIVO, and the Autobiography Contest of 1942," in *Yiddish in America: Essays on Yiddish Culture in the Golden Land*, ed. Edward S. Shapiro (Scranton: University of Scranton Press, 2008), 55–79.

in America. At the same time, immigrants actively maintained their relationships with the old home over decades, through family connections, *landsmanshaftn*, and in other ways.²⁹ While the results were reported in *Commentary* and elsewhere with the explicit aim of revising negative stereotypes about immigrants (as the "defeated" of the East European ghettos and as disillusioned with America), the message for Jews themselves was to emphasize continuity despite the rupture of immigration. The essays show that for those immigrants old enough to have been politicized in Eastern Europe, this politicization had been a more defining experience than immigration. In turn, some contestants placed a larger spiritual gap between themselves and their American-born children than between their pre- and post-immigration selves.³⁰

For the older, first-generation immigrants, the essays were a chance to express, elaborately and publicly, as we will see, an identity, in the literal sense of "sameness," between their lives in Eastern Europe and the United States. Many described as their motivation to emigrate not just an improvement in their social conditions, but also "the chance to develop their personalities."³¹ Echoing Weinreich's psychological language, Soyer points to the "cathartic effect" of crafting such essays as a means of shaping the authors' identities, generalizing the potential for American Jewry as a whole. "In Freudian terms, Yivo would help American Jewry overcome its neurosis by making it 'conscious' of the 'split in its soul.' But it would also help uncover potential sources of emotional strength hidden in its history and cultural heritage."³² The essay contest, therefore, was a small-scale example of the larger coping strategy that Weinreich prescribed for the culturally uprooted immigrant community. At an average length of 100 pages (and with YIVO's encouragement to consider them jumping-off points for full-length autobiographies), the essays worked as a "talking cure": conscious reflection intended to bring suppressed aspects of Jewishness to the fore and integrate them into a continuous and unified individual or communal personality.³³

The notion of an integral Jewishness, of an organic unity encompassing aspects of an individual's or community's life beyond just "religion," provides

---

29 Kligsberg, "The Golden Land," 468, 471–72.
30 Kligsberg, "The Golden Land," 468–69, and Soyer, "Yiddish Scholars Meet the Yiddish-Speaking Masses," 73, 79; Soyer, "Documenting Immigrant Lives," 231. According to Soyer, YIVO originally planned to engage younger Jews through programs like the essay contest, but realized that they could much more easily attract older immigrants, who constituted the majority of contestants.
31 Kligsberg, "The Golden Land," 472.
32 Soyer, "Documenting Immigrant Lives," 223, 230.
33 Kligsberg, "The Golden Land," 468.

another key to YIVO's vision of an ideal Jewishness. Weinreich's psychological rhetoric of insufficient personality integration in the context of an "atomized" American Jewry echoed the broader postwar concerns about the possibility of authentic and meaningful Jewishness, without real community due to individualization, suburbanization, and assimilation. YIVO's language, particularly the institute's public announcements, seems to speak directly to these concerns with its repeated calls for "unity" and "continuity," and its integration of various elements into a comprehensive Jewish culture. At the annual conference in 1964, scholar Marvin Fox stated it succinctly: "For the young Jewish man and woman to find their Jewish identity, there must exist an integral Jewish culture."[34] In the service of this ideal, YIVO scholars invoked the East European past as a model for a culture that would unify its diversity into a meaningful whole. Weinreich in a 1945 address stopped short of suggesting an outright dichotomy between the Eastern and Western concepts of Jewishness, but added that "in essence there is a clear demarcation between the two ways: the atomistic [sic] and the organic, which in their extremest forms, found expression in the figures of Walter Rathenau and Isaac Leib Peretz: the part-Jewish way in contrast to the all-Jewish way."[35] Similarly, Nathan Reich, head of YIVO's research committee, pointed out what distinguished the East European Jewish experience: "There, Jews and Jewishness formed an integral. This is not the case in America. And here the YIVO has a special function to fulfill: to integrate Jews and Jewishness."[36]

In order to realize this vision in the New World, YIVO had to take into account the different socio-political framework of postwar America and the different self-understanding of American Jewry within this framework. The institute had to adjust its program, which had been shaped by the realities of nineteenth and early twentieth-century Eastern Europe. Its original diaspora nationalism and its calls for cultural autonomy bore the marks of its emergence in nineteenth-century tsarist Russia, a multi-ethnic empire run by an interventionist government, where legal and cultural inclusion seemed impossible or undesirable. In the American context of a liberal democracy, a (relatively) open society, religious freedom, and a beckoning majority culture, these ideas were translated into the goal of cultural pluralism. Weinreich saw YIVO's championing of this ideal vindicated by the failure of earlier efforts to integrate immigrant minorities like the Jews into a

---

[34] "Variety of Scholarly Topics Discussed at the 38th YIVO Conference," *News of the YIVO* 89 (February 1964): 1*–2*, 6*.
[35] Max Weinreich, "The YIVO Faces the Post-War World," *YIVO Newsletter* 7 (February 1945): 7*.
[36] "Forty Years of YIVO Existence Outlined at 1965 Conference: Twenty-Five Years of YIVO in America," *News of the YIVO* 93 (February 1965): 1*.

culturally uniform society. YIVO became an advocate of ethnic and cultural diversity, even in a period when it seemed out of touch with the current political and intellectual environment. Its planning committee for a "Guide to Comparative Literature and Intercultural Relation," articulated this position as early as 1944, when ethnic diversity, especially during war time, was rather unpopular. "[The] committee aligns itself with the marked trend in recent years away from the melting-pot theory toward the idea that the different ethnic groups have a definite contribution to make to the American cultural pattern and that the cooperation of these groups for common American ideals does not imply the submersion of their cultural identity."[37]

From YIVO's perspective, however, it was not just US society that needed to be convinced of the value and benefits of ethnic diversity and cultural pluralism; the Jews had to be convinced, too. In the eyes of many observers, American Jewry, for all its material and political security, was not educated enough to create and sustain its own distinct culture. Weinreich was not the only YIVO scholar diagnosing a "cultural lag" of American Jewry, particularly in relation to the spiritual elevation of their East European brethren.[38] Horace Kallen, father of the term "cultural pluralism" and a public intellectual associated with YIVO and the American Jewish Congress, called on American Jews to overcome their ambivalence about their distinctiveness and to develop from their past a distinct character rooted in a group spirit.[39] YIVO researchers Reich and Weinreich claimed for the institute that capturing this "spirit" of the East European Jewish experience would be crucial to shaping young American Jewry into a real community, anchored in the continuity of Jewish history and in a comprehensive Jewish culture. Weinreich argued that it took this imported institution to make American Jews see how much strength

---

37 "The Place of Jewish Cultural Heritage in American Civilization," *YIVO Newsletter* 4 (September 1944): 3*.

38 Cf. comments by Judah Shapiro, quoted in "Yivo Conference Highlights Wide Variety of Scholarly Topics," *News of the YIVO* 56 (March 1955): 1*, and by Sol Liptzin, "Jewish Life in America and the World Over: Papers Read at the 33rd Annual Yivo Conference," *News of the YIVO* 70 (April 1959): 6*.

39 Horace M. Kallen, "The Foundations of Jewish Spiritual and Cultural Unity," *Judaism* 6 (1957): 113. The article was based on a speech at a B'nai B'rith conference. On Kallen's role as the advocate of Jewish distinctiveness within the larger social framework of cultural pluralism, cf. Milton R. Konvitz, ed. *The Legacy of Horace M. Kallen* (Rutherford, NJ: Fairleigh Dickinson University Press, 1987) and Daniel Greene, *The Jewish Origins of Cultural Pluralism: The Menorah Society Association and American Diversity* (Bloomington: Indiana University Press, 2011), 142–45. Kallen's first expression of the theme was his article "Democracy versus the Melting-Pot," first published in *The Nation* in 1915, and reprinted in his essay collection *Culture and Democracy in the United States* (New York: Boni & Loveright, 1924), 67–125.

they could draw from their commonality with a Jewish culture to which they felt superior and with which they therefore did not identify. Reich made YIVO's role in sustaining this unity explicit: "The Yivo Institute for Jewish Research must link the East European past with the American realities of the present."[40]

The link Reich suggested made for both the strength and the limitations of YIVO's voice in the discourse it had initiated. For reasons that were partly beyond YIVO's control, the ideal of a meaningful Jewish culture was severed from the specificity of the Yiddish language and culture as its proposed content. In retrospect, the link turned out to be a predetermined breaking point in YIVO's larger mission, when the demographic reality of American Jewry hit YIVO at the vulnerable intersection of its scholarly neutrality and ideological commitment.

YIVO: Research Institute, Myth, or Instrument of Self-Expression?

The visions of Weinreich and Reich invoked fundamental questions. What would be the basis for the unity and continuity they postulated between pre-war East European and postwar American Jewry, given their original differentness and later dramatic historical changes? Weinreich himself said in 1945 that "one is forced to ask: is there anything substantial, beside a remote past that the Jews of to-day have in common?"[41] Was there an essence to Jewishness that was stable across time, space, and ideological divisions and that supported a positive identity, all under modern conditions of choice and doubt that had undermined the supernatural claims of "religion" and the way of life it had shaped? "[What] would take the place of Judaism as a cohesive force?" Konvitz asked in his analysis for *Commentary* readers, addressing the question to the ideological pantheon of diaspora nationalism. "A common spiritual culture, answered Dubnow. A common culture expressed in Yiddish, said the Galut [diaspora] nationalists. [...] Yiddish was to serve as the foundation for Jewish group survival and as the vessel in which Jews were to pour their cultural riches."[42] YIVO offered a scientific explanation of why and how a broad, culturally based sense of Jewishness was necessary for American Jewry, and insisted

---

[40] "Forty Years of YIVO Existence Outlined," 1*; similarly, Weinreich, "The YIVO Faces the Post-War World," 7.
[41] Weinreich, "Jewish Scholarship Today," 2.
[42] Konvitz, "Yivo Comes to Morningside," 49.

that the culture best nourishing Jewishness was a broad sense of *Yiddishkayt,* as it had sustained East European Jewry for centuries in the past. Such notions of commonalities, essential unity, and trans-historic continuity in the Jewish experience formed the link between the two roles that YIVO played in the postwar conversation about the European past, as organizer and advocate. They connected the framework of the conversation that YIVO had initiated with the content YIVO sought to insert. "For the Jews, said YIVO, social research and Yiddish are two sides of the same coin," Konvitz wrote in his sympathetic account of YIVO's "engaged scholarship."[43]

Yet, the concept of "engaged scholarship" seeks to contain forces that stand in tension with each other: scholarly detachment and political or ideological engagement. Yiddishism as an ideology and a form of Jewish nationalism assumes some degree of universal validity, which is hardly compatible with an anti-essentialist scholarly commitment to contingency, contextual specificity, and constructedness. This tension inherent in YIVO's origins and ideology, combined with its perception among Yiddish-speaking immigrants and American Jewry, shaped the institute's role in the conversation about the East European past. YIVO's leading thinkers were well aware of the various roles the institution blended, not just in postwar America, but from its very beginning. For all of YIVO's self-conception as a research institute devoted to the social sciences, it was not an abstract entity producing scholarship in an ivory tower. Indeed, its founding ideology included its rootedness in and orientation to the concrete political and cultural situation of early twentieth-century (East European) Jewry. Its origin arising out of the needs of the people is an integral part of its founding myth and ideology, as a speech by YIVO historian Jacob Shatzky at the 1951 conference illustrates: "Unlike other institutions of this type, which are generally established by the ruling groups, Yivo was called into being by the masses of the Jewish people. It has remained a folk institution in its rootedness in the people and in its view of Jewish life as a whole."

On its 40th anniversary, the institute prided itself on its function for the people: "YIVO has remained true to its perennial goals of serving the community as its scholarly arm."[44] This understanding is based on the assumption that social science would serve the interests of the community both in practical ways and as a tool for reflection and self-knowledge.

---

43 Konvitz, "Yivo Comes to Morningside," 51–52.
44 "Stages in the Spiritual Growth of the Jewish People Traced at YIVO Jubilee Conference," *News of the YIVO* 40 (March 1951): 3*; "Forty Years of YIVO: The Achievements and Their Meaning," *News of the YIVO* 97 (March 1966): 2*.

Figure 8: Three Jewish youth share a daily Yiddish newspaper; Lithuania, 1939–1941. (United States Holocaust Memorial Museum)

After the institute's relocation to New York, its function for the Jewish "masses" became more complicated. At some point, YIVO's ambition to represent and act on behalf of American Jewry as a whole seemed to be confirmed by the diversity of its board members, its role as a forum, and its recognition by other organizations. Over time, however, the social reality meant that YIVO organized a significant but dwindling sub-segment of American Jewry. In America, "YIVO has not been able to establish the same close connection with the Jewish community as a whole that it enjoyed when its center was in Vilna," Konvitz observed.[45]

Many of the Yiddish-speaking immigrants shared YIVO's perspective on the East European past and American present not on abstract terms, but as a lived experience. Thus, YIVO came to play new symbolic and practical roles for

---

45 Konvitz, "Yivo Comes to Morningside," 52.

American Jewry. Many of the immigrants looked to it as an embodiment of the world that was destroyed in the Holocaust, and as a venue for social practices through which they engaged with both past and present. YIVO became a "myth," in Weinreich's own words, and a place, quite literally, where groups beyond the small circle of scholars would meet for public programs, exhibitions, and conferences.[46] For many, their participation was also a form of Jewish self-expression, sentimentalism, and a public affirmation of their belief in the East European- and Yiddish-based spirit that Kallen invoked as the basis for group continuity. Immigrants of East European origin wanted to meet *landsleyt,* for companionship as much as out of interest in the topics of the meetings; in this sense, YIVO became an umbrella *landsmanshaft.*

The autobiographical essay contest of 1942 illustrates the complex balance YIVO had to negotiate between its interests as a research institute and the needs of its wider audience. YIVO designed the call for entries following principles of social-scientific research, for which it hoped to gather raw material. Among the specifications was that contestants should conceal their identities under a pen name. To the surprise of the organizers, however, "the majority of the contestants ignored these instructions entirely," Kligsberg noted drily. Some even criticized the stipulation and not only included their real names but expressed their hope that their essays would be published, "in order thus to show the world their achievements in life." Contestants thanked YIVO for giving them an opportunity to unburden their souls. "Seemingly, the desire to write has long smouldered [sic] in the hearts of the contestants and has now been kindled into a flame."[47] The immigrants' need for self-expression overwhelmed YIVO's scientific protocol.

YIVO's leaders faced fundamental questions as they tried to calibrate the institute's activities in order to do justice both to their creed as scientists and to the public role which they knew was necessary for YIVO's grounding in a moral and real community. According to literary scholar Dan Miron, Weinreich believed that YIVO, as firmly committed to science as it was, could not flourish unless it struck roots in a pre-rational or even irrational layer of the nation's consciousness. It had to be based on a belief in the continuity and future of the national culture, thus conceived as an act of faith as much as a science. Its scholars would have to work within the framework of the belief in the continued existence of the nation.[48] This new constellation was most clearly visible at the

---

46 Weinreich, "Jewish Scholarship Today," 6 ("Yes, the Yivo has become a myth"); Soyer, "Documenting Immigrant Lives," 234.
47 Kligsberg, "Socio-Psychological Problems," 243–44, 247–48.
48 Dan Miron, "Between Science and Faith: Sixty Years of the YIVO Institute," *YIVO Annual of Jewish Social Science* 19 (1990): 5–6.

annual conferences, which consisted of a sizable number of scholarly papers read in various sessions, and public announcements, particularly the speeches and declarations. The conferences provided the largest and most charged occasion for activities that highlighted the symbolic and ideological aspects of the institute's work – expressed in broad statements and declarations that complemented YIVO's scholarship to project a complex message in the conversation around Eastern Europe and the United States.

The message projected at these conventions was saturated with invocations of the abstract qualities of East European heritage, such as its creativity, vitality, and spirituality. The 1945 conference, the first on American soil, referred to the "life-giving spirit of Jewish creativity" of this past. Three years later, participants of the convention declared, "We have full faith in the ability of Eastern European Jewish spirituality to create a new synthesis of Jewishness and to inspire the Jewish communities all over the world with Jewish creativity." In 1965, the conference pledged YIVO's commitment to the preservation of the spirit of East European Jewry for the benefit of the American Jewish community of today and tomorrow.[49] YIVO scholar Kligsberg found the same over-simplified idealization and spiritualization of the past in the autobiographical accounts of immigrants:

> One observes among the immigrants a distinct hierarchy of preferment with respect to the spiritual values of the old country, intellectual, ethical, abstract values being accorded first place, while the customs and rituals that flourished in the European community are considered much less important. These abstract values are those that can, so to speak, be transported: for the Orthodox, the Torah; for the progressive the party program. It would seem that the Jew believes his most important spiritual values are capable of the easiest transplantation. What he cannot take with him must be inevitably less valuable.[50]

This spiritualization conformed to the way other participants in the American-Jewish discourse at mid-century approached the East European past. It was at odds with YIVO's focus on the material aspects of social history, but linked to postwar ideas about the unifying potential of humanity's spirit, be it religious or civic. More to YIVO's point, this abstraction came with three distinct advantages. It had room for diverse ideas, it could integrate these ideas into some kind of whole, and this whole would not be static but dynamic: East European Jewish life was diverse yet integrated by a spiritual whole which could influence and inspire Jewish life under new conditions, such as postwar America.

---

[49] "Declaration of the 19th Annual Conference," 3*; "From the Declaration Read at the Opening Session of the [22nd Annual] Conference," *News of the YIVO* 25 (February 1948): 2*; "Forty Years of YIVO Existence Outlined at 1965 Conference: Twenty-Five Years of YIVO in America," *News of the YIVO* 93 (February 1965): 1*–2*.
[50] Kligsberg, "The Golden Land," 472.

These notions were explicit in many declarations and speeches at YIVO. The declaration of its first postwar conference in 1946 is an example: "We believe that in this post-war world it is possible to transplant and foster, wheresoever [sic] Jews live, the creativity of Eastern European Jewry which revealed itself in traditional Judaism, in Yiddish and in Hebrew literature, in the struggles of the people for their cultural, political, and economic emancipation, in the upbuilding [sic] of Palestine and of the settlements overseas."[51] Creativity was presented as the unifying and driving force behind a wide range of different political and cultural positions, from traditional Judaism to the radical forms of the struggle for economic emancipation, in both Hebrew and Yiddish, in literature and in practical Zionism, in Palestine and in America. The pluralism that shaped YIVO's scholarly work and its political abstinence served to relativize the ideological commitment to Yiddish. (It also relativized other values that came with it in other formulations of Yiddishism, such as secularism or Socialism.) Yiddish, after all, was mentioned as one expression (besides Hebrew) of the essential creativity that was the legacy of East European Jewry. The sense of *Yiddishkayt* that was inspired and authenticated by this legacy was broad enough to transcend and integrate "Judaism" as one of several forms in which the content of Jewishness manifested itself: "for the Orthodox, the Torah; for the progressive the party program," in Kligsberg's description of the diversity of immigrants' representations of Jewishness.[52] YIVO made it its mission to realize the adaptability of this sense of *Yiddishkayt* to the new environment. But, the participants of the 1949 annual conference admitted that it was "a particularly difficult task [...] to effect in our research a synthesis of Eastern Europe and America."[53]

Forging an American Jewishness – on Yiddish Terms

The glorious Jewishness that YIVO scholars envisioned for America would not be a weak replica of the East European template. Not only was the social scientist Weinreich compelled to challenge nostalgic idealizations (harbored by many immigrants) of the past, by stating, "Traditional Jewish life was fuller of problems than we think

---

[51] "Resolution of the 20th Anniversary Conference of the Yiddish Scientific Institute – YIVO," *News of the YIVO* 13 (February 1946): 1*.
[52] Kligsberg, "The Golden Land," 472.
[53] "Declaration of the 22nd Conference," 2*; "From the Declaration Read at the Opening Session of the [23rd Annual] Conference," *News of the YIVO* 31 (February 1949): 2*, omission in the original.

through our rose-tinted glasses."⁵⁴ He and other YIVO activists, for all their criticism of the current state of American Jewry, also believed in its potential to come into its own, inspired by, but not striving to imitate, the East European model. Reich, head of YIVO's research committee, warned that "we are inclined to gauge the American Jewish community with the standards and criteria of Eastern Europe. Historically, this is a false approach. Just as Jewish Babylonia differs from Judea, Spain from Babylonia, Mainz from Cordoba, and Cracow from Frankfort, so New York, Chicago and Los Angeles differ from Warsaw, Vilna, and Lodz. The Jewish community in America is in the process of evolving its own specific physiognomy, which will be American-Jewish."⁵⁵

YIVO, along with many immigrants, negotiated the complex interplay between Americanization and distinctiveness through the medium of Yiddish. It was the working language of the institution and the subject of numerous scholarly publications and papers delivered at its gatherings. Philologist Yudel Mark emphasized that Yiddish was the basis of YIVO's universality.⁵⁶ Publications targeting the broader constituency also showed the central role that the language played in YIVO's public activities, its symbolic function, and the way the institute positioned itself as embedded both in the old-country culture and its new American environment. In 1944, the newsletter announced the publication of a Yiddish-language analysis by linguist Uriel Weinreich, "now inducted in the US Armed Forces," of four different translations of the national anthem into Yiddish. In the same year, an analysis of the institute's correspondence revealed that "problems of Yiddish language" topped the list of inquiries submitted to YIVO. Several articles approvingly registered a reawakened interest in Yiddish among American Jews, both for practical reasons and as a means of identity expression, motivated as well by the recognition granted the language through its inclusion in college curricula.⁵⁷

---

54 Weinreich, "Jewish Scholarship Today," 14.
55 Quoted in "Jewish Life in America and the World Over: Papers Read at the 33rd Annual Yivo Conference," *News of the YIVO* 70 (April 1959): 1*.
56 A selection of examples: In 1950, linguist Joshua A. Fishman presented the findings of a study on bilingual education: *News of the YIVO* 37 (May 1950): 2*; literary critic Shmuel Niger pointed to the existence of a Yiddish culture in America before the East European immigration: *News of the YIVO* 52 (March 1954): 2*; cf. also Solomon Poll, "The Role of Yiddish in American Ultra-Orthodox and Hassidic Communities," *YIVO Annual of Jewish Social Science* 13 (1955): 125–52; "Jewish History and the Yiddish Language: A Report on the 35th Annual Yivo Conference," *News of the YIVO* 78 (April 1961): 1*–2*, 6*; "The Heart of the Matter: Session of the Board of Directors [on YIVO activities in the US]," *News of the YIVO* 65 (July 1957): 3*.
57 "The Star Spangled Banner in Yiddish," *Newsletter of the YIVO* 4 (September 1944): 7*; "Information Most Frequently Sought from the YIVO," *Newsletter* 5 (November 1944): 7*; "Yiddish on the American Scene," *News of the YIVO* 26 (April 1948): 3*; "City College Introduces Courses

Nevertheless, as the number of Yiddish-speakers dwindled and the Yiddish sub-themes seemed increasingly marginalized and disconnected from the English ones, YIVO added English as a language of its publications, such as in the newsletter or the Peretz edition. Retaining the Yiddish versions became a matter of ideology. The 1946 conference proclaimed, "We believe in the organizing and welding force of the Yiddish language for the dispersed settlement of the Jewish people." Similarly, Weinreich in his 1945 commencement address came close to identifying Yiddish as the essence of Jewishness. He contrasted Yiddish, "a principal carrier of everyday Jewish life for a thousand years or so," with Hebrew, which despite its status as the language of religion, "[cannot] claim the place of *the* Jewish language. English is nowadays the medium of several million Jews, to many of them the only medium, but it is not a Jewish language; abundantly rich and expressive as it is, its etymologies, connotations and images bear the imprint of a civilization that was ready before we came in."[58] The statement illustrates that underlying the validation of Yiddish was the aesthetic program of Yiddishism, which related YIVO to the broader postwar project of presenting Jewishness as dignified and acceptable (albeit to different tastes, as the divergent aesthetics underlying alternative presentations of Jewishness by other ideological groups will show.)

YIVO's roots, its program and its social role in America coalesced and shaped its voice in the postwar discussions on Eastern Europe and the US. This coalescence gave its voice coherence, depth, and authenticity, but in turn made it difficult to separate YIVO's role as an organizer of the broad discussion, which was conducted largely in English, from its aspiration to be an advocate of a culture based in Yiddish. Often, its abstract, lofty ideas collided with the lived experience of mid-century American Jewry. The Yiddish-speakers fought an uphill battle against linguistic and cultural assimilation within their own ranks and in the face of the dominance of English (and, in many cases, disdain for Yiddish) among the American-born generations. This social reality reinforced YIVO's symbolic importance for immigrants as the embodiment of the "old country" culture. Correspondingly, YIVO faced greater difficulties in bonding with a younger generation of American-born Jews of the second generation.[59] It was more successful in highlighting continuities between the two lives of immigrants than in bridging the

---

in Yiddish," *News of the YIVO* 19 (February 1947): 7*; "Yiddish in the Curriculum of American Colleges: Increased Interest in Yiddish," *News of the YIVO* 23 (November 1947): 3*.
58 "Resolution of the 20th Anniversary Conference," 1*; Weinreich, "Jewish Culture in America," 1–2.
59 Soyer, "Documenting Immigrant Lives," 223–24.

Figure 9: YIVO research director Max Weinreich teaching Yiddish at City College New York, not dated. (YIVO Archive)

spiritual gap that participants in the immigrant autobiography contest reported between their own generation and their children. The later generation was more aligned with the *zeitgeist* that had limited tolerance for pluralism, at least if it exceeded the narrow realm of religion. YIVO's broad concept of culture as the basis for distinctiveness smacked too much of ethnic difference and particularism, especially given its proposed Yiddish content.

Yiddish, no matter how much YIVO adapted pragmatically and ideologically to the new American environment after 1940, remained at the heart of its outlook and program. While its practical function decreased as more and more immigrants used both English and Yiddish according to the situation, its symbolic value as a marker of identity grew. Thus, as much as Yiddish-language intellectuals felt marginalized by the demographic development and the linguistic and cultural dominance of the English language, the minority language became a marker of a certain exclusivity that was viewed positively. The use of Yiddish also represented a protected space for self-reflection; in what Weinreich saw as a therapeutic situation, it shielded the vulnerable patient from the gaze or comment of others and provided protection against the concern, mocked by Philip Roth, of "What will the *goyim* think?"[60]

These multiple, interwoven factors shaped YIVO's voice in the postwar American Jewish conversation and, by the same token, limited the effectiveness of YIVO's role as an advocate of its understanding of Jewishness. It served as an intellectual and ideological bridge between the self-understanding of East European and American Jewry and as a social and cultural mediator between immigrants and native-born Jews. Its status as an immigrant institution afforded it a proximity to the former group that came at the expense of its relationship with the latter. Similarly, its refusal to separate in its message the method and form on the one hand – conscious appreciation of cultural group distinctiveness – from its content on the other – Yiddish as the indispensable medium and maybe even essence of such Jewishness – gave YIVO greater coherence than other players in the conversation, but also less flexibility in the light of social and cultural realities to separate its roles as observer, organizer, and mediator from its advocacy of Yiddish.

Finally, the same constellation added force to its perspective that American Jewry was strong and stable merely in members, institutions, and dollars, but in need of psychological, cultural, and spiritual reinforcement from those East European Jews it had supported materially. Setting the tone for a revaluation of a stable and meaningful Jewishness, YIVO was instrumental in preserving and legitimizing Jewishness as a broader concept grounded in culture. It embodied and showcased the virtues of this notion by tirelessly shining a light on the East European past. While it was less successful in its efforts to fill this concept with the specific content it advocated, it provided the historical and conceptual foundation for the postwar conversation on the East European past in the context of the American present: as the construction of a community that was culturally formed by the conscious appreciation and appropriation of its past.

Other actors in the American-Jewish conversation adapted this approach more efficiently to the cultural moment of postwar America, while YIVO became one voice in the multi-vocal exchange it had itself initiated. The institute's leaders hoped that its time was still to come. Late in his life, Weinreich, in a conversation with Dan Miron, insisted that its voice would prevail in the future, when YIVO's existential importance for American Jewry would be realized:

---

[60] Philip Roth, "Writing About Jews," *Commentary* 36 (December 1963): 448. At the 1948 *Commentary* conference, Weinreich argued that little research had been done on American Jewry in English because authors feared the effects of negative findings. "In Yiddish, there is no reason to conceal anything." ("Report on a Conference on the Jewish Experience in America," 35)

> [If] American Jews still dream as a group, Yiddish is the language they speak in their dream. It is still the idiom of their collective unconscious. For their personality to become whole they – or at least some of them – will have to go back to Yiddish one day. Otherwise, their enormous creative force will be blocked by an inner, psychic fragmentation. [...] Somebody will have to spell out for them the contents of their dream, to elucidate the vision they saw with bleary eyes."[61]

This vision has not come true; too many factors conspired against it. At mid-century, the symbolism of YIVO's entering the conversation about the American-Jewish future was greater than the real impact of its call on American Jews to make Yiddish the cornerstone of their Jewishness. However, other actors in postwar American Jewry recognized the importance of YIVO's approach to the problem of Jewish identification and shaped it according to their different needs and ambitions.

---

[61] Miron, "Between Science and Faith," 14–15.

3 New (York) Jewish Intellectuals: The Past as Culture

YIVO's agenda of grounding an unmoored American Jewry in a cultural Jewishness derived from the past attracted other intellectuals' attention soon after the institute arrived in New York. More than anything, it was the program of conscious reflection on the nature of Jewishness under modern conditions that piqued their interest and let them tap into the YIVO approach in their own ways. "When American Jewry [...] learns that the unexamined life is not worth living, then the pursuit of self-knowledge will inevitably bring it to the door of Yivo," Milton Konvitz, legal and Judaic scholar, wrote in *Commentary* in 1947.[1] Historian Oscar Handlin approvingly described YIVO's larger mission as "the transfer into social secular sciences of traditional Jewish cultural values."[2]

It was far from coincidental that both Konvitz and Handlin published their appreciations of YIVO's efforts in *Commentary*, or that Weinreich had made his comments about Jewish identity at the 1948 conference sponsored by the magazine. YIVO and the intellectuals behind *Commentary*, which was founded in 1945, shared a basic perspective on what American Jewry needed to remain vital as a group: it had to come to terms with its Jewish past and make it usable for its American present. At the conference, the journal's founding editor Elliot Cohen bemoaned that American Jews were, so far, quite reluctant to do just that. His journal therefore aspired "to encourage and make available writing on the experience and history of Jews in America" and from other times and places. *Commentary* lived up to this assignment and made the East European past in particular one of its central interests. It published Heschel's narrative of spiritual holism and Parzen's critique; Martin Buber's Hasidic tales and Norman Mailer's drug-infused reflections on them as well as countless other articles, among them writings by thinkers as different as the German-Jewish philosopher Franz Rosenzweig, avantgarde American novelist Isaac Rosenfeld, and poet-philosopher Harold Rosenberg.[3] The journal responded to a growing interest of

---

1 Milton R. Konvitz, "Yivo Comes to Morningside," *Commentary* 3 (January 1947): 54.
2 Oscar Handlin, "The Jewish Historical Sense," review of *Yivo Annual of Jewish Social Science*, *Commentary* 3 (April 1947): 393.
3 Abraham Joshua Heschel, "The Two Great Traditions: The Sephardim and the Ashkenazim," *Commentary* 5 (May 1948): 416–22; Herbert Parzen, "When Secularism Came to Russian Jewry," *Commentary* 13 (April 1952): 355–62; Martin Buber, "Tales of the Hasidim," *Commentary* 3 (January 1947): 73–78; Norman Mailer, "Responses & Reactions," *Commentary* 34 (December 1962): 504–06, and four more installations until August 1963; Franz Rosenzweig, "Discovery of the East European Jew: A Young Visitor in the Old Warsaw Ghetto," *Commentary* 15 (January 1953): 86–89; Isaac Rosenfeld, "Bazaar of the Senses: A Story [from Passage from Home]," *Commentary* 1 (February

American Jews in their history, behind which Cohen saw a search for identity: "For from history alone can contemporary man hope to get what he seems so desperately to hunger for, a sense of himself, his role, and the destiny of himself and his nation on this planet." At the 1948 conference, Cohen also suggested that history had taken on a new quasi-meaning-making function that in pre-modern times had been fulfilled by religion.[4]

The conference itself bespoke the new perspective opened up first by YIVO, which the intellectuals in the *Commentary* orbit made their own, as the get-together of leading American Jewish thinkers constituted a discourse *en miniature* about how the (East European) past could consciously be made usable for the present. Other parallels illustrate the common agenda shared by immigrant and second-generation American Jewish thinkers. Both YIVO and *Commentary* were elite institutions which felt obligated to provide guidance to broader audiences of American Jews. Both reflected a belief in the heuristic and practical value of social science. For YIVO, this approach was part of its DNA; *Commentary* created a special column, "Study of Man," edited by budding scholars, to engage with the latest insights of social science.[5]

Equally significant, however, were the differences between YIVO and *Commentary*, particularly in light of how the two fared in the discourse about Eastern Europe. These differences can explain why the *Commentary* intellectuals were able to take YIVO's approach and develop it according to their own interests, whereas YIVO remained at the margins of the discourse. One crucial reason was the demographics behind the discourse. In contrast to YIVO's background in a first-generation immigrant milieu, *Commentary* was shaped by second-generation, American-born thinkers targeting the second and third generations of by then *American* Jews. Many of these thinkers were rediscovering a past they had not

---

1946): 36–42; Harold Rosenberg, "Jewish Identity in a Free Society: On Current Efforts to Enforce 'Total Commitment,'" *Commentary* 9 (June 1950): 508–14.

4 Elliot Cohen, in "Report on a Conference on the Jewish Experience in America (sponsored by *Commentary*)," May 1948, typescript, YIVO Archives, Max Weinreich Collection, RG 584, folder 225A: 3–4.

5 Examples of texts in this column include Nathan Glazer, "The 'Alienation' of Modern Man: Some Diagnoses of the Malady," *Commentary* 3 (April 1947): 378–85; Moses Kligsberg, "The Golden Land: The Jewish Immigrant in America: Self-Portrait," *Commentary* 5 (May 1948): 467–72; Oscar Handlin, "New Paths in American Jewish History: Afterthoughts on a Conference," *Commentary* 7 (April 1949): 388–94; Moshe Decter, "The 'Old Country' Way of Life: The Rediscovery of the Shtetl," review of *Life is with People*, by Mark Zborowski and Elizabeth Herzog, *Commentary* 13 (June 1952): 600–04; Celia Stopnicka Rosenthal, "How the Polish Jew Saw His World: A Study of a Small-Town Community Before 1939," *Commentary* 18 (July 1954): 70–75.

known first-hand and were therefore free to re-fashion according to their needs. *Commentary's* perspective on the East European past was shaped by a sense of distance, whereas YIVO emphasized continuities between Old World and New. *Commentary* thinkers sought American forms of Jewishness and new ways to translate the East European past in more than just linguistic ways into American terms.

Commonalities and differences shone through a text which Arthur Hertzberg, then a young Conservative rabbi, published in 1950, of course in *Commentary*. It encapsulated the shared perspective underlying the discourse opened up by immigrant and American-born intellectuals:

> One of the dominant spiritual necessities of the present moment is to come to terms with the last several centuries of Eastern European creativity, which recently ended so tragically before our eyes. That world must be assimilated into the canon of the tradition and into the stream of Jewish history. Group memory sanctifies what it chooses to retain by creating symbols and myths which become for it the true picture of the hallowed past.[6]

While, in substance, Hertzberg articulated a common program, between the lines a perspective on the past appeared that illustrated the divide between second-generation, American-born *Commentary* intellectuals and earlier generations of immigrant intellectuals like the YIVO thinkers. Hertzberg invoked the Holocaust, with which the Yiddish-speaking sub-community of American Jewry had engaged more directly and more quickly than the English-speaking majority. His call to assimilate the East European past into American Jewish group memory was premised on a sense of discontinuity and even foreignness, stemming from both the Holocaust and the distance between the two worlds of Jewry even before it. Bridging this distance required a conscious effort, as the natural transmission through living memory passed on through generations had been irrevocably ruptured. Symbolically significant, the textual genre in which Hertzberg expressed these suggestions was an English-language review of two Yiddish books: a translation emblematic of the larger process of rendering something foreign intelligible by expressing it in new terms for an audience unfamiliar with its forms, but interested in its essence.

Hertzberg's statement reflected the perspective from which thinkers around *Commentary* shaped the new discourse they had initiated in order to make the past usable. At its core, this approach suggested a complex effort of identity

---

6 Arthur Hertzberg, "The Worldly Jew," review of *Einems Yidishe Machshovos*, by Melech Ravitch; *Yidish un Yidishkeit*, by Yosef Opatoshu; *Kedushah un Gevurah bei Yidn*, by Y. Efroykin, *Commentary* 10 (July 1950): 87.

engineering for American Jews; Hertzberg pointed out its key dimensions. Referencing the irretrievable loss of the world of East European Jewry, he framed American Jews as its heirs who felt both a need and a responsibility to come to terms with the loss by preserving the East European heritage. The phrase that the East European era had ended "before our eyes" alluded to American Jews' sense of helplessness, guilt, and moral obligation in the face of the Holocaust. Hertzberg translated "coming to terms" with the past into "assimilating" it: accepting what had felt distant and alien, but also appropriating the heritage on one's own terms. He argued that redefining the canon of Jewish tradition was now the responsibility of American Jewry. It involved the construction of "group memory" by making choices about what to retain (and what to shed), and by creating symbols and myths to evoke a past that would feel both true and sacred. A past defined as centuries' worth of "creativity" promised to be usable for American Jewry's present needs; the phrase also hints at the reconceptualization of the tradition in broader cultural terms. Hertzberg hoped that, once assimilated into group memory, the East European past could serve as a source of meaning that would revitalize American Jews' sense of Jewishness.

As a result, thinkers like Hertzberg and Cohen urged their readers to look through the lens of this past at their American present and future. What they really did – and led American Jews to do, too – was the opposite: They looked through the lens of their American present at the East European past and allowed the present to shape the past. Cohen explicitly sanctioned the invention of a past for such purposes. "It is human to want ancestors, and it is an amiable weakness to reshape them, to invent them, in the native tradition," he stated at the 1948 *Commentary* conference.[7]

Different thinkers, depending on how they perceived their present and future in America, chose lenses that showed them different images of the East European past. They competed to define the past in order to define the present: Heschel used his idealized image of the lost world of Ashkenaz to criticize American Jewry, whereas Parzen, in contrast, defended America and de-mythologized Eastern Europe. In the middle decades of the twentieth century, these and other competing narratives, images, and lessons drawn from the past were explored in a rich discourse that was based on a common perception: The East European past provided material for a redefinition of Jewishness, which was required to enable American Jews to find their place in American society and in the Jewish world on their own distinct, American and Jewish, terms. This perspective was the matrix underlying the divergent reconstructions and images that American

---

[7] Cohen, in "Report on a Conference on the Jewish Experience in America," 2–3.

Jewry fashioned out of the East European past: pogrom and *shtetl*, Warsaw and Kasrilevke, Hasid lost in spiritual reverie and Bundists engaged in class struggle. It underlay Heschel's narrative of traditional Ashkenazic Jewish culture as the culmination of Jewish authenticity as much as a narrative sponsored by the Jewish left that claimed Yiddish author Mendele Mokher Sforim as the forefather of revolutionary Communism, as well as many other narratives.[8] These texts formed a debate for which YIVO had provided the original impetus, but it was in how second-generation intellectuals re-conceived the principle behind it that it became dominant in the postwar American-Jewish intellectual discourse.

New York Jewish Intellectuals: Refashioning Their Jewishness Out of the Past

The public debate that sorted out which of these images were assimilated into group memory was shaped in important ways by thinkers who, for their own reasons, were engaging in new ways with their Jewishness. In the process of refashioning themselves, they were refashioning the past as well. This engagement with the East European heritage was an important facet of the larger, oft-analyzed discourse through which Jewish, often New York-based, intellectuals at mid-century re-negotiated the relationship between Jewishness and America.[9] Studies of this loosely grouped collective often emphasized the role of *Commentary* as a vehicle for exploring new forms of Jewishness. *Commentary* gave voice to a new perspective on the past, and gave a space for widely different ways to make it usable. The journal itself presented a range of different images and narratives of this past, since the "New York Jewish intellectuals" did not constitute a homogeneous unit, but a group of highly diverse individuals. While they did not have an explicit common agenda, they shared a sense of intellectual responsibility for their community, to which they related with both detachment and loyalty.

---

[8] Abraham Joshua Heschel, "The Eastern European Era in Jewish History," *YIVO Annual of Jewish Social Science* 1 (1946), 86–105; Sidney Rosenblatt, "Mendele Mocher Sforim," *Jewish Life [Morning Freiheit Association]* 3 (1949), 10–13.

[9] Alexander Bloom, *Prodigal Sons: The New York Intellectuals and Their World* (New York: Oxford University Press, 1986); Neil Jumonville, *Critical Crossings: The New York Intellectuals in Postwar America* (Berkeley: University of California Press, 1991); Alan M. Wald, *The New York Intellectuals: The Rise and Decline of the Anti-Stalinist Left from the 1930s to the 1980s* (Chapel Hill, NC: University of North Carolina Press, 1987); Terry A. Cooney, *The Rise of the New York Intellectuals: "Partisan Review" and Its Circle* (Madison: University of Wisconsin Press, 1986).

They started from a perception similar to Weinreich's diagnosis: that the current state of American Jewry and American Judaism was problematic. They identified different, more viable alternatives, and suggested steps to effect that change. What Hertzberg in 1950 called the "spiritual needs" of the community described a condition which these intellectuals sensed in themselves and found in younger American Jews more generally; it echoed Weinreich's psychological assessment. This condition was condensed in the oft-cited term "alienation," a key word denoting the sense of unease felt by many American Jews vis-à-vis both parts of their hyphenated identity.[10] In his eponymous essay of 1946, young Socialist critic Irving Howe portrayed "the lost young intellectual [as] a marginal man, twice alienated," both from America, which he perceived as hostile to Jewish differentness, and from Jewishness, which he therefore tried, unsuccessfully, to suppress. Being Jewish was to him a mere sociological fact, lacking any positive meaning.[11] Philip Roth traced this insecurity to a pervasive self-consciousness that led many leaders of American Jewry – a group largely coextensive with his most vocal critics – to constantly ask, "What will the *goyim* think?" This mindset, which echoes sociologist David Riesman's concept of "other-directed characters," was in Roth's analysis a response to a loss of Jewish communal cohesiveness and identity, which in postwar America were no longer strengthened by external forces: "The cry 'Watch out for the *goyim!*' at times seems more the expression of an unconscious wish than of a warning: Oh that they were out there, so that we could be together in here! A rumor of persecution, a taste of exile, might even bring with it that old world of feelings and habits – something to replace the new world of social accessibility and moral indifference," Roth wrote in *Commentary*.[12]

---

10 For a condensed description of the psychology and mindset of the second generation, see Norman Podhoretz, *Making It* (New York: Random House, 1967), 120–21. According to Podhoretz, "alienation" related first and foremost to the intellectuals' relationship to America and only in second place to their attitude toward Judaism. (Podhoretz, personal interview, New York, February 7, 2013).

11 Irving Howe, "The Lost Young Intellectual: A Marginal Man, Twice Alienated," *Commentary* 2 (October 1946): 362, published in the "American Scene" department. Writing two years later, fellow *Commentary* contributor David Bernstein extended the assessment to American Jews in general, stating that "of all the insecure people in America (except for Negroes), Jews are the most unhappily insecure." ("Jewish Insecurity and American Realities: A Prescription Against Mental Escapism," *Commentary* 5 (February 1948): 119.)

12 Philip Roth, "Writing About Jews," *Commentary* 36 (December 1963): 448, 451. At the 1948 *Commentary* conference, Elliot Cohen and Max Weinreich emphasized that *Commentary*, in contrast to "official" depictions of Jewry was not afraid to bring problematic aspects of Jewry into the open, for the sake of an honest self-accounting. ("Report on a Conference on the Jewish

Roth and others noted that American Jews were facing an unprecedented opportunity. Moving out of cultural isolation, they had a range of options for understanding, realizing, and presenting their Jewishness (or doing none of that at all); they struggled to locate themselves in the midst of all these options.[13] *Commentary* contributor David Bernstein, later executive director of the 1954 Tercentenary celebrations, saw American Jews as unmoored in both past and present, experiencing themselves as different, but not finding positive meaning in the difference that turned the hyphen of their Jewish-American identity into a separator marking a non-identity as Jews and Americans. "[The problem stems] from the bewilderment of the individual Jew, who often finds himself in social and intellectual limbo because he really does not know what being a Jew means to himself and, therefore, to his world," Bernstein wrote. "He wants very badly to have a 'taken-for-granted' past, present, and future – like everyone else."[14] To overcome this condition of alienation and non-identity, the *Commentary* intellectuals suggested ideas which defined their individual trajectories as much as their common intellectual project. They aimed at the creation of an integral American Jewishness, a concept in which each aspect depended on the other. A historical and cultural sense of Jewishness was a precondition for identifying with America and its cultural pluralism. These thinkers assumed that, like themselves, American Jewry was finally ready to acknowledge its status as a rooted community that was linked on many levels to its non-Jewish environment.

Cohen made this perspective the starting point of *Commentary's* mission. "For at least [some decades] there has been an ambition afloat among Jews – so-called 'intellectuals' and so-called 'laymen' alike – to have a review on matters of concern to American Jews, [...] which would represent the full interplay of Jewish social and cultural interests with the broad intellectual currents of our

---

Experience in America," 11, 35). David Riesman, *The Lonely Crowd: A Study of the Changing American Character* (New Haven: Yale University Press, 1950); on Riesman, cf. also Susan A. Glenn, *The Jewish Cold War: Anxiety and Identity in the Aftermath of the Holocaust* (Ann Arbor: Frankel Center for Judaic Studies, University of Michigan, 2015), 19–23. Nathan Glazer, relevant here as an editor at *Commentary* and later as a scholar of American Jewish sociology, was a collaborator on this study.

13 British participant-observer David Daiches suggested, "a Jew who wants to play his part naturally in a Western environment can do so either by [a] kind of honest self-assurance or by total assimilation. American Jewry seems to me to be aiming at a confused third way." ("American Judaism: A Personal View: A Man of Letters Reflects on Modernist Religion," *Commentary* 11 (February 1951): 132)

14 Bernstein, "Jewish Insecurity and American Realities," 120.

country and of Western culture in general," he stated at the *Commentary* conference.¹⁵ The phrase "our country" signaled that the perspective of a new American Jewishness was based on a new appreciation of America – newly accepted as a politically valuable and culturally relevant reality – and of "Jewishness" – re-conceived as intellectually appealing and identity-inspiring.¹⁶ In the literary realm, the narrator's statement "I am an American, Chicago-born" in Saul Bellow's 1953 novel *The Adventures of Augie March* was perceived as similarly provocative-programmatic.¹⁷ In the ironic description of Norman Podhoretz, then a young writer for the magazine, this was the "Grand Design" of Cohen as the head of the "family" of New York intellectuals: "to lead the family out of the desert of alienation in which it had been wandering for so long and into the promised land of democratic, pluralistic, prosperous America where it would live as blessedly in its Jewishness as in its Americanness, safe and sound and forevermore, amen."¹⁸

The warming of the previously alienated *Commentary* and *Partisan Review* intellectuals to America as "our country" meant a significant turn from their earlier positions.¹⁹ Many of them had been politically identified as Marxists and aesthetically committed to European literary modernism. Both commitments had led them to retain, well into the 1930s, a critical distance from America as a political and cultural phenomenon. In the late 30s and early 40s, however, World War II and the Holocaust, the beginning of the Cold War, and the emergence of cultural space in America for them and their ideas (in the form of university positions and publishing opportunities) let them reconsider their perspectives on America.²⁰ In 1946, Israel Knox, a Russian-born leftist intellectual and

---

15 Cohen, in "Report on a Conference on the Jewish Experience in America," 2. Critic Alfred Kazin reports that his usage of the phrase "our forests" in a book on English literature elicited mockery by his peers for the casual identification with what had previously been seen from an alienated distance (Bloom, *Prodigal Sons*, 294).
16 Nathan Abrams, "'America Is Home': *Commentary* Magazine and the Refocusing of the Community of Memory, 1945–1960," in *Commentary in American Life*, ed. Murray Friedman (Philadelphia: Temple University Press, 2005), 16–18, 30; Ruth R. Wisse, "The Jewishness of *Commentary*," in *Commentary in American Life*, 52–73.
17 Saul Bellow, *The Adventures of Augie March* (New York: Viking, 1953).
18 Podhoretz, *Making It*, 135.
19 I thank Norman Podhoretz and Neal Kozodoy for their helpful input from their personal experiences in leading *Commentary* (Podhoretz, personal interview: New York, February 7, 2013; Kozodoy, personal interview: New York, September 12, 2012).
20 Steven J. Zipperstein, "*Commentary* and American Jewish Culture in the 1940s and 1950s," *Jewish Social Studies* 3 (1997): 18; Benjamin Balint, *Running Commentary: The Contentious Magazine That Transformed the Jewish Left into the Neoconservative Right* (New York: Public

Yiddishist, sounded a passionate call to the leaders of the community to no longer see America as *galut* but to acknowledge "that we – and our children and our children's children – are here to stay, that *this* is home!"[21] Cohen made this the mission of *Commentary,* as announced in his editorial statement in its first issue: "Commentary is an act of faith in our possibilities in America."[22] Consequently, the magazine made a point of engaging with "American topics" beyond narrow assumptions of what made them of particular Jewish interest. It signaled a new Jewish investment in America and the ambition to bring a broad Jewish perspective to larger questions, to speak to an audience beyond the Jewish community, and to fuse what had been separate identities often seen more in tension than as mutually enriching.[23] This ambition grew out of a dedication to cultural pluralism, as articulated a generation earlier by Horace Kallen. *Commentary* was wedded to this philosophy, most directly through Cohen, who had previously edited *Menorah Journal,* which was dedicated to cultural cosmopolitanism.[24] Projecting their own politically and culturally cosmopolitan values on American society and on the Jewish community, the intellectuals around *Commentary* charted a middle course between ideological or factual assimilationism and a parochial Jewish particularism. They envisioned a social order in which Jewish distinctiveness and difference – conceived far more broadly than in mere religious terms and rooted in the Jewish past – would be valorized as political, cultural, intellectual, and moral resources for a liberal polity.[25]

Affairs, 2010), chap. 1; Bloom, *Prodigal Sons,* 137–39; Podhoretz, *Making It,* 84–86; Irving Howe, *World of Our Fathers: The Journey of the East European Jews to America and the Life They Found and Made,* 2nd ed. (New York: Schocken, 1990; orig. publ. 1976), 603–04.
21 Israel Knox, "Is America Exile or Home? We Must Begin to Build for Permanence," *Commentary* 2 (November 1946): 408, emphasis in the original.
22 Elliot Cohen, "An Act of Affirmation: Editorial Statement," *Commentary* 1 (November 1945): 2.
23 Wisse, "The Jewishness of Commentary," 54; Zipperstein, "*Commentary* and American Jewish Culture," 18–19; David Twersky, "Left Right, Left Right: After Half a Century, *Commentary* Remains Defiantly Out of Step," *Moment* 20, (June 1995): 42.
24 Balint, *Running Commentary,* 12–16; Matthew Kaufman, "The Menorah Journal and Shaping American Jewish Identity: Culture and Evolutionary Sociology," *Shofar* 30 (2012); Horace M. Kallen, "Democracy Versus the Melting-Pot." in *Culture and Democracy in the United States* (New York: Boni & Loveright, 1924; orig. publ. 1915), 67–125.
25 Terry A. Cooney, "New York Intellectuals and the Question of Jewish Identity," *American Jewish History* 80 (1991), 355; Wald, *New York Jewish Intellectuals,* 27–30. Later chapters will show how spokesmen for the labor movement and of religious agendas explicitly invoked cultural pluralism in order to legitimize their agendas, e.g. Israel Knox, "America in Jewish History," *Workmen's Circle Call* 23 (1954): 3–4; Morris Adler, "The Freedom of Free Men," *Best Jewish Sermons of 5717–5718,* ed. Saul I. Teplitz (New York: Jonathan David, 1958), 1–11; Konvitz, "Yivo Comes to Morningside," 53.

Bridging the Gap Between the Intellectuals and the Community

So much for the vision. In practice, the intellectuals concluded that the American Jewish community was neither able nor willing to conceive of their Jewishness and Judaism in ways that would make them meaningful resources for themselves and for America. They found American Jewry intellectually mediocre, culturally bland, newly bourgeois, cheaply materialistic, and either parochially Jewish, backwardly religious, or mindlessly assimilationist. "The average Jewish 'community' tends increasingly to be complacent, sentimental, devoid of cultural depth, and babbitized in its social attitudes; people may speak about *Torah*, they care about dollars," Howe pronounced as late as 1952.[26] In response, the intellectuals sought ways to elevate American Jewry culturally, so that it could come into its own as a fully formed community expressing itself through its cultural life. Cohen argued that the community's social and economic achievements had created, with some delay, cultural needs that should now be addressed: "We have reached a stage of maturity where a low level of culture no longer becomes us."[27]

Figure 10: Irving Howe, not dated. (Robert D. Farber Archives & Special Collections Department, Brandeis University)

A higher level of culture would also correct external perceptions of Jews, which had, in turn, been obstacles to a positive Jewish identification. Podhoretz remembered how at Columbia he was taunted for his crudeness (and subsequently worked

---

26 Irving Howe, "[Untitled contribution to symposium Judaism and the 'Lost' Intellectuals]," *Jewish Forum* 35 (1952): 130.
27 Elliot E. Cohen, "Jewish Culture in America: Some Speculations by an Editor," *Commentary* 3 (May 1947): 412.

to re-make himself a WASP). In the early 1950s, the association of Jewishness with vulgarity and lack of cultivation was still widespread among non-Jews and among Jews, particularly Jewish intellectuals who blamed the lack of sophistication on parochialism and cultural inbreeding within secluded organized Jewry. As a result, few of the intellectuals showed any interest in organized American Jewish life. The community's internal debates were noticeably absent from *Commentary*. While the magazine was sponsored by the American Jewish Committee, arguably the behemoth of organized Jewish life, it operated mostly untouched by editorial interference. The writers were at best disinterested in the mundane realities of the lives of religiously or otherwise affiliated Jews. As a result, a gap yawned between the intellectuals and the community.[28] Nathan Glazer wrote in retrospect, "We showed little sympathy for Jewish institutional leaders, rabbis, and writers who made the largest appeal to American Jews. We seemed – and were – outside of established Jewish institutional life."[29] (YIVO, in contrast, formed the center of the Yiddish cultural scene.)

The emotional, cultural, and social distance of the secular intellectuals to organized American Jewish life turned out to be crucial for how they conceived of their identities. When many of them, starting in the 1940s, increasingly re-affirmed their own Jewishness and looked for intellectually appealing ways to realize it, they found in contemporary Jewish life very few ideas, concepts or idioms, let alone organizational structures to do so.[30] Like newly suburbanized American Jews, they could – and had to – invent themselves as Jews, if and how they wanted. They were unbound by the existing patterns of American Jewish life that apparently failed not just their own expectations, but also those of a growing number of spiritually disoriented and dissatisfied rank-and-file members of a community in plain transition. In this situation, *Commentary*

---

[28] Wisse, "The Jewishness of Commentary," 70; Bloom, *Prodigal Sons*, 137–39; Abrams, "America Is Home," 18–19; Balint, *Running Commentary*, 26; Podhoretz, *Making It*, 118.

[29] Nathan Glazer, "Commentary: The Early Years," in *Commentary in American Life*, ed. Murray Friedman (Philadelphia: Temple University Press, 2005), 43.

[30] The historiographical narrative of a move by many of these intellectuals toward a greater affirmation of their Jewishness is controversial and does not always do justice to the complex developments within a loosely connected group of individuals. Stephen Whitfield captures the variegated moves of the members of the group by saying, "Some made gestures of ethnic return, and some had never really left." (Stephen J. Whitfield, "The Ethnicity of the New York Intellectuals," *Revue LISA/LISA e-journal* 1 (2003): 179–89) Cooney dismisses Bloom's account of a return to Jewishness as obscuring the continuities ("New York Intellectuals," 353); for other accounts, cf. Podhoretz, "Jewish Culture and the Intellectuals;" Howe, *World of Our Fathers*, 603–07; and S. A. Longstaff, "Ivy League Gentiles and Inner-City Jews: Class and Ethnicity Around *Partisan Review* in the Thirties and Forties," *American Jewish History* 80 (1991): 325–43.

filled a crucial void. As an intellectual magazine targeting a growing number of well-educated, culturally curious American Jews, it helped to span the gap between intellectuals in search of identification and a community in search of guidance. It provided the vehicle by which the intellectuals reconnected with the larger community and with their heritage.[31] In Podhoretz's words, "Cohen [...] did arrange for certain members of the family to shake hands in public with their own Jewishness for the first time in their lives."[32]

In this process of re-affirmation, the intellectuals around *Commentary* set parameters that shaped much of the larger debate around postwar Jewishness in America, redefining and expanding the concept by turning to culture. In so doing, they built on ideas YIVO had advocated, but adapted them to the new environment, as they conceived Jewishness as a refined American cultural ethnicity. This notion of Jewishness differed from major existing alternatives. "Judaism" as a religious category seemed too narrow for the broad-minded and mostly secular intellectuals; in its traditional expressions it appeared backward, and in its liberal strands as spiritually shallow. Non-religious institutional Jewish life in philanthropic, defense, community, or political institutions was equally unappealing to these highly individualistic, literary-minded thinkers. Howe summed up many secular intellectuals' rejection of the existing options for understanding Jewishness: "Religion I don't want; and as for the Jewish 'community,' what I have seen of it doesn't tempt me. The Jewish organizations are heavy with bureaucratic fat, are parochial in spirit and pedestrian in outlook."[33] The ethnic identity generated in the urban Jewish neighborhoods of the interwar period, on the other hand, seemed uncouth as the offspring of immigrant subculture and as an unreflected, parochial Jewishness. It was also what many second-generation intellectuals in their adolescent, filial rebellion first rejected, before they found in their memories of maternal kitchens the living basis for a more sophisticated Jewishness, refashioned and enhanced by an urbane culture, in which their aspirations for America and Jewishness met. Yiddishism, to the degree a refined Yiddish culture could be recognized behind the off-turning immigrant milieu, meant missing out on the chance to partake in a newly exciting American culture through the English language. Cohen sketched a new concept of Jewishness that would transcend the confines of the other paradigms, integrating a down-to-earth orientation to the present with a spiritual profundity absorbed in the past:

---

[31] Wisse, "The Jewishness of *Commentary*," 69.
[32] Podhoretz, *Making It*, 133.
[33] Howe, "[Judaism and the 'Lost' Intellectuals]," 130.

the Jews, uniquely among all people, developed a cultural tradition in which religion, ethics, and intellectual values are felt as inseparably bound up with [and] expressed through the march of issues and events on this every-day-earth. This gave, some say, their religion and ethics their salty, realistic, this-worldly flavor. And, at the same time, some think it served to lend to their every-day pre-occupations the deeper human meanings that come from a sense of long historic perspective.[34]

Culture appeared, in Cohen's and others' writings, as the magic ingredient to activate the meaning-making potential of Judaism under modern conditions. Critic Shmuel Niger argued that culture would be the best way to give positive direction to the increased, but unguided, identification with Jewishness that he saw among American Jews in general as much as it characterized the thinking of the intellectuals. "The emotional 'Jewishness' in America has increased, but our consciousness of Jewish cultural values has not become sufficiently profound."[35] Cohen himself offered a mission statement for the great project of the intellectuals: to lead American Jews toward a broader, richer, integral sense of Jewishness by drawing on the unrealized cultural potential of a community in search of an identity: "American Jews hunger for some kind of culture," he wrote in 1947. "And yet so little happens. The Jewish community officially still tends to classify culture as a seductive but forbidden luxury – like that second mink coat."[36] If American Jews were finally to give in to their secret desires, they could, in Cohen's optimistic prediction, create a vital Jewish culture. It would include among its sources traditional religious learning, but would derive from them a broader cultural form of Jewishness, by a process of transformation, whose unnamed inspirations would be Ahad Ha'am and Mordecai Kaplan. Cohen and Niger blamed the leadership of American Jewry for suppressing the community's needs for cultural self-expression, which might broadcast more distinctiveness than the American mainstream would tolerate. Parts of the leadership were therefore reluctant to expand the visible expressions of Jewishness beyond activities such as worship or charity, spheres where Jewish distinctiveness was circumscribed and socially accepted. Other, small-minded leaders might reject a broadly cultural understanding of Jewishness for different reasons, as Philip Roth argued. Conceiving Jewishness as tied into and expressible in a wider cultural sphere would undermine the boundaries which separated Jewishness from America and thereby expose Jewishness to, in Roth's words, "the world of social

---

34 Cohen, in "Report on a Conference on the Jewish Experience in America," 5.
35 S. Niger, "The Amalgam Which Is Jewish Life [Address at National Conference for Jewish Education, January 1951]," *Workmen's Circle Call* 19 (1951): 4.
36 Cohen, "Jewish Culture in America," 413, emphasis in the original.

accessibility and moral indifference," risking its cross-pollination with a foreign culture, or its dissolution in an overpowering mainstream culture.[37]

However, it was precisely the urge to explore a budding American *and* Jewish culture combining modernity with time-honored ideas that drove these intellectuals and let *Commentary* occupy an unclaimed position in the intellectual spectrum. It forcefully advocated a Jewish engagement with modern culture. A critique of Heschel's inward-looking particularism illustrates this position. Reform theologian Jakob Petuchowski respectfully faulted Heschel for cheating Judaism out of the fruit of interaction with other cultures, from a misplaced fear of the blinding glamour of foreign ideas. "It would seem [...] that the East European golden age, in contrast to the Spanish golden one, was antagonistic to the broader horizons of Western civilization and could maintain itself only within the limitations imposed from outside," Petuchowski wrote in 1958, asking rhetorically, "Was the God whom the *mitzvot*-observer in Berditshev encountered in his pious deeds really so weak that the dazzling lights of Paris and Heidelberg could put Him to flight? Or is it simply that the results of *mitzvah*-observance which Heschel promises us cannot be guaranteed outside a specific, protected environment?"[38]

Much as it presented modernity and the Jewish tradition as mutually relevant, *Commentary* regarded both Americanness and Jewishness as valuable in their own right and in relation to each other. The distinctness of this approach becomes particularly clear in contrast with the *Partisan Review* perspective on Jewishness. Both journals aspired to contribute to a sophisticated, progressive, modern American culture.[39] They shared a background in political radicalism and literary modernism, a cultural sensibility, and a group of writers, many of whom were Jewish. Still, they differed in a crucial matter. "The main difference between *Commentary* and *Partisan Review*," Elliot Cohen is quoted as saying, "is that we admit to being a Jewish magazine and they don't."[40]

---

[37] Roth, "Writing About Jews," 451.
[38] Jakob J. Petuchowski, "Faith as the Leap of Action: The Theology of Abraham Joshua Heschel," *Commentary* 25 (May 1958): 395. Petuchowski linked Heschel's theology with his image of Eastern Europe, arguing that by the emphasis on "the ineffable" whose presence was intimated in practices shaped by the holistic separateness of the *shtetl* way of life, Heschel largely precluded debates about his theology, protecting it as the source of the separate way of life, whose depiction was, in turn, questionable on historical grounds at least; cf. the following chapter.
[39] Cf. Glazer, "Commentary: The Early Years;" Eugene Goodheart, "The Abandoned Legacy of the New York Intellectuals,"*American Jewish History* 80 (1991): 361–76; Alexander Bloom, "Partisan Review," in *Encyclopedia of the American Left,* ed. Mari Jo Buhle, Paul Buhle and Dan Georgakas (New York: Oxford University Press, 1998), 583–84.
[40] Quoted in Balint, *Running Commentary*, 18.

P.R. refused to subordinate the aesthetic evaluation of a cultural product to external standards, such as the Jewishness of its author, a merely incidental attribute that would not and should not determine the cultural production of individuals or a group. *Commentary*, in contrast, embodied the idea that Jewishness was a legitimate intellectual concern and even a value in itself. *P.R.* prioritized cosmopolitan cultural and political commitments, to which Jewishness and Judaism took, at best, second seat. In a 1962 review of Isaac Bashevis Singer's novel *The Slave* for *P.R.*, Susan Sontag praised the author for taking the ingredients of a specific historical and cultural environment – seventeenth-century Polish Jewry – and transforming them in ways that spoke to modernist sensitivities: "On the face of this highly local and historically dense environment, Singer inscribes the universal conflicts of reason versus the flesh, and of creedal and ritual religion versus a free spirituality. Entirely absent from his work is any merely historical motive, the impulse to evoke this world and thereby to preserve it simply because it is both past and mercilessly destroyed." Historical Jewish distinctiveness is not a value in itself, Sontag seems to be arguing, but a means to a higher end, such as getting to the core of universal issues.[41] In a similar vein, Isaac Rosenfeld in a text about Y. L. Peretz re-interpreted Hasidism as a means to an end, here artistic creativity and cultural progress. "The Chassidic ecstasies to him [Peretz] were appearances in real historical time, but they are seen under a holy light," he wrote in a review of Maurice Samuel's book *Prince of the Ghetto*. "It is the holy light of progress, enlightenment, brotherhood, the revelation of that face of the Godhead in which liberalism seeks its own image."[42] When *Partisan Review* reconstructed East European Jewishness, it did so as a resource for spiritual sensitivity which begat aesthetic creativity. Eastern Europe provided the venue and the cultural matrix for this creativity. But, whatever was specifically Jewish about this past, including traditional religion, was assimilated into its modernist concept of literature. The Jewishness of a writer was incidental to his or her larger perspective. Jewishness meant a shared sensitivity,

---

[41] Susan Sontag, "Demons and Dreams," review of *The Slave*, by Isaac B. Singer, *Partisan Review* 29 (1962): 461.

[42] Isaac Rosenfeld, "The Ghetto and the World," review of *Prince of the Ghetto*, by Maurice Samuel, *Partisan Review* 16 (1948): 210. In another example, literary critic Elizabeth Hardwick reviewed Isaac Babel's collection of stories, *Benya Krik, the Gangster*. She offered the highest praise for Babel as "a magical Russian writer." But she concluded the review by scolding the publisher, Schocken, for the decision "to present him so meekly and meagerly by isolating the Jewish stories." ("Fiction Chronicle," *Partisan Review* 15 (1948), 1352) On the interaction between Jewish and non-Jewish writers (like Hardwick) at *P.R.*, cf. Longstaff, "Ivy League Gentiles and Inner-City Jews."

in aesthetic and political terms. If it had a contribution to make, it would be to the modern American culture to which the journal was committed. The revitalization of Jewishness as such, let alone of organized Jewish life, was not part of the magazine's brief. Its writers were socially even less attached to any community beyond themselves, let alone the organized Jewish community, than the *Commentary* family. While both journals were products by and for an elite, *P.R.* worked with a more narrow, high-brow concept of culture than *Commentary*, which one may call "upper-middle brow."[43] Editor Cohen created the department "From the American Scene," which covered topics so seemingly mundane that *P.R.* would not touch them. It explored American Jews' expanding social and cultural horizons by surveying ritual objects on sale at "Macy's," analyzing the popular radio show "The Goldbergs," and revaluating the Jewish delicatessen as "an important Jewish cultural institution in the American scene."[44]

Dialectics of Jewish Pastness and American Presentness

As these intellectuals sought to overcome the previous bifurcation between Jewishness and Americanness, the place of this new American Jewishness in the continuum of Jewish history became a prime concern. Cohen, Niger and other thinkers were confident, albeit with a dose of reservation in the mix, that some kind of a viable, perhaps even vibrant, American Jewish culture could be developed to satisfy the spiritual needs of American Jewry. In the 1940s and into the 1950s, however, this matter was tied into the larger debate about the make-up of the Jewish world after the Holocaust. This debate would also shape how American Jews related to the Jewish past. After the Holocaust, Jewish leaders worried whether American Jewry, just coming into its own, would be able to serve a greater purpose than perpetuating itself. Would their numerical and material

---

43 Podhoretz, *Making It*, 130–31.
44 Examples include Ruth Glazer, "The Jewish Delicatessen: The Evolution of an Institution," *Commentary* 1 (March 1946): 58–63; A.A. Roback, "From Sarah to Sylvia to Shirley," *Commentary* 2 (September 1946): 271–74; May Natalie Tabak, "My Grandmother Had Yichus: The Great Jewish Intangible," *Commentary* 7 (April 1949): 368–72; Ruth Glazer, "The Jewish Object: A Shopper's Report," *Commentary* 12 (July 1951): 63–67; Ruth Glazer, "The World of Station WEVD," *Commentary* 19 (February 1955): 162–70; Sylvia Rothchild, "Sixty-Five and Over: '... When Our Strength Expires, Forsake Us Not,'" *Commentary* 18 (December 1954): 549–56; and Morris Freedman, "The Real Molly Goldberg: Baalebosteh of the Air Waves," *Commentary* 21 (April 1956): 359–64.

strength equip them to take over from Eastern Europe the spiritual leadership of world Jewry?[45] Some elevated the East European past to the role of arbiter of authentic Jewish culture and of Jewish legitimacy.[46]

Many Americanized intellectuals rejected the idea that East European Jewish culture should be the yardstick for Jewish vitality and cultural creativity, which alone would legitimize American Jewry. Cohen may have had "contemptuous disdain" toward European-Yiddish values, as one scholar has argued, or nobler reasons for his position that American Jewry could not merely perpetuate East European *Yiddishkayt*, or live off the memories of it.[47] He took the new responsibility that had devolved on American Jewry as another argument to fashion a Jewish culture on its own, new, American terms. "[Out] of the opportunities of our experience here, there will evolve new patterns of living, new modes of thought, which will harmonize heritage and country into a true sense of at-home-ness in the modern world."[48] In the face of this complex project, Cohen took to dialectics as he described the relationship of the new Jewishness to past forms: "It will be similar, it will be different. It will be old, it will be new. It will be real, and it will have a fresh identity never seen before."[49]

Statements of other intellectuals further illustrate the contradictory impulses shaping American Jews' attitudes to the past, particularly the East European past. Moses Lasky, an American-born AJC official, was torn between the authenticating and constricting effect of the East European heritage: "Until recently,

---

45 Cf. Hasia R. Diner, *We Remember with Reverence and Love: American Jews and the Myth of Silence after the Holocaust, 1945–1962* (New York: New York University Press, 2009), 331–38; Riv-Ellen Prell, "Triumph, Accommodation, and Resistance: American Jewish Life from the End of World War II to the Six-Day War," in *The Columbia History of Jews and Judaism in America*, ed. Marc Lee Raphael (New York: Columbia University Press, 2008), 116–17.
46 On this question, some saw the jury still out even in the 1960s. "One, the pessimistic opinion, maintained that the European heritage would never take root on American soil and that in vain would the toilers labor. The optimists foresaw a revival of Jewish learning in New York and other cities of America, rivaling and perhaps excelling Vilna and other former centers," Yiddish scholar Sol Liptzin stated in 1964. "The realization of the vision of the optimists [...] is in the hands of the Jews of America." ("Three Hundred Years of Jewish Life and Activities in America: A Summary of Papers Read at the Yivo Conference," *News of the YIVO* 52 (1954): 1*) The text summarizes Liptzin's remarks as if spoken in his voice.
47 Abrams quotes Cohen registering his disdain, taking it as an indication of *Commentary's* conscious rejection of mere nostalgic engagement with the East European past ("America is Home," 34).
48 Cohen, "Act of Affirmation," 2.
49 Cohen, "Jewish Culture in America," 414; see also Niger, "Amalgam," 4.

our Jewishness was constantly renewed by drops of the concentrated Judaism of Europe, latterly of Eastern Europe. These infusions [...] have supplied the essence of Jewishness here. At the same time, they have served to retard the development of our own Jewish culture."⁵⁰ Jewish studies scholar Judah Goldin found different reasons for American Jews' ambivalence to this past. He pointed to a post-Holocaust sense of loss and guilt, but emphasized yet another factor: "I cannot help feeling that the contemporary Jew's difficulty with the world of East European Jewry lies [...] in an inability to understand it. It seems utterly irrelevant to his idiom; at best it appears quaint, epigrammatic, otherworldly," Goldin wrote in 1950 in *Commentary*. "If he is to take that world seriously, it needs to be made intelligible before it is held up as a model to him."⁵¹

Historian Eli Lederhendler has taken these inner tensions as part of a larger development which pitted "retrievalists" of the past against those taking a more optimistic, future-oriented approach to American Jewish culture. In his analysis, the former perspective, at least in the 1960s and at least in New York, was consolidated in a "culture of retrieval," which responded to the perceived shallowness and cultural barrenness of present Jewishness by trying to retrieve from the past what was irretrievably lost. The result was an identity not integrated but split between its two components: "Self-validation in the American idiom turned toward the future, while self-validation in the Jewish idiom turned toward the past."⁵² Against the hopes of many American-born intellectuals, this split that linked America to the present and Jewishness to the past became a common trope in postwar American Jewish debates. Leon Baritz, an intellectual historian, made this point based on personal experience. Writing in 1962, he recalled how his immigrant family first embraced the newness of the New World, as "they have wrapped their children in a thick layer of America so that they and their children may forget their participation in recent Jewish history as well as their membership in the wider, non-American community of Jews." But the Holocaust shattered the illusion that such a flight from the bonds of Jewishness was possible and morally defensible. Baritz modified a classical argument often invoked by European critics of America,

---

50 Moses Lasky and Herbert B. Ehrmann, "Jewish Culture for America? Two Commentaries," *Commentary* 3 (March 1947): 250–55; Lasky and Ehrmann responded critically to Israel Knox's article "Is America Exile or Home?", quoted above). Cf. also Lester Seligman, "A Second Look at the Tercentenary," *Judaism* 4 (1955): 110–15.
51 Judah Goldin, "Remembrance of Things Past," review of *The Testament of the Lost Son*, by Soma Morgenstern, *Commentary* 10 (November 1950): 502, 503.
52 Eli Lederhendler, *New York Jews and the Decline of Urban Ethnicity, 1950–1970* (Syracuse: Syracuse University Press, 2001), 68–69.

as he suggested that America's conscious opting-out of history was fundamentally opposite to the essence of Jewishness. "Because of America's rejection of the past, of the fierce commitment to the notion that this land will start anew, the American Jew is pulled apart. To be a Jew is to remember. An American must forget."[53] In marked contrast to the rhetoric of congenial American and Jewish values which characterized the 1954 tercentenary, Jewish pastness here becomes the mark of distinctiveness in America.[54]

Accepting Ambivalence – Vis-à-Vis Eastern Europe and America

The dissenting voices of these intellectuals suggest that in the 1940s and into the 1960s, the balance of pastness and orientation toward an American future, as well as the nature of the pastness and its role in present American culture, were open and contested. This was particularly true in the case of the East European past. Mindful, albeit not in all cases conscious, of this constellation, intellectuals approached the East European past in highly selective and creative ways, as they followed Hertzberg's outline: choosing what to retain and absorb into group memory that would serve the present spiritual needs of American Jews.[55] By the 1950s, as Podhoretz observed, many of the secular intellectuals were "enthusiasts of Martin Buber, while the whole of the New York literary world was ringing with praise of the Yiddish storytellers, [and] the Hasidim," as well as of other aspects of Jewish history.[56] As a collective, embodied by *Commentary*, they turned to the East European past, claiming or constructing continuities in the service of legitimacy for their overall project: an expanded concept of Jewishness, distinctly American and distinctly Jewish, intellectually appealing and spiritually rich, translated into modern cultural terms.

In an analysis limited to Eastern Europe-related texts, several themes stand out in *Commentary* and illustrate how the authors creatively drew connections

---

53 Loren Baritz, "A Jew's American Dilemma," *Commentary* 33 (June 1962): 523, 525; Cohen similarly spoke of the Jews' "talent for history" and their "history-focused mentality" ("Report on a Conference on the Jewish Experience in America," 5).
54 It is also a foretaste of the countercultural valorization and invocation of difference for the purpose of critiquing America after the loss of the societal consensus in the 1960s.
55 Cf. Hertzberg, "The Worldly Jew," 87.
56 Norman Podhoretz, "Introduction – Jewishness and the Younger Intellectuals: A Symposium," *Commentary* 31 (April 1961): 307–08.

Figure 11: Martin Buber, 1957. (Robert D. Farber Archives & Special Collections Department, Brandeis University)

between past and present. The range of dimensions of East European Jewish life that were brought to life in these texts points to the writers' concern with the value of internal diversity in Jewish life. The magazine presented both Heschel, scion of a Hasidic family, who sublimated poverty, and Vladimir Medem, son of an assimilated family, who through the *Bund* fought poverty as a product of the capitalist order; they appeared as equally legitimate, alternative ways to express Jewishness as a commitment inspiring meaningful agendas. Similarly, the decision to include thinkers as different as Franz Rosenzweig and Hayyim of Volozhin in the column "Cedars of Lebanon" suggested that both could equally inform American Jews' identification with Judaism. *Commentary* itself was the forum in which the contest of ideas took place. Norman Podhoretz extolled the behavioral concept of Jewishness that he found in Sholem Aleichem's *Adventures of Mottel the Cantor's Son* – a notion of Jewishness which reader Ivan B. Abrams in a letter to the journal dismissed as "pseudo-Jewish."[57] Numerous texts explicitly called for a pluralism that would liberate the Jews from the monopoly of religion as the only legitimate expression of Jewishness, and for a broader, culture-based identity. Editor Cohen himself listed "religious thinking" as but one expression of a broader cultural Jewishness. Reviewing Heschel's *The Earth Is the Lord's*, Irving Kristol argued that missing from the idealized picture were "our harassed and disbelieving ancestors, who fled to America, not only from the pogroms, but – very many of them – also from the rebbe, the Hasid, the ghetto." Hebrew

---

[57] Vladimir Medem, "Youth of a Bundist: A Jewish Labor Leader Recalls His Beginnings," *Commentary* 10 (November 1950): 477–82; Rosenzweig, "Discovery of the East European Jew;" Hayim Ben Isaac, "Man, the Master of All Created Worlds [Cedars of Lebanon]," *Commentary* 14 (December 1952): 595–97; Norman Podhoretz, "Sholom Aleichem: Jewishness Is Jews: The Unregenerate Tribe," *Commentary* 16 (September 1953): 261–63; Ivan B. Abrams, "The Need to Clarify," *Commentary* 16 (December 1953): 591–92.

scholar Ezra Spicehandler extolled the secular humanism of Ahad Ha'am as relevant for American Jews. Hertzberg called on American Jews to add the *"veltliche yid"* (secular Jew) to their reservoir of images of Eastern Europe, on which they drew for inspiration and guidance in their own time.[58] Similarly, Yiddish educator Saul Goodman urged a "revaluation" of the ideas of Simon Dubnow, which "have either been forgotten or ignored, perhaps because the exponents of a religious point of view have come to dominate the discussion of Jewishness." Goodman's essay is a model for how an intellectual translates the East European past to make it speak to his or her contemporary American agenda, and a succinct articulation of an agenda shared by many postwar American Jewish intellectuals. Goodman concludes his essay by asking, what American Jews can learn from Dubnow:

> First of all, in secularizing the idea of Jewishness, and in giving meaning to Jewish history without benefit of theology, he provided a rationale [...] for the free-thinking Jew's impulse to remain Jewish and to transmit the heritage of Jewishness to future generations. Those who assert that a creative Jewish culture is impossible without a firm religious commitment might reflect on Dubnow's analysis of how the Jews maintained their spiritual character in various periods of history. [...] Is it, however, at all likely that American Jews will remain committed to Jewishness in a broad cultural sense? My own feeling is that the signs point in this direction. Surely the much heralded religious revival of recent years has less to do with religion (as many observers agree) than with cultural identification. If we adapt Dubnow's conception of the three national types to the American Jewish community, we might say that it has passed through the first two stages of Americanization and integration and is now entering into the third stage – the search for its ancestral roots and its authentic "self." And in this search, Dubnow deserves to be considered one of the best and most helpful guides.[59]

A guide like Dubnow seemed necessary for American Jews who in the middle decades of the century expressed great ambivalence vis-à-vis their East European past. The spectrum of perspectives found in the writings of the period shows that many cross-currents of ideas and images had to be navigated in order to arrive at a coherent position vis-à-vis the past and the American present. Again, differences between immigrant intellectuals and American-born ones came into play. YIVO's Weinreich saw a tendency in English-language Jewish publications

---

58 Cohen, "Jewish Culture in America," 413; Irving Kristol, "Elegy for a Lost World," review of *The Earth Is the Lord's,* by Abraham Joshua Heschel, *Commentary* 9 (May 1950): 490–91; Ezra Spicehandler, "A Jewish Humanist," review of *Ahad Ha-Am – Asher Ginzberg,* by Leon Simon, *Commentary* 32 (September 1961): 266–68; Hertzberg, "The Worldy Jew," 88.
59 Saul Goodman, "Simon Dubnow: A Revaluation," *Commentary* 30 (December 1960): 515.

to whitewash Jewish life in Eastern Europe and Jewish life in general, lest its mundane, salty, ethnic particularity overtax middle-class American tastes and expectations of Jews as representatives of a dignified, bourgeois religion. At the 1948 *Commentary* conference, he argued that Yiddish publications were much less protective "than the things written on similar subjects in English, excluding, of course, *Commentary*."[60] Weinreich may have exempted the journal from his criticism out of politeness for his hosts. Still, a survey of *Commentary* texts on Eastern Europe gives credence to his differentiation. The journal did print essays, not just by Heschel, that expressed unalloyed admiration and reverence for the authentically Jewish and spiritually profound life of East European Jewry. On the other hand, it also gave room for perspectives that undermined such efforts at idealization and apotheosis. The selection of letters by Rosenzweig, published by *Commentary* in 1953, in which he described to his mother and friends his first encounter with Eastern Jews in 1918 Warsaw, is a case in point. Rosenzweig's own description of his sudden attraction to the intensity and fervor of their distinct Jewishness is counterbalanced by the editorial introduction by Nahum Glatzer, who reports that Rosenzweig's highly Germanized mother was initially worried by her son's identification with these Polish Jews, but soon "realized that Franz remained a Western Jew, yet one of a new kind: his Judaism became all-inclusive, universal, and of a profound tolerance."[61]

The perspectives on both Eastern Europe and America ranged from exaltation to rejection, with plenty of room in between for more measured, complex, or ambivalent positions. For every critique of American Jewry by Heschel, there was a counternarrative such as Parzen's. Ideologically motivated and simplifying depictions that idealized Jewish life in the Old World were contrasted by images of its harsh reality. "The lachrymose recollections of the *shtetl* (which are still with us) fail to recall its narrowness of mind, its cruelty, especially to school children [...], and its invidious stratification," Daniel Bell wrote in 1961. Midge Decter argued that many of those who left the *shtetl* did so less due to outside pressure, but due to "the heavy hands of their own fathers."[62] Clement Greenberg, the journal's leading critic, represented an extreme case, as he extended the criticism from the backwardness of Jewish life in Eastern Europe to

---

[60] Weinreich, in "Report on a Conference on the Jewish Experience in America," 35.
[61] Rosenzweig, "Discovery of the East European Jew," 86. For a contrast, cf. Julius Fisher, "The Great Repentant: Franz Rosenzweig," *Jewish Forum* 37 (1954): 37–38, and subsequent issues.
[62] Daniel Bell, "Reflections on Jewish Identity," *Commentary* 31 (June 1961): 474; Midge Decter, "Belittling Sholom Aleichem's Jews: Folk Falsification of the Ghetto," *Commentary* 17 (May 1954): 389–92.

the parochial and self-hating mentality he found in contemporary Jewish leaders in America: "They cannot, in their political function, wholly escape the effects of the backward environment in which they grew up," he charged in his blistering attack on "positive Jewishness," an ideology opposed to the cosmopolitan values of the intellectuals. "These stigmata of political backwardness will probably not disappear until Eastern Europe becomes a less vivid memory, the Oriental Jews are successfully absorbed."[63] On the other hand, in the decision to give space to Heschel, Buber, and other exponents of an idealizing perspective on Eastern Europe, *Commentary* destabilized the quasi-official narrative that painted the Old World past in dark colors, and used it as a foil to affirm modern, liberal, prosperous, and pluralist America as hospitable to Jews and congenial to Jewish values.[64]

Translating the East European Past for the American Jewish Present

It was this wide range of images and narratives that allowed the *Commentary* intellectuals to pick up YIVO's urge to make the East European past usable for the American present – and to make it their own. Where YIVO was limited by its

---

[63] Clement Greenberg, "Self-Hatred and Jewish Chauvinism: Some Reflections on 'Positive Jewishness,'" *Commentary* 10 (November 1950): 431.

[64] This narrative dominated the official rhetoric at the 1954 tercentenary; cf. Norman Belth, *Everyman's Guide: The American Jewish Tercentenary, 1654–1954* (New York: American Jewish Tercentenary, December 1953; American Jewish Archives, Horace Kallen papers, MS-1, box 46, folder 6); American Jewish Tercentenary Committee, *The American Jewish Tercentenary Community Manual* (New York: American Jewish Tercentenary Committee, 1954; American Jewish Archives, Horace Kallen papers, MS-1, box 46, folder 6). Cf. also Knox, "America in Jewish History;" David Bernstein, "The American Jewish Tercentenary," in *American Jewish Yearbook 1956*, ed. Morris Fine (New York: American Jewish Committee, 1956), 101–18. As for the Cold War context, the great number of articles on the suppression of Judaism and persecution of Jews in the Soviet Union and its satellites made up much of *Commentary's* writing on Eastern Europe in the period under consideration; cf. Nathan Reich, "Jewish Life in the Russian Satellites: The Prospects for Recovery under Totalitarianism," *Commentary* 7 (April 1949): 328–34; Peter Meyer, "Soviet Anti-Semitism in High Gear: What Can the Kremlin Hope to Gain?" *Commentary* 15 (February 1953): 115–20; Franz Borkenau, "Was Malenkov Behind the Anti-Semitic Plot? The Doctors' Frame-up and Its Reversal," *Commentary* 15 (May 1953): 438–46; Walter Z. Laqueur, "Soviet Policy and Jewish Fate: In Russia and Israel," *Commentary* 22 (October 1956): 303–12; and Lucy Dawidowicz, "What Future for Judaism in Russia? The Dark Record of the Past," *Commentary* 22 (November 1956): 401–07.

ideological commitment to Yiddishism and opposing demographic and cultural trends, *Commentary* was open enough to provide a forum to dissect various images and narratives of the past in order to select those that could best be made usable for the present. Complementing a genuine interest in Judaism as a positive source of identity and ideas by its openness to the new opportunities America offered its Jews, the journal probed the intersection of the two and their fusion in a specifically American concept of Jewishness. Writing in English, it targeted a potentially growing audience, whereas Yiddish publications fought an uphill battle against demographic and cultural trends. The second-generation, American-born intellectuals as a group were culturally potent enough to take YIVO's conceptual framework and make it their own. The result was a framework that Yiddish translators would have called "fartaytsht un farbessert" – improved by its translation into a new cultural formation. By providing a forum for the exploration of the East European past and for its translation into American terms, *Commentary* helped to weave Jewishness into the American texture and vice versa. Thereby, it was instrumental in grounding American Jewry in a past that made Jewishness more meaningful. At its helm, "Cohen explicitly appealed to Jewish memories drawn from the past and located them within a new American context, producing a radically new covenant to be formed between America and its Jewish intellectual community," Abrams wrote of the early years of the journal. "It became an agency for the refocusing of the community of memory by its refashioning of Jewish memories." Refashioning included rejecting the practice of merely preserving memories or retrieving from the East European past what seemed usable to perpetuate previous modes of Jewishness; rather, it meant aspiring "to produce a new type of Jew" through the discourse about the Jewish past and the American present.[65]

Commentary's openness made it a forum for the intellectual and spiritual unrest which characterized much of postwar American Jewish thought. This unrest resulted in the creation of several other journals that gave space to the questions a growing number of highly educated, self-reflexive, and curious thinkers raised about the future of Judaism in a modern, liberal, prosperous society.[66] With the ferment of change at work within the community going well beyond the circles *Commentary* could speak for and to, the secular intellectuals, try as they might, could not control the debate around the future of Judaism in America.

---

[65] Abrams, "America is Home," 31.
[66] Robert G. Goldy, *The Emergence of Jewish Theology in America* (Bloomington: Indiana University Press, 1990); Arnold M. Eisen, *The Chosen People in America: A Study in Jewish Religious Ideology* (Bloomington: Indiana University Press, 1983).

They became just one voice in a debate that took directions different from what they had intended, as other powerful voices spoke up. Other thinkers brought their own, different and distinct perspectives to the questions facing American Jews in mid-twentieth century – a time of deeply upsetting events on the world stage and of disorienting changes on the domestic scene, all of which led many Americans, Jews and non-Jews, to look for religious answers.

4 Religious Culture as an Antidote to Liberal Judaism and Secular Jewishness

If there was one segment within the American Jewish elites that would not let the secular *Commentary* intellectuals have their way with the future of Judaism in America, it was a diverse but like-minded set of religious thinkers. These rabbis and academic theologians shared the secularists' diagnosis that there was a dire need to make Jewishness more meaningful. But, they also recognized that the Jewishness peddled by the secular intellectuals was diametrically opposed to their own ideas.

As the chief purveyor of the secularist heresy, *Commentary* became the *bête noir* for religious thinkers like Milton Steinberg (1903–1950), a prominent Conservative rabbi of Reconstructionist outlook. His eponymous 1949 lecture at his Park Avenue Synagogue asked, rhetorically, "*Commentary* Magazine – Benefit or Detriment to American Judaism?" His polemic answer spelled out how dangerous the journal was, as it filled a crucial void with highly problematic content. Steinberg started out by warning that the chance to achieve a vital Jewish life in America was slim and rapidly diminishing. The alternative he feared was a "dejudaized American Jewry, bereft of its God and Torah, its will to live and joy in life, a mass golem of five million persons kept alive only by the evil spell of anti-Semitism." In this dangerous situation, criticism and alternative visions of Judaism were urgently important, and Steinberg acknowledged that *Commentary* had drawn new thinkers into the public debate about these problems.[1] Other than that, however, Steinberg had only crushing criticism for the journal. Its typical writer was a "negative Jew" lacking love for Judaism, a "rootless intellectual [who is] alienated from yet drawn to the Jewish faith, tradition and people, ambivalent to them, that is to say, loving and hating them at the same time." As a result, *Commentary* ignored or distorted the most important aspects of Jewish life, first and foremost the synagogue. What Steinberg found instead was a dangerous, cultural-aesthetic concept of Jewishness:

> Now perhaps we can account for the air of dilletantism and literary dandyism which hovers over *Commentary*, the impression it lends of being so very much in "the high aesthetic line." What is wrong in this respect is not that *Commentary* concerns itself with problems of the creation and criticism of Jewish literature, real issues and deserving of concern, but that it fails so generally to concern itself with the issues of Jewish life.[2]

---

[1] Milton Steinberg, "Commentary Magazine–Benefit or Detriment to American Judaism?" November 18, 1949, typescript, American Jewish Archives, Julian Morgenstern papers, MS 30, box 10, folder 30, 2; also published in Milton Steinberg, *A Believing Jew: The Selected Writings of Milton Steinberg* (New York: Harcourt Brace, 1951), 136–65.
[2] Steinberg, "Commentary Magazine," 3, 6, 9, 13, 15.

In Steinberg's reading, the rootless intellectuals compensated for their distance from the religious life of the present by vicariously identifying with the past. This hypothesis, he wrote, "would account for the warmth which the magazine so often displays toward the Jewish past and Jewish life at a distance, where it does not come too close to the editors or touch them too intimately." This indictment – lack of love for Judaism, distance from actual Jewish life, and misuse of the heritage for the sake of a dejudaized Judaism – points, in turn, to the positive vision that Steinberg shared with many religious thinkers. They hoped to create a "vital Jewish religious, ethical, cultural and communal life in this land."[3] It was for this vision of the future that they, too, would make the past usable.

Judaism: Eastern Europe as a Resource for a Broader Concept of Judaism

Like their secular rivals, mid-twentieth century religious thinkers presented their ideas to a public debate, which itself reflected the unsettled religious landscape of American Judaism. The sense of an urgent need for change fueled a proliferation of religious, and specifically theological, reflections by Jewish thinkers who challenged established patterns of Jewish thought and life, most of all liberal Judaism.[4] Heschel, Will Herberg, Emil Fackenheim, and Joseph B. Soloveitchik were key thinkers in a scattered movement constituted by shared generational experiences. Heschel and Soloveitchik in particular consciously harnessed the East European past for their respective religious agendas. Several religious journals, denominational and trans-denominational, sprang up in this period, serving as forums to air, test, and refine new ideas about Judaism. They reflected the intellectual ferment at work within the religious elite of rabbis and academic theologians. This ferment also shaped an emerging segment of university-trained, American or Americanized rabbis whose intellectual interests informed their practical work as pulpit rabbis, educators, and communal leaders. They were readers and writers for the journals that also targeted a growing audience of religiously educated American Jewish laypeople.[5]

---

3 Steinberg, "Commentary Magazine," 2, 12, 15.
4 Cf. Robert G. Goldy, *The Emergence of Jewish Theology in America* (Bloomington: Indiana University Press, 1990).
5 Arnold M. Eisen, "Theology, Sociology, Ideology: Jewish Thought in America, 1925–1955," *Modern Judaism* 2 (1982): 91–103.

Among those publications, the ambitiously named journal *Judaism* was of particular influence among religious professionals. Somewhat surprisingly, it was the secular American Jewish Congress that founded it in 1952 with an explicit commitment to Judaism as a religion and a value in itself. The statement of sponsorship defined its purpose as "foster[ing] the affirmation of Jewish religious, cultural, and historic identity."[6] Its writers and readers, many of them rabbis, but also academic and other religious thinkers and professionals, had a stake in revitalizing Judaism under new circumstances. They responded to problems, such as low levels of observance and great ambivalence about Jewishness, as well as to opportunities, such as the new openness of American society to religion in general and to Judaism in particular.

In light of this constellation, the journal was committed to a distinctly religious concept of Judaism and Jewishness. Founding editor Robert Gordis, himself a Conservative rabbi and Biblical scholar, spelled out the constitutive belief that Judaism as a religion could offer meaning to Jewishness as an identity, but it could also speak to the spiritual needs beyond the Jewish group. In a programmatic article opening the journal's inaugural issue, he identified "the spiritual unease of modern man" as the main factor driving the new interest in Judaism. But American Jewry, he argued, was intellectually unprepared for this new role, because it was not aware of the contribution it could offer in response to the religious questions Americans asked. *Judaism* made it its mission to change that. "It would be little short of tragic if the Jewish people, which gave the Bible and the basic postulates of God and morality to the world, should play no recognizable part in the resurgence of religious and ethical standards in our time."[7]

As the writers for *Judaism* publicly developed their ideas around the role that Judaism should play for Jews and non-Jews, they had to position them vis-à-vis competing ideologies. The most obvious target of many of their articles was secularism. In 1959, Herbert Parzen issued a powerful call to secularists to wake up and realize that they were clinging to illusions rendered obsolete by the march of history toward religious identification. Like other religious thinkers, he optimistically dismissed secularism as a one-generation phenomenon doomed to die

---

[6] American Jewish Congress, "Statement of Sponsorship," *Judaism* 1 (1952): 2. Gordis, in his account of the founding history, adds organizational considerations of the American Jewish Congress and human aspects, like the need to find a position for Herberg, to the intellectual and spiritual need for a new journal; Robert Gordis, "The Genesis of *Judaism:* A Chapter in Jewish Cultural History," *Judaism* 30 (1981): 390–95.

[7] Robert Gordis, "Toward a Renascence of Judaism," *Judaism* 1 (1952): 4, 5.

out with the immigrant generation because it was foreign to America.[8] In some cases, the secularists themselves admitted defeat. Saul Goodman, director of the New York Sholem Aleichem schools, even did so in *Judaism*, in a 1960 article that recognized the need for a Jewishness grounded in religion: "Jewish humanists or secularists realize that their most precious ideals and values [...] must be rooted in the spiritual soil of their ancestry." Given the social realities of postwar America, he concluded: "Were we to give an American twist to the concept of Jewish secularity we could designate it *religious secularism*."[9]

While the decline of secularism as an ideology was gratifying to the religious thinkers, they still feared the powerful secularizing effects of the day-to-day American social reality. To insulate American Jews from both, some invoked the East European past to advocate for a more assertive role of religious Judaism in the American present. Ben-Zion Bokser, an unusually learned Conservative pulpit rabbi, pointed out that the saintly leaders of East European Jewry stood by in helpless passivity to allow secularism to undermine traditional life. Lest American Jews repeat this mistake, he urged that "[religion] will also have to enter more boldly into the war of ideas, [...] to undertake with vigor the intellectual defense of religion against secularism."[10] Others echoed this call to actively engage with the challenges and opportunities of modern society. Parzen presented Jewish secularism as a reaction to traditional Judaism's rejection of modernity; thus, it was out of place in America, where religious Judaism had been modernized.[11] Hebrew literary critic Baruch Kurzweil found the most pernicious response to the secularizing forces in a cultural Judaism à la Ahad Ha'am that relegated religion to an inferior role. The error was all the greater, since this descendant of a Hasidic family born near Kiev should have known better: "As a Russian Jew, steeped in Jewish tradition, Achad Ha-am knew that religion occupies a position so dominant in Jewish culture as to make the latter inconceivable without it."[12]

---

8 Herbert Parzen, "The Passing of Jewish Secularism in the United States," *Judaism* 8 (1959): 195, 198. Cf. also Harold M. Schulweis, "[Review of *Secularism Is the Will of God*, by Horace Kallen]," *Judaism* 4 (1955): 367–71; Will Herberg, "Religious Trends in American Jewry," *Judaism* 3 (1954): 229–40; Melvin M. Tumin, "Conservative Trends in American Jewish Life." *Judaism* 13 (1964): 135–36.
9 Saul Goodman, "Jewish Secularism in America – Permanence and Change," *Judaism* 9 (1960): 329–30, emphasis in the original.
10 Ben Zion Bokser, "Religion and Secularism," *Judaism* 1 (1952): 156–57.
11 Parzen, "Passing of Jewish Secularism," 197.
12 Baruch Kurzweil, "Judaism – The Group Will-to-Survive? A Critique of Achad Ha-Amism," *Judaism* 4 (1955): 211, 215. Cf. also Goodman, "Jewish Secularism in America;" C. Bezalel

Kurzweil's last sentence hinted at the second major theme on the journal's agenda for the revitalization of American Judaism. His use of the phrase "Jewish culture" illustrated many religious intellectuals' insight that the modern concept of religion, as realized in particular in postwar America, was reductive and deprived Judaism of its full meaning-making potential. Gordis warned that "in the past, protagonists of Judaism as a 'religion' have all too often been advocates of a minimal, scarcely identifiable Jewish content in their lives;" he called such a narrow concept "un-Jewish." Therefore, the understanding of religion should be expanded so that Judaism could be conceived more broadly and in distinctly Jewish terms: "Torah embraces the law, the lore, and the learning of Israel, the world-view of Judaism, and the Jewish way of life through which it is expressed."[13] Similarly, Orthodox rabbi Eliezer Berkovits urged that "Judaism, representing a comprehensive philosophy of life and living," be re-vitalized in its traditional, broad scope, at least to the degree this was possible under modern, American conditions.[14] The call for an expanded concept of Judaism was the common basis of many of the ideas that the eponymous journal presented in order to invigorate American Jewish life. Taken together, they unfolded a panorama of diverse expressions of Judaism. This pluralism was deduced both from the greatness of the task and from the ideal of a broadly inclusive Judaism that would transcend previous boundaries and concepts. Gordis programmatically emphasized the journal's non-dogmatic openness to fresh ideas: "New and unconventional interpretations, whatever their standpoint, will be welcomed from every source."[15]

In search of such new ideas for a broader and deeper, hence more meaningful, understanding of Judaism, the writers for *Judaism* again found a treasure trove in the East European past. It yielded a range of motifs that could be used to inform and inspire the American Jewish present in different ways. Many authors, Gordis among them, expounded on what may be the most important trope in postwar American Jewish accounts of the past: East European Jewish life radiated its spiritual and human warmth to American Jewry and infused it with dignity and distinctiveness. Gordis approvingly pointed to an inherited ethno-religious identification with the group: "This Jewish loyalty is the heritage of American

---

Sherman, "Nationalism, Secularism and Religion in the Jewish Labor Movement," *Judaism* 3 (1954; Tercentenary issue): 354–65.
13 Gordis, "Toward a Renascence," 7, 8.
14 Eliezer Berkovits, "Jewish Living in America," *Judaism* 2 (1953): 72. Berkovits qualified his hopes for such a development in America by stating that ultimately "Jewish living" was possible only by living in one civilization in the State of Israel, "the natural home of Judaism." (73) "Jewish living in America is not fully realizable." (74)
15 Gordis, "Toward a Renascence," 10.

Jewry from Eastern Europe," he wrote on the occasion of the 1954 Tercentenary.[16] Others pushed the notion of a spiritual heritage toward an aesthetic sense of Jewishness. Stephen Kayser, a friend of Heschel's, used an essay on Jewish art to highlight the rich, organic, holistic Jewishness which shaped the creativity of East European Jewish artists: "Their Jewishness was but a natural part of their lives."[17] Fellow art critic Maurice Schmitt echoed the notion of an aesthetic Jewish distinctiveness, by describing East European Jewish art, such as Marc Chagall's, as embodying a sense of beauty distinct from Western standards. Martin Buber's dialogical philosophy as much as Sholem Aleichem's stories bespoke a spiritual depth that impressed with their alien grandeur, he claimed.[18] The shift from narrowly defined religious understandings to broader notions of Jewishness was also palpable in a glowing tribute to Yiddishist critic Shmuel Niger. *Judaism* embraced his notion of *Yiddishkayt,* derived, as it was, from the East European experience, including the transformation of a religious concept of Jewishness into a cultural one.[19] These and many other invocations of the East European heritage pointed to the ideal that Kurzweil had presented in his critique of Ahad Ha'am: a "Jewish culture" dominated by religion, or a spiritual culture, which would draw its vital energy from religion rather than relegating it to a minor role.[20]

Yet, Gordis and his stable of writers insisted on keeping "religion" and "culture" separate. They often walked linguistic and conceptual tightropes as they sought to relate the two in a different way from their secular intellectual counterparts. The impetus as well as the problems of this approach crystallized in *Judaism's* strenuous rejection of cultural pluralism, which many writers dismissed as insufficient in practice to stem the mighty tide of assimilation. "Cultural pluralism is little more than a retarding factor, useful in making the process of assimilation more gradual and thus reducing the tension between immigrant and native generations," Gordis declared. "The only enduring type of pluralism which the structure of American life envisages lies in the field

---

16 Robert Gordis, "American Jewry Faces Its Fourth Century," *Judaism* 3 (1954; Tercentenary issue): 300.
17 Stephen S. Kayser, "Visual Arts in American Jewish Life," *Judaism* 3 (1954, Tercentenary issue): 444. Kayser became the first curator of the Jewish Museum in New York; cf. Edward K. Kaplan, *Spiritual Radical: Abraham Joshua Heschel in America, 1940–1972* (New Haven: Yale University Press, 2007), 78.
18 Maurice Schmidt, "Marc Chagall – The Jewish Painter," *Judaism* 13 (1964): 328–34; cf. also Alfred Werner, "Max Weber: Hasidic Painter," *Judaism* 9 (1960): 260–68; Ernest M. Wolf, "Martin Buber and German Jewry," *Judaism* 1 (1952): 346–52.
19 Samuel Kreiter, "Sh. Niger: Yiddish Humanist," *Judaism* 6 (1957): 334–39.
20 Kurzweil, "The Group Will-to-Survive," 215.

of religion."²¹ The difference between a cultural pluralism à la *Commentary*, which translated traditional religious concepts into modern cultural terms, and the religious pluralism that *Judaism* advocated was abstract but crucial. In order to expand the scope of religion, Gordis and other writers associated with *Judaism* contracted the scope of culture; this allowed them, in a second step, to order the two in a hierarchy: "to stimulate Jewish creativity in the fields of literature, music, and art alone, while neglecting the areas of religion, philosophy, and ethics, would mean presenting Hamlet without the Prince of Denmark."²² In other words, Judaism as a religion, expanded to mean a way of life, was at least equal in rank, if not foundational to culture, which had been reduced to "literature, music, and art." Here was the deeper reason why these writers went to such great lengths to dismiss cultural pluralism. The cultural reconstruction of Judaism that was required for this approach meant, to them, the very subordination of religion to culture that Steinberg and others found in *Commentary*. In the words of poet and *Judaism* contributor Richard Fein, the "subjective 'aestheticizing' of religion [as] the personal literary-cultural imagination replaces the communal religious one."²³ In response, they sought to strengthen religion, Judaism, defined more expansively as the primary sphere of Jewish expression and identification.

And yet, on a larger plane, the missions of the religious and the secular intellectuals were quite similar. The writers in *Judaism* strove to shape a new, expanded and distinctly American concept of Judaism, which, like the East European Jewish life on which it was patterned, would touch American Jews more deeply and more broadly than the contemporaneous shallow, compartmentalized, and de-spiritualized sense of Jewishness. For the same reason, *Commentary* advocated a broad cultural definition of Jewishness drawing on a translation of the traditional heritage into new terms. Crucially, both sets of thinkers, secular and religious intellectuals, agreed on the need to create a new, American sense of Jewishness, for which the East European past could be an inspiration, but not the yardstick by which to measure its authenticity. Gordis in several texts presented the emerging American Jewish culture as a synthesis transcending the antithesis of the East and West European Jewish experiences. To him, it was "a 'mutation,' an amalgamation of both types of community," drawing its spiritual vitality from

---

21 Gordis, "Toward a Renascence of Judaism," 7. Gordis's polemic appeared some twenty pages away from a text by Horace Kallen, which re-affirmed the concept that Kallen created, albeit without using the term: "What Price 'Jewish Living?'" *Judaism* 1 (1952): 27–35. Cf. also Parzen, "Passing of Jewish Secularism," 195; Schulweis, "[Review of Kallen]," 367; Herberg, "Religious Trends;" Tumin, "Conservative Trends," 135–36.
22 Gordis, "Toward a Renascence of Judaism," 10.
23 Richard J. Fein, "Jewishness – The Felt Ambiguity," *Judaism* 16 (1967): 140.

the East European heritage. "American Jewry is a *novum*," not an attempt to replicate previous patterns of Jewish life.[24] By this perspective alone, *Judaism* was crucial for the religious discourse about the revitalization of Judaism. It greatly expanded the range of legitimate options for how Judaism might be reconceived under new, American conditions. For this purpose, it turned to the East European past, while rejecting a mere retrieval or transplantation of the East European past to the American present.

Some of *Judaism's* authors had to navigate the balance between past and present, American newness and the East European past in their own lives. One of its most prominent contributors was in a unique position to do this, as he raised his voice in the discourse about the future of Judaism in America: Abraham Joshua Heschel.[25]

Heschel's Apotheosis of Ashkenazic Jewish Life

Heschel was, quite literally, the public face of the venerable East European heritage for many Americans, both Jews and non-Jews. They saw him prominently featured in news media as a religious intellectual and political activist in the civil rights and anti-war movements of the 1950s and 60s. Heschel's physical appearance contributed to the shaping of the image of an archetypal East European Jew. His visibility and biography combined to make him one of the most influential Jewish thinkers to harness the East European past for the revitalization of American Judaism. Heschel seemed predestined for this role, as he had to integrate in his biography a wide range of experiences that informed how postwar American Jewry

---

[24] Gordis, "American Jewry Faces Its Fourth Century," 298–99. English professor Lester G. Seligman (in an article otherwise atypically dismissive of the East European heritage), agreed that American Jewry would form a way of life in its own right: "East European Jewish life is no prototype for America." (Lester G. Seligman, "A Second Look at the Tercentenary," *Judaism* 4 (1955): 115) In this declaration of American Jewry's independence, Seligman states: "The period of life when the American Jewish community lived under the shadow of the Old World culture is at an end. The umbilical cords with the past have been severed." (110–11)

[25] The first issue of *Judaism* featured a piece by Heschel, whose thought dominated its third issue and was discussed over time in a number of texts in the journal. Cf. Abraham Joshua Heschel, "Architecture of Time," *Judaism* 1 (1952): 44–51; Heschel, "Space, Time, and Reality," *Judaism* 1 (1952): 262–69; Trude Weiss-Rosmarin, "[Review of *The Sabbath*, by Abraham Joshua Heschel]," *Judaism* 1 (1952): 277–78; Nachum Glatzer, "[Review of *The Sabbath*, by Abraham Joshua Heschel]," *Judaism* 1 (1952): 283–86; Joseph H. Lookstein, "The Neo-Hasidism of Abraham J. Heschel," *Judaism* 5 (1956): 248–55; Maurice Friedman, "Hasidism and the Contemporary Jew," *Judaism* 9 (1960): 197–206; Norman E. Frimer, "The A-Theological Judaism of the American Community," *Judaism* 11 (1962): 144–54.

reflected on itself.[26] Born in Warsaw in 1907 and groomed as the scion of a Hasidic dynasty, Heschel was raised in a traditional, yet modernizing Jewish environment. His foray into Yiddish poetry in Vilna and later his training in philosophy at Berlin University and the *Hochschule für die Wissenschaft des Judentums* exposed him to vastly different cultures of Judaism. More than was immediately visible from his English-language publications, he grappled with the Holocaust, during which many of his family were killed and the world that had shaped him was destroyed.[27] Heschel himself barely escaped the murderous Nazi troops when he came to America in 1940. There, he served as a living bridge to the various European Jewish heritages he had encountered and even embodied at different times in his life.

Figure 12: Abraham Joshua Heschel, with students, 1972. (The Library of The Jewish Theological Seminary)

---

[26] In this arena, he was rivaled in stature by Martin Buber, whose influence was greater among non-religious and non-Jewish readers. Buber's role will be analyzed in the sections on Hasidism. Information on Heschel's life is drawn from the two-volume biography: Edward K. Kaplan and Samuel Dresner, *Abraham Joshua Heschel: Prophetic Witness* (New Haven: Yale University Press, 1998); Kaplan, *Spiritual Radical*.

[27] On the Holocaust in Heschel's English and Yiddish texts, see Morris M. Faierstein, Abraham Joshua Heschel, and Gershon Jacobson, "Abraham Joshua Heschel and the Holocaust," *Modern Judaism* 19 (1999): 255–75.

Most of all, Heschel resurrected the world of traditional Ashkenazic Jewry in his work to make it usable for American Jewry. He put forth his understanding of the East European Jewish experience in a series of publications. The most comprehensive and sustained images came in a Yiddish address that he delivered on January 7, 1945, "The East European Era in Jewish History," at the annual YIVO conference and for a broader audience in the bestselling 1949 book *The Earth Is the Lord's*.[28] He presented East European Jewry as a moral community, living a holistically Jewish life based in a profound spirituality that pervaded the lives of the folk and set them apart from the surrounding people. It sublimated poverty, persecution, and other hardships that were inflicted on them from the outside. For Heschel, this Ashkenazic Jewish life represented the essence of Jewishness in its highest concentration and at its purest. "In eastern Europe, the Jewish people has come into its own," he wrote. "Spiritually above the neighbors, the Jews developed a unique Jewish collective life, based upon their own traditions [. . .] to the utter disregard of the outside world." This made the East European era "the golden period in Jewish history, in the history of the Jewish soul," which was realized in a spiritual culture.[29] The YIVO speech, by its tone and timing, came across as a eulogy for this very culture. Accordingly, it is reported that as Heschel concluded, many in the audience were moved to tears, spontaneously rose, and recited the Kaddish.[30]

In the speech and in the book, Heschel not only praised and elevated Ashkenazic Jewry, but also aestheticized it. The text and illustrations made *The Earth Is the Lord's* an early example of how a distinct sensual image of the essentialized East European Jew was defined, or recast, in a positive way.[31] The many re-printings of

---

28 Abraham Joshua Heschel, "The Eastern European Era in Jewish History," *YIVO Annual of Jewish Social Science* 1 (1946): 86–105; reprinted in Deborah Dash Moore, ed. *East European Jews in Two Worlds: Studies from the YIVO Annual* (Evanston, IL: Northwestern University Press, 1990), 1–21. This is an English version of the Yiddish speech. The book is *The Earth is the Lord's: The Inner World of the Jew in Eastern Europe* (Woodstock, VT: Jewish Lights, 1995; orig. publ. 1949; republ. as paperback in 1963). Basic motifs and arguments of the original 1945 speech appeared in different forms and texts, among them "The Inner World of the Polish Jew," an essay introducing photographs by Roman Vishniac: *Polish Jews: A Pictorial Record* (New York: Schocken, 1947), 7–17. Jeffrey Shandler has examined the modifications among these texts, particularly between the Yiddish and English versions, in "Heschel and Yiddish: A Struggle with Signification," *Journal of Jewish Thought and Philosophy* 2 (1993): 245–99.
29 Heschel, "The Eastern European Era," 87–88.
30 Moore, "Preface," *East European Jews in Two Worlds*, viii.
31 The effect of the text was further strengthened by the woodcut illustrations by Ilya Schor, who shared Heschel's perspective on their common "old country" *shtetl* culture as grounded in "folk feeling" and the "traditional religious spirit;" cf. Ilya Schor, "A Working Definition of Jewish Art," *Conservative Judaism* 16 (1961): 29. This text was published on the occasion of Schor's death. Heschel gave the eulogy (Abraham Joshua Heschel, "Ilya Schor ז״ל," *Conservative Judaism* 16 (1961): 20–21).

the popular book perpetuated the highly spiritualized image of how East European Jews looked and sounded: "The vocabulary of their heart consisted of one sound: '*Oy!*'" he wrote in a chapter entitled "The Sigh." "Their authentic chants are consistently in the minor key. [...] But the Jews all sang: the student over the Talmud, the tailor while sewing a pair of trousers, the cobbler while mending tattered shoes, and the preacher while delivering a sermon."[32] The flip side of this all-out spiritualization was a disregard for the material, time- and space-bound dimensions of Jewish life in Eastern Europe. Heschel put in a nutshell a trope that runs through much of the imagery American Jews constructed of their past in the old country: the interrelated co-existence of spiritual wealth with material poverty: "The stomach is empty, the home overcrowded; but the heads are full of spiritual and cultural riches, and the Torah is free and ample," he wrote in the elevated prose that is characteristic of his work and which itself contributed to the spiritualization and aestheticizing of its subjects. Poverty, like physical persecution in pogroms, political inferiority in the Pale, and sometimes even cultural parochialism, seemed like the prerequisite conditions under which Jewish spirituality and distinctiveness flourished and which this spirituality transcended. Stripping the East European past of its concrete materiality, Heschel presented the essence of the Ashkenazic tradition as timeless. He obliquely referred to "the thousand years of tradition [preceding the] three generations of enlightenment," suggesting that the corrosive forces made themselves felt sometime in the nineteenth century or so.[33] Yet, he did not ground his account in material history, but rather let it hover above it, in *Heilsgeschichte,* the salvific history of East European Jews. "To them, history was only an intimation, things were like palimpsests, heaven the tangent at the circle of all experiences."[34] Heschel placed his own work within the same framework. Rather than rendering a disinterested, scholarly account of the past, he practiced religious memory, following a biblical imperative: "If I forget the Jews of Russia, may my right hand wither," he solemnly stated in an interview, substituting Ashkenazic Eastern Europe for the psalmist's Jerusalem as the vanishing point of Jewish spiritual longing.[35]

---

32 Heschel, *The Earth Is the Lord's*, 15–17, emphasis in the original. The details of the spelling in the book and the English version of the YIVO speech may not have been Heschel's decision; the shift from "eastern Europe" in the 1945 speech to "Eastern Europe" in the 1949 book indicates a move toward the reification of the image he constructed.
33 Abraham Joshua Heschel, "YIVO's Task Now," *News of the YIVO* 64 (March 1957): 2*. (The bilingual *News of the YIVO* uses an asterisk to distinguish English-language pages from the Yiddish section.)
34 Heschel, *The Earth Is the Lord's*, 88, 56.
35 Gershon Jacobson, "An Interview with Professor Heschel about Russian Jewry," *Der Tag – Morning Journal*, September 13, 1963 [Appendix to Faierstein et al. "Abraham Joshua Heschel and

For Heschel, this particular reconstruction of the East European past served several related objectives. The most obvious one, suggested by his biography and his life-long association with the scientifically-oriented YIVO, was to preserve the memory of one of the richest cultural traditions in Jewish history for its own sake.[36] However, he urged YIVO publicly not to place this past in a virtual museum, but to keep it alive, so that it would continue to give life and meaning to Judaism – the central objective of his work.[37] Heschel's main mission was to revitalize American Jewry by admonishing them to return to the sense of Jewishness that had inspired the lost Eden of Ashkenazic Jewry. The heritage of this era should become part and parcel of the lives of Jews born in America – of whom he was often harshly critical. To him, American Jews had been lured into a compartmentalized Jewishness expressed by a reductive, hence uninspiring Judaism, mostly severed from any meaningful continuity with the vital past. A 1948 article in *Commentary* was the first of many polemics by Heschel on the topic. He contrasted his idealized reconstruction of the dynamic culture of Ashkenazic Jewry with a pointedly negative depiction of the static Sephardic "cultural pattern" which echoed his perception of American Jewish spiritual culture. Brilliant it may be, he wrote, but shaped by external expectations and therefore more interested in Judaism's outward edifices, physical, intellectual, and institutional, and less in its living, spiritual depth. As a result, Jewish life was at risk of losing its vital core. "Magnificent synagogues are not enough if they mean a petrified Judaism," Heschel stated acerbically.[38] The allusions to a middle-class Jewish community attracted by what is external to its own tradition, and from which it selected only what fit into the reductive category of religion, are obvious. Driven by considerations of the present, the community willfully ignored its rich past. "With certain exceptions, American Jews have made great efforts to forget their roots," he lamented as late as 1963, and warned that "in forgetting Eastern Europe we dissipate our essence, our spirit and the sense of our existence."[39] For Heschel, the malaise of American Jewry typified the modern Jewish condition more generally. In his perception, the existential crises of modern individuals were connected to

---

the Holocaust," 274] The obvious reference is Psalm 137:5: "If I forget you, O Jerusalem, let my right hand wither." (NJPS translation)
36 According to Kaplan, Heschel was one of the few religiously committed members of YIVO's Board of Directors. (Kaplan, *Spiritual Radical*, 16)
37 Heschel, "YIVO's Task Now," 2*. Cf. also Daniel S. Breslauer, "Abraham J. Heschel's Politics of Nostalgia," *Journal of Church and State* 22 (1980): 307–13.
38 Abraham Joshua Heschel, "The Two Great Traditions: The Sephardim and the Ashkenazim," *Commentary* 5 (May 1948): 416–18, emphasis in the original.
39 Jacobson, "An Interview with Professor Heschel," 273; Heschel, "YIVO's Task Now," 2*.

the fact that Western modernity had led Jews into a spiritual dead end. In a 1948 interview he said (originally in Yiddish)

> Many of us began to think about a spiritual accounting, about revising assumptions and principles in which modern Jews believed with stubbornness and naiveté during the last three of four generations. Whoever has open eyes and examines the fruits that we have matured knows that we have set off in a direction which leads to spiritual death. [...] When we were blinded by the light of European civilization, many of us overlooked the incomparable beauty of our old, poor home. [...] Dazzled by the big city street lamps we lost our inner vision.[40]

Here, Heschel's critique of American Jewry and his apotheosis of the East European past fed into his larger intellectual-spiritual mission. Playing on the infatuation of many *maskilim* and thinkers in the paradigm of *Wissenschaft* with what they saw as the proto-modern, enlightened rationalism of the Sephardic tradition, he saw American Jewry as the child of an ill-fated liaison between liberalism and Judaism – and presented it as a spiritual cripple.[41]

To construct a positive vision for American Jewry, Heschel also drew heavily on his own East European past. The present generation was still in possession of the keys to the treasure, which could become an inspiration for all American Jewry, he urged his listeners.[42] Its spiritual *Yiddishkayt* should inspire them to embrace a broad and deep sense of Jewishness that would break the mold of "religion" and instead suffuse all of American Jewry with its vital spirit. Characteristically, and in line with the program of the journal *Judaism*, Heschel raised the question of a *cultural* pattern and gave distinctly *religious* answers. His use of "culture" for what Mordecai Kaplan had called "civilization" implied more than just the all-encompassing scope of what he was advocating. It also emphasized

---

40 Abraham Joshua Heschel, "After Majdanek: On Aaron Zeitlin's New Poems," *Yidisher Kemfer* 29, 1 October 1948 [Appendix to Faierstein et al., "Abraham Joshua Heschel and the Holocaust," 266, 268].
41 Ismar Schorsch, "The Myth of Sephardic Supremacy," in *From Text to Context: The Turn to History in Modern Judaism* (Waltham: Brandeis University Press/Hanover: University Press of New England, 1994), 71–92. In the larger perspective of Jewish intellectual history, Heschel's attack was a replay of the early-twentieth century rebellion of East European thinkers, like Simon Dubnow, against the German-Jewish tradition of scholarship focused on the liberal model of individual emancipation – another sign of the parallel between the intellectual constellation in 1920s' Europe and post-1945 America. In "The Two Great Traditions," Heschel criticized the *Wissenschaft* view and singled out Hermann Cohen for his disparaging view of East European Jews (420–21).
42 Heschel, "The Eastern European Era," 106.

that the ideas, rituals, and symbols making up a religious culture point to "meaning" beyond structures, that is beyond the community as a goal in itself to the transcendent, or in Heschel's term, the "ineffable."[43] This concept of a spiritual culture flowed from Heschel's philosophy of Judaism, which was informed by an idiosyncratic confluence of existentialism, phenomenology, prophetic elements, and his Hasidic heritage. Heschel's call to understand Judaism on its own terms, and for Jews to open themselves up to a sense of awe and wonder in encounters with the divine, represented a radical shift from the functionalist and liberal concepts of Judaism represented by Kaplan. Heschel offered American Jews a timeless, unchanging Jewish essence. If they recognized it for what it was, they would be able to renew their connection to the true understanding of Judaism. Grounding this perspective in an ahistorical past was a key move by which Heschel sought to legitimize this message and defend it against criticism.[44]

Given the diversity of the American Jewish intellectual landscape at midcentury, it is not surprising that Heschel came in for criticism from various quarters.[45] While only a small section of the critique was directed specifically at his image of the East European past, it is difficult to separate his religious thought from its grounding in this idealized past, his biography, and his political activism. After all, it was from the perception of an integrated persona in which these various strands were seen to coalesce and be held together that Heschel's image of the past derived much of its impact. Some critics engaged Heschel on his own terms when they questioned his depiction of the East European past as a foundation of his larger intellectual program.[46]

---

43 Abraham Joshua Heschel, *God in Search of Man: A Philosophy of Judaism* (New York: Farrar, Straus, and Giroux, 1976; orig. publ. 1955), 103–04.
44 On Heschel in the context of the New Jewish Theology, cf. Goldy, *Emergence of Jewish Theology*, chap. 7; Kaplan, *Spiritual Radical*, 117–25.
45 Irving Kristol in a *Commentary* review of *The Earth Is the Lord's* gave Heschel a pass for his sentimentalism, but found him guilty on various other charges: artificially eloquent language, "romantic simplification," unjustified disparagement of the Sephardim and, most germane to our topic, his removal of Ashkenazic Jewry from history, and omission of its problematic aspects. (Irving Kristol, "Elegy for a Lost World," review of *The Earth Is the Lord's*, by Abraham Joshua Heschel, *Commentary* 9 (May 1950): 491) According to Heschel's biographer, Kristol, on the grounds of the quality of Heschel's literary writing, fought against an appreciative review of *Man Is Not Alone* (Kaplan: *Spiritual Radical*, 121–22). Modern Orthodox rabbi Gersion Appel in *Jewish Life* applauded Heschel's sensitive depiction of the East European past, but found the critique of modernity excessive ("The Lost Sanctuary," review of *The Earth Is the Lord's*, by Abraham Joshua Heschel, *Jewish Life* 18 (1951): 68).
46 Cf. Reform theologian Jacob Petuchowski's previously mentioned critique of Heschel's depiction of Ashkenazic Jewry's beneficial inwardness, which aimed at the larger issue of

In the context of the post-1945 debate about liberal Judaism, Heschel has been recognized as a trail blazer for the religious subjectivity that made itself felt in American Jewry in the late 1960s as well as in the *havurah* movement, not to speak of neo-Hasidic thinkers, and movements like "Jewish Renewal." All these expressions of American Judaism found it meaningful to relate to a reconstructed East European Jewish past as they imagined a vital American Judaism that would draw on the religious tradition in new ways.[47]

Heschel inspired American Jews across denominational lines. Many of those committed to Orthodoxy, however, could look to one figure distinctly their own who served as a biographical and intellectual bridge to the East European past.

Soloveitchik: Bringing "Halakhic Man" from Lithuania to America

Joseph B. Soloveitchik (1903–1993) was less visible to the American Jewish (and non-Jewish) public than Heschel, the public intellectual. If he nevertheless shaped the perspective of important sectors of postwar American Jewry on the East European heritage, it was through his formative influence on generations of Orthodox rabbis and as the intellectual giant leading the movement. Moreover, Soloveitchik's thought was also disseminated within Conservative and Reform rabbinical elites, since in the postwar decades Orthodoxy's distancing from the other denominations was less rigid than today and was transcended by Soloveitchik's standing.[48] For his students and many admirers beyond, he was "the Rav," an ideal example of the traditional yet modern Judaism embodied through his ancestry, biography, and intellectual force — all of which pointed back to the world of the Lithuanian *yeshivah*.

Soloveitchik was born in Pruzhan (Poland), into an illustrious dynasty of Talmudic scholars. His *mitnagdic* family traced its roots back to the Vilna Gaon and Hayyim of Volozhin. He was raised in Khaslavichy (Belarus) where he encountered Hasidism, both in the Jewish community and in the person of a *melamed*. In

---

Judaism's engagement with modern culture; "Faith as the Leap of Action: The Theology of Abraham Joshua Heschel," *Commentary* 25 (May 1958): 395.

47 Cf. Susannah Heschel, "Imagining Judaism in America," in *The Cambridge Companion to Jewish American Literature*, eds. Hana Wirth-Nesher and Michael P. Kramer (Cambridge: Cambridge University Press, 2003), 31–49; Zalman Schachter, "Hasidism and Neo-Hasidism," *Judaism* 9 (1960; special issue on Hasidism): 216–21.

48 Goldy, *Emergence of Jewish Theology*, 27.

1920, his family moved to Warsaw. In his traditional education, Soloveitchik was schooled in the intellectually rigorous "Brisker" method of conceptual-abstract Talmud study. It had been developed by his grandfather Hayyim Soloveitchik, himself a student and teacher at the Volozhin Yeshivah, before moving to Brisk (Brest-Litowsk). The *Brisker Derekh* came to dominate the way Talmud was studied in Lithuanian *yeshivot*. Soloveitchik also received a secular education, first through a private tutor, later studying political science and philosophy in Warsaw and Berlin. He wrote his dissertation at Berlin University on Hermann Cohen, which placed him philosophically in the neo-Kantian school.[49] (Menahem Mendel Schneerson was a contemporary at Berlin University, and so was Heschel.[50]) In 1932, Soloveitchik moved to the US. After serving as the rabbi for an Orthodox community in Boston, he was appointed in 1941 professor of Talmud at the Rabbi Isaac Elchanan Theological Seminary (RIETS) in New York,

Figure 13: Joseph B. Soloveitchik, not dated. (American Jewish Archives)

---

49 Aaron Rakeffet-Rothkoff, "Rabbi Joseph B. Soloveitchik: The Early Years," *Tradition* 30 (1996): 193–94; Chimen Abramsky, "Soloveitchik Family," in *YIVO Encyclopedia of Jews in Eastern Europe*, ed. Gershon D. Hundert (New Haven: Yale University Press, 2008), 1782–83; Samuel C. Heilman, *Sliding to the Right: The Contest for the Future of American Jewish Orthodoxy* (Berkeley: University of California Press, 2006), 34. For "inside" descriptions of the "Brisker" method, cf. several essays in Menachem D. Genack, ed. *Rabbi Joseph B. Soloveitchik: Man of Halacha, Man of Faith* (Hoboken: Ktav, 1998).
50 According to Heschel's biographer, Heschel and Soloveitchik probably did not meet in Berlin (Kaplan, *Prophetic Witness*, 119).

a constituent part of what became Yeshiva University, the pre-eminent institution to train Orthodox rabbis. He also taught philosophy at the University's graduate school. Until his retirement in 1985, Soloveitchik as *rosh yeshivah* in the East European tradition influenced and ordained hundreds of rabbis over the course of more than 40 years.[51]

Soloveitchik's influence on how Orthodoxy related to the East European past must be placed in the shifting context of how the movement understood itself in the modern American environment of the postwar years, particularly in the changing fate of "modern Orthodoxy" within the larger movement. By his personal engagement with broader culture, modern philosophy, and issues of interfaith dialogue, Soloveitchik embodied the core perspective of modern Orthodoxy, enshrined in Yeshiva University's motto "Torah u-maddah" (Torah and secular knowledge). Yet, over the middle decades of the twentieth century, this segment's constitutive engagement with modern culture and the more universalistic openness behind this approach were questioned and delegitimized as forces grew in influence which placed ever greater emphasis on Torah and an inward-looking particularism.[52] This development included an increasingly hagiographic perspective on traditionalist East European Jewish life. The apotheosis of this often ahistorical past served to legitimize an agenda of tightening religious and social norms designed to insulate the Orthodox community from the corrosive forces of American modernity, particularly its secular and non-Jewish aspects.[53] Against this larger development, the depiction of Soloveitchik and the interpretation of his thought are highly contested to this day. The East European heritage has played a crucial role in this contest, via divergent interpretations of a key question for Orthodoxy in the modern world. Did Soloveitchik *integrate* traditional Jewish commitments with those to modern culture and thought into an organic whole? Or, did he rather envision their mere *co-existence* without a

---

[51] Jeffrey S. Gurock, *Orthodox Jews in America* (Bloomington: Indiana University Press, 2009), 207–08. Beyond his role in the training of rabbis, Soloveitchik influenced Orthodoxy at large through his leadership of its commission on Halakhah.

[52] The back story behind Soloveitchik's appointment in 1941 already reflects the university's search for a role vis-à-vis East European Judaism and America, and within the then wider tent of Orthodoxy; cf. Jeffrey S. Gurock, *The Men and Women of Yeshiva: Higher Education, Orthodoxy, and American Judaism* (New York: Columbia University Press, 1988), 130–31; cf. also Heilman, *Sliding to the Right*, 31–61.

[53] This hagiographic approach also colors a number of outwardly scholarly texts on Soloveitchik, among them Rakeffet-Rothkoff's essay in *Tradition* ("Soloveitchik: Early Years"), in which the author draws on plainly admiring sources about "the Rav" and juxtaposes his learnedness with the "ignorance of the American Jewish community." (201) See also the essays in Genack, *Rabbi Joseph B. Soloveitchik*.

synthesis? The latter compartmentalized model would be better suited to regard the modern commitments as inferior and subordinate to separatist Jewish values, or dismiss modernity as dangerously un-Jewish.[54] Recently, revisionist interpreters have looked for, and found, more evidence for such a separatist approach than for earlier ones. Some elements of *haredi* Orthodoxy, from within the Soloveitchik dynasty, no less, which aimed to protect the "true" Brisker legacy, forcefully rejected the openness to non-Jewish modernity, which "the tyrant from Boston, product of the cursed Berlin Haskalah, and poisoner of the hearts of the Children of Israel" embodied in their view.[55]

The tension that gives rise to such controversies, particularly to the fundamental issue of balancing particularism and universalism in the modern world, runs through several of Soloveitchik's works, among them his seminal essay "Confrontation" on interreligious relations. In this 1964 article, Soloveitchik argued that despite their integration into American society and culture at large, (Orthodox) Jews would have to retain some consciousness of being "strangers and outsiders" and of constitutive "homelessness and loneliness."[56] This paradox has been the defining challenge of Orthodoxy in modern social, intellectual, and political environments. Negotiating the seemingly contradictory impulses in order to balance or integrate them requires complex intellectual skills that employ the respective values of "tradition" and "newness" to legitimize the desired outcome. Sociologist Samuel Heilman called these construction processes "contemporization and traditioning."[57] Their interplay forms the backdrop of the reception and influence of Soloveitchik's book-length essay *Halakhic Man*, one of the relatively few works by Soloveitchik published under his control and during his lifetime.[58]

---

[54] Walter Wurzburger, "Rav Joseph B. Soloveitchik as Posek of Post-Modern Orthodoxy," *Tradition* 29 (1994): 5–20; Gurock, *Orthodox Jews*, 207.
[55] Lawrence Kaplan, "Revisionism and the Rav: The Struggle for the Soul of Modern Orthodoxy," *Judaism* 48 (1999): 290–311; Norman Lamm, warning against revisionism: "The Rav: Stranger in a Foreign Land," in: *Rabbi Joseph B. Soloveitchik*, ed. Genack, 234; Moshe Sokol, "'Ger ve-Toshav Anokhi': Modernity and Traditionalism in the Life and Thought of Rabbi Joseph B. Soloveitchik," *Tradition* 29 (1994): 32–47; Wurzburger, "Rav Joseph B. Soloveitchik as Posek." The *haredi* attack on Soloveitchik is documented in Pini Dunner and David N. Myers, "A Haredi Attack on Rabbi Joseph Ber Soloveitchik: A Battle Over the Brisker Legacy from 1984," *Jewish Quarterly Review* 105 (2015): 131–38.
[56] Joseph B. Soloveitchik, "Confrontation," *Tradition* 6 (1964): 5–29.
[57] Heilman, *Sliding to the Right*, 36.
[58] Since his death, disciples have edited and published numerous lectures and sermons Soloveitchik delivered over the years at Yeshiva University. These posthumous publications are part of the ongoing contest of his position and legacy. Cf., for example, *Rabbi Joseph B. Soloveitchik*, ed. Genack.

This condensed religious treatise articulated a perspective on the East European heritage that radiated, via the author's students and disciples, into postwar traditional American Judaism. The text is an elegy and a memorial to the intellectual culture of the East European *yeshivah* and a call to reconstruct this ideal of scholarship under new conditions in America. Published in Hebrew in 1944 and translated into English only in 1983, the essay stands as a classic text of modern Jewish religious thought, as it combines traditional Jewish ideas and epistemology with modern existentialist and phenomenological approaches to questions of religious experience.[59] Soloveitchik portrayed the eponymous "halakhic man" as the exemplar of Lithuanian *yeshivah* scholarship, but did so by using modern, specifically neo-Kantian, categories.[60] He employed the breadth of his philosophical and religious learnedness by inserting his hero into the matrix of modern Western philosophy, invoking Immanuel Kant, Soeren Kierkegaard, Karl Barth, and Martin Heidegger, but also placed him alongside Talmudic sages, Maimonides, Hasidic leaders, and the *gedolim* of East European Judaism. As a result, his depiction of "halakhic man" in relation to "cognitive man" and *homo religiosus* transcended extant philosophical categories and laid claim to an ideal type that was comprehensively Jewish yet modern, as Soloveitchik stated: "All of the frames of reference constructed by the philosophers and psychologists of religion for explaining the varieties of religious experience cannot accommodate halakhic man as far as his reaction to empirical reality is concerned."[61]

By placing this ideal type in the environment of the Lithuanian *yeshivah*, Soloveitchik had "halakhic man" and the authentic intellectual and spiritual culture of East European Judaism legitimize each other. Soloveitchik made numerous references to East European Jewish scholarship and spiritual culture, often by relating the experiences of his father and earlier ancestors, through anecdotes and vignettes. He presented the Volozhin Yeshivah and the Vilna Gaon as examples of the ideal he advocated: the intellectual value of rigorous scholarship and

---

[59] Joseph B. Soloveitchik, *Halakhic Man* (Philadelphia: Jewish Publication Society, 1983); orig. published as "Ish ha-Halakhah," *Talpiot* 1 (1944): 651–735. Cf. Oliver Leaman, "Jewish Existentialism: Rosenzweig, Buber, and Soloveitchik," in *History of Jewish Philosophy [Routledge History of World Philosophies, vol. 2]*, eds. Daniel H. Frank and Oliver Leaman (London/New York: Routledge, 1997), 799–819.
[60] For a thorough philosophical analysis of *Halakhic Man*, cf. Reinier Munk, *The Rationale of Halakhic Man: Joseph B. Soloveitchik's Conception of Jewish Thought* (Amsterdam: Gieben, 1996).
[61] Soloveitchik, *Halakhic Man*, 17. Soloveitchik makes reference to William James, whose work *The Varieties of Religious Experience* (1902) the English translation of this passage echoes. Cf. Jeffrey Saks, "An Index to Rabbi Joseph B. Soloveitchik's 'Halakhic Man,'" *Torah U-Madda Journal* 11 (2002–2003): 107–22.

its spiritual effect in shaping a person's character and behavior. The invocations of dynastic ancestors and spiritual leaders were often tinged with a hagiographic undertone. The brief stories echoed the genre of orally transmitted tales best known from the Hasidic tradition, beginning with the *Praises of the Ba'al Shem Tov*, the movement's founder. Similarly, in *Halakhic Man* the anecdotes postulated the authenticity of the theological positions that were attributed to them. In a passage on death as the arch-opposite of the holiness associated with a life pursuing a halakhic ideal, Soloveitchik called on the pantheon of Lithuanian scholarship for proof: "The Gaon of Vilna, R. Joseph Dov Soloveitchik, his son, R. Hayyim, his grandson, R. Moses, R. Elijah Pruzna [Feinstein] never visited cemeteries [...] The memory of death would have distracted them from the intensive efforts to study the Torah."[62]

Soloveitchik employed such anecdotes to illustrate and fortify his ideal of a life infused by Halakhah, which is understood as a scholarship-based religious philosophy and perspective on God, man, and the world, rather than as a code of laws governing ritual behavior.[63] Halakhah inspires a comprehensive Jewish way of life in Soloveitchik's presentation, by which he articulates from a distinctly Orthodox perspective an ideal pervading much of postwar American Jewish religious thought. Soloveitchik contrasted this ideal forcefully with alternative religious philosophies, notably Christianity as the most influential expression of an unhealthy mind-body dualism and an escapist orientation toward the transcendent rather than this world. "We have here a manifestation of a deep fissure in one's psychic identity," he wrote of Christians; in the same breath, he set up a contrast with the ideal he was promoting: "The Halakhah, however, rejects such a personality split, such a spiritual schizophrenia."[64] The authentic Jewish philosophy of religion and spiritual culture is comprehensive, the opposite of fragmented identities and world views. "Halakhic man does not compartmentalize reality," he stressed, nor does he escape to a transcendent world in order to commune with God. "Even when halakhic man enters the synagogue or study house, he does not leave his this-worldly life behind." He is concerned with this world in an all-encompassing way, since Halakhah "penetrates into every nook and cranny of life. The marketplace, the street, the factory, the house, the meeting place, the banquet hall, all constitute the backdrop for the religious life."

---

62 Soloveitchik, *Halakhic Man*, 36. The reference "[Feinstein]," to Soloveitchik's maternal grandfather, is by translator Lawrence Kaplan. For other passages related in anecdotal tone, cf. *Halakhic Man*, 30, 52, 60, 77, 87, 90.
63 On Soloveitchik's concept of Halakhah, cf. Goldy, *Emergence of Jewish Theology*, 82–83.
64 Soloveitchik, *Halakhic Man*, 93.

By relating this ideal to the East European heritage, Soloveitchik claimed an authentic understanding of religion for Judaism grounded in a past that he retold in the service of this objective. In this basic sense, his message was similar to Heschel's, who also claimed authenticity for his vision based on his ancestry and biography. Both thinkers called for a return to a spiritual culture that would heal modern Jews' unease at the alienation stemming from the non-identity they experienced in their divergent roles and from the absence of meaning-making holiness in their lives. Still, the images that Soloveitchik and Heschel presented of East European Jewishness differ in style and in substance, due to the deep differences in their respective ideals representing authentic Jewish life. Not only was Heschel a romantic in style, he also hoped for the spiritual elevation of humanity to the ineffable divine – the opposite perspective from Soloveitchik's call to bring the divine into this world. Moreover, the existentialist strand in Heschel's thought allowed more room for religious subjectivity, a characteristically modern aspect of religion that many Orthodox thinkers dismissed. Soloveitchik defended Halakhah as objective, even though he recognized that religious experience was a matter of subjective inwardness for "halakhic man," too. His insistence on the objective nature of Halakhah and his emphasis on its this-worldly focus and comprehensive nature let Soloveitchik claim authenticity for a specific strand within Judaism, making him less universal in substance and orientation than Heschel and other modern American Jewish thinkers. In all these efforts, the East European heritage remained the backdrop and source of the ideals he presented.

The exact relationship between Soloveitchik's thought in *Halakhic Man* and other works with the East European world of Jewish life and ideas has been fiercely debated. His rivaling interpreters have addressed not only Soloveitchik's thought, but also the way in which the East European world conditioned him biographically and intellectually. At least one scholar has argued that the religious anthropology of *Halakhic Man* fundamentally differs from the early *mitnagdic* perspective to which Soloveitchik tied it by way of his spiritual and familial ancestors.[65] Another, very critical, assessment of the essay emphasizes the immediate personal and historical context of the time in which Soloveitchik reconstructed the ideal Lithuanian, specifically Brisker, *yeshivah* past in the essay. "'Halakhic Man' [...] was written in the early 1940s, at a time when Lithuanian Jewry was being destroyed by the Nazis, and when Soloveitchik was still mourning the death of his father," scholars David Singer and Moshe Sokol

---

[65] Allan Nadler, "Soloveitchik's Halakhic Man: Not a 'Mithnagged,'" *Modern Judaism* 19 (1993): 119–47.

argued.⁶⁶ They claimed that the personal pain Soloveitchik experienced not just in this particular situation, but as a modern religious intellectual more generally, showed through in the book. Even though halakhic man's Litvak intellectualism was supposedly unshakeable, his pent-up emotional side broke through its seams. So invested was Soloveitchik in preserving the Brisker heritage of rationality that the anecdotes he related about his ancestors "seem like nothing so much as Hasidic parodies of the brainy but soulless Litvak." In this sense, Singer and Sokol argued, Soloveitchik "recapitulates the religious debate between the Hasidim and the *Mitnaggdim*."⁶⁷

Hasidism did indeed appear as a highly ambivalent expression of Judaism in *Halakhic Man*, as Soloveitchik veered between recognition of its spiritual potency and criticism of key elements of its theology. He clad a basic theological disagreement in an anecdote about R. Hayyim and a friend discovering Habad Hasidic works in the Vilna house of an acquaintance. R. Hayyim categorically rejected the ideas presented therein about God's motivations for creating the world. Soloveitchik marshaled the writings of Maimonides, Solomon Ibn Gabirol and Duns Scotus to support the stance that, in contrast to Hasidic thought, the world was created solely for the sake of God's will. In the framework of his ideal types, Soloveitchik portrayed Hasidism as the search for transcendence characteristic of *homo religiosus*, a negative foil for "halakhic man." Hasidism's potential for ecstatic spirituality runs against the moderation that Soloveitchik espoused in expressing one's religious experience. On the one hand, Habad's founder, R. Shneur Zalman of Lyady, was hailed as a "great luminary of Halakhah and mysticism," but the latter went against the religious rationalism of the Litvak tradition that Soloveitchik extolled. Rationality and moderation were hallmarks of the religious life that Soloveitchik advocated and by which he measured competing strands within East European Judaism. He pointed out, for example, that the Volozhin Yeshivah rejected the early *musar* movement because the latter was driven by an irrational fear of death.⁶⁸

Regardless of whether or not Soloveitchik's depictions of early *mitnagdism* and the *musar* movement were historically sound, and whether his ideal type of "halakhic man" contained larger elements of (Hasidic) spiritual emotionality than he might have acknowledged, an idealized memory of the spiritual world of East European Jewry remained the reference point for his theological stance. It was

---

66 David Singer and Moshe Sokol, "Joseph Soloveitchik: Lonely Man of Faith," *Modern Judaism* 2 (1982): 257.
67 Singer and Sokol, "Joseph Soloveitchik," 259–60.
68 Soloveitchik, *Halakhic Man*, 52–53, 56–57, 60–61.

a stance which – on the opposite end of the spectrum from Hasidic mysticism – also rejected liberal religion as an equally problematic attempt to cope with the dialectic of man's need for wholeness.[69] In Soloveitchik's assessment, written in the context of modern American society, liberal Judaism erred too far on the side of disenchanting the world by separating its divine core and confining it to a circumscribed sphere of life: "liberal Judaism expelled the *Shekhinah*, the Divine Presence, from the broad area of Jewish life," Soloveitchik charged. By setting the divine aside from the reality and breadth of life as a whole, liberal Judaism deprived the world of the holiness that can come only from the never-ending human effort to bring the divine into the mundane, in order to bring it closer to the halakhic ideal. The true sanctuary, Soloveitchik wrote, is not the synagogue, but "the sphere of our daily mundane activities, for it is there that the realization of the Halakhah takes place." For human beings in their daily lives, this realization of the scholarly ideal is ultimately a matter of spiritual-ethical behavior. "The great Torah giants, the halakhic men, par excellence, were indeed champions of truth and justice."[70] Soloveitchik, again, pointed to East European role models: his grandfather R. Hayyim of Brisk, his father R. Moses Soloveitchik, whom he calls "a halakhic man par excellence," and other spiritual ancestors.[71] They represented a spiritual culture: broader than the modern sphere of "religion," and determined by Halakhah as understood by Soloveitchik: objective, comprehensive, rational, and infused by a divine presence.

This spiritual culture bears resemblance to the ideals presented by Heschel and other religious thinkers in *Judaism*, yet Soloveitchik's is distinct in the emphatically rational character of the spiritual culture he advocated. By this vision of authentic Judaism, Soloveitchik influenced the way postwar American Orthodoxy related to the East European heritage as a crucial factor in its shifting role. Along with Heschel and the writers of *Judaism*, he provided theological resources for the transformation of the American Jewish denominational landscape in the middle of the twentieth century.

---

69 For a balanced discussion of *Halakhic Man* in light of the criticism by Singer/Sokol and others, cf. David Hartman, "The Halakhic Hero: Rabbi Joseph B. Soloveitchik, Halakhic Man," *Modern Judaism* 9 (1989): 249–73.
70 Soloveitchik, *Halakhic Man*, 94–95.
71 Soloveitchik, *Halakhic Man*, 38, 95.

5 Spiritual Needs, the Past, and the Denominational Landscape

The ferment that moved religious thinkers to explore new perspectives on Judaism and theology also affected rank-and-file religious Jews. Not only may their rabbis have read *Judaism* or studied with Heschel or Soloveitchik; in the early 1940s and into the 1950s, the same sense of fluidity and openness that characterized American Jewry as a whole also affected organized religious life.[1] Different ideas about ways to revitalize Judaism shaped the contours of a new denominational constellation, as Reform, Conservative, and Orthodox Judaism responded in different ways to the challenges and opportunities of the moment. The emergence of a broad Jewish middle class of native-born, suburbanized descendants of East European immigrants raised new questions for religious thought and practice. They ranged from halakhic issues like the use of automobiles on the Sabbath to the role of women in synagogue life, the reading lists of congregational book clubs, and the pronunciation of liturgical Hebrew. The renewed public interest in religious topics, growing financial and intellectual resources invested into organized Jewish religious life, and the interests of an increasingly distinct cadre of professionals in religious institutions added to the crystallization of denominational profiles, as they made for a lively religious sub-discourse that included questions of Jewish history and memory.

Important differences that drove the differentiation of the Jewish religious scene had intellectual underpinnings that were articulated in denominational journals. A number of the competing answers engaged the East European past in the face of an uncertain present and future. Even the intellectual and spiritual leaders of Reform Judaism, the segment of American Jewry demographically and ideologically most removed from East European *Yiddishkayt*, drew on this past in an effort to situate their denomination in a profoundly changed context.

Reform: Taking a New Look at a Distant Past

The relationship of Reform Judaism to the East European past has been a study in contrasts and conflicts since the encounter of Classical Reform with the first generation

---

1 Cf. Jeffrey S. Gurock, "American Judaism Between the Two World Wars," in *The Columbia History of Jews and Judaism in America,* ed. Marc Lee Raphael (New York: Columbia University Press, 2008), 93–113; Arnold M. Eisen, "Theology, Sociology, Ideology: Jewish Thought in America, 1925–1955," *Modern Judaism* 2 (1982): 91–103.

DOI 10.1515/9783110499438-006

of East European immigrants in the 1880s.[2] The 1885 Pittsburgh Platform defined Reform Judaism as a consciously modern, liberal religion, subordinating key components like Halakhah and Jewish peoplehood as well as concrete markers of ethno-religious distinctiveness to the criteria of rationalism, universalism, and progressivism, which characterized the American intellectual *zeitgeist* at the time. The immigrants, in contrast, came from an environment that was slowly modernizing in fits and starts and with many setbacks. For most of them, Judaism was not a liberal religion, but a comprehensive way of life, supported by a sense of proudly particularistic Jewishness, rooted in Halakhah, and expressed by the very markers of distinctiveness that Reform Judaism played down, such as dress and language. The modernization of East European Jewry was playing out less in the form of liberalizing changes to the religion, and more in other spheres instead.[3] These processes had been shaped by political and economic conditions that often gave rise not to optimism, but to a sense of despair, one which also fueled mass immigration to America from the 1880s to the 1920s.

American conditions transformed this original constellation of starkest contrasts in processes that were still going on by the mid-twentieth century. By 1940, American Reform Judaism was still defined by the German origins of much of its religious ideology and rabbinate, but was already on its way to a major demographic and ideological transformation resulting from the influx from Eastern Europe. The Columbus Platform of 1937 had revised key tenets of the Pittsburgh Platform. Reform Judaism was moving closer to the center of the religious landscape, as the children and grandchildren of immigrants came to dominate the community numerically and began to shape the future of American Judaism. At stake in this ongoing transformation were crucial elements of original Reform: the scope of Judaism as a pure "religion" as opposed to broader ethnic and national concepts, the style and atmosphere of its liturgical practices, and the defining focus on ethics and social action. The journal of the Reform Central Conference

---

2 For the historical background, cf. Michael A. Meyer, *Response to Modernity: A History of the Reform Movement in Judaism* (Detroit: Wayne State University Press, 1995; orig. publ. 1988), esp. chaps. 7 and 8.

3 For accounts of Jewish modernization that point to the East European Jewish experience in order to revise previous paradigms (which used the transformation of numerically smaller, hence arguably less influential Central and West European Jewry), cf. Eli Lederhendler, "Modernity Without Emancipation or Assimilation? The Case of Russian Jewry," *Assimilation and Community: The Jews in Nineteenth-Century Europe,* ed. Jonathan Frankel and Steven J. Zipperstein (Cambridge: Cambridge University Press, 1992), 324–33; Gershon D. Hundert, *Jews in Poland-Lithuania in the Eighteenth Century: A Genealogy of Modernity* (Berkeley: University of California Press, 2004).

of American Rabbis (CCAR) was a major forum to discuss how these ideas made Reform stable or static in the face of new realities.[4] Reform intellectuals, many of whom were rabbis, recognized the importance of accommodating the needs of a different constituent base and the potential their heritage represented for renewing Judaism. Addressing these questions from the pulpit and through their writings, they turned to the East European past and created a complex mixture of narratives of discontinuity and continuity that selectively engaged this past.

Since only a few of these rabbis could draw on a biographical background in Eastern Europe, the starting point for much of Reform thinking on this heritage was a sense of distance. After all, American Reform Judaism considered itself the expression of progress away from the very East European heritage that now caught up with them – in light of its destruction and of the needs and memories which the children and grandchildren of the immigrants now brought to the synagogues and community centers. Some thinkers responded by emphasizing the contrasts between East European darkness and American light, even placing traditional East European Jewry on the wrong side of history.[5] Eastern Europe seemed forever trapped in darkness, as Reform publications saw continuities between the Czarist regime and Communism, the contemporaneous state of Soviet Jewry, and the Holocaust. These texts depicted East European Jewish life as dead or dying, and alien to the experience of contemporary American Jews. A report in the *CCAR Journal* on a visit to an Orthodox service in Leningrad spiced up the image of Eastern Europe as the deathbed of Jewish life by means of vivid, or rather morbid, sensual details: "The overriding impression was one of senility, ill health and poverty. [...] The cacophony of prayer and the bits of whispered private conversation [...], coughing and spitting, filled the stifling room with an atmosphere reminiscent of a poorly managed aged men's rest home." The author contrasted the East European dead end with the vitality of Jewish life in the US, letting his interlocutors make the point: "Judaism, they said, was already dead in Russia. They were the last remnants, and with their death nothing would be left. One man added hopefully, 'But Judaism will still live on in America, won't it?'"[6]

---

4 The *CCAR Journal* was founded in 1953 and published quarterly.
5 Prominent Chicago-based Rabbi Jacob J. Weinstein wrote, "The keepers of the tradition preferred to bear the curse of Rome and Moscow and the ills of segregation and persecution than venture into the dangers of submitting religious verities to scientific review and evaluation." ("Trends in Reform Judaism," *CCAR Journal*, October 1957: 2.)
6 Cf., for example, ["An Expert on Soviet Affairs"], "Anti-Semitism in the Soviet Union," *CCAR Journal*, October 1956: 30, 32. The author was kept anonymous to protect him after his candid account of a trip that had to be authorized by Soviet authorities; cf. also S. Andhil Fineberg,

Writing East European Judaism off, with sadness or with glee, in order to shore up America as the new home of (modern) Judaism, was not the only approach, however. For other authors, the need to find or construct some meaningful continuity between the East European past and the American present mitigated the stark contrast. Rabbi Jacob Shankman, the US-born leader of Temple Israel in New Rochelle, reflected on his father's life. "His was the world of Eastern Europe – with its *schul*, now deserted and locked, its *cheder* become a nostalgic etching, its *yeshivah* ground into the dust and forgotten. It is a world now gone. It was a different world into which I was catapulted." In a dialectical turn, Shankman then found this very distance transcended by the American promise of Jewish continuity across such ruptures: "My father's world will never be known to my daughter, but isn't she part of the history which he lived? And isn't this the promise of the new century? And isn't this why we are celebrating the Tercentenary?"[7] The strong sense of difference between East European and American Jews, which stood in for the differentness between backward, authoritarian Russia, Communist USSR, and the liberal, progressive US often served to affirm America and American Jewry, particularly in Tercentenary-themed texts, like Shankman's.

At other times, particularly later into the 1950s and 1960s, this same sense of difference could also work the other way, when these thinkers described East European Jewishness as vital and authentic in contrast to bland, bloodless American Jewishness. In a sermon, Ukrainian-born rabbi Charles E. Shulman turned the table on American Jewry, whose inner distance from their East European ancestors to him represented a deficiency: "Because the Jews of the Russian ghettos of yesterday will probably always remain a mystery to those who live in the western world, it is difficult to measure the amazing spiritual depths of their commitment. Poor for the most part in the world's goods, they were rich beyond measure in imagination, in saintliness and in piety."[8] While Shulman made the common move of juxtaposing material poverty with spiritual wealth, he used it for an image of East European Jewry that was less romanticized and more nuanced than Heschel's depiction. Acknowledging the distance from this past, like Shulman did, some Reform thinkers looked to it as a positive model for the changes they wanted to work in American Judaism and Jewry in order

---

"Religion Behind the Iron Curtain," *CCAR Journal*, June 1962: 12–16, 37. This attitude may also have reflected contempt for Orthodox Judaism, which Reform thinkers conflated with East European Jewry.

7 Jacob K. Shankman, "My Father and I: Thoughts on Approaching the Tercentenary," *CCAR Journal*, October 1954: 6–8, 9.

8 Charles E. Shulman, "Three Came to Israel," in *Best Jewish Sermons of 5715–5716*, ed. Saul I. Teplitz (New York: Jonathan David, 1956), 189.

to revitalize both. Quite a number of Reform leaders were concerned about the moral-spiritual state of their constituents, who rapidly integrated economically and socially into the American mainstream. They sensed an insalubrious identification with materialistic middle-class norms that undermined Reform's constitutive understanding of a "prophetic" Judaism concerned with ethics and social justice. Romanticizing poverty may not have seemed the most effective strategy. Rather than focusing on material status, Reform rabbis shifted to the moral stature and behavior that made East European Jews models for a spiritual life. Reviewing a biography of Israel Salanter, *CCAR*'s Ely Pilchik depicted the spirit of East European *musar* as a sorely needed corrective to self-satisfied, complacent American Jewry. "Would that an Israel Salanter rise again and stride up and down the land pointing his accusing finger at our country-club devotees with: 'Truly, the wickedness of man is great upon the earth; no one seeks after righteousness, nor is there anyone who has understanding of the Fear of God.'" Elsewhere, he juxtaposed the profound values Sholem Aleichem conveyed in his stories with American materialism, when he suggested that teenage children may learn from *Mottel the Cantor's Son* "that men have lived by something other than station wagons, television and comic books. And who knows: perhaps something better."[9] Comparisons such as these illustrate what historian Lila Corwin Berman has described as the American Jewish "ambivalence of middle-classness;" in this instance, the concern was particularly about the effects of socioeconomic comfort on moral and spiritual life.[10]

The texts by Pilchik and others represented a trajectory from a broad integration-minded affirmation of America as congenial with Jewish values to a more critical stance that placed greater emphasis on the need for Jews to retain some critical distance from America – for the sake of Jewish distinctiveness and the existential meaning Judaism could offer. Religious philosopher Emil Fackenheim

---

9 Ely E. Pilchik, "Of Books and Papers," *CCAR Journal*, June 1954: 32; Pilchik, "Of Books and Papers," *CCAR Journal*, June 1953: 49. Similarly, Connecticut-based rabbi Jerome A. Molino presented an archetypal Hasidic *zaddik* as a moral guide for a perplexed American Jewry ("[Review of *The Zaddik*, by Samuel Dresner]," *CCAR Journal*, January 1962: 69–70.

10 Lila Corwin Berman, "American Jews and the Ambivalence of Middle-Classness," *American Jewish History* 93 (2007): 409–44. Not all thinkers, however, were critical or apologetic of the new status, but rather saw it as a challenge to create something new. In a twist on the more common trope that romanticized poverty and hardship as a means to achieve spirituality, Bernard Bamberger, a prominent rabbi, called for a new conception of piety: "We are faced with the opportunity and the challenge to produce a new kind of piety, which has depth and vigor even though the people who practice it are not constantly struggling for physical and economic survival;" Bernard Bamberger, "Charting the Future of Reform Judaism," *CCAR Journal*, January 1958: 15.

acknowledged in a programmatic article the danger that liberal religion, Reform Judaism included, would in the face of increasing acceptance, "turn into friendly but innocuous platitudinousness."[11] Reform thinker Eugene Borowitz picked up on the doubts around how economic success and social inclusion affected Jewish authenticity and spiritual survival: "America has not been an unmixed blessing to us." Jews have integrated too well into American life. "What we need now is to learn to stand off a little from it."[12] Descendants of early to mid-nineteenth-century Jewish immigrants, more likely to be Reform, were by the mid-twentieth century more integrated socially and economically into the American middle-class mainstream than those whose ancestors arrived later.[13] Therefore, when in the 1950s and later the price paid for successful inclusion was questioned, it was Reform Judaism's ability to attract a different demographic base that was at stake. Would the newly suburbanized descendants of East European immigrants accept the reduction of Judaism to a faith that was inherent in both societal expectations and the tradition of classical Reform à la Pittsburgh Platform? The Jews who established new Jewish structures and practices in the suburbs had few models with which to reshape religious life. The majority felt unconstrained by classical Reform ideas in their creation of suburban Judaism. The synagogues they built incorporated more ritual, ceremony, and Hebrew and less of the "high church" atmosphere of Reform temples two generations earlier, and instead encouraged a greater sense of sociability among congregants, based on an often unideological sense of ethnic kinship that would come to favor the growth of more traditional and peoplehood-oriented Conservative Judaism at mid-century.[14]

The intellectual elite of the Reform movement meanwhile fought over the historical and ideological underpinnings of these developments and, predictably, turned to the East European past in their quest for a new understanding of Judaism. Calling for a broadened concept, the Chicago-based rabbi Morton M. Berman struck a revisionist tone with regard to his own movement: "Early Reform had weakened the sense of Jewishness in Jews by repudiating the 'peoplehood' of Israel. With this rejection, the folkways that constitute the ingredients in a people's

---

[11] Emil Fackenheim, "Liberalism and Reform Judaism," *CCAR Journal*, April 1958: 1–7.
[12] Eugene Borowitz, "Divinity and Dividends," in *Best Jewish Sermons of 5719–20*, ed. Saul I. Teplitz (New York: Jonathan David, 1960), 24–25.
[13] Marshall Sklare and Joseph Greenblum registered such socioeconomic differences between descendants of Central and East European immigrants, respectively, in their study *Jewish Identity on the Suburban Frontier: A Study of Group Survival in the Open Society*, 2nd ed. (Chicago: University of Chicago Press, 1979; orig. publ. 1967; the study was conducted in 1957/58), chap. 2.
[14] Leon Jick, "The Reform Synagogue," in *The American Synagogue: A Sanctuary Transformed*, ed. Jack Wertheimer (Cambridge: Cambridge University Press, 1987), 98–104.

culture ceased to have meaning." Only a return to a greater sense of ethno-national Jewishness could create a "home-feeling" for Jews, he argued.[15] Shulman in another sermon reflected on Y. L. Peretz, whose idea of Jewishness, as he pointed out, had a broader scope than religion, as it included a "national creative will."[16]

Writers who, in contrast, expected or advocated for a narrower concept of Jewishness, one closer to Judaism as a religion, were less likely to invoke classical Reform ideas or the East European past, instead emphasizing contemporary American norms. As they sought a compromise between historical ideals and present realities, they painted a vision of a Reform-oriented, American type of Judaism that would be religion-based but have room for an ethnic dimension of Jewishness. Rabbi Roland Gittelsohn, famous for his Iwo Jima eulogy and his progressive activism, acknowledged "that Jews constitute an ethnic people which must maintain its corporate identity if its culture and faith are to be preserved." And yet, he averred, "for a variety of reasons it seems manifest that the Jew in this land is destined to be considered and consider himself increasingly part of a religious rather than a national group."[17] Bernard Bamberger, a prominent rabbi and Bible translator, concurred, also suggesting that the self-presentation of America's Jews as a religious group was not ideological or theological, but tactical: "because of the circumstances in which they live, they find it necessary to give their group survival a religious character. This strategy is hardly conscious and deliberate. Nevertheless it can be successful only if the Jewish communities become in fact what they claim to be – genuinely religious bodies."

As a result of the complex considerations going into mid-century Reform thinking, the lesson its leaders took from the East European past for the American present was a somewhat broadened concept of Judaism: incorporating a sense of peoplehood, but largely shaped by rationalist concepts making for a distinctly liberal type of religion. Like thinkers writing in *Commentary* and *Judaism*, they expected the emergence of a uniquely American Judaism, which would absorb ideas associated with the East European Jewish experience, such as peoplehood, particularistic pride, and spiritual warmth. They recognized the need

---

15 Morton M. Berman, "Reform Ritual," *CCAR Journal*, October 1953: 9, 10.
16 Charles E. Shulman, "On Being a Jew," in *Best Jewish Sermons of 5714*, ed. Saul I. Teplitz (New York: Jonathan David, 1954), 171–72. Others used the debate about the traditional Ashkenazic or growing Sephardic pronunciation of liturgical Hebrew as a vehicle through which to demand a greater sense of loyalty to the East European tradition; cf. Harold Silver, "'An Oy for an Eye or an Eye for an Eye:' Some Reactions Towards the Trend Away from Ashkenazic Pronunciation," *CCAR Journal*, June 1962: 41–49.
17 Roland B. Gittelsohn, "A Tribute to Mordecai M. Kaplan," *CCAR Journal*, June 1956: 24; Gittelsohn, "Reform Judaism's Chances for Survival," *CCAR Journal*, January 1958: 6.

and the potential of paying greater attention to aspects of the Jewish heritage that were associated with the East European past. But, they were too distant from it culturally to fully embrace them; instead, they opted for a mix of responses: rejection, selective adoption, and spiritualization of a past for which they had only limited use.

Conservative Judaism: East European Jewishness as *ersatz Yiddishkayt*

Based on a different religious ideology and history, Conservative Judaism engaged the East European Jewish past in ways very different from Reform. From the time of its ideological origins in nineteenth-century Central Europe, it had always placed greater emphasis on peoplehood and retained more of the traditional religious practices. In the early period of East European immigration to the US, the ideas and practices of what would become Conservative Judaism were indeed part of "traditional Judaism," the social basis of which were immigrants who strove to retain a commitment to the religious tradition under new circumstances.[18] It was only in the middle decades of the twentieth century that developments in opposite directions led to the full parting of the ways between Conservative Judaism and Orthodoxy as distinct denominations. As a result, Conservative Judaism needed to bolster its identity through its own sources that would have to vouchsafe for its legitimacy by providing a past with which it could claim continuity.[19] Still, more than the ideological considerations of the JTS-associated,

---

18 Marshall Sklare, *Conservative Judaism: An American Religious Movement* (Glencoe, IL: Free Press, 1955), 32–40; Neil Gillman, *Conservative Judaism: The New Century* (New York: Behrrman, 1993), 39–40. For a nuanced picture of the complicated relationship between JTS, early Conservative Judaism, and the immigrants, see David Weinberg, "JTS and the 'Downtown' Jews of New York at the Turn of the Century," in *Tradition Renewed: A History of the Jewish Theological Seminary of America [vol. 2]: Beyond the Academy*, ed. Jack Wertheimer (New York: JTS Press, 1997), 3–52. Sklare explains *ex negativo* the attraction of Conservative Judaism to Jews of East European descent: Orthodoxy could not be simply transplanted to America, the venue of the bulk of their adjustment to modern life (*Conservative Judaism*, 23–25). Cf. also Michael R. Cohen, *The Birth of Conservative Judaism: Solomon Schechter's Disciples and the Creation of an American Religious Movement* (New York: Columbia University Press, 2012).

19 Cf. Jeffrey S. Gurock, *From Fluidity to Rigidity: The Religious Worlds of Conservative and Orthodox Jews in Twentieth Century America* (Ann Arbor: Frankel Center, 1998). Despite the establishment of Conservative institutions, such as JTS in 1886 and the United Synagogue of America in 1913, leading actors of the emerging movement well into the 1940s upheld an ideal of American

tradition-minded, and observant elite, it was the social reality of the rank-and-file stratum of the developing movement that shaped – and complicated – the quest for a positive identity for Conservative Judaism.[20] In their religious practices, these rank-and-file Jews were often closer to the more recent type of Reform Judaism than to Orthodoxy, but upheld higher standards of observance as the ideal of Jewish authenticity. Many Conservative Jews associated authentic and total Jewishness with Orthodoxy and with the East European Jewish past.[21] From this past, they derived a strong loyalty to a comprehensive sense of Jewishness, in which religion informed a broad set of behavioral norms rooted in an ethnic culture. At the same time, a strong urge to integrate into the American mainstream counterbalanced this sense of broad distinctiveness. Postwar American society's reduction of Jewish distinctiveness to the private and circumscribed realm of religion challenged the East European-derived notion of Jewish peoplehood and ethno-cultural Jewishness, thus complicating the second and third generations' efforts to express a meaningful Jewish identity and locate themselves within the American social mainstream.

These competing considerations also complicated and shaped the development of a Conservative Jewish identity based in a distinct religious ideology. Rather than resolve the tension between traditional peoplehood loyalties and the privatization of religion in the modern nation state, as Reform Judaism tried to do, Conservative Judaism tried to navigate and manage them. It owed its growth in the 1940s and 1950s to a successful self-presentation as both American and Jewish, integration-minded and distinct, modern and traditional. It achieved this feat by refraining from articulating a clear ideology that would have threatened its flexibility to hold the tensions in balance. Conservative

---

Jewish unity, avoiding in particular an overt secession from what they hoped would remain one Orthodox-traditionalist camp. Louis Finkelstein is quoted to have said in the 1950s that Conservative Judaism was the gimmick to bring Jews back to "authentic" Judaism; see Daniel J. Elazar and Rela Mintz Geffen, *The Conservative Movement in Judaism: Dilemmas and Opportunities* (Albany: SUNY Press, 2000), 17.

20 Sklare, *Conservative Judaism*, 185–90. For the idea that this gap is an inherited pattern of Litvak religious culture, see Elazar/Mintz Geffen, 74.

21 Elazar/Mintz Geffen, 97; Hasia Diner, *The Jews of the United States, 1654 to 2000* (Berkeley: University of California Press, 2004), 297. For the Orthodox background of many JTS faculty members, see Harvey E. Goldberg, "Becoming History: Perspectives on the Seminary Faculty at Mid-Century," in *Tradition Renewed: A History of the Jewish Theological Seminary of America [vol. 1]: The Making of an Institution of Jewish Higher Learning*, ed. Jack Wertheimer (New York: JTS Press, 1997), 388–89; for students, see Aryeh Davidson, "Seminary Rabbinical Students: Who Attended and Why," *Tradition Renewed*, 441–70.

thinkers found that the East European past offered a rich repertoire of ideas, images, and symbols in which to ground this ambivalence.

This was all the more important at mid-century, when these masterminds had to acknowledge that their management of the tensions did little to prevent the spiritual attrition that left many American Jews without enough iron filings of positive Jewish content to still feel an attraction to the magnet of authentic Jewishness. For all the success of Conservative Judaism, the elite of the movement found that the general perception of American Jewry in crisis was true for its constituency, too.[22] Rabbi and scholar Samuel Dresner offered a brutally succinct diagnosis: "Judaism – if not the Jew – is vanishing."[23] While thinkers like Dresner distinguished between religion and social group, they recognized that, with Judaism, *Jewishness* was in crisis as well. Dresner's quip suggested the insight that Jewishness would continue to exist as a social attribute, but without content – a *leitmotif* of the Conservative discourse. Many thinkers worried that Jews found little in Judaism to identify in positive ways with their Jewishness. In their search for new sources of a positive identity for post-traditional American Jews, some invoked "civilizational patterns," showing the influence of Mordecai M. Kaplan's thought.[24] The idea of such an expanded concept of Judaism that would make for "identity" in the sense of an integrated sameness of the individual and the community ran through many texts in Conservative Judaism's discourse, particularly in the eponymous denominational magazine that was founded in 1945.[25] The new

---

[22] In line with their personal background, the rabbinical elites measured the spiritual malaise they observed in the low level of observance among its constituents, particularly of the Sabbath. "[How] has it been permitted to fall into virtual obsolescence in America?" Samuel Dresner asked despairingly ("The Sabbath," *Conservative Judaism* 14 (1960): 25). Finkelstein bemoaned "American Jewish apathy" in the face of existential crises ("Hasideanism and the Modern World," *Conservative Judaism* 14 (1960): 3). Jacob Neusner even polemically predicted the imminent "religious and cultural suicide" by American Jewry ("The Future of American Judaism," *Conservative Judaism* 18 (1964): 30). Cf. also Marcus Wald, "What Does World Jewry Expect of American Jewry?" *Conservative Judaism* 7 (1950): 1–8; Richard Rubenstein, "The Intellectual and Contemporary Jewish Life," *Conservative Judaism* 14 (1960): 40–46.

[23] Samuel Dresner, "Renewal," *Conservative Judaism* 19 (1965): 57.

[24] Sidney Greenberg, "Disturbing the Comfortable," in *Best Jewish Sermons of 5717–5718*, ed. Saul I. Teplitz (New York: Jonathan David, 1958), 106. Similarly, Rabbi Seymour J. Cohen stated that many American Jews even denied their Jewishness, as they mistook it for an obstacle to being fully at home in America; the result, he said, was restlessness and rootlessness. ("Being 'At Home,'" in *Best Jewish Sermons of 5719–20*, ed. Saul I. Teplitz (New York: Jonathan David, 1960), 39–45) For a Kaplanian approach, cf. Herbert Ribner, "Waning Traditionalism Among American Jews," *Conservative Judaism* 9 (1952): 33.

[25] The sermon "The Freedom of Free Men" by Rabbi Morris Adler explicitly addressed the question of such an identity; *Best Jewish Sermons of 5717–5718*, ed. Saul I. Teplitz (New York:

magazine's vision of an emphatically *cultural* concept of Judaism, as opposed to its reduction to religion, was explicit in the programmatic choice to reprint in the first issue a 25-year-old "prophecy" for Judaism in America by Israel Friedlaender. In a section of his book *Past and Present*, published in 1919, a year before the rabbi and educator was killed on a relief mission in Eastern Europe, Friedlaender challenged the Emancipation-era conceptualization of Judaism as a creed, rather than an all-encompassing culture:

> It was the fatal mistake of the period of emancipation, a mistake which is the real source of subsequent disasters in modern Jewish life, that in order to facilitate the fight for political equality, Judaism was put forward not as a culture, as the full experience of the inner life of the Jewish people, but as a creed, as the summary of a few abstract articles of faith, similar in character to the religion of the surrounding nations.
>
> If, therefore, Judaism is to be preserved amidst the new conditions – it must again break the narrow frame of a creed and resume its original function as a culture as the expression of the Jewish spirit and the whole life of the Jews. It [...] will encircle the whole life of the Jew and give content and color to its highest functions and activities.[26]

In response to this call, many Conservative thinkers summoned the East European past as a model of a more encompassing cultural heritage that gave content and meaning to a positive identification with Jewishness. East European Jews had "something in their culture which – for all our education and culture – we lack," JTS-ordained rabbi Herman Kieval wrote. "They had a pattern and a purpose for living."[27] This pattern, or way of life, had its basis in a spirituality that differed from disenchanted modern societies. Critic Marshall R. Lifson overtly contrasted "the brittle, mechanized world of twentieth-century America [and] the warm emotional life of the Eastern European *shul*."[28] Invoked in sermons, these East European Jews were made to live their wholesome, meaningful, and integrated Jewishness vicariously for American Jews whose fragmented, Jewishly limited lives sorely lacked such a *Yiddishkayt*. This spiritual ethnicity constituted the heart

---

Jonathan David, 1958), 1–11. Cf. also Leo Trepp, "Peace of Mind," review of *Peace of Mind* by Joshua Liebman, *Conservative Judaism* 3 (1947): 43–46.

26 Israel Friedlaender, "Judaism in America: A Prophecy," *Conservative Judaism* 1 (1945): 25. Cf. also Robert Gordis, "The Task Before Us: A Preface to Our Journal," *Conservative Judaism* 1 (1945): 6.

27 Herman Kieval, "[Review of *The Earth Is the Lord's* by Abraham Joshua Heschel]," *Conservative Judaism* 7 (1951): 28.

28 Marshall R. Lifson, "The Kosher Dybbuk," *Conservative Judaism* 14 (1960): 48. Cf. also Benjamin M. Kahn, "The Sabbath: Symbol of Jewish Living," in *Best Jewish Sermons of 5714*, ed. Saul I. Teplitz (New York: Jonathan David, 1954), 59–60.

of the expanded understanding of Judaism as a culture that Conservative thinkers hoped to inspire.[29] The question of how this particular notion of Jewishness was rooted in tradition and relatable to the present was at the core of the Conservative discourse at mid-century. In sermons and essays, rabbis and other intellectuals discussed how the movement's brand of Judaism could be informed and legitimized by its continuity with traditional models of Judaism, which would make it relevant to Jews keen on acceptance in America. On the coincidence of Shavuot and Memorial Day, Rabbi Kieval spent an entire sermon on the question of how American Jewry could nurture living ties to the past without being tied down by them in the task of renewing Judaism:

> This is what our tradition has to teach us at Yizkor time, when we think of those who have gone before us. We do not have to agree with everything they did or said or thought. We do not have to imitate their ways of thought and behavior without the slightest deviation. On the other hand, if we are interested in producing fine, mature, sweet fruit for the future – for our own children and grandchildren – it is disastrous to fly in the face of all wisdom and experience and turn our backs on the rich values of Jewish tradition. [...] Let us therefore resolve this day that we shall neither forget them [our ancestors] nor worship them, neither abandon them nor carry them, but *Stand Upon Their Shoulders and See Farther*.[30]

His rabbinical colleague Wilfred Shuchat preached a similar message. "We can't live in the past, but not in the future, without the past, either. The solution is to live not as it was or as it will be, but as it ought to be," he said in a sermon that linked this insight to the East European past. His point of reference was the popular anthropological study *Life is with People*, published in 1952, which shaped the view that many American Jews had of the East European *shtetl*: "'Life is with People' gives us the beauty and sweetness of the shtetl – but there can be no shtetl without the ghetto, which we wouldn't want to trade it for," Shuchat said in a trope often used by others to express the ambivalent relationship of many American Jews to that complex past. This ambivalence was reflected in the diversity of sources on which Benjamin Kahn, another Conservative rabbi, drew to portray East European Jewish life. He referenced Heschel, quoted a vignette by Mendele, retold a Hasidic folktale, and used material from *Life is with People*, all in one sermon.[31] This diversity signaled

---

[29] Cf. Leon Roth, "Back to, Forward from, Ahad Haam?" *Conservative Judaism* 17 (1962/63): 20–30; Philip Sigal, "Whither Diaspora Judaism?" *Conservative Judaism* 14 (1960): 45; Leon S. Lang, "Jewish Education for the American Jew," review of *The Future of the American Jew*, by Mordecai Kaplan, *Conservative Judaism* 4 (1948): 24.
[30] Herman Kieval, "Stand on Your Father's Shoulders," in *Best Jewish Sermons of 5715–5716*, ed. Saul I. Teplitz (New York: Jonathan David, 1956), 97–98, emphasis in the original.
[31] Wilfred Shuchat, "How to Face A New Age," in *Best Jewish Sermons of 5715–5716*, ed. Saul I. Teplitz (New York: Jonathan David, 1956), 177–83; Kahn, "The Sabbath."

that Jewish life in Eastern Europe was dynamic and had room for competing perspectives, such as Mendele's satirical take versus the earnest morality of Hasidic tales. The reference to *Life is with People* represented both the distance from a world that was now the subject of scholarly reconstruction, and the relevance of this past for the present, for its own sake and as a repository of ideas and ideals that could be made usable for diverse contemporary needs.[32]

This preoccupation of Conservative thinkers with the past suggests that to them, a conscious attitude to it, even in the form of explicit ambivalence, was required to ground contemporary Jewish life. A sense of positive continuity with the past was a necessary condition for a vital Judaism, which in turn would foster identification with Jewishness. Conservative thinkers used reconstructions of the East European past as a model for Judaism as a spiritual culture, which would inform the lives of Jews more forcefully than a truncated "religion." It would be traditional, like Orthodoxy, but also modern, as it developed into new expressions in America. This vision was grounded in a more nuanced and often positive image of the East European past than that of Reform thinkers, who used pre-modern East European Jewish life as a foil for their teleology of progress toward an enlightened, modern Judaism. By incorporating a wide range of time periods and phenomena from East European Jewish history, Conservative thinkers could claim legitimacy for a broader spectrum of their forms and practices of Judaism and Jewishness. This was all the more the case for thinkers like Heschel and artist Ilya Schor, who pointed to the folk as the authentic bearers of the tradition.[33] This representation of the past fit the foundational tenet of Conservative Judaism and its European predecessor, namely that Judaism was not eternal, but historical: an evolving set of practices and ideas co-shaped in its development through time by God and man, particularly by *klal Israel* as the authenticating authority.

Thus, reconstructions of the East European past served Conservative Judaism as a means to several ends that preoccupied the movement in the middle decades. It provided legitimacy for a religious ideology and culture that would distinguish Conservative Judaism from both Reform and Orthodoxy and still be flexible enough to accommodate the intra-denominational spectrum of different practices and ideas. The historical references would show rank-and-file Jews ways to locate themselves imaginatively in a continuity with the past that provided models of a dignified and aestheticized Jewishness. It would form the basis of

---

[32] Cf. Barbara Kirshenblatt-Gimblett, "Introduction," in Mark Zborowski and Elizabeth Herzog, *Life is with People: The Culture of the Shtetl* (New York: Schocken, 1995), ix–xlviii.
[33] Abraham Joshua Heschel, *The Earth is the Lord's: The Inner World of the Jew in Eastern Europe* (Woodstock, VT: Jewish Lights, 1995; orig. publ. 1949), 7, 37; Ilya Schor, "A Working Definition of Jewish Art," *Conservative Judaism* 16 (1961): 29.

a sense of vicarious *Yiddishkayt*, a symbolic ethnicity summoned in sermons and expressed in the social practices of suburban Jews that would allow for a positive sense of Jewish identification. Not least due to the dominant role of the Conservative movement in mid-century American Judaism, this identity, vague in propositional content and mostly symbolic in its expressions, was a key ingredient of the religious discourse about the cultural transformation of American Jewry.

Orthodoxy: Silencing, Historicizing, Idolizing the Recent East European Past

For all of Conservative Judaism's ambivalences, the relationship of Orthodoxy to the East European Jewish past may be the most complex among the denominations. Over the first half of the twentieth century, an early version of "modern Orthodoxy" developed. Its adherents were initially not so much ideologically modern, but pragmatically more open than later members to behavioral accommodation to American society, as they were navigating the tensions inherent in the Americanization of an immigrant or even "old world" culture.[34] As a result, Orthodoxy at the time both institutionally and ideologically constituted a rather unstructured, diverse, and internally discordant phenomenon. Like American Jewry in general, it was characterized by low levels of observance, affiliation and identification, and, consequently, debates about ways to revitalize it.[35]

Some factors, however, were particular to the emerging Orthodox denomination. The Holocaust with its destruction of the spiritual centers of religious Jewry in Eastern Europe forced the question whether and how traditional Judaism could stay its course in America. In response, out of shock and shame, Orthodox Jewry turned inward, more than the other denominations in America. Orthodoxy's experience of Judaism's revival in the 1940s was also distinct from the other movements. Due to its higher average age and broad reluctance to move to the suburbs, where synagogues would be out of walking distance for most, Orthodoxy remained more focused on the (big) cities in the Northeast, particularly the

---

34 Jeffrey S. Gurock, *American Jewish Orthodoxy in Historical Perspective* (Hoboken, NJ: Ktav, 1996), chap. 14; Jenna Weissman Joselit, *New York's Jewish Jews: The Orthodox Community in the Interwar Years* (Bloomington: Indiana University Press, 1994), chap. 1; Cimmy Kaplan, "The Ever-Dying Denomination: American Jewish Orthodoxy, 1824–1965," in *The Columbia History of Jews and Judaism in America*, ed. Marc Lee Raphael (New York: Columbia University Press, 2008), 171–82.
35 Jonathan D. Sarna, *American Judaism: A History* (New Haven: Yale University Press, 2004), 278.

New York area. The revitalization of Judaism in the cities was more qualitative than the quantitative "religious revival" in the suburbs, with its record levels of construction and enrollment in Conservative and, to a lesser degree, Reform synagogues. A crucial factor in this regeneration and for the complicated relationship to the East European past was the influx of Orthodox immigrants from Europe in the 1930s and 1940s, some of whom re-created Yiddish-speaking religious communities in the US. The re-creation of East European *yeshivot* in America in these decades made the distinctly East European religious culture a first-hand point of reference for how American Orthodoxy would define itself. The arrival of European Orthodox leaders and rank and file strengthened the resolve of the small group of committed traditionalists in America; in turn, the immigrants challenged the existing, distinctly American reconstructions of the tradition. As the analysis of the thought and role of Joseph B. Soloveitchik showed, balancing the competing impulses of some commitments to modern ideas and values with the (increasingly dominant and antagonistic) impulse toward supposedly traditional stringency in behavior and ideology was an intellectually difficult and communally controversial ongoing process within postwar American Orthodoxy.

The journals *Orthodox Union/Jewish Life* and *Jewish Forum* mirrored over the decades the internal development of American Orthodoxy. *Orthodox Union*, published by the eponymous umbrella organization (and succeeded by *Jewish Life* in 1946), represented institutionalized modern Orthodoxy in this period. The *Jewish Forum,* institutionally independent of organized religious life, was founded in 1918; its own fate illustrates the developments of Orthodoxy. Committed in its mission statement to "traditional Judaism," it was an important agent of Orthodoxy's Americanization. Founded in 1918, it gave a strong voice, particularly through its long-time editor Charles Raddock, and an open forum to this early, undogmatic version of "modern Orthodoxy."[36] As the movement forged a sharper religious ideology, the magazine reflected the "shift to the right," becoming critical of what was now the movement's left wing. Still, it did not itself shift fast and far enough, and as a result declined while in parallel a younger generation expressed the new approach in the journal *Tradition*, founded in 1958; the *Jewish Forum* folded in 1962, one year after an attempted re-launch.[37] The monthly journal *Dos Yiddishe Vort,* published by Agudas Israel beginning in 1953, will provide additional insight into the perspective of the Yiddish-speaking section of Orthodoxy.

---

36 "Mission Statement," *Jewish Forum* 23 (1940): back cover.
37 Ira Robinson and Maxine Jacobson, "'When Orthodoxy Was Not as Chic as It Is Today': The *Jewish Forum* and American Modern Orthodoxy," *Modern Judaism* 31 (2011): 285–313. The membership of Gordis on its board illustrates its inclusive approach; so does Finkelstein's contribution to the magazine: Louis Finkelstein, "Cyrus Adler as I Knew Him," *Jewish Forum* 23 (1940): 85–86.

Figure 14: The journal *Jewish Life* was a forum of modern Orthodoxy at mid-century (cover of the February/March 1951 issue)

Orthodoxy: Silencing, Historicizing, Idolizing the Recent East European Past — 135

At the beginning of the middle decades of the century, the first urge by many Orthodox Jews was to Americanize, which in turn shaped how Orthodoxy related to the East European past. The positive orientation toward American norms in products, ideas, aesthetics, and behavior was obvious in the journals, whose mission statements and programmatic articles identified traditional Judaism with American political values, such as democracy and tolerance.[38] Patriotic declarations of loyalty were flanked by advertisements and statements that illustrated the identification with America in its everyday material culture and behavioral norms. They emphasized the compatibility of American consumer culture with Jewish religious concerns, like the advertisement "Pepsi Cola is sanctioned for Passover Use by the Union of Orthodox Jewish Congregations of America."[39] Distinctly Jewish products were explicitly Americanized: "Everybody's Favorite! Manischewitz AMERICAN Matzos."[40] In a parallel development, the number of English-language ads grew in *Dos Yiddishe Vort*.[41] The commitment to American norms included new aesthetics for the synagogue service, as in a programmatic article by the Orthodox Union: "For Dignity and Decorum in Religious Services."[42]

As these examples support the historiographical narrative of the Americanization of Orthodoxy, they also illustrate one specific way in which the East European past figured in these processes: through the absence of explicit references. Suggestive as it may be to associate an Orthodoxy focused on becoming American with silence toward its East European past, a closer look leads to a more ambiguous picture, however.[43] Even the absence of explicit references to the past is not easily

---

38 Leo Jung, "Democracy and the Torah," *Orthodox Union* 8 (1941): 3. Cf. also Samuel Umen, "Democracy and Jewish Culture," *Jewish Forum* 23 (1940): 65; "Democracy in Defense of Religious Freedom [Symposium]," *Jewish Forum* 23 (1940); William Weiss, "Democracy on Trial," *Orthodox Union* 8 (1941): 4.
39 *Jewish Forum* 24 (April 1941): inside back cover.
40 *Orthodox Union* 8 (1940): 7, emphasis in the original.
41 Examples include publisher Philip Feldheim, Inc., "Torah-True Literature in English," *Dos Yiddishe Vort* 66 (1960); Horowitz Margareten, "The Matzoh with the taste!" *Dos Yiddishe Vort* 70 (1961): 30; Feldheim, "Fountain of Jewish Learning: Hebrew-English Mishnayoth," *Dos Yiddishe Vort* 90 (1963): back cover.
42 *Orthodox Union* 7 (1939–40): 2. The successor journal's music critic based his favorable review of a record of Hasidic tunes on its adherence to Western aesthetics, such as the "disciplined voices [that] belong to a group of nine devoted Chassidim." (Eric Offenbacher, "Modzitzer Nigunim [On the Jewish Record]," *Jewish Life* 24 (1956): 43–44)
43 Robinson and Jacobson state that the magazine presented "an Orthodoxy compatible with Americanism and modernity, adaptable, inclusive, and *free of its East European image*" ("When Orthodoxy was not as chic," 292, emphasis added). This may be true for an early editorial program, but hardly so for the magazine's later stage.

interpreted, as several texts in the *Jewish Forum* illustrate, which show appreciation for Maurice Schwartz, founder of the Yiddish Art Theatre and recipient of the 1947 Louis D. Brandeis Medal. Neither the citation nor the articles on Schwartz and on the Yiddish Art Theatre referenced the East European background of their subjects.[44] However, the texts mentioned long lists of East European Yiddish authors, and the award ceremony was, according to the reports, rich in references to East European Jewish culture, as well: Schwartz accepted the medal in the costume of "Tevya," as acts from this and from one other piece by Sholem Aleichem and I. J. Singer's "Yoshe Kalb" were performed during the ceremony. How is the absence of explicit verbal references to this past alongside the presence of cultural products rooted in this past to be interpreted? Does it suggest avoidance or even suppression of the past? Or do the costumes and most of all the Yiddish language of the performances speak to a ubiquity of this past that made explicit references superfluous? Was Eastern Europe nowhere because it was everywhere, at least in people's minds?[45] Other examples suggest that the pre-American past was an important element of Orthodoxy's mental and emotional setup, in ways that, again, illustrate the trajectory from an Americanizing, approvingly modern movement to one that brought an idealized past into position against a threatening present.

Some Orthodox thinkers, sounding like their Reform counterparts, expressed great distance from a past that they portrayed as constricted, alien to the conditions of American Jewry, and untranslatable, in every respect far away. Critic Harold Berman described late nineteenth-century Eastern Europe as "a period of medieval darkness and superstition [...] when the greatest majority of Russo-Polish Jews lived in the circumscribed circle of the Talmud, in the narrow, straitened 'four cubits of the law.'"[46] The world of East European Jewry, at least in the earlier part of the middle decades, was firmly placed in the distant past. The most significant example of this historicization is the multi-part series "Thirty

---

44 "Citation," *Jewish Forum* 30 (1947): 21; Leon Crystal, "Maurice Schwartz," *Jewish Forum* 30 (1947): 40; William Mercur, "The Yiddish Art Theatre," *Jewish Forum* 30 (1947): 27.

45 In the case of American Orthodoxy, this question is related to larger shifts from the "osmotic" and implicit transmission of cultural attachments and norms within the community to more conscious and prescriptive formulations of such norms that are consciously learned from books and authoritative professionals; cf. Haym Soloveitchik, "Rupture and Reconstruction: The Transformation of Contemporary Orthodoxy," *Tradition* 28 (1994): 64–130.

46 Harold Berman, "Peretz Smolenskin," *Jewish Forum* 32 (1949): 67. Similarly, Harry Cushing, principal of a Massachusetts Hebrew school, played the East European past off of the American future. "We must realize that we cannot transplant the Jewish environment of Russia and Poland to America. American Israel is slowly creating a new Jewish culture." ("The Future of Yiddish," *Jewish Life* 17 (1950): 62) Yiddishist Gertrude Hirschler similarly emphasized the alienness of the world of Yiddish to Americans ("Say It in Yiddish!" *Jewish Forum* 45 (1962): 12–13, 22, 34).

Generations," which the *Jewish Forum* ran from 1943 into the 1950s. This series, by academic-author Edward Herbert, gave a comprehensive, scholarly overview, soberly told and largely free of nostalgia or even identification, of Jewish history in Eastern Europe from its beginnings in the eleventh century.[47] Such texts and their emphasis on the remoteness and pastness of the East European Jewish experience were complemented by others that tried to link it in a meaningful way to the American present. Like their counterparts in other denominations, Orthodox journals made the familiar move of distilling a timeless spiritual essence from the past that would be abstract enough to be applicable in a totally different setting. A report in *Jewish Life* found that the spirit of the Telz Yeshivah could be transplanted to Cleveland, where it informed practice-oriented Jewish higher education in 1941. "With the core of the Yeshiva's ideological and practical principles independent of time and place, the system as a whole has proven itself remarkably flexible in adjusting to external conditions as necessary."[48] Yet, other authors used a common technique as they highlighted the spiritual nature of East European Jewish life by juxtaposing it with the material hardship Jews had to endure, as in a fictional account of nineteenth-century *shtetl* dwellers in the Mogilev province, tellingly entitled "Blood Libel" and running in several installments.[49] An autobiographical text by a former visiting student of the Mir Yeshivah, Theodore Lewis, spelled out the spiritual transcendence: "I heard a voice of yearning, a yearning towards spiritual uplifting, a voice sublime, which made all things material recede."[50]

---

47 Selected installments: Edward Herbert, "Thirty Generations (The Jews in Poland)," *Jewish Forum* 26 (June 1943): 95–96; "Before the Beginning of Polish History" (July 1943); "Jews Under King Casimir the Great" (September 1943); "Early Jewish Settlement in Lithuania" (November 1943); "The First Intellectual Celebrities in Poland" (May 1944); "The Beginning of Jewish Autonomy in Poland" (June 1944); "The Creator of Jewish Pilpul" (October 1944); "The Great Yeshivah in Lublin" (January 1945); "Synagogues Used as Forts" (September 1950); (January, April, November 1951). Historian Cecil Roth also emphasized the pastness of the East European era by constructing a succession of linguistic civilizations in Jewish history which is now numerically (and must soon be culturally) dominated by English-speaking Jewry. ("The English-Speaking Era," *Jewish Life* 20 (1952): 15–19) The editorial decision to publish these texts in a journal targeting Orthodox readers makes them relevant as statements by an Orthodox elite, irrespective of the individual authors' denominational identification.
48 T. Laedun and L. Davids, "The Way of Telz," *Jewish Life* 26 (1958): 60; cf. also Jacob Avi-Melekh, "[Review of *Israel Salanter*, by Menahem G. Glenn]," *Jewish Forum* 39 (September 1956): 137.
49 Philip Getson, "The Blood Libel: A Story," *Jewish Forum* 23 (April 1940): 39–40; continued until December 1940.
50 Theodore Lewis, "Reminiscences of Mir Yeshiva," *Jewish Life* 16 (1949): 6, 8.

These reminiscences of the Mir Yeshivah are an early example of the idealization of the East European past that became more pronounced over the middle decades. As the interest in this past grew (particularly in the *Jewish Forum*), the approach of "silence" increasingly gave way to idolizing embraces of East European Jewish life. Looking back at his years at the Mir Yeshivah, Lewis declared them to be "the happiest years of my life."[51] Portraits of figures representing this past become increasingly hagiographic, like a multi-part portrait of the Maggid of Dubno. The same process occurred in the Yiddish-language Orthodox press.[52] This development reflected Orthodoxy's increasingly ambivalent stance vis-à-vis America and modernity, to which the idealized reconstructions of a pre-modern East European past offered counter-cultural antidotes. Moreover, Orthodoxy's "shift to the right" entailed the need for conscious strategies for legitimizing religious practices (as opposed to less reflected forms of transmission through behavior). A reified, a-historical East European tradition had to be reconstructed as a source of such legitimizing authenticity.[53]

Given the demographic and ideological impact of Yiddish-speaking refugees from Eastern Europe on American Orthodoxy at mid-century, it is worth tracing briefly the changing images of the *alte heym* appearing in the Yiddish press. The imagery presented in *Dos Yiddishe Vort* brings into particularly clear relief the changing interrelationship of the reconstructed East European past and the American present – in this case, in the writings of a single author over the short span of about two years. Between 1957 and 1959, Rabbi Simcha Elberg, Talmudic scholar and leader of the Orthodox rabbinate and of Agudat Israel, wrote several articles addressing the situation of Judaism in America. In "Winter Night," America represents the loud, superficial, fleeting type of life and relationships, a foil against which the old country "*bes medresh* in a winter night" is elevated

---

[51] Lewis, "Reminiscences of Mir Yeshiva," 12.
[52] Harry A. Savitz, "The Maggid of Dubno: Fabulous Fabulist (1741–1804)," *Jewish Forum* 36 (1953): 27, 28; Cf. also Herbert who, in contrast to other installments of his history series, paints a hagiographical picture of Moses Isserles ("Rabbi Moses Isserles, Codifier and Philosopher," *Jewish Forum* 28 (1945): 56). *Dos Yiddishe Vort* published a growing number of hagiographic portraits, occasioned by anniversaries of leading East European (-descended) *g'dolim*; a selection (all in Yiddish): Meir Shapiro, "The 'Hatam Sofer' has Won," *Dos Yiddishe Vort* 29 (1956): 11; Shmuel Pliskin, "The Rabbi of a Generation," *Dos Yiddishe Vort* 48 (1958): 24–25 (on Hafetz Hayyim); Ava Siones, "Brisk – A Look Back," *Dos Yiddishe Vort* 58 (1959): 17–18 (on the Brisker Rebbe); Avraham Semba, "The Rabbi and the Way of Israel," *Dos Yiddishe Vort* 86 (1963): 20–23 (on the Gerer Rebbe).
[53] Samuel C. Heilman, *Sliding to the Right: The Contest for the Future of American Jewish Orthodoxy* (Berkeley: University of California Press, 2006); Soloveitchik, "Rupture and Reconstruction."

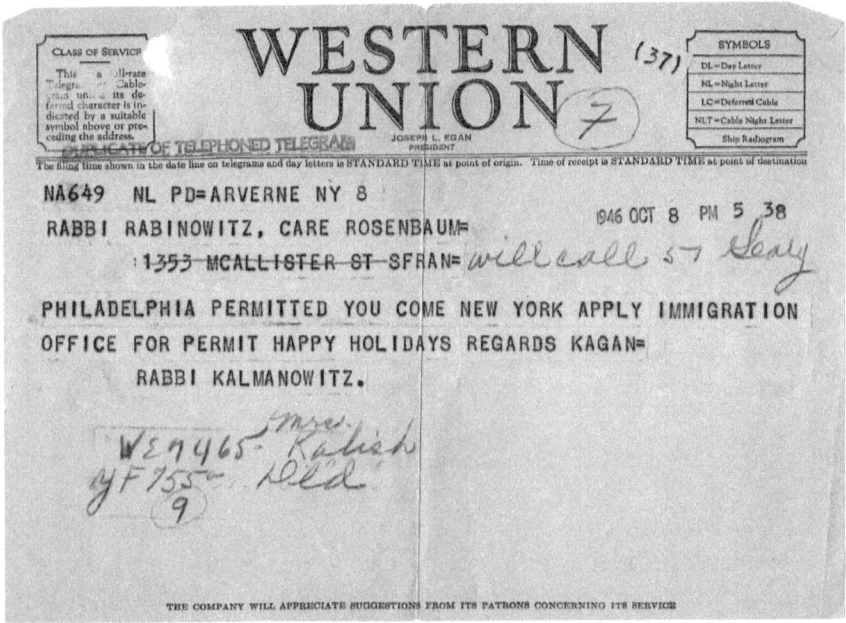

Figure 15: Telegram, October 8, 1946, by rabbi Avraham Kalmanowitz, head of the Mir Yeshivah transplanted to Brooklyn, to his student Jacob (Yankiel) Rabinowitz, who had attended the *yeshivah* before the war and was now allowed to come to New York to apply for an immigration permit. (United States Holocaust Memorial Museum)

to an ideal. "What a treasure did the East European Jew represent," Elberg continues, describing the *beit midrash* as "the collective home of the whole *shtetl*." In one paragraph, he shifts from the historical specificity of East European Jewry to "the Jew," concluding his argument by stating, "The bes medresh in a winter night has been the foundation of historical Jewry."[54] Only a little later, in a similar setup, Elberg compares city and *shtetl*, coming at first to what may be the expected apotheosis of the latter: "The Jew of the *shtetl* has always been closer to G'd." However, Elberg moved on to warmly appreciate the religious renaissance in America, which he found inspired by traditional East European Judaism: "We have been convinced in the past years that one can transplant to America, too,

---

54 Simcha Elberg, "Winter Night" [Yiddish], *Dos Yiddishe Vort* 39 (1957): 8–9. Similarly, in "Back to Historical Rabbanut" [Yiddish], he juxtaposes enlightened ideas of American rabbis and their notion of the rabbinate as a "career" with the deep spirituality of traditional rabbis. (*Dos Yiddishe Vort* 49 (1958): 17–19)

the East European lifestyle, which has for generations preserved the form of traditional Judaism." Like other observers, he found that American Jewry was at mid-century still unformed, just coming into its own. Later, however, Elberg elevated America to an unprecedented historical and moral status, declaring that the term "American Jewishness" no longer described a "spiritual cripple." Going even farther, he effectively repented for East European Orthodoxy's majority opposition to Jewish immigration to America (and does so not only from retrospective knowledge of the Holocaust):

> Not to move from one's place and not emigrating to America, even though its doors were wide open, not to realize the great potential opportunities for the creation of a new, pulsating religious Jewish settlement, has been the greatest punishment for the Jewish people.[55]

Noting the dominant role of American Jewry, he calls on his readers to make American Jewry not only the "gold reservoir" for Jews in other countries, but to see it as the spiritual center it has to become. And yet, Elberg noted again what he had emphasized in the previous texts: the essentially different character of American Jewry as a community in a modern context, which precludes the wholeness ("*shleymusdiker*" Judaism) of the *alte heym* and makes for a fragmented, compartmentalized Jewishness. "A single 'pious' Jew often consists of several Jews. One Jew in him is strictly pious, and the second Jew in him is already made up of a different type."[56]

Starting from a sense of distance and ambivalence, Orthodox writers in Yiddish and English increasingly embraced the East European Jewish past as they reconstructed it for their own purposes in the American and Jewish contexts. Positioning Judaism and Jewishness in a critical stance toward the American mainstream gained importance over time and fueled the development of a clearer denominational profile of Orthodoxy. Again, Raddock wielded the sharpest pen: "[In] our own days, the so-called 'Reform' Jews, despite their many congregations in North America, have been going the way of total assimilation," he charged, and "while Reform is dying," transplanted East European *yeshivot* were vital in recharging authentic Judaism in America.[57] Conservative Judaism was faulted for accepting false compromises in its search to become both fully American and authentically Jewish. Orthodox rabbi Moses Mescheloff accused it of subscribing

---

55 Simcha Elberg, "City and Shtetl" [Yiddish], *Dos Yiddishe Vort* 55 (1959): 12–13; Elberg, "A New Era of Jewishness in America" [Yiddish], *Dos Yiddishe Vort* 59 (1959): 12.
56 Elberg, "A New Era," 13.
57 Charles Raddock, "Judaism and The Lost Intellectuals," *Jewish Forum* 35 (1952): 97; Raddock, "Imprint of a Unique Personality: Baruch Baer of Kaminetz," *Jewish Forum* 41 (1958): 58.

to the model of "a Jew at home and a man in the street," which had to result in a fragmented, hence inauthentic, Jewishness. "Our religion is our whole life," he countered. "Being a part-time Jew is not only religiously inconceivable; it is morally wrong and psychologically undesirable."[58] Mescheloff and other Orthodox thinkers pointed to an East European-inspired ideal of an integral Jewish life, which brought them into the broad intellectual camp made up of thinkers of various ideological stripes. United by this objective, however, Orthodox writers presented quite different suggestions on how to accomplish it. They suggested that an integral Jewishness could rest not just on Halakhah, but also on new forms of spirituality, on ethnic concepts of Jewishness, or on a cultural understanding of Judaism. A hagiographic portrait of the Ba'al Shem Tov described a highly subjective spirituality, a clear contrast to the objective force of Halakhah. Besides spirituality, a sense of ethnic or cultural commonality was also hailed as an authenticating fundament, as in the editorial introduction to a text by Raddock, which was announced as an "uncompromising defense of traditional Yiddishkeit."[59] In some texts, Yiddish and Yiddish culture were presented as one such common ground; others explicitly connected the fate of the language to the spiritual state of Judaism in America.[60]

Yiddish Orthodoxy was particularly pressed to clarify its position on the status of the language as the embodiment of a spirit of Jewishness, and whether it could define religious Judaism in particular. After all, YIVO and its Yiddishist adherents understood the language as the fundament for a very different sense of Jewish authenticity. Therefore, Orthodox writer Nissim Gordon in *Dos Yiddishe Vort* distinguished his (and Yiddish Orthodoxy's) spiritual affirmation of the language from the secularist approach that sought to make it the basis of a cultural Jewishness. "Yiddish is a holy language, a language that was created by Jews in

---

58 Moses Mescheloff, "Split-Personality Judaism," *Orthodox Union* 13 (1946): 5.
59 Raddock, "Judaism and the Lost Intellectuals," 98. Others described the ideal of a *national* religious life. "The spiritual fate and the national survival of the Jewish people, in the Diaspora and in its ancient homeland, are bound up with its total commitment to the national ideals and the Torah laws which constitute the heritage of Israel," stated Appel in a text on Dubnow. (Gersion Appel, "Dubnow's Philosophy of History," review of *Nationalism and History,* by Simon Dubnow, *Jewish Life* 29 (1961): 55)
60 Irvin Michlin, "The 30th Yahrtzeit of Mendele Mokher Sefarim," *Jewish Forum* 43 (1960). Cf. also Abraham Berger, "The Last Word on Yiddish," review of *Great Dictionary of the Yiddish Language, Jewish Forum* 45 (1962): 27–28; Josef Fraenkel, "A World Organization for Yiddish," *Jewish Forum* 42 (1959): 12–13; Hirschler, "Say It in Yiddish!" Isaac Rosengarten, "Is Yiddish Declining?" [Editorial], *Jewish Forum* 34 (1951): 113; Jacob B. Glenn, "Assimilatory Tendencies in American Jewry," *Jewish Forum* 39 (1956): 79–81.

order to be different from the goyim," he stated. It had become sanctified by generations, each of which lived in Yiddish how Jews had to live, in Eastern Europe and in America. But, in the end, Yiddish was only an expression and a means, not an end in itself. "Yiddish is traditionally Jewish only when it is part of a whole, living Yiddishkayt/Jewishness. Yiddish without Jewishness/Yiddishkayt is like a branch torn off a tree." This was the crucial difference from the secular Yiddishists, whose ideology he called "bankrupt" and whom he feared nevertheless: "you should know that no other movement in Jewish has the propaganda instruments at its disposal that the Yiddishists have," he wrote, pointing explicitly to the contemporary interest in Y. L. Peretz and neo-Hasidism – the very cultural reconstructions of the East European heritage which Orthodoxy so abhorred.[61]

This, then, was the sum and crux that Orthodox thinkers shared with others who searched for ways to revitalize Judaism. They strove for a Judaism that would be deeper and broader than the present one they found in postwar America: it should shape deeper spiritual lives for Jews and inform larger parts of their lives than mere religion. On that quest, they pushed against the reductive term of religion and searched for an understanding of Judaism that would make for an integral Jewishness, without sliding into cultural concepts that defined Judaism according to external criteria and subordinated it to other ends. They were trying to square the circle set up by the liberal concept of society that relegated religion to the status of one of various distinct spheres that follow their own internal logic. They tried to protect religion as an autonomous sphere with its own internal logic, but also pushed against the inherent limitations of this sphere as they tried to bring other spheres under its domination. Orthodox thinkers like Raddock suggested already in the 1950s that the ideal of an integral Jewishness based on traditional Judaism was incompatible with the role assigned to "religion" within American society and with the moral state of that society. Over time, more and more Orthodox and other American Jewish thinkers would use the East European past to construct a sense of distinctiveness and difference to set Jews apart from mainstream society, or call for their withdrawal. The multi-layered and variegated images of this past, which competed in the mid-century Orthodox discourse about the future of Judaism in America, helped to pave the way for this turn.

---

[61] Nissim Gordon, "Jewishness and Yiddishism" [Yiddish], *Dos Yiddishe Vort* 2 (1954): 8; cf. also N'hurai [pseud.], "Abraham, Isaac and ... Toby" [Yiddish], *Dos Yiddishe Vort* 9 (1954): 12.

Renewing American Judaism on Religious Terms Found in the Past

In its themes and trajectory, the religious debate mirrored the larger American Jewish discourse at mid-century. The initial openness of the discourse, as exemplified by the range of positions discussed in *Judaism*, over time gave way to more defined positions, as the denominations sharpened new profiles and, more than before, policed the boundaries of their understanding of Judaism. The shared diagnosis of Jews' psychological fragmentation led to a search for ways to understand Judaism and Jewishness as more than a taxonomic label or as one pillar of "tri-faith America."[62] This early consensus, shared with many secular intellectuals, stopped at the question regarding to what extent the reconstruction of Judaism would incorporate external ideas that seemed to threaten its defining role in the lives of Jews. Jewish creativity expressed in culture was fine, as long as it did not come at the cost of Judaism as the core of Jewishness. The denominations put varying degrees of distance between the spiritual culture they advocated and purely cultural reconstructions of Judaism. They ranged from a mere fine line to a fundamentally different approach.

Religious thinkers' efforts to renew Judaism from out of its past for the American present involved processes of abstraction and essentialization. These processes became possible and necessary, as the living memory of the original culture was no longer refreshed by significant immigration, but was gradually embodied in cultural products. This shift to cultural memory was the background for the proliferation of texts addressing this past and trying to make sense, and use, of it. Given the often negative images of Eastern Europe and its (Jewish) culture as backward, parochial, and poor, the spiritualization of this past also involved its aestheticization, as Heschel's and others' writings illustrated.

Religious thinkers reconstructed, essentialized, and aestheticized the East European past typically by isolating its spiritual dimension. In this, they competed not just with secular, literary-minded thinkers focusing on the aesthetic potential of this past, but also with a sub-segment of American Jewry that mined the East European heritage for a political essence that would serve their present American agenda.

---

[62] David Riesman, *The Lonely Crowd: A Study of the Changing American Character* (New Haven: Yale University Press, 1950); Joshua Loth Liebman, *Peace of Mind* (New York: Simon & Schuster, 1946).

6 From East European Radicalism to Postwar American Progressivism

The American Jewish left, bitterly divided as it was internally, constituted a social and intellectual milieu of its own in mid-century America. Even though it was related in many ways to the Yiddishists around YIVO, it was a distinct force in the debate about the past, present, and future of American Jewry. Its perspective on the East European past was shaped by several factors specific to the left. The emergence of radical Socialism in nineteenth-century Russia made for biographical connections and a common myth of origin. As a result, Eastern Europe was a more immediate and politically important point of reference for leftists than for other groups within American Jewry. The Soviet Union, positioned as the "motherland" of Socialism, further strengthened this aspect. It provided a current, common point of reference, but also inspired bitter sectarian divisions within the left, adding a layer of ideological-emotional orientation toward Eastern Europe. Within the American context, in turn, the postwar Jewish left found itself marginalized on at least two accounts. Its Socialism went against the broadly anti-Communist social climate and its secularism defied the *zeitgeist* of postwar America and its affirmation of religion.

Even though sectarian divisions characterized the Jewish as much as the larger left, it is possible to discern major lines of commonality among leftist Jews. In the search for meaningful Jewishness, the Jewish left offered a sense of ethno-cultural, secular, politically progressive *Yiddishkayt* that very much bore the marks of the historic moment. Historian Paul Buhle has described *Yiddishkayt* as a "wild card" on the left, a category that cut across the grain of Marxist theories, yet a powerful force in the generation of immigrant Jewish workers with their roots in the "old country."[1] This segment of American Jewry, while dwindling in numbers, was passionately politicized and vocal in its uphill struggle for an alternative to the religious understanding of Jewishness. In doing so, they sought to transform an East European-born ideology, which had been further shaped in interwar America, into postwar progressive Jewishness. Leftists, like others in the debate, invoked the East European past. Still, as a force aiming to be disruptive with the past and present, the left could not claim continuity with the past as easily as religious thinkers could for their respective agendas.[2]

---

[1] Paul Buhle, "Yiddish Left," in *Encyclopedia of the American Left*, ed. Mari Jo Buhle, Paul Buhle and Dan Georgakas (New York: Oxford University Press, 1998), 912–13.
[2] David G. Roskies, *The Jewish Search for a Usable Past* (Bloomington: Indiana University Press, 1999), 9.

Figure 16: Members of the Socialist *Bund* march in a May Day parade in Bialystok, Poland, May 1, 1934. (United States Holocaust Memorial Museum)

The Jewish left had to play to its near-mythical origin in Eastern Europe in its effort to make the past useful: as proof of the left's legitimacy and as a guide for American Jewry.

The myth of the Jewish left's heroic and idealistic origin in Eastern Europe is grounded in historical facts. One of its ur-types, the *Bund*, was founded in 1897 and became the largest of the radically leftist movements. It was formed in opposition to the oppression of Jews by czarist policies, as well as in opposition to internal traditional and religious restrictions on social progress. The *Bund's* connections to the mid-century American Jewish left existed not just in the realm of ideological identification; both incarnations of the Jewish left, East European and American, were closely intertwined.[3] Ideas, ideologies, and programs flew in steady streams across the Atlantic, through newspapers and pamphlets, and through immigration.[4] Many future American Jewish labor leaders, particularly

---

[3] Jonathan Frankel's analysis has shown that their development is a case of transnationalism *avant la lettre,* as by the eve of World War I there was a subculture of Jewish Socialism in all major centers of Jewish life; *Prophecy and Politics: Socialism, Nationalism, and the Russian Jews, 1862–1917* (Cambridge: Cambridge University Press, 1981).

[4] Tony Michels, "Exporting Yiddish Socialism: New York's Role in the Russian Jewish Workers' Movement," *Jewish Social Studies* 16 (2009): 1–26; Goldstein, Eric L. "A Taste of Freedom:

of the Workmen's Circle, were politically socialized in the ethnically Jewish, secular-leftist Bundist milieu before they came to the US, often in the first decades of the twentieth century.[5] The coupling of the political-ideological and ethnic-cultural dimensions of Jewishness was the basis for the American Jewish left's self-understanding, from the early into the mid-decades of the twentieth century.[6] During the early interwar years, the social constellation still favored a Jewishness conceived as an ethnic category expressed in cultural terms and associated with class-based politics. While American Jewry gradually shifted from a majority immigrant to a second-generation, middle-class community, political radicalism, in Americanized forms, remained attractive to significant numbers of American Jews for some time. However, the larger trajectory of the social, political, cultural, and intellectual forces pointed in a different direction, which challenged both aspects of the Jewish left's identity – class and culture, or political and ethnic conceptions of Jewishness. Historian Tony Michels has described the changes that reduced Jewish labor's importance in American society and within American Jewry as a return to "normalcy." For the left, this "normalcy" meant the specter of irrelevance and the worry that its political influence and cultural appeal would be a single-generation exception to a general rule.[7]

At mid-century, this seemed like an open question, as the same factors that made for American-Jewish uncertainties and ambivalence applied equally to the Jewish left. The answer to the question soon became clear, and the left had reason to worry. The new emphasis on political and social consensus and on commonalities between the various groups in American society was diametrically opposed to an ideology premised on being different from the established structures of power. Two specific factors, both related to American Jews' rise into the middle class, stand out as shaping the new "normalcy:" their consent to let religion be the primary category to express Jewish distinctiveness, and their shift toward political liberalism – two crucial elements of the Americanization

---

American Yiddish Publications in Imperial Russia," in *Transnational Traditions: New Perspectives on American Jewish History,* ed. Ava F. Kahn and Adam D. Mendelsohn (Detroit: Wayne State University Press, 2014), 105–39.

[5] Ezra Mendelsohn, *Class Struggle in the Pale: The Formative Years of the Jewish Workers' Movement in Tsarist Russia* (Cambridge: Cambridge University Press, 1970); Henry J. Tobias, *The Jewish Bund in Russia from Its Origins to 1905* (Stanford: Stanford University Press, 1972). For contemporaneous claims of continuity between the *Bund* and the Workmen's Circle, cf. Joseph Schlossberg, "A Half Century of Jewish Labor," *Workmen's Circle Call* (henceforth: *WCC*) 8 (1940): 9; Joseph Baskin, "Fifty Years of the 'Bund,'" *WCC* 16 (1948): 4, 14; Benjamin Tabachinsky, "62 Years of the 'Bund,'" *WCC* 29 (1960): 4.

[6] Tony Michels, *A Fire in Their Hearts: Yiddish Socialists in New York* (Cambridge: Harvard University Press, 2005), 128–78, 253.

[7] Michels, *Fire in Their Hearts*, 254.

of the former immigrant community. What many leftists saw, in contrast, was a process of cultural homogenization that threatened Jewish distinctiveness. Leftist aesthetic and moral sensibilities could easily be offended by the new "all-rightnik" infatuation with an American mainstream culture that seemed (petit) bourgeois, materialistic and consumerist, self-satisfied, self-congratulatory, and self-righteous.[8] The overall domestic and international political climate, particularly Cold War liberalism, put the left on the defensive.[9] Communism was ostracized as "un-American," as McCarthyism and the "Red Scare" of the first half of the 1950s demonstrated. In the case of the Jewish left, the arrest, conviction, and execution of the Rosenbergs between 1950 and 1953 added the element of an alleged linkage of Jews, Communism, and treason to the troubles.[10] If Jewishness had been equated with secular ethnicity and overlapped with leftism in previous decades, the postwar constellation forced Jews on the left to look for new ways to position themselves. Leftist thinkers crafted narratives about Eastern Europe to support their vision of a politically progressive-leftist and culturally distinct Jewishness.

Journalistic Infighting Over Communism and Jewishness

Re-constructing the East European past was part of a larger process of self-fashioning, and as such it was contested within the Jewish left. A plethora of journals served as vehicles of this infighting, three of which covered a large part of the ideological spectrum within the Jewish left at mid-century: The *Workmen's Circle Call,* led by its outspoken editor Israel Knox, was the English-language

---

[8] Such criticism was occasioned by various events, e.g. anniversaries such as the Tercentenary, or by cultural products: Moses Z. Frank, "In a Glass House," review of *The American Jew,* ed. by Oscar Janowsky, *WCC* 11 (1943): 17–18; Louis Harap, "Is Sammy Levenson Funny?," *Jewish Life* 3 (1949): 17–20; Nathaniel Buchwald, "'Shund' on Broadway," review of *Borsht Capades, Jewish Life* 6 (1951): 29; Louis Harap, "'Marjorie Morningstar' Shines Dimly," *Jewish Currents* 12 (1958): 26–27; Joseph C. Landes, "Yiddishkeyt and Mentschlekhkeyt," *WCC* 31 (1962): 17–18.
[9] Louis Harap singled out *Commentary* as an example of the "revisionist liberalism" he decried. ("Literary Breakthrough – To What?" *Jewish Currents* 19 (1964): 16–22); cf. also the editorial, "Towards American Democracy" in *WCC* 8 (1940): 2.
[10] The Communist *Jewish Currents* raised questions about the trial and the entire case and was attacked by other leftists, among them the *Jewish Frontier* and the *WCC.* Cf. William Reuben, "Truth About the Rosenbergs' Case," *Jewish Life* 6 (1951): 4–7; Editors, "The Rosenberg Case," *Jewish Frontier* XX (1953): 4–5; Walter K. Lewis, "Behind the Fronts," *WCC* 25 (1956): 8.

journal of the originally Yiddish-speaking Socialist *Arbeter Ring*. The creation of the English section in the 1930s reflected a shift toward Americanization, which also meant a gradual transition toward a quasi-social-democratic program.[11] The monthly *Jewish Life* was founded in 1946 as the English-language offshoot of the Yiddish Communist *Morning Freiheit* association.[12] It was consistently pro-Soviet and disputed the existence of anti-Semitic policies and campaigns in the USSR, until revelations in 1956 of Stalin's anti-Jewish political actions forced it to change course.[13] The post-1956 shift was also associated with a change in editorship from Louis Harap, who ran the paper from 1948 to 1958, to Morris Schappes, and a change in name to *Jewish Currents*.[14] The *Jewish Frontier*, published since 1934, represented the numerically small but vocal force of anti-Communist Labor Zionism. Its co-founder and editor-in chief was Hayim Greenberg, a non-religious, anti-Marxist, Socialist Zionist co-founder.

The sectarian fights among the factions behind the journals were conducted with a maximum of passion and rhetorical volume. Their differences also colored the journal's perspectives on the Jewish experience in Eastern Europe. In 1940, the *Jewish Frontier* noted with satisfaction the dissolution of the American committee for the settlement of Jews in Birobidjan, as "the end of another pipedream." Ten years later, it suggested with bitter irony that Ilya Ehrenburg be awarded the "Khmelnitski Medal" for lending (Jewish) support to Soviet policies.[15] On the defensive, the Communists virtually shouted back

---

11 Daniel Soyer, "Workmen's Circle," in *Encyclopedia of the American Left*, ed. Mari Jo Buhle, Paul Buhle and Dan Georgakas, 2nd ed. (New York: Oxford University Press, 1998), 905–06. The *Call* generally appeared monthly. Knox later became a professor of philosophy at New York University.
12 While in other chapters, the publisher "Morning Freiheit Association" is added to the journal's name in footnotes, in order to avoid confusion with the Orthodox journal of the same name, references to *Jewish Life* in this chapter are solely to the Communist journal and the publisher's name is omitted.
13 The change in course was signaled by the (partial) publication of the text, by which the Warsaw *Folks-Shtimme* (Yiddish) had pointed out the crimes: "What Happened to Soviet Yiddish Culture?" *Jewish Life* 11 (1956): 3–7, 27, 40; Editors, "A Ten-Year Look," *Jewish Life* 11 (1956): 3–4; Aaron Kramer, "For Peretz Markish and Itzik Feffer," *Jewish Life* 11 (1956): 23; "A Memo to Soviet Leaders," *Jewish Life* 11 (1956): 27–30. By the time the journal changed course, it had lost three out of four of its readers; cf. David A. Hacker, "Jewish Life/Jewish Currents," in *Encyclopedia of the American Left*, ed. Mari Jo Buhle (New York: Oxford University Press, 1998), 401–02; Gennady Estraikh, "Metamorphoses of *Morgn-frayhayt*," in *Yiddish and the Left*, ed. Gennady Estraikh and Mikhail Krutikov (Oxford: Legenda, 2000), 148–51.
14 The journal announced the change in name in its October 1957 issue, explaining that it acted in order to avoid a lawsuit by the Orthodox journal *Jewish Life*.
15 "The End of Another Pipedream [Editorial]," *Jewish Frontier* VII (1940): 3; "Editorial Comment: A Medal for Mr. Ehrenburg," *Jewish Frontier* XVII (1950): 7. The *Workmen's Circle Call*

Figure 17: Morris Schappes, longtime editor of the Communist journal *Jewish Life*, re-named *Jewish Currents* in 1956; not dated. (American Jewish Archives)

at their critics from *Jewish Life's* pages. They also attacked the anti-Communist *Forverts* for slander.[16] The greatest passion was invested in fights about the direction of Jewish history, and it is here that the differences affect the imagery of the East European past most sharply.[17] Unsurprisingly, *Jewish Life* presented Communism, as it developed until the Bolshevik revolution of 1917 and shaped Eastern Europe afterward, as the most important transformation in recent East European (Jewish) history. A five-part series entitled "Jews of the USSR" related how Communism liberated Jewry from the reactionary and anti-Semitic policies of czarism, turned *luftmentshen* into productive people, and banned harmful

---

attacked Soviet leader Nikita Khrushchev directly for the deterioration of the situation of Jews in the USSR (David Ben-Mordechay Bligh, "Moscow Retaliates ... While Khrushchev Forgets How Jews Befriended Him in His Youth," *WCC* 27 (1958): 3–4).

16 Louis Harap, "X-Ray on 'Commentary,'" *Jewish Life* 1 (1947): 24; "'Soviet Anti-Semitism:' The Big Lie," *Jewish Life* 3 (1949): 3; Louis Harap, "Ludwig Lewisohn: Prophet of Delusion," *Jewish Life* 5 (1951): 27–29.; Joseph Nover, "Reply to Slander," *Jewish Life* 3 (1949): 27–28. In 1951, the *Jewish Frontier* issued a direct editorial "challenge to *Jewish Life*" over its position on Soviet policies toward the Jews ("[Editorial Comment]," *Jewish Frontier* XVIII (1951): 4–5).

17 Jack Greenstein, "Rise of an American 'Judenrat,'"*Jewish Life* 6 (1952): 9–11; Nathaniel Buchwald, "'Shund' on Broadway," *Jewish Life* 6 (1951): 29; Harap, "Is Sammy Levenson Funny?" Julius Horwitz, "Self-Abasement of Broadway," review of shows *Borscht Capades* and *Bagels and Yox*, *Jewish Frontier* XVIII (1951): 15–17; cf. also Israel Knox, "'The Goldbergs:' Pseudo-Humor," *WCC* 18 (1950): 5; Knox, "In the Jewish World," *WCC* 19 (1951): 6–7.

religious activities, while supporting a national culture that flourished again after the destruction of the war.[18] Articles dealing with pre-1917 East European Jewish history took the same ideological perspective. Authors like Mendele, Sholem Aleichem, and Y. L. Peretz were presented as pre-revolutionary pioneers in the struggle for social justice and change. In a 1949 tribute, literary critic Sidney Rosenblatt portrayed Mendele as a sympathizer of the Bolshevik revolution. "[In] the last months of his life, in 1917, Mendele saw the earthshaking October revolution. [...] Mendele the Bookseller must have smiled a smile of peace when he closed his eyes for the last time."[19]

The Labor Zionist *Jewish Frontier* articulated a markedly different ideology.[20] East European Jewish life was presented as a stronghold of separateness from other groups and, until the nineteenth century, insulated from the corroding forces of modernity. In this protected space, a de-facto national culture developed, first in an organic and unreflective manner, before the modern political movements shaped a conscious understanding of the Jewish condition.[21] Labor Zionism, as articulated in the *Jewish Frontier*, did not reject Jewish life in the diaspora as illegitimate *per se*; rather, it defined *galut* as the absence of a national identity and the lack of will to act against the assimilating force of emancipation.[22] The journal asserted the legitimacy of both pre-modern European Jewry and modern East European Jewry after the advent of the modern national ideologies that shaped such a consciousness. Thus, the *Jewish Frontier* drew on the post-emancipatory East European past as a model for nationally-minded American Jewishness.[23]

---

18 L. Singer, "Jews of the USSR: I – Out of the Pale," *Jewish Life* 3 (1948): 20–22. The other parts were published from December 1948 to March 1949; Editorial, "Jewish Life," *Jewish Life* 1 (1946): 3; Itzik Feffer, "Fact and Fancy on Birobidjan," *Jewish Life* 3 (1949): 9–10; Samuel Sillen, "A Visit With Polish Jewry," *Jewish Life* 4 (1950): 21–24; Peter Furst, "The Jews of Eastern Europe," *Jewish Life* 5 (1951): 9–11, and in numerous other issues; Nathan Samaroff, "Jews in New Poland," *Jewish Life* 5 (1951): 16–19.
19 Sidney Rosenblatt, "Mendele Mocher Sforim," *Jewish Life* 3 (1949): 10–13.
20 "End of Another Pipedream," 3; C. Bezalel Sherman, "Jews Under the Soviets," review of *The Jews in the Soviet Union*, by Solomon Schwartz, *Jewish Frontier* XVIII (1951): 23–26; Erich Goldhagen, "Vergelis: The Commissar and the Jew," *Jewish Frontier* XXXI (1964): 8–11.
21 Jacob Lestshinsky, "New Conditions of Jewish Survival," *Jewish Frontier* XIV (1947): 48. Kiev-born Lestshinsky, a sociologist with YIVO, lived in the US at the time of this article; he later emigrated to Israel.
22 Hayim Greenberg, "Zionism and Diaspora," *Jewish Frontier* XVIII (1951): 7–9.
23 Author Ludwig Lewisohn enunciated the underlying ideology in the first of six programmatic articles in 1950 ("Reflections on the Jewish Situation, Part I: Re-Examination," *Jewish Frontier*

The Workmen's Circle's role as a mainstream organization within the left resulted in a more nuanced perspective than those displayed by the Communists and Labor Zionists. Moreover, whereas the latter two factions turned to the Soviet Union and the State of Israel, respectively, as points of reference and laboratories for their ideological programs, the Workmen's Circle had only America. The *Call's* positions were frequently more measured or pluralistic than those of the more ideological journals. Mendele was presented as "a real fighter for social justice," but not as a predecessor of the revolutionary Communism that the journal repeatedly attacked.[24] As for Zionism, the journal stated its support for the State of Israel, but took care to emphasize that this stemmed from its belief in Jewish peoplehood rather than in the nation state.[25] The cultural stirring of East European Jewry in the second half of the nineteenth century and the political responses to the new circumstances were presented as key developments of relevance to the American Jewish present. The *political* transformation that gave direction to the new group consciousness was concentrated in the foundational events of 1897, as Israel Knox wrote on their 50th anniversary: the founding of the "Bund," the first Zionist Congress, and the publication of Simon Dubnow's "Letters" and the founding of the *Forverts,* which Knox presented as the most significant of the events. It symbolized yet another late-nineteenth century response by East European Jews: immigration to America. Its appreciation illustrated that the *Call* also provided more space than the other two journals for explorations of the new American environment of East European Jews. Here, the rivalling factions of the left found common ground among themselves and with other observers of mid-century American Jewry.

American Jews: Mindlessly Assimilating, or Forming a New Spiritual Center?

Like many other players on the scene, the left saw American Jewry as essentially unsettled and unformed, at a crossroads and in need of guidance on

---

XVII (1950): 5–8. The articles, running from February to August 1950, were incorporated in Lewisohn's book *The American Jew: Character and Destiny* (New York: Knopf, 1950).
24 Nathan Goldberg, "Mendele the Bookseller," *WCC* 11 (1943): 9–10; Walter K. Lewis, "Behind the Fronts," *WCC* 25 (1956), 8; Lewis, "Commie Confessions Conceal Old Confidence Game," *WCC* 25 (1956): 10.
25 Israel Knox, "The Workmen's Circle: Past – Present – Future," *WCC* 20 (1952): 4.

what to do with its considerable potential, lest it fall prey to the assimilating powers of America. "In the United States even Jews who withstood the test of assimilation in Russia are drawn into its vortex," Polish-born journalist Eliezer Liebenstein warned in 1940 in the *Jewish Frontier*.[26] Many thinkers blamed this problem on their ignorance of the past. "A generation has arisen in America without knowledge of, and therefore without love of that world," Knox wrote. He bemoaned a lack of intellectual leadership, as even teachers and rabbis had grown distant to this world. Without their guidance, he suggested, many Jews falsely believed that acceptance in America required shedding not just visible and audible reminders of their East European and immigrant past, but also their memory and consciousness of this heritage. He lamented the rootlessness of the community in several articles addressing American Jews' willful ignorance of the East European past.[27] Whether purposeful or negligent, the scenario of rapid and broad assimilation appeared as a dramatic threat to individual and communal stability and to Jewish continuity. "Even here in the United States where the attitude towards Jews is most tolerant, the attempt to flee one's own Jewishness ends in spiritual tragedy," a critic for the *Workmen's Circle Call* wrote in a review of the 1947 novel *Wasteland* by Jo Sinclair. Its existentially insecure, alcoholic protagonist Jake finds new meaning in his life when he begins to appreciate the Jewishness from which he had tried to flee. The reviewer concluded that Jewish life in America could only be healthy if more Jews, like Jake, came to feel at ease with their Jewishness.[28]

---

26 Eliezer Liebenstein, "A Zionist Look at the Diaspora," *Jewish Frontier* VII 8 (1940): 8. (Lodz-born journalist Liebenstein, under his Hebraized name Livneh, became an influential figure in the Israeli labor party.) Cf. also C. Bezalel Sherman, "What American Jewish Youth Ask," *Jewish Frontier* XXXII (1965): 8; Israel Knox, "Towards Our Goal," *WCC* 9 (1941): 12–13; M.P. [Reader's letter], "Assimilationism and Yiddish," *Jewish Life* 3 (1948): 29; James G. Heller, "Confessions of an American Zionist," *Jewish Frontier* XXI (1954): 10–19.
27 Israel Knox, "Portrait of a World that Was," *WCC* 25 (1956): 6, emphasis in the original; Knox, "Sholem Aleichem," *WCC* 28 (1959): 6; Kox, "A World to Remember," 5, 15. For the discussion of the role of Jewish intellectuals, cf. Daniel Bell, "A Parable of Alienation," *Jewish Frontier* XIII (1946); Nathan Ausubel, "Challenge to American Jewish Intellectuals," *Jewish Life* 2 (1948): 18–22; Moise Katz, "The Development of Jewish Culture in America," *Jewish Life* 2 (1948): 19–22; Shlomo Katz, "The Sins of The Jewish Intellectual," *Jewish Frontier* XVIII (1951): 11–14; William Stern, "Tipping the Scales," *WCC* 30 (1961): 7.
28 Zalman Efron (Yefroiken), "Our Approach to Jewish Life," *WCC* 22 (1953), 7; Jo Sinclair [pseud.], *Wasteland* (Philadelphia: Jewish Publication Society, 1987; orig. publ. 1947). Other examples include Frank, "In a Glass House;" Zalman Yefroiken (Efron), "Why Jewish Education?" *WCC* 33 (1962): 7–8; Lewisohn: "Reflections." Both spellings of Efron/Yefroiken's name were in use.

These issues of (un-) stable personalities, fictitious or real, were often presented in terms of an accelerated and forced coming of age. Maurice Samuel saw American Jewry as still depending on East European Jewry when the Holocaust cut off their source of nourishment and threw American Jewry into a premature state of daunting responsibility.[29] Hence, American Jews found themselves facing a double task: to craft a sense of Jewishness that would provide meaning for their lives in America, and to take intellectual and spiritual leadership of world Jewry. Like intellectuals of other segments of American Jewry, many leftists worried that American Jewry was too immature to uphold the continuity and tradition that was threatened in its very existence. Yiddishist Jacob Lestshinsky summed up the appraisal of many observers within the Jewish left and without: American Jewry, he stated, was spiritually unprepared to take over the responsibility for continuing the golden chain of Jewish cultural life and for beating back the assault upon the survival of the Jews as a people. "The American Jewish community is even less prepared to become the spiritual center of the Jewish communities which are scattered over some 90 countries throughout the world."[30]

However, it seemed that all was not lost. Some observers did see hope in the ferment that transformed American Jewry and pointed to a greater commitment to Jewishness and to a communal responsibility for its heritage. The *Workmen's Circle Call* as early as 1945 took note of a new consciousness arising among Jews to speak and act as a national entity.[31] Tellingly, it found them in the realm of culture. "There are cultural stirrings in the American Jewish community, which signify heightened awareness of Jewishness and a conscious effort to develop to the full the cultural potentialities of this largest community in the world," the *Jewish Frontier* agreed, even though these stirrings were "in the groping stage."[32] The left sought to give direction to the groping, recognizing in it an attempt to find deeper meaning than what organized Jewish life at the time could offer. Philanthropy and relief efforts were not enough to create a meaningful and creative

---

[29] Maurice Samuel, "The Story That Must Build Itself: On Jewish History and John Hersey's 'The Wall,'"*Jewish Frontier* XVII (1950): 17.
[30] Lestshinsky, "New Conditions of Jewish Survival," 48; cf. also Maurice Samuel, "Chalutziut from America," *Jewish Frontier* XVII (1950): 5–8. An editorial in the *Jewish Frontier* criticized (in 1944) that "[the] future of American Jewry is discussed as though its function among Jewish communities could still be the same as when there were those millions in Eastern Europe upon whom to lean. We have not yet given ourselves an honest accounting of our place in the world in the light of the new reality." ("Minsk, Vilna, Pinsk, Grodno," *Jewish Frontier* XI (1944): 5)
[31] "Seventy-five Years of the Yiddish Press," *WCC* 13 (1945): 14.
[32] "Culture for the People's Sake [Editorial]," *Jewish Life* 3 (1948, Cultural Supplement): 3.

Jewish existence, *Jewish Life* argued; a conscious effort was required.³³ A 1943 editorial in the *Call* articulated a programmatic basis common to the American Jewish left at large, as it related American Jewry to its East European ancestry:

> The tragic dismemberment of the Jewish community in Eastern Europe imposes upon the Jews of America great historic responsibilities, not only in the way of providing aid for our brothers and sisters across the ocean, but also in the recognition of our allegiance to a common culture, a common set of values. That allegiance will be tenuous unless it is anchored in self-knowledge, in self-awareness, unless the American Jewish center is capable of realizing these responsibilities and their implications.³⁴

For leftists, this hoped-for cultural consciousness would be the crucial phenomenon by which American Jewry would come into its own, come to terms with its heritage, and find meaning in its *American* Jewishness.³⁵ To achieve this goal, Jewry had to "reorder their spiritual strategy," Maurice Samuel stated, pointing to the East European heritage as the crucial resource.³⁶

East European Folk Culture as Part of Jewish Leftists' Political Project

The left found such a new spiritual strategy for American Jewry in a cultural notion of Jewishness inspired by the past and intertwined with the political identity that the left sought to impress on American Jews. Thus, the depiction of the East European Jewish experience in the leftist journals was dominated by two motifs, which together formed a core theme of much of the postwar American Jewish imagery of the past: Eastern Europe was presented as a place of oppression by czarism, capitalism, and rabbinic rigidity; at the same time, it was a place of rich and highly variegated Yiddish-based Jewish civilization. The hostile environment set the stage for heroic idealism in the face of persecution and made for a powerful myth of origin that nourished the American Jewish left well into the postwar

---

33 "Culture for the People's Sake;" similarly Adolph Held, "Jewish Culture and the American Jewish Community," *WCC* 28 (1959): 2–3.

34 "Book and School Month [Editorial]," *WCC* 11 (1943): 3. The same sentiment is expressed in the Workmen's Circle's "Resolution on Jewish Affairs," passed at its 1948 national convention (*WCC* 16 (1948): 17–18).

35 S. Niger: "The emotional 'Jewishness' in America has increased, but our consciousness of Jewish cultural values has not become sufficiently profound." ("The Amalgam Which Is Jewish Life," *WCC* (1951): 4)

36 Samuel, "The Story That Must Build Itself," 18.

years. The unalloyed hopes of the broad masses for revolutionary change from a clear-cut, morally corrupt opponent to a secular-messianic future made for easier identification than the uphill struggle of a shrinking minority toward the gradual improvements that the left could dare to hope for in America. The story of the early years of Jewish radicalism in Russia, as presented in the journals, was therefore a picture of black and white, good and evil, with some red mixed in for the blood that was spilled for the cause of humanity's progress.

The depiction of Jewish life was more variegated and colorful: a dazzling panorama of events and places, persons and ideas, experiences and stories. A reader of the August 1955 issue of *Jewish Life* could find texts about Mendele and Solomon Maimon.[37] Readers of the *Workmen's Circle Call* in January 1964 were offered an article about Israel Ben Eliezer, the eighteenth-century founder of Hasidism, and an editorial recalling the anti-Semitism of the 1913 "Beilis Affair" in Russia.[38] In October 1951, the (rare) reader of all three journals would have found a story by Sholem Aleichem in *Jewish Life,* a eulogy for *Forverts* editor Abraham Cahan in the *Workmen's Circle Call,* and in the *Jewish Frontier* a fantastical story about Reb Levi-Yitshak's experience in heaven.[39] Taken together, the journals presented the world of East European Jewry as "filled with the sounds and movements, the screams, curses, and prayers, the dirt and disorder, the warmth and tenderness, the superstitions, the struggles, the spirituality and hopefulness by means of which the Jews of the last century sustained themselves," as Yiddishist author and educator Henry Goodman wrote. The stories covered big-city Warsaw and small Russian villages, the Socialist movements and Zionism, Yiddish and Hebrew, the new ideological secularism and Hasidism, the corroding effects of modernity and the dissolution of communities by immigration, pogroms, and the Holocaust.[40] This world was populated by

---

[37] Louis Lerman, "A Book Peddler and His Nag," review of *The Nag*, by Mendele Mokher Sforim, *Jewish Life* 9 (1955): 9–10; Ber Mark, "The Story of Solomon Maimon," *Jewish Life* 9 (1955): 20–22.

[38] Anon., "Mendel Beilis – Lest We Forget," *WCC* 35 (1964): 10; "[Review of *Rabbi Israel Baal Shem Tov*, by Menashe Unger]," *WCC* 35 (1964): 16.

[39] Sholem Aleichem, "Some Way to Do Business," *Jewish Life* 5 (1951): 21; Joseph Baskin, "Abraham Cahan," *WCC* 19 (1951): 3–4; Menashe Unger, "Levi Itzhak Goes to Heaven: A Hassidic Story," *Jewish Frontier* XVIII (1951): 16–17.

[40] A selection: Fishel Lakhover, "Warsaw: Metropolis of Polish Jewry," *Jewish Frontier* XII (1945): 11–13; Hilda Auerbach, "[Review of *Song of the Dnieper,* by Zalman Shneour]," *Jewish Frontier* XIII (1946): 45–46; Viktor Erlich, "A Monument to the Brave," review of *Fun a Jugnt*, by J. S. Hertz, *WCC* 14 (1946): 14–16; Samuel Adinoff, "Memories of Remez," *Jewish Frontier* XXVIII (1961): 50–53; Chaim Nachman Bialik, "Is There One Jewish Language?,"*Jewish Frontier* XXIX (1962): 16–21; Elias Schulman, "Yiddish in the Contemporary Jewish World," *WCC* 30 (1961): 13–15; Abraham Bick, "Rabbi Levi-Itzhok of Berdichev," *Jewish Currents* 14 (1959): 26–27, 42; Steve Nelson,

artists and tailors, rabbis and *luftmentschen,* most of them poor and oppressed, but at the same time carrying the grandeur of tradition and purpose in life.[41] East European Jewish life drew on traditional sources and modern impulses alike, and on the tensions among them, as they played out in the folk culture of the common people.

It was in this implicit notion of a folk-based cultural core of Jewishness that the diversity of images and the political message of the American Jewish left cohered. It offered its adherents the model of a vital, modernizing Jewishness that was as much cultural as it was political. Culture was in no way an escape from harsh political and material realities, but inextricably tied to the political core of Jewish leftism. Many journal articles that point to the absence of equal rights, political freedom, and economic opportunities for East European Jews note in the same breath the suppression of cultural self-expression in czarist Russia. "The people [were] as hungry for culture as they were for bread," wrote leading Yiddishist and leftist Itche Goldberg.[42] Yiddish culture was a vehicle of the politicization of East European Jewry, as it was through communal self-reflection that it constituted itself as an actor with distinct interests in cultural and political self-determination, to which Jewish Socialists gave expression and direction.[43] They valued cultural distinctiveness as part of their ideology. Jewish Socialism was predicated on the assumption that, in capitalist societies, ethnic identity was a constituent

---

"The National Question in the Soviet Union," *Jewish Life* 1 (1946): 8–14; "Minsk, Vilna, Pinsk, Grodno," 5.

41 Henry Goodman, "Mendele's Great Beginning," *Jewish Currents* 19 (1964) 7; Israel Knox, "A World to Remember," review of *The World of Sholem Aleichem*, by Maurice Samuel, *WCC* 13 (1944): 15; Knox, "Sholem Aleichem" (1946), 6. Similar tropes can be found in Hayim Greenberg, "What Is Happening to Soviet Jewry? An Open Letter to the Soviet Ambassador to the U.S.," *Jewish Frontier* XVIII (1951): 5; Ludwig Lewisohn, "Creative Nostalgia," review of *The World of Sholem Aleichem*, by Maurice Samuel, *Jewish Frontier* X (1943): 27; Max Rosenfeld, "The World of Yiddish Folksong: Ruth Rubin's 'Treasury' Opens a Window on Our Heritage," review of *Treasury of a People*, ed. by Ruth Rubin, *Jewish Currents* 18 (1964): 14.

42 I[tche] Goldberg, "Our Yiddish Literary Heritage: Its Meaning and Value for the English-Speaking Jew," *Jewish Currents* 15 (1960): 15; Baskin, "Fifty Years of the 'Bund,'" 4.

43 David E. Fishman, *The Rise of Modern Yiddish Culture* (Pittsburgh: University of Pittsburgh Press, 2005); Fishman, "The Bund and Modern Yiddish Culture," in *The Emergence of Modern Jewish Politics*, ed. Zvi Gitelman (Pittsburgh: Pittsburgh University Pr., 2003), 107–19; Jonathan Frankel, *Prophecy and Politics: Socialism, Nationalism, and the Russian Jews, 1862–1917* (Cambridge: Cambridge University Press, 1981); Emanuel S. Goldsmith, *Architects of Yiddishism at the Beginning of the Twentieth Century: A Study in Jewish Cultural History* (Rutherford, NJ: Farleigh Dickinson University Press, 1976), chap. 3; David H. Weinberg, *Between Tradition and Modernity: Haim Zhitlovsky, Simon Dubnow, Ahad Ha'am, and the Shaping of Modern Jewish Identity* (New York: Holmes & Meier, 1996), 83–86.

of class, historian Daniel Katz writes: "the struggle to assert cultural identity is a class struggle as well."⁴⁴ The struggle pointed to a revolution that would be initiated by workers rooted in various ethnic folk cultures, whose development would be part of the progress toward the social ideal of the historical process.⁴⁵

Readers of the American Jewish leftist publications were introduced to this message of political and cultural progress through the heroes of modern East European Yiddish culture. They captured their community in its struggle for material improvement, physical safety, political self-determination, and cultural expression. The journals, particularly *Jewish Life/Jewish Currents*, published numerous stories by Mendele, Sholem Aleichem, and Y. L. Peretz, the trio of "classic" Yiddish writers. They reviewed the growing number of translations and offered special editions and commemorative articles on important anniversaries.⁴⁶ Often, the Yiddish authors were employed as field guides to the East European past as the left saw it: a world in the throes of modernization, between tradition and modernity. Among its many functions, the *Fiddler* version of Sholem Aleichem's "Tevye" stories served as a prism for the left's perspective on the past. Reviewers presented Tevye as embodying the experience of his people: "a people tormented

---

44 Daniel Katz, *All Together Different: Yiddish Socialists, Garment Workers, and the Labor Roots of Multiculturalism* (New York: New York University Press, 2011), 5–6.

45 For the left, this applies to folk culture as much as to the more elevated Yiddish culture that emerged in the nineteenth century. Leftists would likely not make this distinction, or would try to obliterate it in the concept of one culture serving as a means to the spiritual survival of its bearers. Cf. B. A. Botkin, "Jewish Salt on Jewish Wounds," review of *A Treasury of Yiddish Folklore*, ed. by Nathan Ausubel, *Jewish Life* 3 (1948, Cultural Supplement): 27–29; Goldberg, "Yiddish Literary Heritage," 15.

46 Sholem Aleichem, "The Trial of Shomer: A Critical Essay," *Jewish Life* 3 (1949): 21–23; "A Proposal of 'Marriage,'" *Jewish Life* 7 (1953): 18–19; "'Heder' of Bygone Days," *Jewish Life* 7 (1953): 19–20; "An Easy Fast," *Jewish Life* 7 (1953): 20–22; "The Couple," *Jewish Frontier* XXI (1954): 16–21; Mendele Mocher Seforim, "Hershele," *Jewish Life* 1 (1946): 17–19; "What Does Chanukah Mean?" *Jewish Life* 2 (1947): 11–13; Y. L. Peretz, "Sisters," *Jewish Life* 5 (1951): 20–21; "Bontshe Silent," *Jewish Life* 4 (1949): 20–22; David Bergelson, "The Witness," *Jewish Life* 3 (1948): 12–16; Abraham Reisin, "The Revolution in the Little Synagogue," *Jewish Life* 9 (1956): 21–23. *Jewish Currents* devoted a special edition to Sholem Aleichem's centennial in 1959 (March 1959); the journal ran a column "News about the Sholem Aleichem Centennial." Reviews of Yiddish authors in translation include Israel Knox, "Peretz in English," review of *Prince of the Ghetto*, by Maurice Samuel, *WCC* 17 (1949), 8; Frances Butwin, "A New Translation of Peretz," review of *Three Gifts and Other Stories*, by Y. L. Peretz, *Jewish Life* 2 (1948): 29–30; H. Ben Elias, "The Yiddish Don Quixote," review of *Travels of Benjamin III*, by Mendele Mokher Sforim, *Jewish Life* 10 (1949): 28–29; Ludwig Lewisohn, "Of Yiddish Literature ," review of *A Treasury of Yiddish Stories*, ed. by Irving Howe and Eliezer Greenberg, *Jewish Frontier* XXII (1955): 27; Jacob Sloan, "The Education of Sholem Aleichem," review of *The Great Fair*, by Sholem Aleichem, *Jewish Frontier* XXII (1955): 28–30.

by the daily struggle for existence, repressions, and pogroms, a people stirred, at the same time, by dreams of new social developments."[47] The Workmen's Circle's Joseph Baskin described to his American comrades how this empowering development began to change the self-conception of East European Jewry: "Like an electric current these ideas spread among the Jewish masses. [... The] blind began to see, the deformed straightened up, and the lame began to walk. It is no exaggeration to say that the Jewish people took on a new countenance."[48] By the time Baskin wrote this, in 1948, the struggle was far from over for the left, given the condition of Jewry in postwar America, and the Jewish left set out to apply the spirit of its East European origin to its re-incarnation in the US.

Memory as Content, From a Means to an End

As it turned to the past in conceiving the American present, the left utilized a number of strategies familiar from other players, particularly the Yiddishists; however, it contributed a motif that other actors in the discourse used less often, but that had appeal beyond the left: the elevation of memory to a quasi-religious status.

One of the familiar perspectives the left espoused was the conviction that American Jewry would have to come into its own, inspired, but not measured, by the East European past. Several authors on the left therefore warned against gauging the authenticity of the emerging American Jewish culture by previous forms of Jewishness. "Our style of life, our *nusach,* cannot be a replica of a style which emerged out of other conditions and circumstances. But if it is to be an authentic and blessed style, it must build on that which was and not annul it," Knox declared, mixing cultural and religious terms of Jewish life. Despite its indebtedness to the East European past, some thinkers predicted that the new style or culture would be essentially American, and all the better and more authentic for it.[49] This new, American Jewish culture should be internally pluralistic and diverse, the left demanded. The editorial introduction to the *Workmen's Circle Call's* new supplement "Point of View" praised diversity as being constitutive of a

---

[47] H. Ben Elias, "Tevye Speaks English," review of *Tevye's Daughters*, by Sholem Aleichem, *Jewish Life* 3 (1949): 29; cf. also Robert Arnow, "Elegy for a Milkman," review of *Fiddler on the Roof*, *Jewish Currents* 20 (1964): 34–37.
[48] Baskin, "Fifty Years of the Bund," 4.
[49] Israel Knox, "Judaism as Insight," *WCC* 31 (1962): 15; cf. also Katz, "Development of Jewish Culture," 19–20.

healthy, vibrant community, which should be wary of uniformity. "Indeed, if there be cause for concern it is not because the American Jewish community speaks with many voices but because frequently these voices sing the same tune and recite the same text."[50] The diversity that the left advocated for American Jewry was based in the belief that the East European Jewish experience had been vital and authentic because it drew on an essence of Jewishness that integrated traditional and modern forms, enriched by exchange with local cultures. The result was a unique composition that united the best of many contributing cultures into a unique whole. Maurice Samuel stated this notion succinctly in a post-Holocaust eulogy in the *Jewish Frontier*:

> The Yiddish form of Jewishness, a particular and irreplaceable expression of eternal Jewishness, was a creation *sui generis*. Here was a world which achieved one of the most fascinating syntheses in human experience. Rooted spiritually in the old faith and philosophy we know as Judaism, it had found new and subtle expression for its values in media acquired locally: in the Yiddish language, in Polish dress, in Ukrainian melodies. Essential Judaism was not diluted or deflected thereby; it was enriched, it was confirmed in its direction.[51]

Just as East European *Yiddishkayt* was one particular expression of "eternal Jewishness," so would be American Jewishness, if it came of age and learned from Eastern Europe that, to be meaningful, Jewishness had to shape the individual and the community as a whole. "What was truly unique about the Eastern European Jewish communities and made their tradition *viable*, and indeed transformed it into a total civilization, was the fact that it also had a *style of life*," Knox wrote in the *Workmen's Circle Call*.[52] Tellingly, especially given the left's fundamental secularism, Samuel invoked Heschel's *The Earth Is the Lord's* in support of his portrayal of a comprehensive, spiritual sense of Jewishness. The left shared with Heschel and the Yiddishists around YIVO the perception that American Jewry was Jewishly too alienated and fragmented to be wholesome (spiritually in Heschel's reading, socio-psychologically from YIVO's perspective). The common diagnosis was: lack of a grounding in the Jewish past. Knox dismissed Sinclair's *Wasteland*, without even mentioning the author's name, for the distorted picture of Jewish life presented in the novel: "It is a tale of a family without a 'past,' or a 'heritage,'

---

50 "A Word of Introduction [to 'Point of View']," *WCC* 30 (1961): 9.
51 Samuel, "The Story That Must Build Itself," 18, emphasis in the original.
52 Knox, "To Cherish and to Preserve," 4, emphasis in the original; cf. also Knox, "Academic Committee for Yiddish Arts," *WCC* 26 (1957): 5–6; Knox, "[Review of *A Treasury of Yiddish Stories*, ed. by Irving Howe and Eliezer Greenberg]," *WCC* 26 (1957): 8–9; Knox, "The Arbeter Ring at Sixty," *WCC* 31 (1962): 13–15.

to light up its present, and with a present that is crude and meaningless," he fumed. "The final impression [...] is that of a *wasteland* – with a psychiatrist as king."⁵³ Just as the psychiatrist of the novel tried to reconcile the protagonist-patient Jake with his Jewish background, accomplishing a sense of identification and belonging, the left prescribed a therapy for American Jewry. Besides the defining political-ideological content of Socialism/Communism, it advocated a broad sense of cultural Jewishness, for individual Jews and the community; in doing so, like other groups within American Jewry, leftists drew on the East European past. A reviewer of poet Zalman Shneour's novel *Song of the Dnieper*, set in a shtetl, used the term "wholeness" three times on a single page in her reflections on Jewish life there and then. She suggested that such a wholesome Jewishness could inspire American Jews to develop a sensitivity and consciousness of their place within the continuity of Jewish history.⁵⁴ A Jewishness understood in this way as broadly cultural and progressively political would be the source of meaning for the modern Jew, as the religious tradition had been for previous generations.⁵⁵ In Knox's words: "Our task in America is to integrate our Jewishness and our socialism, loyalty to our people and devotion to America, to shape them into a seamless continuity and a meaningful pattern of life."⁵⁶

Culture was the intersection at which the various prescriptions for the future of American Jewry – aesthetic, religious, leftist – met. The meeting was based on some overlap in the understanding of what culture meant and what its role would be in the hoped-for new American Jewishness, but it was not without complications. Just as denominational thinkers warily sought to delineate its scope by subordinating it to religion, the left had to define how much religion could go into its secular Socialist understanding of cultural Jewishness. In this regard, too, the left shared a predicament with YIVO. Some on the left responded in a similar fashion by elevating Yiddish to the status of a secular mystique, from a medium to the

---

53 Israel Knox, "Wasteland It Remains," review of *Wasteland*, by Jo Sinclair, *WCC* 14 (1946): 8. Whereas he takes the description to be merciless realism, the reviewer for the *Jewish Frontier* praises the book for exposing a neurosis (Harry Salpeter, "Two Novels," review of *The Street*, by Ann Petry; *Wasteland*, by Jo Sinclair, *Jewish Frontier* XIII (1946): 46.
54 Auerbach, Review of *Song of the Dnieper*, 45. Other examples are Nathan Goldberg, "Solutions for the Jewish Problem/Simon M. Dubnow," *WCC* 11 (1943): 6–7; Ludwig Lewisohn, "Reflections on the Jewish Situation, Part II: What Are We?," *Jewish Frontier* XVII (1950): 7–11; Knox, "To Cherish and Preserve;" "Our Point of View," *WCC* 29 (1960): 4, 10; Zalman Yefroiken, "Our Schools: Meeting the Challenge of Change," *WCC* 35 (1964): 9; Goodman, "Mendele's Great Beginning."
55 Caroline Bunton, "The Road to Integration," *Jewish Frontier* XV (1948): 55. Ben Halpern urged self-proclaimed "alienated intellectual" Daniel Bell to find "community in history" ("Letter to an Intellectual [Response to Daniel Bell, 'Parable of Alienation']," *Jewish Frontier* XIII (1946): 15).
56 Israel Knox, "A Lesson for Us," *WCC* 16 (1948): 7.

embodiment of the spiritual values, cultural sensitivities, and mass-based political progressivism that together constituted the legacy of East European Jewry, which American Jews should accept and continue.[57] Without Yiddish, a Jewish child "can never be in complete communion with the Jewish spirit," Zalman Efron (Yefroiken), Yiddishist Labor activist, agreed in a programmatic article.[58] Knox took this approach to an extreme, by arguing that Yiddish was the vessel of all of Jewishness and thus ultimately untranslatable:

> Yiddish is more than a medium; it is more than content; it is a concept, a category in Jewish history and in Jewish experience. It is the summation of a thousand years of Jewish life. It is the Tzeena Urena of our grandmothers, the Talmudic chant of the heder; it is Hassidism and it also links us to the Sage of Vilna; it is the Jewish labor movement and it is also Zionism; and it is above all Yiddish literature which contains *lacrimae rerum* (the tears of things), the tears and joys of Jewish life. Jewish experience, traditions, values, history, dwell in Yiddish as they do not dwell in anything else – since Yiddish is inseparate from several hundreds of years of Jewish life. But the reverse is also true. Yiddish, if it is still to be significant, leads us back to Jewish values and traditions.[59]

However, this mystical linguistic essentialism was not uncontroversial. The *Jewish Life* rejected such ideas as exclusionary and so far removed from realities on the ground as to be politically harmful. "These people actually turn Yiddish into a weapon of reaction. They seek not only to split the ranks of the Yiddish-speaking cultural masses, but also consciously ignore the actual bi-lingualism of the Jewish national group in America. They thereby help to deepen the harmful cleavage between Yiddish and English speaking [sic] Jews."[60] Given the sectarian divisions within the left, its ambivalent relationship to the religious tradition, and the difficult balance between political universalism and ethno-cultural particularism, an apotheosis of the Yiddish language was bound to be controversial.

Historical memory offered safer ground for the left and other segments of American Jewry on which to meet and shape the future of a community in transition. "Never before, in our entire history, has self-awareness and knowledge of the true meaning of the Jewish past and present, a recognition of our part in the drama of the world, been so essential for well-being and spiritual health," the *Workmen's Circle Call* emphasized in a 1943 editorial, again echoing YIVO's per-

---

57 William Stern, "Tipping the Scales," *WCC* 25 (1956): 9.
58 Efron, "Our Approach to Jewish Life," 7.
59 Israel Knox, "In the Jewish World," *WCC* 25 (1956): 6–7.
60 Katz, "Development of Jewish Culture," 21. Even Stern, to whom Knox responded, had qualified his call for Yiddish education by stating that Yiddish "as a language [...] can only be a vehicle and not the heritage itself." ("Tipping the Scales (1956)," 9)

spective. "It would be tragic for Jewish youth to go on living in this world without an awareness of their history, their contribution to the civilization of mankind, their folk-language and folk-culture."[61]

What was required in the face of fundamental, unsettling disruptions was the conscious affirmation of the meaning that the unbroken chain of the Jewish tradition could offer to American Jewry, particularly by its links to the East European past. This required some deliberate lobbying in order to influence the processes of remembering and memorializing. The left repeatedly called for greater recognition of the contribution of East European Jews in America, which they felt was under-acknowledged in the quasi-official narratives crafted for the 1954 jubilee. "In the observance of the Tercentenary of Jewish life in America, we regard it as our particular responsibility [...] to depict the great contribution of the Eastern European Jews in America and that of the various branches of the Jewish labor movement of this country," the Workmen's Circle stated in an editorial.[62] Leftist journals warmly welcomed books preserving the heritage of East European Jewry as another means to anchor and legitimize it as valuable in the public consciousness. *Life is with People* was a case in point. "Its implications are particularly important for those of us who wish nowadays to come to terms with the Jewish tradition," reviewer Jacob Sloan wrote in the *Jewish Frontier*. "The *shtetl* is dead [but ...] we are still its epigones."[63] Given the role of Yiddish folk culture as the embodiment of the East European heritage, such works were often presented as cultural bridges across which a sense of meaning could be transmitted from past to present.[64] Knox hailed Maurice Samuel's presentation of Sholem Aleichem as one such bridge that would allow American Jews to find meaning and wholeness in their Jewishness by linking it to their East European heritage. "As we shape our own world here in America we must hold dear, we must cherish and preserve the memory of that world. Otherwise ours will be a world built on sand, without a foundation. Sholem Aleichem's tales will help us preserve that memory."[65]

---

61 "Back to School [Editorial]," *WCC* 11 (1943): 3, 5.
62 "Our Stand on Public Questions: Three Hundred Years of Jewish Life in America [Resolution adopted by W.C. Convention in Atlantic City]," *WCC* 23 (1954): 11. Similarly, C. Bezalel Sherman, "Reflections on the Tercentenary," *Jewish Frontier* XX (1953): 8–12; Morris U. Schappes, "The Tercentenary Celebration," *Jewish Life* 7 (1953): 12–15; J. C. Rich, "Jewish Labor in the Tercentenary," *WCC* 24 (1955): 2–4; Knox, "300 and 70."
63 Jacob Sloan, "The Shtetl in Retrospect: Life is also Within," *Jewish Frontier* XIX (1952): 28.
64 Cf. Rosenfeld, "The World of Yiddish Folksong," 9.
65 Israel Knox, "Books: The World of Sholem Aleichem, by Maurice Samuel," *WCC* 11 (1943): 17. Another example: Knox, "A Peretz Reader," *WCC* 20 (1952): 5–6; Knox, "Sholem Aleichem" (1946), 6.

Memory, of both the East European and the general Jewish past, emerged as the most important form of "content" for Jewishness in the writings of many leftist authors. It was not purely instrumental; it became an end in itself, providing content to the higher end of Jewish continuity. "Without continuity, Jewish life is bloodless, devoid of content," Efron wrote in his manifesto.[66] To legitimize the notion that memory was content, *Jewish Life* invoked and quoted philosopher Khayim Zhitlovski: "Then, what is the content of Jewish culture, secular or otherwise? 'The life of the Jewish people in its past insofar as it lies in the memory of the generations; its present, with all its struggles and conflicts [...]; its future, as it is striven for by various Jewish movements – that will always be the chief content of Jewish cultural expression.'"[67] Building on this conceptual foundation, Knox was the most articulate advocate of memory and historical consciousness, never tiring of the topic. "The pity is not that the world of Mendele, and Peretz and, above all, of Sholem Aleichem has vanished; the pity is that the *memory* of that world is vanishing and the knowledge of its meaning, its wisdom, its vision, its lore and – let us add quickly – its *language*," he wrote in 1944 and again in 1959.[68]

Preserving the Heritage – Sacred Duty in the Service of Continuity

In all this, the Jewish left took a position vis-à-vis the Jewish past to which other ideological actors may have subscribed: "We of the Workmen's Circle have an historical-cultural approach to Jewish life," read the opening line of the association's 1953 statement of principles. What followed, however, was a distinctly leftist program, which at the surface level divided the left from other segments of American Jewry, but at a deeper level offered common ground. "Our Jewishness is secular rather than religious, holding as we do that we are people bound together by a common destiny and common instincts," the statement continued, and clarified: "Our secularity is not a negative one, since we do not deny religion as such." The Workmen's Circle vowed to do everything possible "to

---

66 Efron, "Our Approach to Jewish Life," 8.
67 Max Rosenfeld, "Philosopher of Jewish Secularism," *Jewish Currents* 19 (1965): 31.
68 Knox, "A World to Remember," 15, emphasis in the original. Knox recycled this and other passages verbatim in his 1959 article "Sholem Aleichem." Cf. also Knox, "Portrait of a World That Was;" "Academic Committee for Yiddish Arts," *WCC* 26 (1957): 5–6.

preserve our culture, our language, our literature, our folkways, our traditions, and our customs, except for the religious aspects."[69]

The conceptual tightrope of winnowing "religion" from culture, folkways, and traditions – an exercise reminiscent of what religious thinkers attempted in *Judaism* – was resolved through a move that once again transcended the limits of what would appeal only to leftist American Jews: memory of the Jewish past in all its vital breadth became a sacred duty, in which the force of traditional religion coalesced with the modern need for a grounding in history; together, they formed a secular-sacred obligation for the sake of Jewish continuity. A connection was established between cultural memory and values held sacred: peoplehood, commemoration of the dead, Jewish survival and continuity. For Knox, this connection was formative, as his appreciation of Heschel's spiritual reconstruction of Ashkenazic Jewry and his linguistic mysticism further suggest.[70] If he spoke for more than just himself, the Jewish left acknowledged the religious dimensions of Judaism not only for tactical reasons, in order to tap into the religious *zeitgeist* of postwar America. Rather, it addressed the spiritual needs of a community which responded to the conflicting demands of the past and present in a complex way. On the one hand, American Jews bristled against the reduction of Jewishness to Judaism, a mere religion, by seeking out a broader concept, as even religious thinkers did. On the other hand, American Jews seemed unwilling to let go of the links in such a cultural notion between Jewishness and Judaism, an essentially religious tradition that had been severed and needed to be reconstructed. Several texts suggest that it was the Holocaust in particular that drove the move to draw together Jewishness and Judaism, cultural memory and sacred commemoration. It worked like a prism converging the different forces, as in the 1948 resolution by the Workmen's Circle that declared cultural continuity to be a quasi-religious obligation for American Jewry: "It is our sacred duty to become a constructive and creative Jewish community. We must strive to strengthen the national consciousness of the Jews in America. We must build our cultural heritage – the Jewish school movement, the Jewish theater, Jewish literature and every other form of spiritual enlightenment."[71]

---

[69] Efron, "Our Approach to Jewish Life," 6.
[70] Knox, "To Cherish and to Preserve;" Knox, "In the Jewish World" (September 1956).
[71] Workmen's Circle National Convention, "Resolution on Jewish Affairs," *WCC* 16 (1948): 17–18. Other authors countered the conflation of cultural memory and spirituality and insisted on a realism that would preserve in memory the mundane reality rather than a spiritual essence of East European Jewry. Art critic Harold Rosenberg in the *Jewish Frontier* criticized *Polish Jews*, the book of photographs by Roman Vishniac, introduced by a version of Heschel's 1945 YIVO speech, for presenting Jews "as pure spirits" rather than in their unidealized humanity (Harold Rosenberg,

By giving memory a sacred dimension, or channeling religious impulses into secular history, the left espoused a modern notion of culture as a secularized form of religion. The *Workmen's Circle Call's* editor, Israel Knox, came close to scholarly theories of modern religion, as he located cultural memory within the religious realm:

> the cultural activity of such 'secularist' Jewish groups as the Workmen's Circle, the Congress for Yiddish Culture, the Yiddish Scientific Institute [YIVO], fits into the pattern of America's Constitutional democracy. It is truly *spiritual* activity, concerned as much with the conscience as with the mind of the Jew in America. Unless one insists upon a tight and narrow definition of religion, as the Constitution does not, such activity – and all Jewish cultural activity – falls under the rubric of *religious equality or religious pluralism*.[72]

This emphasis on culture as a response to the spiritual needs of an unmoored American Jewry counterbalanced the materialism and universalism of the Jewish left's political agenda. It advocated *cultural* continuity for several reasons. Its fight against discrimination and suppression – under czarism in Russia and liberal capitalism in America, and by traditional Judaism – made it an agent of change and discontinuity in spheres in which continuity could have been located, such as traditional religion. Therefore, the American Jewish left, to borrow Roskies' imagery, could not and would not kidnap and repurpose important aspects of the Jewish past by embracing and romanticizing a pre-modern, a-political traditionalism for its present agenda. The left, like YIVO, therefore, faced an uphill struggle in postwar America. It suffered from the same thinning basis of first-generation immigrants who did not discard their own roots in Yiddish culture in favor of new commitments to American culture. Moreover, its Socialism further marginalized the left within a broadly liberal polity engaged in a Cold War with the motherland of this ideology. In the postwar decades, a Yiddish-based leftism was doomed to decline. Nevertheless, the left lent support to an understanding of Jewishness that would become the basis for broader segments of American Jewry. By advocating the secular sacredness of memory, the left offered American Jews a crucial way to channel traditional-religious impulses in modern ways that spoke to their spiritual needs. By preserving an understanding of *Yiddishkayt* as a distinct cultural and political sensitivity that could make for a broad and meaningful sense of Jewishness, it threw its weight behind the transformation that several other actors in the debate pushed.

"Pictures of Jews," review of *Polish Jews,* by Roman Vishniac; *The Vanished World,* by Raphael Abramovitch, *Jewish Frontier* XIV (1947): 30.

72 Israel Knox, "America in Jewish History," *WCC* 23 (1954): 4, emphasis in the original.

Elevating culture (and memory as a cultural phenomenon) as a source of meaning, replacing religion in this traditional function, is a development characteristic of Western modernity. In postwar America, it was a common move by various players to undermine the mid-century reduction of Jewishness to religion. While different groups within American Jewry – Yiddishists, secular intellectuals, religious thinkers and rabbis, leftists of different stripes – engaged with different periods, places, and persons of the past in elite journals, a broader American Jewish public encountered such cultural reconstructions of the past in more accessible, popular forms: on the radio, in schools, and in popular books.

7 Presenting a Rich Jewish Culture: *The Eternal Light* and *Life Is with People*

The elite discourse described in previous chapters shaped, and was shaped by, the imagination and self-understanding of rank-and-file Jews, who engaged competing reconstructions of the East European past in a vast number of popular cultural products. Which images and narratives of the East European past did these listeners and readers encounter? Were these images similar to the ones the elites discussed? What agendas did they serve and which functions did they have for the American Jewish community at mid-century? And (how) did mass-based, sometimes commodified depictions of the past shape the outcome of the competition among the different narratives vying for a dominant place in American Jewry's collective memory, which the elites tried to influence through memory engineering?

As different types of cultural products representing the past targeted different strata of American Jewry, the boundaries between scholarship and popular ideas, history and memory became blurred. Beginning in 1944, a popular radio show, *The Eternal Light*, set out to shape its audience's collective memory of the past for the sake of the present. A bestselling work of ethnography, *Life is with People* (1952), was undertaken under scholarly auspices, but was largely based on the memories of former East European Jews and shaped a romanticized imagery of the "old country" for American Jews. Textbooks for Jewish schools sought in their depictions of this past to balance a commitment to historical veracity with the mandate to socialize young Jews by helping them to link themselves with a collective, meaningful Jewish past.

The individuals and institutions involved in the dissemination and popularization of the East European Jewish heritage were driven by a heterogeneous mixture of motivations. Commercial interests, idealistic impulses, pedagogical methods, scholarly considerations, legal questions, and other factors shaped how the East European past was depicted. A brief look at the deliberations by publishers like the Jewish Publication Society (JPS) can illustrate the considerations that went into the cultural products that shaped the popular imagination of the Jewish past at mid-twentieth century.

An internal JPS paper, "The Search for a Policy," prepared for its publications committee in 1961, reflected how an idealistic elite felt a responsibility for the broader Jewish community in a time of transition. The JPS leadership aspired to provide cultural guidance by publishing books that would make the Jewish past meaningful to American Jews:

> A reading public exists; authors can be found. But the ultimate aim of creating a constructive, interpretive literature has been hardly begun. The fact is that such a literature must be created

DOI 10.1515/9783110499438-008

by each generation in its own terms. The creation of such a literature is more imperative now than ever before, lest we lose the mind of the present literate generation. Just because there are people ready to read and books to sate their appetites, we now have the obligation to plan for them and to lay before them an interpretation of Jewish thought and experience that is both truthful and stimulating. Just because there are other publishers who give them what they want, we must offer them what they need for understanding themselves as Jews.[1]

The final section of the quote suggests the perception of a risk that commercial interests and mass taste might jointly result in the commodification of a past that had to be protected as a resource for building Jewish identity. What was true of JPS, a non-profit publisher, also applied to commercial publishing houses like Schocken Books. Schocken's decision to make foundational texts of the Jewish experience available to broad audiences – as part of what turned out to be the "paperback revolution" – originated from a blend of idealistic and commercial considerations similar to those reflected in the JPS strategy paper.[2]

Publishers chose which texts on the East European past would be offered to the reading public.[3] In such decisions, often the interests of publishers and authors clashed. Maurice Samuel and his wife and executor Edith Samuel left a trail of letters in which they negotiated with their publishers, including Schocken, about revenues, new editions, and other practical aspects of bringing the East European heritage to American Jewry. In one case, Edith Samuel complained that the financial and advertising arrangements for a Schocken paperback edition of *The World of Sholom Aleichem* were inadequate: "Their payment was piddling, and their silence about it deafening – this at a time when FIDDLER ON THE ROOF which derives from THE WOLRD OF SHOLOM ALEICHEM was having a tremendous worldwide success."[4]

---

[1] Anon. [Solomon Grayzel?], "The Publication Committee of the JPS: Agenda For The Meeting on October 15, 1961," typescript, American Jewish Archives, JPS records, MS-388, folder 3, 2–3. On JPS in general, cf. Jonathan D. Sarna, *JPS: The Americanization of Jewish Culture, 1889–1989: A Centennial History of the Jewish Publication Society* (Philadelphia: Jewish Publication Society, 1989).

[2] Cf. Altie Karper, "A History of Schocken Books in America, 1945–2013," in *Konsum und Gestalt: Leben und Werk von Salman Schocken und Erich Mendelsohn vor 1933 und im Exil*, ed. Antje Borrmann, Doreen Mölders and Sabine Wolfram (Berlin: Hentrich & Hentrich, 2016), 272–76. In 1962, *Life is with People* was a prominent Schocken publication; David G. Roskies, "The Shtetl as Imagined Community," in *The Shtetl: Image and Reality*, ed. Gennady Estraikh and Mikhail Krutikov (Oxford: Legenda, 2000), 6.

[3] The JPS publications committee decided in 1961 "to give up the plan of co-publishing with Yivo the translation of [Elias] Cherikower's book on the History of Jewish Labor in America," whereas Bernard Weinryb's *A History of the Jews of Poland* was listed as "well on the way to acceptance." (Solomon Grayzel, "Minutes of the Publication Committee, April 30, 1961," typescript, American Jewish Archives, JPS records, MS-388, folder 3)

[4] Cf. Maurice Samuel, "[Letter to Alfred A. Knopf]," November 16, 1947; "Letter to Joseph C. Lesser of Alfred E. Knopf]," December 30, 1951; [Edith] Mrs. Maurice Samuel, "[Letter to William

Copyright and licensing aspects may have actually determined even the genre of *The World of Sholom Aleichem* (1943), Maurice Samuel's seminal book – one of the most influential vehicles to reconstruct an East European past for American Jewish readers. In a 1942 letter to Maurice Samuel, Olga Rabinovitz, Sholom Aleichem's widow, expressed her support for the planned book, provided that it would not merely translate Sholom Aleichem's original texts, but "describe persons, places, incidents, customs, folklore etc., by way of illustrating the world which Sholom Aleichem re-created," and use translated quotations – "of not more than two or three paragraphs" – as Samuel should need.[5] Further letters illustrated yet other aspects of the publishing process for texts on the East European past. Maurice Samuel urged his publisher Alfred E. Knopf to sell *The World of Sholom Aleichem* and *Prince of the Ghetto* as a boxed set, as "they form, together, an introduction to the Yiddish-speaking world."[6] If Knopf had agreed, the status of the books as authoritative texts on the East European past might have been further enhanced by their material presentation, as dictated by commercial considerations.

Questions of scholarly and aesthetic authority versus emotional needs and attendant commercial potential drove the discourse made up of elite and popular reconstructions of the past. The different perspectives on the past co-existed and competed – until those who had started the discourse in earnest, the secular, literary-minded intellectuals, conceded defeat. As a later chapter will show, searching for Jewish meaning in aesthetics, they turned to Hasidism and to literary depictions of the East European past as reservoirs and vehicles of its spiritual depth – only to find out that American Jewry at large voted with their feet for representations that seemed to fulfill much less existentially deep yearnings and, by these intellectuals' rating, a much less existentially deep meaning of Jewishness.

The Eternal Light: East European Spiritual Jewishness Made Audible

On the spectrum between elite, highbrow reconstructions of the past and its commodification for entertainment purposes, the radio show *The Eternal Light*

Koshland of Alfred E. Knopf]," December 26, 1972, typescripts, American Jewish Archives, Maurice Samuel papers (MS-89), box 36, folder 20, 25; emphasis in the original.
5 Mrs. [Olga] Sholom Aleichem Rabinowitz, "[Letter to Maurice Samuel]," May 28, 1942, typescript, American Jewish Archives, Maurice Samuel papers (MS-89), box 36, folder 25.
6 Maurice Samuel, "[Letter to Alfred E. Knopf]," November 16, 1947, typescript, American Jewish Archives, Maurice Samuel papers, (MS 89), box 36, folder 20.

occupied a middle ground. It started in October 1944 as a cooperative effort between NBC and the Jewish Theological Seminary in New York. The 30-minute episodes were produced by JTS and given free airtime each Sunday as public service programming for religious groups.[7] JTS president Louis Finkelstein jumped at the opportunity to create the first major Jewish equivalent to existing Christian radio shows, and invested considerable resources in the project.[8] *The Eternal Light* presented original radio dramas, then a new genre, performed by professional actors and a live orchestra. Often, the dramatic portion of an episode was followed by a three-minute commentary by a Jewish religious or communal leader, building on the drama's topic or relating it to a current event. The show explained Judaism's basic religious concepts, retold Biblical and Talmud stories, and recounted pivotal events in Jewish history.[9] Even though it was placed in the "Sunday ghetto" of religious programs, when it aired first at 11 a.m. and later at 12.30 p.m., *The Eternal Light* turned out to be a great success, as measured by the growing number of NBC affiliates carrying it, its critical reception, listener responses, and ratings: JTS claimed up to six million listeners, which made the program an influential popularizer of the topics it broadcast.[10] Listening to the show became an important Sunday ritual for many families, who dressed up for the occasion and gathered around the radio. Listeners could order scripts of the original dramas, which were then staged as school plays.[11] Much of the credit for the show's appeal goes to

---

[7] Michele Hilmes, "NBC and the Network Idea: Defining the 'American System,'" in *NBC: America's Network*, ed. Michele Hilmes (Berkeley: University of California Press, 2007), 20–21; cf. also Stewart M. Hoover and Douglas K. Wagner, "History and Policy in American Broadcast Treatment of Religion," *Media, Culture and Society* 19 (1997): 7–27. JTS holds the copyright of the program scripts.

[8] Cf. Henry Sapoznik, "Broadcast Ghetto: The Image of Jews on Mainstream American Radio," *Jewish Folklore and Ethnology Review* 16 (1994): 37–39; see also David S. Siegel and Susan Siegel, *Radio and the Jews: The Untold Story of How Radio Influenced America's Image of Jews, 1920s–1950s* (Yorktown Heights: Book Hunter Press, 2007).

[9] The analysis of the show is based on the scripts preserved by JTS. The topics of shows from which no scripts were preserved were gleaned from Eli Segal, *The Eternal Light: The Unauthorized Guide to the Superb NBC Broadcast Series* (Newtown, CT: Yesteryear Press, 2005), a non-scholarly tribute by the son of the show's long-time cantor, Robert Segal.

[10] Undated printed brochure (late 1940s?) produced by JTS (JTS Archive, RG 11-C, box 27, folder 11). JTS collected numerous listeners' responses; they were preserved in processed form (typed-up quotes from selected letters, without full information on senders, dates etc. (JTS Archive, RG 11-C, box 26)

[11] JTS, *Eternal Light*. In his 1979 novel *The Ghost Writer*, considered autobiographical, Philip Roth relates such a ritual. (Cf. Jeffrey Shandler and Elihu Katz, "Broadcasting American Judaism: The Radio and Television Department of JTS," in *Tradition Renewed: A History of the Jewish*

head writer Morton Wishengrad, a labor organizer for whom work on the show was a way to return to the Judaism from which he had been alienated.[12]

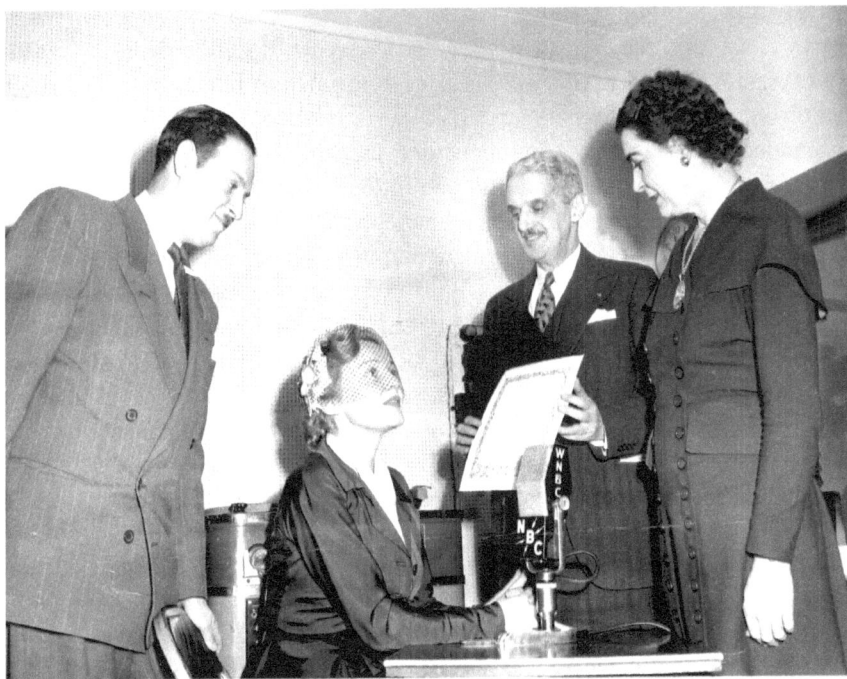

Figure 18: Protagonists of *The Eternal Light* at the ceremony of the Annual Brotherhood Award, which the radio show received for the second time in 1950. From left: Moshe Davis of JTS, program editor; Madeleine Carroll of the National Conference of Christian and Jews, which sponsored the award; Edgar J. Nathan, Jr., NY Supreme Court Justice and chairman of the *Eternal Light* Committee; and Doris Corwith, Director of Religious Radio for NBC. (The Library of The Jewish Theological Seminary)

Finkelstein regarded *The Eternal Light*, which ran well into the 1970s and spawned an eponymous hour-long TV show, as a key component of his larger project: to restore Judaism (and religion in general) to its former importance, by presenting it as a source of spiritual coherence, values, and meaning for Jews and American

---

Theological Seminary of America [vol. II:] Beyond the Academy, ed. Jack Wertheimer (New York: JTS Press, 1997), 390)
12 Morton Wishengrad, *Eternal Light* (New York: Crown, 1947).

can society more broadly. The program was therefore deliberately aimed at both Jewish and non-Jewish listeners.¹³ In this approach, *The Eternal Light* reflected the spirit of postwar America in bringing the insights religion offered into human nature to bear on the spiritual malaise of the time, when wars, perceptions of urban crisis, and technological acceleration seemed to undermine the stability of American society and polity, or even the fate of humanity. Like Joshua Loth Liebman with his bestselling advice book *Peace of Mind*, *The Eternal Light* responded to the exigency by employing Judaism as a solution.¹⁴ The radio program specifically addressed the perception that American Jews, facing the new challenges and opportunities in America and the Jewish world, were in need of orientation in finding the meaning of their Jewishness, an adolescent community in search of its identity. "We [...] are very much in need of spiritual guidance," a listener from Lyndonville, Vermont, admitted in a letter to *The Eternal Light*.¹⁵ The program aimed to provide such guidance by presenting the Jewish tradition as a wellspring of spiritual experience, honed over the centuries, that could benefit non-Jews and Jews alike, often by drawing on the richness of Jewish history since Biblical times.

Among the approximately 800 episodes that aired between 1944 and the early 1960s, more than 50 dealt explicitly with the East European Jewish past.¹⁶ These segments portrayed the founder of the *musar* movement, Israel Salanter, the Vilna Gaon, the Ba'al Shem Tov, and the Hasidic rebbe Levi-Yitshak of Berditchev; they dramatized stories by Sholem Aleichem, Y. L. Peretz, and Isaac Bashevis Singer; retold Hasidic tales as well as stories of the fools' town of Chelm and of Hershel Ostropolier; recounted the 1648 Khmelnytzkyi massacres and the destruction of the Volozhin Yeshivah, the rescuing of YIVO's Vilna library and the persecution of Jewish writers in post-1945 USSR.¹⁷

---

13 Shandler/Katz, "Broadcasting American Judaism," 366–68; Marjorie G. Wyler, "The Eternal Light: Judaism on the Airwaves,"*Conservative Judaism* 39 (1986/87): 18–22 (Wyler oversaw the program as JTS director of public relations). Jeffrey Shandler, *Jews, God, and Videotape: Religion and Media in America* (New York: New York University Press, 2009), 83; JTS, *Eternal Light: A Historical Perspective* (DVD; New York: JTS 2006).
14 Joshua Loth Liebman, *Peace of Mind* (New York: Simon & Schuster, 1946).
15 "Excerpts from letters received by Eternal Light program," 1946, typescript; RG 11-C, box 26, folder 39.
16 Even more episodes were set in Eastern Europe, but used the setting only as a backdrop to address more universal questions. The growing number over time of repeat productions of earlier shows make a precise tabulation of both the absolute number of (original) shows and the share of East European-themed ones difficult.
17 "Rabbi Israel Salanter," January 21, 1945, "His Excellency of Vilna," December 19, 1948, "The Fourth Crown," May 6, 1951, "The Song of Berditchev," February 23, 1947; Sholem Aleichem stories

Through engaging presentations on topics like these, *The Eternal Light* partook in the lively public discourse about at least one East European Jewish past, presenting key concepts, events, and personalities in accessible, entertaining, often humorous but also profound ways. The wide range of topics and periods covered by the program did not make for a single consistent narrative of *one* East European past. Yet, several larger motifs ran through a number of segments and shaped how this past was made usable for the present.

Several such motifs were expressed by "Joseph," a fictitious American lawyer and the narrator of a segment that presented his pre-immigration life in Poland to his largely uncomprehending, American-born offspring. "[My] first life, my youth in the old country, is a lost world to my children. This first life of mine is a sort of museum piece. But, perhaps, if I set it down, my children may see its strange beauty and terror."[18] Joseph's speculative monologue made the East European past appear far away, detached geographically and culturally from the American present. For Joseph, linking the two seemed like a difficult, but ultimately rewarding, process. The strangeness of the past lay in its paradoxical nature: the "terror" of hostilities, poverty, persecution, and destruction, and a "beauty" that seemed strange for its otherworldly piety, naïve innocence, and self-contained coherence.

Such demarcations between inside and outside the Jewish world formed a crucial, pervasive aspect of the presentation of the East European Jewish past in the *Eternal Light* as much as in other cultural products. The dividing line between inside and outside was sharply drawn to strengthen the Jewish world against its antitheses. The otherness against which it was defined included a wide range of social groups, ideas, and phenomena that highlighted the social, spiritual, and ethical distinctiveness of Jews. The "others" included Czarist officials and peasants, Nazi invaders and Soviet officials. In some cases, more abstract developments intruded on what seemed the time capsule of East European Jewry: Technological innovations such as railroads and the telephone challenged its quaint, innocent insularity embodied by the *shtetl*, which defined something

---

(selection): "The Great Purim Scandal," March 17, 1946, "The Miracle of Hashono Rabo," October 13, 1946, "The Fiddle," May 4, 1947; Peretz stories (selection): "The Man Who Flew to Heaven," July 29, 1945, "If Not Higher," September 16, 1945/November 11, 1951, "Transmigration of a Melody," March 11, 1951; Singer story: "The Little Shoemakers," May 1, 1955; Chelm stories: "The Melamed, His Wife, the Rabbi and the Goat," February 29, 1948, "The New Synagogue of Chelm," May 25, 1952;" "The Merry Jests of Hershel of Ostropolier," January 9, 1949; 1648: "The Choice," May 27, 1951; Volozhin: "The Voice," December 26, 1954; YIVO: "The Golden Chain," April 24, 1960; Soviet persecution: "Wipe the Stain Away," September 29, 1957.

18 "Hear, Ye Sons," July 15, 1945, 1–2; "Hear, Ye Sons, Part II," July 22, 1945.

of an ideal world. The distinctions between this ideal and its adversaries could run within Jewry rather than against the outside world, such as in stories that contrasted mass poverty with the new class of wealthy Jewish magnates. In such stories, the *Eternal Light* transmitted a familiar stereotype which cultural historian Alissa Solomon has called "the most enduring and endearing shtetl ideal: that its 'prosperity was spiritual rather than material.' This became the overriding trope of American remembrances of Eastern European Jewry."[19]

This spiritual character was indeed the catch-all quality which made the past seem coherent and allowed the producers of the show to present the world of East European Jewry as appealing and usable for their distinctly religious agenda. In keeping with the legal requirements of the programming, JTS's mission, and the mid-century American embrace of religion, many *Eternal Light* installments conflated "spirituality" with "piety," which they suggested was characteristic of East European Jewry – and relevant for their contemporary American listeners. The narrator of the segment on Israel Salanter introduced him as "a man of piety and wisdom [living] a life of gentle and scrupulous devotion to the Law." His humble and compassionate spirit was illustrated by a scene in which Salanter, despite being in a hurry, waited for a lame man, and, chastised for it by his wife, defended himself by invoking a Talmudic precept. In the commentary following the dramatic portion, Samuel Kramer, introduced as a leader of Orthodoxy, spoke about the importance of Salanter as a model character for later generations.[20] In the segment "Once Upon a Time" broadcast in 1955, Samuel, a young man, came to a village. He explored the pious way of life of the archetypal villagers, looking for answers to his own doubts and questions. Following the dramatic portion, commentator Louis Stein, identified for the radio show as a prominent civic leader, spelled out the show's message: "It was only when he understood the villagers, did Samuel realize that they held the secret to the treasure he had been seeking all his life. He knew then that a full and happy life was the result of devotion and kindness: faith and charity, and not wealth and luxury."[21]

---

[19] Alisa Solomon, *Wonder of Wonders: A Cultural History of "Fiddler on the Roof"* (New York: Henry Holt, 2013), 55.
[20] "Rabbi Israel Salanter," 2–4, 11–12. Other prominent personalities of East European Jewry are depicted in similar terms of piety, cf. programs on the Vilna Gaon and the various Hasidic figures.
[21] "Once Upon a Time," January 30, 1955, 12–13; "The Song of Berditchev," February 23, 1947, 9. Other segments depicting East European piety include "The Sabbath of Chayim, the Porter," February 3, 1946; "The Tender Grass," March 30, 1947; "The Fiddle," May 4, 1947; "The Fourth Crown," May 6, 1951; "The Transgressions of Judel Kirschenstein," February 6, 1955; "Once Upon a Sabbath," January 13, 1957; "Investigation at Medziboz," April 23, 1961.

Piety was, in these and other episodes, closely connected to other aspects that fit the American context of the program. East European Judaism was depicted as infused with a profound ethics, making it the source of universal values. Some of the East European-themed episodes focused on large and abstract ethical questions, such as the show on the Khmelnytzkyi massacres, in which several characters disagreed about the legitimacy of violent resistance. Other episodes humorously described an otherworldly, innocent saintliness of one "Reb Yisroel," whose naïve selflessness stretched the patience not just of his wife, but also of the angels sent to investigate him. More programs, however, focused on smaller-scale, everyday questions of ethical behavior, such as Salanter's empathy for the lame.[22]

Portraying religious commitment and ethical ideals as hallmarks of East European Judaism, the *Eternal Light* reflected Finkelstein's mission to present Judaism to mid-century America as a venerable resource, or even as the ultimate source, of values that linked the Jewish and American traditions as congenial. Programs that presented Jewish suffering from, and occasional resistance against, Czarist tyranny and Soviet persecution pointed to the shared Jewish and American desires for political and religious freedom. The dramatization of the rescuing of the YIVO library was a case in point. It emphasized the American role in the effort and gave former US military commander General Lucius D. Clay the opportunity to admonish listeners to "remain determined never again to let those who would destroy the lives and culture of any people to attain the power to accomplish their ruthless aim."[23] Similarly, the shared religious values made Judaism the senior partner in the newly coined concept of a Judeo-Christian heritage that underlay the American value of interfaith brotherhood.[24] The civil-religious patriotism, which the East European past was made to serve, was illustrated succinctly by a quote from Sholem Aleichem's *Adventures of Mottl, the Cantor's Son* which was used as the title for its *Eternal Light* dramatization: The show "Try Not to Love Such a Country" juxtaposed the poverty and limitations of

---

22 "The Choice," May 5, 1951; "The Parable of Reb Yisroel," January 13, 1946; "A Chassidic Tale," December 16, 1945; "The Four Spinsters of Gimel," January 23, 1949.
23 "The Golden Chain," April 24, 1960, 12–13; cf. also "My Son, the Convict," March 30, 1958; "The Voice," December 26, 1954; "Touro Synagogue: A Rhode Island Refuge," October 8, 1944; "Emanu-El – God Is With Us," October 15, 1944; "The Tender Grass," March 30, 1947; "A Duty of Conscience," October 8, 1950.
24 "How the World Came to Yanovke," March 4, 1951; "How Rabbi Kalman Disappeared," February 20, 1955; non-East European-themed programs of this focus included "The Legend of the Mountain," February 16, 1947; "Esther," March 21, 1948; "The Man from Omaha," May 2, 1948; "Gandhi," February 20, 1949; "Passport to the World," February 19, 1950.

Jewish life in the old world with the new opportunities of the immigrants.²⁵ If the depiction of piety as a constitutively human trait and the religious legitimization of American values implied a universalist outlook of the *The Eternal Light*, the show balanced it, however, with elements that supported a sense of Jewish distinctiveness, albeit one limited to the sphere of religion. Salanter invoked the Talmud and Reb Levi-Yitshak of Berditchev sang a form of the *Kaddish*, thus introducing distinctly Jewish expressions of ethical norms and religious spirituality. These moves mirrored the general thrust of the program. Its topics, speakers, and advertisements clearly identified it as an emphatically Jewish show, and it portrayed Judaism as the oldest of several religions, with which it sought to live in brotherly cooperation.²⁶

Aestheticizing Judaism – On a "High Church" Note

Part of the program's double mission – to secure acceptance for Judaism within the Judeo-Christian heritage while preserving meaningful Jewish distinctiveness – was the aestheticizing of Judaism and Jewishness according to postwar American middle-class norms: in other words, an Americanization of Jewishness. Besides avoiding stereotypical and disfavored ethnic markers, such as the Yiddish-inflected speech associated with ethnic humor driving shows like "The Goldbergs," the use of music played a key role. The show's opening musical theme, "Shomer Israel," established its "high church" musical proclivities.²⁷ The aesthetic choices were shaped by the needs of the medium radio. It called for acoustic elements to structure the show, set its tone, and enhance the dramatic effect. The producers of the *Eternal Light* frequently picked Hasidic melodies for this purpose. Assuming that for many listeners these tunes

---

25 "Try Not to Love Such a Country," December 27, 1953.
26 Cf. Markus Krah, "Role Models or Foils for American Jews? *The Eternal Light*, Displaced Persons, and the Construction of Jewishness in Mid-Twentieth-Century America,"*American Jewish History* 96 (2010; publ. 2012): 280–81.
27 Shandler, *Jews, God, and Videotape*, 68–71, 84–86; Sapoznik, "Broadcast Ghetto," 38. For an analysis of an entertainment program playing on the ethnic dimension, cf. Donald Weber, "The Jewish-American World of Gertrude Berg: The Goldbergs on Radio and Television, 1930–1950," in *Talking Back: Images of Jewish Women in American Popular Culture*, ed. Joyce Antler (Waltham: Brandeis University Press/Hanover: University Press of New England, 1998), 85–99. For contemporary perspectives, see Morris Freedman, "The Real Molly Goldberg: Baalebosteh of the Air Waves [From the American Scene]," *Commentary* 21 (April 1956): 359–64; Israel Knox, "'The Goldbergs': Pseudo-Humor," *Workmen's Circle Call* 18 (1950): 5.

embodied what "Joseph" called the "strange beauty" of the old country, this choice served both to express particularistic self-confidence and to lodge these Jewish aesthetics into a more universal canon of acceptable religious music. The historical association of Hasidism with music was an important factor that made the Hasidic movement more easily accessible than other ideological groups within the Jewish tradition. Moreover, the use of folk-inspired music to express Judaism and Jewishness, as dictated by the needs of radio as a medium, contributed to their reconstruction in cultural terms, albeit safe ones, rather than religious terms.

For this key development, another aspect of the *Eternal Light* was crucial. It depicted the East European past as part of a folk identity that transcended the narrow, religious definition of "Judaism" and pushed it toward a broader category of "Jewishness" as a coherent civilization based on a religiously-grounded common culture. This sense of a comprehensive folk Jewishness was transmitted in many episodes, particularly, again, those based on Sholem Aleichem stories. In a dramatization of Maurice Samuel's *World of Sholom Aleichem*, the various characters of the fictitious townlet of Kasrilevke appeared, "Tevye" most prominent among them, as archetypes of the folksy, good-natured but proud, pious but irreverent, half-learned but *shtetl*-street smart, proud East European Jew. The Yiddish writer as narrator of the radio show made explicit how the folk piety of his characters made for an all-encompassing sense of Jewishness: "There was no division between life and faith. Religion wasn't something tacked on to life. It was life itself. ... And yet they never speak of religion ... it is something understood ... like being human."[28]

Other episodes similarly presented innocent, comprehensive folk piety as characteristic of East European Jewry. On one program, the *shtetl* rabbi got lost in the forest for several days. When rescued, he had lost track of the days of the week, but was adamant that what was actually a workday was Shabbat. Out of respect, the entire town played along for weeks. Ultimately, the new order caused chaos, as it collided with external factors, such as economic relations with peasants; but, before that, it seemed like an innocent attempt to preserve the stability and coherence of a community based on Jewish norms. The commentator on another show spelled out this motif. Looking at the complexities and tensions of modern societies, he asserted that "because of the tenacious preservation of the Jewish tradition, a sense of community could be established, and people could warm to each other because of their similar beliefs, practices and

---

28 "Sholom Aleichem," March 4, 1945, 6–8, omissions in the original.

language," core elements of a common culture.²⁹ Not coincidentally, the commentary was related to a show that emphasized the role of Yiddish as a vehicle and expression of spiritual coherence and social homogeneity. Another Sholem Aleichem-based program portrayed a close-knit, closed-off community based in a common culture, so distinct that it required a dramatized glossary of key terms:

> One: Nasch. A nasch, the noun. To nasch, the verb.
> Narrator: What is a nasch? A between-meals snack, a sample, a lick of the tongue, a tidbit. Not good enough. A nasch is a nasch.
> Two: Hamantasch.
> Narrator: Hamantasch. A special Purim cake, a Haman's hat, triangular in shape with a sweet hard crust and a stuffing of poppyseed, ground nuts, and honey. Purim without hamantasch is Hamlet without the Prince.³⁰

Purim cakes, Yiddish, Hasidic melodies, or food, language, and music as expressions of the folk spirit, show that while the Jewishness of Eastern Europe was based on religion, it was lived in a comprehensive folk culture. In the depiction by *The Eternal Light,* the basis of this specific culture in timeless religious values suggested that continuities across time and space were possible. The East European past was presented as distant, but still so much in transition that it could be made usable for the present. An East European Jewish culture trying to preserve its spirit in the throes of modernization could serve as a model, the *Eternal Light* argued, as it tried to make Judaism meaningful and beautiful for American Jews and non-Jews in search of new expressions of spirituality. Thus, more than other depictions of the East European past, the program subscribed to the concept of Jewishness by Judaism, letting religion, as narrowly defined in postwar America, determine Jewish distinctiveness. *The Eternal Light* did portray East European Jewish life as a spiritual culture, emphasizing the comprehensiveness, it expanded the scope of Judaism as the basis of Jewishness. Adhering closely to notions pondered by religious thinkers in the journal *Judaism,* the program – run by a rabbinical seminary and regulated by quasi-legal definitions of religious programming that reflected Christian understandings of religion – it placed even greater emphasis on the *spiritual* foundation of the culture that had to be compatible with a more universal, interreligious American culture.

---

29 "The Broken Sabbath of Rabbi Asher," November 3, 1946; "The Way of My Uncle Gedalia," April 4, 1957. The commentator was Moses Hornstein, identified as a community leader associated with JTS.
30 "The Great Purim Scandal," March 17, 1946, 3; cf. also "The Miracle of Hashono Rabo," October 13, 1946.

Life Is with People: Ethnography Presents a Rich East European Jewish Culture

If *The Eternal Light* gave its listeners "high church" Judaism, *Life is with People* gave them *shtetl* Jewishness. The study was published in 1952, midway through the 25-year period under consideration here.[31] Whereas for book publishers it was commercial considerations and for radio it was the medium that shaped representations of the East European past, for *Life is with People* it was the scholarly discipline of cultural anthropology. Its rise flanked the shift toward social history and the scholarly interest in the day-to-day experience of broader segments of society. In *Life is with People,* this approach led to a portrayal of an East European Jewish culture as spiritually suffused and thoroughly Jewish, which made it eminently usable for readers looking for an authentic Jewishness beyond what mere "religion" could offer.

Over some 430 pages, the book cast a sympathetic eye across the breadth of pre-World War I *shtetl* life. Based on interviews with former inhabitants and their descendants, written documents, literary texts by Sholem Aleichem, Mendele, Peretz, and others, as well as on secondary sources, it described the community from the inside: activities and atmosphere on Shabbat and on weekdays, the life cycle ("from the kheyder to the grave"), social hierarchies and gender roles, synagogue life and the functions of the rabbi, superstition and ignorance in worldly matters, life at home and the *shtetl* perspective on children, economic life, and holidays.[32]

In her foreword, prominent cultural anthropologist Margaret Mead, who with her late colleague Ruth Benedict supported the project, stated the purpose of the book in the context of anthropology: to study and preserve cultures "outside the

---

[31] Mark Zborowski and Elizabeth Herzog, *Life is with People: The Jewish Little-Town of Eastern Europe* (New York: International Universities Press, 1952). Zborowski (1908–1990) was the senior author. Born in Uman near Kiev, he drew on some personal recollections of East European Jewish life. Before coming to the US in 1941, he studied in Berlin and Paris toward a degree in anthropology. In Paris, he was recruited by Stalin's Soviet intelligence service, mainly to spy on Trotskyites. During his work on *Life is with People* in the 1940s, his activities as a spy went publicly unnoticed; they were exposed in the mid-1950s and resulted in a prison sentence (Frank Fox, "Mark Zborowski: The Spy Who Came Out of the 'Shtetl,'" *East European Jewish Affairs* 29 (1999): 119–28).

[32] Elizabeth Herzog and Mark Zborowski, "Preface," in *Life is with People*, 23. The notion that literary texts could serve as primary sources much like first-hand memories suggests a perception of Yiddish literature as a genre of ethnography that is addressed in greater detail in the following chapter.

main currents of history," as they were disappearing or, in the case at hand, after they had been destroyed. "This book is an attempt to bring our anthropological discipline to the task of preserving something of the form and the content, the texture and the beauty, of the small-town life of Eastern European Jews, as it was lived before World War I, in some places up to World War II."[33] Controversially, the authors, Mark Zborowski and Elizabeth Herzog, constructed from their raw material a synthetic *shtetl*, rather than locating contingent phenomena in their respective historical and geographical contexts; nor did they attribute the information gained from their interviews.[34] They called the result a composite portrait: "The effort has been made to capture the core of continuity running through the Jewish culture of Eastern Europe rather than the details in which localities and regions differed."[35] Mead explained that the study was "devoted to catching the essence of a culture." In the process, with little explanation or justification, the authors came to equate the *shtetl* culture they constructed with a generic East European Jewish culture in general (and thereby compromised its credibility as an anthropological documentation).[36] This culture was described in loving, nostalgic terms and in a literary style that immersed the reader in the *shtetl* world of yore. A section from the chapter "Sabbath Eve" serves as an illustration:

> The shtetl housewife wakes up earlier than usual with the thought, "Today is Erev Shabbes – I must hurry!" Even if she usually works at the shop or market, on this day she will stay at home to prepare for the reception of the Queen Sabbath. First of all she pours over her hands the "fingernail water" – water that stood by her bed overnight in a glass or a cup to be at hand for the ritual ablution that must start each day, and says the short morning prayer with which each day must begin. Then she puts on her oldest dress, her work apron, ties a kerchief over her head, and rolls up her sleeves.
>
> Before the others are awake she "fires the oven" with logs so that it will be ready for use. She feeds her family as they appear, as quickly as possible, and bundles the boys off to school. Meanwhile she inspects the dough that she set to rise last night for the Sabbath loaf, the *hallah*. She begins to clean the chicken that she bought yesterday, watching anxiously – "it shouldn't happen!" – for any forbidden flecks of blood, blister on the gizzard or other calamity that would raise doubts whether her chicken was *kosher* – ritually fit to eat.

---

[33] Margaret Mead, "Foreword," in *Life is with People*, 9, 11. On the genesis of the project within the context of American cultural anthropology, cf. Barbara Kirshenblatt-Gimblett's introduction to the 1995 edition of the book (New York: Schocken), xxv.
[34] For contemporaneous methodological criticism, cf. Yudel Mark, "The Shtetl in Retrospect: Pseudo-Science,"*Jewish Frontier* XIX (1952): 26–27; Moshe Decter, "The 'Old Country' Way of Life: The Rediscovery of the Shtetl," *Commentary* 13 (June 1952): 601; an example of later criticism is Ben Cion Pinchuk, "Jewish Discourse and the *Shtetl*," *Jewish History* 15 (2001): 173.
[35] Herzog/Zborowski, "Preface," 21.
[36] Mead, "Foreword," 9.

If it did happen, somebody would have to hurry to the rabbi asking breathlessly, "Is it kosher?" and waiting in painful suspense until the rabbi, after studying the chicken and the relevant laws, declared "Kosher!"

The chapter goes on to describe at length many other elements of a quintessential Erev Shabbat, from the visits by beggars, to the cleaning of the house, visits to the *mikveh*, dressing up for Shabbat, lighting the candles, the *kiddush*, and finally the meal with its dishes, prayers, and songs. The activities and material culture are portrayed as resonating with spiritual depth that derives from the transcendent and communal meaning of the day. The Jews know that all others in the *shtetl*, which is implied, ahistorically, to be 100% Jewish, and Jews all over the world are sharing the Shabbat experience, Zborowski and Herzog wrote. The result is "a sense of proud and joyous identification with the tradition, the past, the ancestors, with all the Jewish world living or gone. On the Sabbath the shtetl feels most strongly and most gladly that 'it is good to be a Jew.'"[37]

Other chapters in *Life is with People* support this last sentiment, as they describe the sense of mutual social responsibility, the warmth of the Jewish family, and the coherence of a shared calendar of holidays.[38]

The picture of the *shtetl* that emerges from *Life is with People* is one of a comprehensive, organic, homogeneous, and self-contained civilization: a reconstruction of the past that is as powerful as it is a-historic. The core of this civilization is portrayed as timeless, frozen in an unspecified moment sometime before World War I. Modernizing intellectual, religious, social, and political developments like the Haskalah, urbanization, Socialism, or Zionism are declared to be outside the focus of the study, as they undermine (but ultimately strengthen) the core message.[39] This portrait reflects not only the methodological limitations of "long-distance ethnography," but also the forces that shaped the authors' perspectives and readers' interest, as later researchers have pointed out. Historiographical shifts and new research have emphasized the dynamic and diversity of East European Jewish life, as it developed in mutual exchanges with the surrounding culture and in the face of modernizing forces that, contrary to the image in *Life is with People*, transformed religious life, too.[40]

---

37 *Life is with People*, 38–39, 48.
38 "Charity Saves from Death" (191–213), "Peace of the Home" (291–307), "Gut Yontev" (381–405).
39 Herzog/Zborowski, "Preface," 21.
40 Kirshenblatt-Gimblett, "Introduction," xvi. A number of later publications explicitly or implicitly work as correctives to the representation of the past by *Life is with People*; among them are David G. Roskies and Diane K. Roskies, *The Shtetl Book* (New York: Ktav, 1975); Lucjan Dobroszycki and Barbara Kirshenblatt-Gimblett, *Image Before My Eyes: A Photographic History of Jewish Life in Poland* (New York: Schocken, 1977).

Beside later scholarly correctives, Lucy Dawidowicz's book *The Golden Tradition* responded with an engaged counter-narrative that illustrated how a different ideological perspective resulted in a markedly dissimilar picture, only 15 years later. Written by a Zionist in the midst of a shift to greater American Jewish particularism, *The Golden Tradition* pays special attention to the very modernizing ideological movements that *Life is with People* marginalized, as they responded to a crisis of East European Jewish life that ran counter to the image of parochialism, piety, and poverty. "East European Jewry was not, as the sentimentalists see it, forever frozen in utter piety and utter poverty," Dawidowicz stated.[41] Her emphasis on national Jewish renewal spoke to the changed sensitivities of late-1960s American Jews, whereas *Life is with People* was in tune with a different outlook. It was the very timelessness and folkloristic essentialism of its portrait of the East European past that made *Life is with People* so successful with American Jews. It spoke to their impulses and needs: ethnography in the service of commemoration and authenticity.

The commemorative function of the book, particularly with regard to the Holocaust, was directly linked to its idealization of the *shtetl*, as the "vanished world" motif was its dominant perspective. In the words of historian Ben Cion Pinchuk, "the book carries the Shoah's tragic imprint, lovingly describing a world that was brutally destroyed."[42] Readers must have perceived the vividly immediate descriptions of East European life with the ever-present knowledge of its destruction. "The present tense is used, but it is the historical present," Zborowski and Herzog explained in their preface. "The life described here no longer exists. People and culture have been destroyed, and soon it will be too late to find the models for a living picture."[43] After the Holocaust (and the suppression of traditional Judaism in the Soviet Union), *Life is with People* performed "salvage ethnography," in the words of anthropologist Barbara Kirshenblatt-Gimblett. "The annihilation of six million Jews was irreversible. Nevertheless it was felt, the *world* that had been destroyed with them could be recovered. Indeed it was now a moral requirement that this world not suffer a double death." The book was therefore pivotal for how American Jews viewed the past, as it called for a moral perspective: "ambivalence towards the world [that East European Jews] had created became a desecration of their memory."[44] Mead already identified this trope in her foreword to the book. "From such historical studies,

---

[41] Lucy S. Dawidowicz, *The Golden Tradition: Jewish Life and Thought in Eastern Europe* (New York: Holt, Rinehart and Winston, 1967), 6.
[42] Pinchuk, "Jewish Discourse," 173.
[43] Herzog/Zborowski, "Preface," 22.
[44] Kirshenblatt-Gimblett, "Introduction," xi, emphasis in the original.

something is saved to become part of the rich inheritance of all future men and women – often enough is saved to fire the imagination and evoke the nostalgia of the gifted in many succeeding generations."[45]

"Fire the imagination" and "evoke nostalgia" the book did. It sold briskly and became a reference point for American Jews engaging their heritage in postwar America. *Life is with People* appealed to very different sections of the community, who found it useful for their religious, communal, or political agendas. Conservative Rabbi Benjamin M. Kahn used the book's description of the *shtetl* Sabbath in a sermon to urge his congregants toward greater observance. His colleague Wilfred Shuchat, in a sermon on the confusion caused by modern society, invoked ambivalent images of the East European past, quoting Zborowski and Herzog: "beauty and sweetness" on the one hand, but also the ghetto, as the flip side.[46] At the other end of the spectrum, *Commentary*'s Norman Podhoretz placed the book in the context of the secular intellectuals' "process of rediscovery" of their Jewishness.[47] The American Jewish Committee had supported the research for the book with a substantial grant. Behind the support was the hope that the book would not just be a resource to combat prejudice against Jews but would also help Jews develop integrated personalities, as a community and as individuals. While these perspectives were in line with the AJC's traditional policies, its support for *Life is with People* also pointed to a more recent focus on Jewish ethnic distinctiveness, for which the book was regarded as a scholarly and popular source.[48] It was welcomed at the time by those who sought a basis for such distinctiveness, particularly leftists finding it in East European folklore. *Jewish Currents* reviewer Max Rosenfeld placed the book alongside *The World of Sholom Aleichem* and Ruth Rubin's *Treasury of a People*, which together form "a little bookshelf which comes close to being a sociological record of the *shtetl* folkways" and thereby a meaningful heritage.[49]

---

45 Mead, "Foreword," 9.
46 Benjamin M. Kahn, "The Sabbath: Symbol of Jewish Living," in *Best Jewish Sermons of 5714*, ed. Saul I. Teplitz (New York: Jonathan David, 1954), 57–65; Wilfred Shuchat, "How to Face a New Age," in *Best Jewish Sermons of 5715–5716*, ed. Saul I. Teplitz (New York: Jonathan David, 1956), 177–83.
47 Norman Podhoretz, "Jewish Culture and the Intellectuals: The Process of Rediscovery," *Commentary* 13 (May 1955): 452.
48 "Acknowledgments," in *Life is with People*, 6; Barbara Kirshenblatt-Gimblett, "Imagining Europe: The Popular Arts of American Jewish Ethnography," in *Divergent Centers: Shaping Jewish Cultures in Israel and America*, ed. Deborah Dash Moore and Ilan Troen (New Haven: Yale University Press, 2001), 155–56; Kirshenblatt-Gimblett, "Introduction," xxix–xxx.
49 Max Rosenfeld, "The World of Yiddish Folksong: Ruth Rubin's 'Treasury' Opens a Window on Our Heritage," review of *Treasury of a People*, ed. by Ruth Rubin, *Jewish Currents* 18 (1964): 9.

"Sex, Taboo, and Superstition:" Attracting American Jewish Interest in the *Shtetl*

Ethnography, like other social sciences, was seen as a way to make the past usable for the present, as the *Commentary* department "The Study of Man" illustrated, in which another ethnographic reconstruction of the *shtetl* past was published in 1954.[50] As a discipline, the rise of ethnography marked not only the social scientific shift from racial concepts to cultural ones (hence AJC's support for such projects), but also a constitutive assumption of legitimate cultural pluralism. Particularly small, vulnerable cultures "outside the main currents of history," in Mead's words, were worth studying, not just for their own sake, but as relevant for those facing the same questions in different cultures.[51] Zborowski and Herzog made this function of their study explicit, linking the past they described to the present of their second- and third-generation readers.

> It is a culture that is not remote. On the contrary, it is one with which many have had direct or indirect contact, through its representatives or their descendants. Therefore the bringing together and interrelating of its features and details [...] may have a special significance for many people. Brought together so that main culture themes and patterns can be perceived, these heretofore scattered items permit an understanding that for many feels fresh and new. [...] "Now I understand – " is a very frequent response to this material. It may be an understanding of one's parents, of one's friends and neighbors.[52]

It was the very notion of Jewishness as a culture, which ethnography vouchsafed, and its particular presentation of East European Jewish life, that made the book's offer of an identity so attractive and powerful. It was grounded in a comprehensive Jewishness, which the book portrayed as time-tested and infused with spiritual depth so as to make it meaningful for everyday life in the present. *Life is with People* connected the Sinaitic covenant to issues of personal hygiene, and described ideals of beauty as much as instances of violence in Jewish life. The authors were open in the premises of their work, setting it

---

50 Celia Stopnicka Rosenthal, "How the Polish Jew Saw His World: A Study of a Small-Town Community Before 1939," *Commentary* 18 (July 1954): 70–75. *Life is with People* was modeled theoretically on the Yale Seminar on the Impact of Culture on Personality, in which YIVO researcher Max Weinreich participated in 1932–33 and which shaped his work at YIVO. (Barbara Kirshenblatt-Gimblett, "Coming of Age in the Thirties: Max Weinreich, Eduard Sapir, and Jewish Social Science," in *YIVO Annual of Jewish Social Science* 23, ed. Deborah Dash Moore (New York: YIVO, 1996): 1–2.)
51 Mead, "Foreword," 9.
52 Herzog/Zborowski, "Preface," 20; similarly, Mead, "Foreword," 10–11.

not just in the scholarly context of anthropology, but also of the social sciences at large with their broad interest in a community's life-world. At a YIVO conference, Zborowski criticized reductive conceptions of Jewishness under the category of religion and called for a broad ethno-cultural perspective, which he spelled out with Herzog in the book's introduction: "The Jews of Eastern Europe had one culture, possessing the characteristics that mark a culture: a language, a religion, a set of values, a specific constellation of social mechanisms and institutions, and the feeling of its members that they belong to one group."[53] As the study started with the question of what distinguished East European Jewish life from others, this holistic, coherent, and highly distinct culture was defined against the external, non-Jewish world and set a norm of what was authentically Jewish.

Therefore, the image presented by *Life is with People*, like other depictions of the East European Jewish experience, could be and was invoked as a model of committed Jewishness, as in the sermons, or served as a distant reference for a distinct geographic and cultural origin, supporting a symbolic Jewish ethnicity through vicarious identification with a radically different life. Some contemporary critics, however, criticized the book and the underlying methods, as well as the message the study presented to its readers. They took the authors to task for factual errors or distortions, citing lack of Judaic knowledge, or the limitations of the scholarly approach. Historian Abraham Duker presented a long list of errors, attributing them to the lack of specialized expertise, particularly in ritual aspects of traditional Jewish life, among the researchers.[54] Moshe Decter, in *Commentary*, called *Life is with People* a good book, but criticized that the intensity of social tensions and the "unbelievable poverty" were underplayed, turning the *shtetl* into a "stable utopia." The perception of a superficial treatment of a profound phenomenon also drove the negative review left by Yiddishist Yudel Mark in the *Jewish Frontier*. His critique, entitled "Pseudo-Science," was more fundamental: He blamed the shortcomings of the book on its ethnographic approach. In his judgment, "a description of the externals of ritual detached from their essential content" made for the impression of *shtetl* Jews as "extremely primitive and ritualistic creatures." The effect would be pernicious on two levels, as later generations of young Jews would get a false image of their heritage, and non-Jews would see them as "backward and uncultured."[55] Mark's choice of words reveals

---

53 Mark Zborowski, "In the American Community: Problems Discussed at Twenty-Sixth Annual Conference of Yivo," *News of the YIVO* 44 (March 1952): 3*; Herzog/Zborowski, "Preface," 21.
54 Abraham G. Duker, "A Shady Portrait of the Shtetl," *Congress Weekly* 19 (22 September 1952): 23–24; Decter, "'Old Country' Way of Life," 601–02.
55 Mark, "Pseudo-Science," 25.

a normative concept of culture, from which he distinguished a spiritual dimension that defined authentic Judaism. Ethnography's descriptive understanding of culture had to result in an inadequate depiction of East European Jewish life, as it was not equipped to capture its spiritual essence.

Life is with People's popular appeal may have led the *Jewish Frontier* to pair Mark's negative review with a more positive one by literary editor and translator Jacob Sloan. He praised the book for making the East European past usable as a guide for American Jews in search of a meaningful sense of Jewishness: "The *shtetl* is our past; obviously we cannot and would not accept or reject, revive or deny, that past *in toto*. But what shall we do with it?" he asked rhetorically. Sloan sensed that the fascination with the past stemmed from its place in the distance, which, in turn, made it difficult to establish more than symbolic connections to ancestors who, particularly after their murder, seemed too elevated to serve as models. Rather than defensively accepting that they lacked religious commitment and Jewish identification, American Jews should apply a yardstick more fitting to their contemporary situation in America, a modern society with different standards of Jewish authenticity: "To us [*shtetl* Jews] a good Jew meant an authentic human being – one who was concerned with where he had come from and where he was going. Life is with people; life is also within."[56] Sloan employed a subjective sense of authenticity – "life within" – as something very modern and transferable to American Jewry. This reading of *Life is with People* re-defined an earlier, communally sanctioned set of public values of authentic Jewishness as individual values of the private, subjective realm – a move very much in line with modern notions of religion, and one that could legitimize Judaism in its American context.

If this was one of the messages that made *Life is with People* relevant to American Jews, yet another reading could provide an even more specific way to legitimize their community within the continuum of Jewish history. The static timelessness of the East European past presented in the book, the elision of modernizing forces within East European Jewry and, by extension, the elision of new, different forms of Jewishness, would, at first sight, seem like the very opposite: a de-legitimization of American Jewishness. After all, American Jewry was a quintessentially new and modern phenomenon that developed in the aftermath of mass immigration and was a complex mixture of rejection and continuation of East European Jewish life. At second glance, however, a different way to link American Jewry and the *shtetl* emerges. If *shtetl* Jewishness could not change and develop, leaving the *shtetl* was the only option available to modernizing Jews (as

---

56 Jacob Sloan, "The Shtetl in Retrospect: Life Is Also Within," *Jewish Frontier* XIX (1952): 29.

was additionally confirmed by the Holocaust).⁵⁷ According to *Life is with People*, immigration does not belong to the category of forces that undermined and eroded East European Jewish civilization. Rather, it brings some of the "home" culture to new arenas of Jewish life, like America, where its essence and patterns live on, albeit in altered form. The essentializing and spiritualizing of a pluriform Jewish culture with significant material expressions made the culture transportable across time and space, in this ethnographical depiction as in narratives from other quarters of American Jewry.

In the terms of "Hansen's Law," according to which "[what] the son wishes to forget the grandson wishes to remember," *Life is with People* was written for third-generation American Jews who looked back past their second-generation parents to re-discover the Jewishness of their grandparents.⁵⁸ Unencumbered by the need to prove that American and Jewish values were congenial and unburdened by the idea that distinctiveness had to be reduced to religious categories, these third-generation Jews found in the book a past that gave historical and spiritual, hence deeper, meaning to their distinctiveness. This approach became more pronounced over the period under analysis, from the 1940s into the 1960s, as American society moved toward cultural pluralism. More and more American Jews invoked the East European past as a fertile source of ethno-cultural distinctiveness, which took on a life of its own, increasingly independent of the nourishing source. In 1955, the journal *Judaism* printed a polemic by Lester Seligman, a Hillel-affiliated English professor, who declared that American Jewry, a culture in the midst of late adolescence and just coming of age, had emancipated itself from its East European heritage: "The period of life when the American Jewish community lived under the shadow of the Old World culture is at an end. The umbilical cords with the past have been severed," he declared. "That complete world of Eastern Europe, known to us through orthodox practice and belief, its rich folkish life of custom and story, and its insightful Jewish social thought has come to an end. It exists faintly in the romantic nostalgia that motivated the volumes of translation of Sholom Aleichem and Peretz, and Zborowski's and Herzog's '*Life is with People*.'" To him, *Life is with People* was a eulogy to be read only by a dwindling group of mourners.⁵⁹

In retrospect, Seligman seems to have been wrong, as the fate of *Life is with People* suggests. Its publication in the accessible Schocken paperback edition

---

57 Cf. Kirshenblatt-Gimblett, "Introduction," xvi.
58 Cf. Marcus Lee Hansen, "The Third Generation in America," *Commentary* 14 (November 1952): 495. Cf. introduction for background on "Hansen's Law."
59 Lester G. Seligman, "A Second Look at the Tercentenary," *Judaism* 4 (1955): 110.

made it into a defining text for a new generation of American Jews in the 1960s. "In its 1960s reincarnation, *Life is with People* became an adolescent romance for third-generation American Jews, the kind of fiction one read when searching for one's identity," literary scholar David Roskies recalled. "It told of a life that was anti-bourgeois, simple, down to earth. What's more, because this life seemed to stand still, it did not require any knowledge of history or geography, the very subjects that American teenagers are so poorly tutored in. There was just enough about sex, superstition and taboos to keep it interesting."[60] Sex, superstition, and taboos – it was the stuff of ethnography that made the book so popular and influential. It served as a guide for *Fiddler on the Roof*, in which the link between commemoration and idealization of the "vanished world" reached a climax, and as a reference work for academic scholarship on the *shtetl*. The new subtitle of the paperback edition, "The Culture of the Shtetl" introduced the term into the American Jewish vocabulary; Zborowski later wrote the definition of *shtetl* in the 1972 edition of the *Encyclopaedia Judaica*.[61] Ethnography of the East European past had turned out to be a useful tool with which postwar American Jews could navigate and re-navigate the complex balance between external expectations and communal needs, Judaism and Jewishness, as the community came of age.

As it turned out, American Jews literally coming of age (and thus particularly interested in sex, superstition, and taboos) also confronted the East European past, in textbooks that sought to socialize them into a Jewish identity – a parallel to the search of secular intellectuals, whose fascination with unconventional expressions of Judaism took them on a different path.

---

60 Roskies, "The Shtetl as Imagined Community," 6–7.
61 Seth Wolitz, "The Americanization of Tevye or Boarding the Jewish 'Mayflower,'" *American Quarterly* 40 (1988): 526; Solomon, *Wonder of Wonders*, 119; Pinchuk, "Jewish Discourse," 173; Kirshenblatt-Gimblett, "Introduction," xxi.

8 Making Jewishness Meaningful: In School and in Hasidism

If the preoccupation of mid-century American Jewry with the East European past was a function of their coming of age – defining a communal identity in relation to their ancestors (parents or grandparents) – there may be a parallel to the processes in which individual American Jews fashioned their Jewish identity by relating to their heritage. Textbooks dealing with Jewish history can be a revealing source for both processes. They present a unique case of disseminating and popularizing the past, as they reconstruct it with the explicit purpose of making it usable as an identity resource. The pedagogical need to simplify and spell out for young readers that which is transmitted more indirectly and subtly in other textual genres makes textbooks a particularly rich indicator of what concerns a community at a given time and place with regard to their collective future.[1] History textbooks shape the collective memory of the group, condensing and dispensing "truths" about the past and the present and how they are linked. The past is studied not just for its own sake, but as a means to an end.[2]

Harnessing the past to instill a positive sense of Jewishness in the younger generation was a motive that shaped the depiction of the East European past in textbooks used in mid-century Jewish schools. The American Jewish educational landscape in this period was variegated, but dominated by congregation-linked supplementary schools. Three textbooks, written and used under the auspices of the religious movements, were widely in use: Mamie Gamoran's *New Jewish History* (Reform, 1957), Deborah Pessin's *The Jewish People* (Conservative, 1953), and Gilbert and Libby Klaperman's *The Story of the Jewish People* (Orthodox, 1958/61).[3] While by the mid-1950s Yiddish schools had been in decline for some twenty years, they still taught a

---

[1] Cf. Walter Ackerman, "Let Us Now Praise Famous Men and Their Fathers in the Generations: History Books for Jewish Children in America," *Dor Ledor: Studies in the History of Jewish Education in Israel and the Diaspora* II (1984): 5–6.
[2] Deborah Pessin, *The Jewish People, Book III* (New York: United Synagogue of America, 1953), 7; Emanuel Gamoran, "Editor's Introduction," *The New Jewish History, Book 3: From the Discovery of America to Our Own Day*, ed. Mamie Gamoran (Cincinnati: Union of American Hebrew Congregations, 1957), viii.
[3] Gilbert Klaperman and Libby Klaperman, *The Story of the Jewish People, vol. 3: From the Golden Age in Spain Through the European Emancipation* (New York: Behrman House [in cooperation with the Rabbinical Council of America], 1958); Klaperman/Klaperman, *The Story of the Jewish People, vol. 4: From the Settlement of America through Israel Today* (New York: Behrman House [in cooperation with the Rabbinical Council of America], 1961). For information on which textbooks were widely used, cf. Jonathan Krasner, "Constructing Collective Memory: The Re-Envisioning of Eastern Europe as Seen

DOI 10.1515/9783110499438-009

significant number of students. Among the various branches of Yiddish schools, the Socialist Workmen's Circle system was one of the largest.[4] An analysis here of a Yiddish-language textbook published under its auspices – *Dos Lebendike Vort* by Zalman Yefroiken and Hyman B. Bass (1954/1959) – supplements the examination of the English-language educational material; it represents the prevailing approach to teaching history via Yiddish language and literature.[5]

In this period, the crucial changes associated with the suburbanization of large parts of American Jewry shaped developments in the field of education. The shift from the "osmotically" transmitted Jewishness of the urban neighborhoods to the conscious engagement with Jewish identity was reflected in the transition from "incidental" to "intentional" Jewish education, as historian Jonathan Sarna wrote, applying the categories defined by philosopher John Dewey.[6] Dewey's ideas were formative in the rapidly growing and professionalizing field of Jewish education, as in the 1940s developments begun in the interwar years came to fruition. Modern approaches to the teaching of history, associated in particular with Samson Benderly and his students, drew heavily on the ideas of Dewey and Mordecai Kaplan, who advocated a broad understanding of Jewishness within a culturally pluralistic society. Embracing one's historical heritage became an important resource for Jewish identification. Positive depictions of Jewishness in formal Jewish education also reflected a (delayed) concern that the negative stereotypes that had been widespread during the interwar period needed to be proactively counter-balanced.[7] New pedagogical tools were employed, among them youth journals like *World Over* (founded in 1940, by the Jewish Education

---

Through American Jewish Textbooks," in *Polin [vol. 19]: Polish-Jewish Relations in North America*, ed. Miecyzslaw B. Biskupski and Antony Polonsky (Oxford: Littman, 2007).

4 David E. Fishman, "Yiddish Schools in America and the Problem of Secular Jewish Identity," in *Religion or Ethnicity*, ed. Zvi Gitelman (New Brunswick: Rutgers University Press, 2009), 72; Nancy Sinkoff, "Yiddish Schools," in *Encyclopedia of the American Left*, ed. Mari Jo Buhle, Paul Buhle and Dan Georgakas (New York: Oxford University Press, 1998), 917–18; Yudel Mark, "Changes in the Yiddish Schools," in *Jewish Education in the United States: A Documentary History*, ed. Lloyd P. Gartner (New York: Teachers College Press, 1969, orig. publ. 1949), 190–91. (According to Shandler, the original text was published already in 1947, in contrast to the year 1949 given in Gartner's book; Jeffrey Shandler, *Adventures in Yiddishland: Postvernacular Language and Culture* (Berkeley: University of California Press, 2006), 222n93).

5 Zalman Yefroiken and Hyman B. Bass, *Dos Lebendike Vort [for third year]* (New York: Workmen's Circle, 1954/1959).

6 Jonathan D. Sarna, "American Jewish Education in Historical Perspective," *Journal of Jewish Education* 64 (1998), 10–11.

7 Cf. Beth S. Wenger, *History Lessons: The Creation of American Jewish Heritage* (Princeton: Princeton University Press, 2010), 144–50; Krasner, "Constructing Collective Memory", 242–48.

Committee of New York) and *Keeping Posted* (1952, by the Union of American Hebrew Congregations). This development toward a deliberately crafted, more intense, positive identification with a distinctive Jewishness was strengthened by larger intellectual and social changes brought about by the Holocaust. With this turning point, the educational goal of identity formation took on unprecedented meaning for American Jews. Physical survival and cultural self-preservation made the issue of Jewish continuity the most determinant impulse driving Jewish education. Pessin used the motif of continuity six times over little more than three pages in a prefatory address to the reader, tying it explicitly to knowledge of the past and a commitment to its values.[8] Similarly, William B. Lakritz, education professional in the Conservative movement, defined continuity as a key objective of congregational schools: "Our final goal is an upright participating Jew, who finds in Judaism a worthy way of life and thereby makes possible the continuation of the Jewish people and the tradition it bears."[9] Addressing the student directly, Mamie Gamoran made the notion of continuity particularly intense and personal, as she pointed the reader to the present and future: "The kind of history that follows now will be decided by your feeling of kinship with Jews in the rest of the world, and by your adherence to the Jewish religion and its teachings."[10] This new focus on continuity shaped the textbooks' depictions of the East European past. If there were any doubt about this past's importance to postwar American Jews, the sheer amount of space the textbooks spend on it will dispel it. Gamoran devoted about a fifth of her description of modern Jewish history to the subject; Pessin and the Klapermans even more than a quarter.

Within these depictions, education scholar Jonathan Krasner diagnosed a "return to reductionism" in the postwar decades: a trend away from an earlier, interwar-period focus on commonalities and interaction between Jews and surrounding East European groups. He attributes this change to the "turning inward" of the post-1945 American Jewish community and to a more sympathetic perspective on the East European past. Particularly after the Holocaust, textbooks also corrected previous depictions of Eastern Jews as unenlightened and primitive, as their depiction now served a new function. "Having rehabilitated and claimed the Ostjuden, the books adopted the common tactic of using

---

8 Pessin, *The Jewish People*, 12–13.
9 William B. Lakritz, "Congregational School Curricula – An Evaluation," *The Synagogue School* 13 (1955): 14. Lakritz was director of education for the Philadelphia branch of the United Synagogue.
10 Gamoran, *New Jewish History*, 353.

Figure 19: Jewish education, here at Congregation Emanu-El B'ne Jeshurun, Milwaukee, WI (1952–53), became a primary way of attempting to transmit a conscious Jewish identity. Hebrew schools were often affiliated with congregations. (American Jewish Archives)

the Other as a foil."[11] Targeting young Jews as they learned to define themselves in relation to others, Gamoran made the juxtaposition of sameness and difference overt and transferred it from Eastern Europe to America: "Your mother and father, as far as looks are concerned, are doubtless no different in appearance, dress, and speech from all their non-Jewish friends," she wrote, adding, "Being alike is not a virtue in itself. Being different may mean holding on to worth while [sic] ideas and observing customs which bind you with a historic past."[12] This message of sameness and difference is supported in less overt ways by the presentations of the East European past in the textbooks, as they construct Jewishness by juxtaposing Jews and others and probing commonalities and contrasts. The

---

[11] Krasner, "Constructing Collective Memory," 249–52. Krasner finds that textbooks reflect with some delay broader shifts in historiography, as they typically rely on academic studies rather than original research.

[12] Gamoran, *New Jewish History*, 343–44.

results are intensified versions of familiar images, as general pedagogical needs to simplify converged with the post-1945 need to sharpen particularistic Jewish self-conceptions. The most prevalent contrasts are described to distinguish Jews from peasants, scholarliness from illiteracy, and material poverty from spiritual wealth. The figure of the (non-Jewish) peasant, or rather, peasants, served as a foil for several of these juxtapositions. The most frequently used attributes for peasants were "poor" and "ignorant." Pessin wrote of "millions of ignorant, poverty-stricken peasants," Gamoran of "a huge number of poor and unlearned peasants."[13] Both attributes, poverty and ignorance, highlighted stereotypically negative depictions of peasants, all in the service of balancing distinctiveness and integration. Material poverty was an existential condition that linked Jews and peasants and distinguished both groups from the Polish nobility. In this sense, Jewish and peasant poverty was sometimes associated with ethical purity and compassion, whereas material wealth was tantamount to greediness and corruption.[14] More importantly, peasant material poverty was associated with intellectual dearth, and thereby served as a contrast to the spiritual wealth of East European Jewry and their love of learning, the most dominant motif. "The Jews of Poland loved learning. They loved studying the word of God in His Holy Torah," the Klapermans wrote. Pessin entitled a chapter on Jews in Poland "A Nation of Students," a subsection of which, "Torah and Honey," relates the innocent joy of a young boy's first day at the *cheder*. The same motif runs through "A Cheder Story" in *Dos Lebendike Vort*, one of five texts in the section "The Jewish Child in the Old Home." The story concludes with a song by the teacher, the last line of which reads, "And remember my child: he who will not learn, will forever remain blind."[15] Gamoran described how spiritual learnedness and practice in school and the home infused a student's whole life: "Abraham, Isaac, and Jacob became familiar friends of the pupils. Joshua, Saul, and David were their heroes. Their games were based on Jewish themes."[16] All this was often contrasted with the lives and habits of the intellectually and spiritually unrefined peasants, as presented by the Klapermans. "In the early hours of the morning, while the Polish peasants

---

13 Pessin, *The Jewish People*, 232; Gamoran, *New Jewish History*, 57.
14 "The Miraculous Pipe" [Yiddish], in Yefroiken/Bass, *Dos Lebendike Vort*, 35–36; "The Peasant and the Treasure" [Yiddish], *Dos Lebendike Vort*, 111.
15 Klaperman/Klaperman, *Story of the Jewish People*, vol. 3, 157; Pessin, *The Jewish People*, 78; "A Kheder Meyseh," "Dos Yidishe Kind in der alte Heym" [all Yiddish], in Yefroiken/Bass, *Dos Lebendike Vort*, 241.
16 Gamoran, *New Jewish History*, 162. The journal *World Over* reinforced the imagery, writing in a special issue on Jewish life in the Middle ages: "Polish Jews devoted much time to the study of Torah, and Jewish learning flourished throughout the land," *World Over* 22 (October 7, 1960): 5)

still snored in their beds, the ancient Jews of the community would wend their way to the 'shul,' the synagogue."[17]

While part of the idealization of studying was certainly meant to spur on the student reader in an American congregational school, it also points to larger objectives in constructing a positive sense of Jewishness, in contradistinction to an essentialized non-Jewish other. However, the depictions of peasants as poor and primitive could also serve a condescending, but more charitable perspective. Gamoran wrote how the serfs could be influenced by the other estates to become friend or foe.[18] Here, the peasants appeared as tools of elites, who manipulated them for their own purposes. The Klapermans wrote that "[for] the most part, the poor Polish peasant, who lived side by side with the Jew, had no hatred towards him."[19] In such widely ranging depictions of non-Jews in Eastern Europe, Krasner observes changing Jewish views of their American present, as the community gradually consolidated its post-Holocaust perspective. A pre-1945 angle, driven by the unfulfilled urge toward social inclusion, resulted in more universalist attitudes toward others. Later, concerns about Jewish physical and cultural survival engendered by the Holocaust would result in a more inward-turned, particularistic perspective.[20]

Textbook Cases: Spiritual Culture as a Source of Fortitude in the Face of Persecution

The post-Holocaust outlook also drove the larger narrative of persecution in Eastern Europe. The Cossack revolts beginning in 1648 and the Polish partitions are presented as major turning points in a story that moves from a largely blissful Jewish existence in Poland to the hostile policies of the Russian czars and the pogroms beginning in the 1880s, then climaxing tragically in the Holocaust (and, to a lesser degree, in the Communist suppression of Judaism in the Soviet Eastern bloc, which became an issue particularly in the context of the Cold War).[21] Again,

---

17 Klaperman/Klaperman, *Story of the Jewish People*, vol. 3, 157.
18 Gamoran, *New Jewish History*, 57.
19 Klaperman/Klaperman, *Story of the Jewish People*, vol. 3, 171.
20 Krasner, "Constructing Collective Memory," 240, 255.
21 "Light and Shadow" is the title of the second unit of Pessin's book (*The Jewish People*, 61–112); the fourth unit begins with a chapter called "Oppression under Czarism" (147–59). A similar pattern runs through other textbooks, e.g. Dorothy F. Zeligs, *A History of Jewish Life in Modern Times* (New York: Bloch, 1938) and Mordecai I. Soloff, *How the Jewish People Lives Today* (Cincinnati:

a familiar trope leads back to the overarching narrative of Jewish continuity: the warmth, depth, and beauty of the inner life of the community are presented as bulwarks and consolation in the face of external oppression and violence. "The Jews, huddled together in the crowded towns of the Pale, drew what happiness they could from the study of their Torah, from the Sabbath and their beautiful festivals bringing memories of their people's past," Pessin wrote in her chapter on Jewish life under czarism.[22] In a poem printed in *Dos Lebendike Vort*, "In the Evening" by Nokhem Yud, the idyllic childhood memory of a peacock in a forest, "vald," rhymes with "gevalt," the force by which *khappers* kidnapped Jewish children for military service. The two final stanzas of the poem, which is narrated by a child sitting in its grandmother's lap, condense various key motifs of the post-Holocaust American-Jewish perspective: the mediating role of grandparents, nostalgia, and grief for a bygone world, and the (retrospective) foreboding implied in the concluding image:

> And I listen, enchanted,
> To Grandmother's talking
> And from my eyes fall
> Tears, silently.
> Nobody is in the room
> Only we, together
> And the dancing shadows
> On the white wall.[23]

The Holocaust was present in different ways in American Jewish textbooks, sometimes more as a shadow than as an explicit topic, particularly in the English-language texts. Often, it was invoked in generic terms and used to emphasize Jewish survival, as in statements such as one by Emanuel Gamoran, who pointed to an "inner fortitude" preserved over history which allowed for "Jews and

---

Union of American Hebrew Congregations, 1952, orig. publ. 1940). The journal *Keeping Posted* was very vocal in its criticism of the Soviet Union and its suppression of religious life, anti-Jewish policies and, later, prohibition on Jewish emigration. Examples include "Soviet Russia and the Iron Curtain," *Keeping Posted* I (March 18, 1956): 2; "Jews Under Communism," *Keeping Posted* III (December 1958): 7; "Soviet Union Opposes Jewish Immigration," *Keeping Posted* IV (March 1959): cover.

22 Pessin, *The Jewish People*, 232.
23 Nokhem Yud, "In Ovent," in Yefroiken/Bass, *Dos Lebendike Vort*, 240; An extract of Sholem Aleichem's *Mottel, the Cantor's Son* in *Dos Lebendike Vort* introduced the motif of intra-Jewish tensions and conflicts ("I'm fine – I'm an Orphan"/"Mir is gut – Ikh bin a Yosem", 243–51). Its focus on contrasts between poor and rich reflects the Socialist ideology driving the sponsoring Workmen's Circle.

Judaism to survive, hold aloft their social, religious, and cultural ideals, despite tragedy."[24] It was this inner strength that also fueled the courageous and heroic acts of Jewish pride and resistance in the face of persecution to which the post-1945 books give much greater play than their predecessors.[25]

It is also this notion of an "inner fortitude" that makes the Jewish past, as depicted in the textbooks, usable as a resource for their present readers. Their narratives point to a strong, empowering, all-encompassing, communal Jewish identity, which serves as the proven guarantor of a coherent and meaningful sense of Jewishness that alone would safeguard continuity. This concept of Jewishness is by no means limited to a narrowly religious definition, but owes more to Kaplanian notions of Judaism as a civilization. The Klapermans prize such a distinctly cultural notion of Judaism, as illustrated by their favorable view of the affirmatively Jewish Russian Haskalah, which contrasted with the weakening effects they attributed to its German version: "Instead, the Russian Haskalah brought forth great new poets, profound historians, thinkers, and philosophers." Pessin's peoplehood-oriented perspective credited an amalgam of customs, religion, and memories for the broad identity that Jews transmitted over time: "Unlike other people who were conquered and exiled, they did not disappear, because their own way of life continued from one generation to the next." Gamoran, whose Reform perspective focused on a timeless spiritual essence of Judaism, emphasized the coherence that the tradition gave East European Jewry: "Whether they dwelt in village or town, their life was similar in many ways. Even when the modern world broke through to them, their daily life changed very little."[26] The books' depictions of Jewish life gave support to these programmatic statements. Both Pessin and Gamoran used the fair at Lublin to illustrate a range of aspects of distinctly Jewish life in Eastern Europe, among them the role of Yiddish,

---

[24] Emanuel Gamoran, "Editor's Introduction," vii. In his introduction to the 1952 re-issuing of Soloff's *How the Jewish People Lives Today* from 1940, Gamoran writes that events moved too fast for a writer of Jewish history to keep pace.

[25] Pessin in a programmatic prefatory statement speaks of the "illustrious and heroic story" of the Jewish people *(The Jewish People*, 7). Similarly, Gamoran calls on her readers "to follow in the footsteps of the sages and heroes of the Jewish people." She also entitles her chapter on the 1648 Cossack revolts "The Heroes" and emphasizes Jewish courage in the face of the attacks *(New Jewish History*, 3, 65). In a supportive text announcing her book, the journal *Keeping Posted* wrote in 1955 that "Mrs Gamoran is trying to show the brighter side of the Jewish past. She tells of the courage of the Jews and the way they overcame their trials." ("Husband and Wife Writing Teams," *Keeping Posted* I (November 13, 1955): 3)

[26] Klaperman/Klaperman, *Story of the Jewish People*, vol. 3, 233; Pessin, *The Jewish People*, 13; Gamoran: *New Jewish History*, 169.

along with trade practices, matchmaking, religious rulings, and communal autonomy.[27] The Klapermans illustrated their ideal of a comprehensive, cultural, lived Jewishness by their characterization of Yiddish:

> It was more than a language. A remarkable literature in Yiddish and a deep attachment to it had grown up. It was the language of instruction in the cheder and the yeshiva. It was the language of the mother's lullaby. It was the language of the everyday businessman, as well as the spiritual language of the rabbi. It was the language of the fable and story. It was the stream in which Jewish culture passed from generation to generation.[28]

Matchmaking, business activities, lullabies – the textbooks' focus on the daily life of East European Jews rather than just on political events and religious developments represented a recent shift in scholarship toward social history and in pedagogy. Pessin and Gamoran in particular reflected the new sociological approach in historiography and the modern pedagogical methods to make the material relevant. These included efforts to address students directly and draw them into the Jewish past by emphasizing its link to their American present. The depiction of Jewish life in America was closely connected to the presentation of the past, particularly when, in another set of juxtapositions, the East European past was portrayed in dark terms and contrasted with the Jewish opportunities in America for the immigrants and later generations.[29] Extending the historical development to postwar America, the textbooks brought the story full circle and overtly tried to transmit lessons from the recent past. They emphasized the new responsibility of the by now most stable Jewish community in the world, which had to mature by becoming more self-conscious and self-confident. In recent decades, Gamoran wrote, "American Jews began to cast an inward look upon themselves. They became aware of their responsibilities as the wealthiest and most stable Jewish group in the world. The American Jewish community learned that its most pressing need was to build up its own inner strength. It could no longer draw on the vast reservoir of scholarship which came from Eastern Europe." When she formulated this self-understanding of mid-century American Jewry, she may have thought both of her student reader and of the American Jewish community who were both coming of age and taking on new responsibilities for ensuring a Jewish future.[30]

---

27 Pessin, *The Jewish People*, 61–77; Gamoran, *New Jewish History*, 55.
28 Klaperman/Klaperman, *Story of the Jewish People*, vol. 4, 145, 149.
29 Klaperman/Klaperman, *Story of the Jewish People*, vol. 3, 223; Pessin, *The Jewish People*, 147; Gamoran, *New Jewish History*, 181; cf. also Wenger, *History Lessons*, 161–66.
30 Gamoran, *New Jewish History*, 268.

While the "coming of age" motif is a useful metaphor for the English-language segment of American Jewry, its Yiddish-language counterpart faced a different and more painful passage. The demographic decline of Yiddish speakers was compounded by the effects of the Holocaust. The destruction of East European Jewry hit the Yiddish-speaking community from a much shorter biographical and cultural distance. The Yiddish educational system mirrored this effect. "The children of the Yiddish schools may be said to have lived through the happenings themselves," educator Yudel Mark observed shortly after the Holocaust.[31] This was even more true for the teachers, almost all of whom had been born in Eastern Europe. Whereas the raw experience of the Holocaust distinguished the Yiddish-speaking community from the English-speaking majority, other developments pointed toward greater proximity and commonality, beginning in the mid-to-late 1930s. Disillusionment with the reality of Communism in the Soviet Union pulled a large segment of Yiddish-oriented leftists closer toward the political mainstream. More importantly, however, the general trajectory that moved American society toward a greater appreciation of religion – and specifically toward a greater appreciation of its tradition – also affected staunchly secularist-progressive Yiddishists. "The turn to tradition among Yiddish educators was, consciously or unconsciously, an expression of their rapprochement with the rest of Jewry – with the non-socialist and non-Yiddishist Jews – in a time of common peril," historian David Fishman wrote.[32] The practical effect was a more conscious inclusion of Jewish content in the Yiddish schools," as Mark explained. "From all sides, more Jewishness was streaming into the schools [...] in general, through the acceptance of ideas which would earlier have called forth a storm of protest from the guardians of the pure secular line." As a result, students were more consciously and deliberately Jewish. "They live more Jewishly; they are more bound up with Jewish symbols and ceremonies."[33]

Dos Lebendike Vort reflected many of these larger developments. It was named to honor and continue a textbook of the same title, whose authors "perished with the textbook on the saddest day of the greatest atrocity against our people," as authors Yefroiken and Bass stated in their message to the teachers. In the same text, they pointed out that the work was more traditionally religious than earlier works.[34] This shift was reflected in the selection of topics, which included a heavy emphasis on religious holidays. In contrast to earlier decisions, the selection went

---

31 Mark, "Changes in the Yiddish Schools," 193.
32 Fishman, "Yiddish Schools in America," 83; cf. also Wenger, *History Lessons*, 141.
33 Mark, "Changes in the Yiddish Schools", 192–94.
34 Yefroiken/Bass, *Dos Lebendike Vort*, 252.

beyond those holidays that had been re-interpreted in terms of political progressivism, such as Passover and Hanukkah, as symbols of liberation from slavery and rebellion against tyranny. *Dos Lebendike Vort* contained segments on holidays less prone to re-purposing, like Shavuot. Its long section *Shabbes* also focused on that day's religious dimensions. Another poem by Nokhem Yud bathed the onset of the Sabbath in the warm light of pure holiness: the mother lights the candles "with quiet, solemn piety/the white hands, the noble ones/cover her face."[35]

By affirming the religious tradition, Yiddish educators moved their community closer to the increasingly dominant discourse which reconstructed the (East European) Jewish past in terms of a tradition-based spirituality. This rapprochement with religious tradition drew the culturally conceived, progressive sense of *Yiddishkayt* closer to notions of Judaism and Jewishness as essentially spiritual phenomena. In this sense, the Yiddish-speaking segment of American Jewry also partook in the spiritualization of the lost world and the sacralization of its memory for the sacred task of Jewish continuity. Yudel Mark found this development to be driven by "the desire to get to the roots of eternal Jewishness." It represented a radical continuation of a premise of Yiddishism: the notion that Yiddish embodied a Jewish essence. After the Holocaust and in light of the new role of "religion" as the expression of Jewishness, this tendency gained in potency, as Mark's outline of the meaning of Yiddish illustrated:

> Yiddish as a bridge between various Jewish groups throughout the world; as the language of our recent, concrete, clearly understood past; as the language of that East European kernel which though it perished, succeeded in causing all modern movements to sprout from it, and from which the Jewish community in America basically stems; as a language of recent martyrs; as a language which has absorbed thirty generations of folk quality and became the vehicle of valuable, original Jewish creativity; as the language which bears upon itself the sheen of folk sanctity and has become a holy language, as it were, of a modern and peculiar character.[36]

As the notion of Yiddish as a "holy language" suggests, cultural self-preservation became a sacred task, for educators and for American Jewry at large. Since textbooks served as a primary vehicle for this message, they shaped their material accordingly, illustrating how external factors determined the way in which reconstructions of the East European past were made usable in a particularly influential medium of its popularization and dissemination.

---

35 Yefroiken/Bass, *Dos Lebendike Vort*, 67.
36 Mark, "Changes in the Yiddish Schools," 197.

Hasidism: Everyone's Third Way

For adults out of school, one specific element of the East European past played an unexpectedly crucial role, which proved a fifty-year-old prophecy to be true: "No renewal of Judaism is possible that does not bear in itself the elements of Hasidism," Martin Buber declared in the 1907 preface to his German book on the founder of the movement, and again in the 1955 edition of *The Legend of the Baal-Shem*.[37] By that time, some 200 years after the death of Hasidism's founder, Israel Ben Eliezer – the Ba'al Shem Tov (BeShT) – significant parts of American Jewry were fascinated with Hasidism, whose spiritual nature and holism they projected onto the East European experience in general. In sermons, Hasidic tales were used as proof texts of universal wisdom from Jewish sources.[38] Hasidic music, adapted for American Jewish bourgeois taste, made Hasidism accessible. With this growing popularity, Hasidism gained official recognition, such as for the 1954 Tercentenary.[39] The culturally-minded, secular intellectuals were particularly smitten with their reconstruction of Hasidism, which competed with those of other subgroups trying to make it usable for their agendas. As mentioned before, in 1954, Norman Podhoretz looked back at the 1944 *Commentary* symposium "Under Forty" and the prevalent hostility or indifference of many contributors regarding their Jewishness, and remarked: "ten years later at least half of them had become enthusiasts of Martin Buber, while the whole of the New York literary world was ringing with praise of the Yiddish storytellers, the Hasidim," and other affirmatively Jewish phenomena.[40] The fascination of American Jews (and Christians) with Hasidism

---

37 *The Legend of the Baal-Shem* (New York, Harper), xii–xiii. This is a translation of the introduction, dated "Ravenna 1907," to the German original *(Die Legende des Baalschem* (Frankfurt: Rütten & Loenig, 1918), xi).
38 Richard C. Hertz, "How To Be Happy As a Jew," in *Best Jewish Sermons of 5714*, ed. Saul I. Teplitz (New York: Jonathan David, 1954), 51; Benjamin M. Kahn, "The Sabbath: Symbol of Jewish Living," 63–64; Orthodox writer Aaron Rosmarin registered surprise that "Conservative and reform [sic] rabbis pen essays on the history of Hassidism, render Hassidic literature into English and even deliver sermons on Hassidism with neo-Hassidic pathos" ("Hassidism and Its Founder (On the 200th Anniversary of His Demise)," *Jewish Forum* 43 (1960): 189).
39 The *American Jewish Tercentenary Community Manual* in the chapter "Music and the Tercentenary" listed "Three Hasidic Dances; Dance of the Joyous, Dance of the Enraptured, Dance of the Exultant" as music appropriate for events related to the anniversary (New York: American Jewish Tercentenary Committee, 1954, 64).
40 Norman Podhoretz, "Introduction: Jewishness and the Younger Intellectuals: A Symposium," *Commentary* 31 (April 1961): 307–08. Philosopher and Buber translator Walter Kaufman called the fascination with Buber an elite phenomenon; "The Stature of Martin Buber," *Commentary* 26(October 1958): 355–59.

owed much to Buber's presentation of the phenomenon. Buber provided the occasion and point of entry for these thinkers, with the publication of *Tales of the Hasidim, Legends of the Baal-Shem*, and many other texts, as well as by his visits to the United States in the 1950s.[41] Secular thinkers around *Commentary* were especially open to his message. "If there is a neo-Hasidism, it is the creation of Martin Buber," Leslie Fiedler declared in 1949 in the journal.[42] Will Herberg in 1952 called Buber's recent lecture tour of the United States "an event of major intellectual signification."[43] These thinkers' infatuation with the Jerusalem-based bearded sage from Galicia and his ideas was mocked as "Buber mayses."[44]

Hasidism played a special role in their trajectories toward a positive Jewish identity. Through its reconstructions in mid-twentieth-century America, many thinkers explored innovative ways to tap into an authenticating tradition within the American present. It served them as the gateway to the East European past and became, particularly for intellectuals, a *pars pro toto,* or even its essence. It was most prominently Buber and Heschel who asserted that Hasidism contained the spiritual essence of East European Judaism, which was, in turn, the most authentic form of Judaism as such. Buber wrote, "The Hasidic teaching is the consummation of Judaism."[45] His presentation of the Hasidic movement shaped the influential perspective that Hasidism was the last unadulterated Jewish phenomenon that emerged before closer social and intellectual contact with the outside world injected non-Jewish modernity into Judaism. *Commentary's*

---

41 *Tales of the Hasidim: The Early Masters* (New York: Schocken, 1947); *Tales of the Hasidim: The Later Masters* (New York: Schocken, 1948); *Hasidism* (New York: Philosophical Library, 1948); *Commentary* published excerpts of Buber's books. Articles include "The Man of Today and the Jewish Bible: How the Modern Can Recapture Faith," *Commentary* 6 (1948), 327–33; "The Silent Question: About Henri Bergson and Simone Weil," *Judaism* 1 (1952): 99–105; "National and Pioneer Education," *Jewish Frontier* VIII (1941): 39–43.

42 Leslie A. Fiedler, "Hasidism and the Modern Jew," review of *Tales of the Hasidim, Hasidism,* et al. by Martin Buber, *Commentary* 7 (January 1949): 196. Such statements obscure the role of other thinkers, particularly Heschel, as his biographers noted. On the relationship between Buber and Heschel, cf. Edward K. Kaplan and Samuel Dresner, *Abraham Joshua Heschel: Prophetic Witness* (New Haven: Yale University Press, 1998): 142–45, 164–66, 222–28, 245–47.

43 Will Herberg, "How Can You Say 'God'? review of *Eclipse of God*, and *At the Turning*, by Martin Buber, *Commentary* 14 (December 1952): 615. Buber's first visit to the US, a lecture tour in the fall of 1951, was arranged by JTS to gain further publicity (Kaplan, *Spiritual Radical*, 134–35).

44 Milton Himmelfarb makes reference to the double meaning of the Yiddish term: for "stories" but also for "old wives' tales," in his introduction to the *Commentary* symposium, "The State of Jewish Belief," *Commentary* 42 (August 1966): 72.

45 Buber, "Silent Question," 105; cf. Abraham Joshua Heschel, "The Two Great Traditions: The Sephardim and the Ashkenazim," *Commentary* 5 (May 1948): 416.

editorial introduction to Buber's "Tales" called Hasidism the last positive gesture made by East European Jews before the disintegration of their civilization.[46]

Buber's and other popular narratives drew on diverse scholarly findings on Hasidism, as they served American Jewish needs for memory and identity. Scholarship on the movement at mid-century agreed that Hasidism played a distinct role as a reaction to the crisis of East European Jewry and Judaism in the eighteenth century. It appeared as an agent of change threatening traditional structures, or as representative of backward traditionalism, but initially not as a positive, modern spiritual force. Dubnow's influential writings had placed its rise within the context of socioeconomic crisis. He dismissed its spiritual dimensions out of a rationalist social-scientific view of Hasidism as a *social* movement. Historian Jacob Katz interpreted Hasidism as the functional equivalent of the Haskalah, both of which undermined the traditional society he constructed as the baseline of Jewish modernization. Other and later interpretations provided images that, informing popular depictions, would make identification with Hasidism easier for American Jewish readers by assigning it a moderating role in the modernization processes. Lucy Dawidowicz described Hasidism as "a buffering third force in the conflict between traditionalism and modernity and a source of life-giving energy to both a desiccated rabbinism and an arid rationalism." She also pointed to Hasidism's cultural creativity. Other mid-century scholars told a (since revised) story of innocent founders (like the BeShT) whose free spirituality challenged existing communal and rabbinic power structures.[47] Distance from organized religion and the life-shaping power of a vital spirituality were prominent

---

[46] Editors, "[Note introducing Buber, "Tales of the Hasidim,]" *Commentary* 3 (January 1947): 73; Buber, *Tales: The Early Masters*, 11. Cf. also Buber, "Interpreting Hasidism," *Commentary* 36 (September 1963): 221–22; Grace Goldin, who describes Hasidism as "moving from within" ("For the Sake of Neo-Khassidism," review of *For the Sake of Heaven*, by Martin Buber, *Jewish Frontier* XII (1945): 4); Fiedler, "Hasidism and Modern Man," 195. The notion of Hasidism as a purely Jewish phenomenon is also a key idea of Jacob Katz's *Tradition and Crisis: Jewish Society at the End of the Middle Ages* (New York: New York University Press, 1993; orig. publ. 1958, Hebrew; 1961 English).

[47] Cf. Simon Dubnow, *Weltgeschichte des jüdischen Volkes: von seinen Uranfängen bis zur Gegenwart [vol. 7: Die Neuzeit: die zweite Hälfte des XVII. und das XVIII. Jahrhundert]* (Berlin: Jüdischer Verlag, 1928), 213–25; Katz, *Tradition and Crisis*, part III; Lucy S. Dawidowicz, *The Golden Tradition Jewish Life and Thought in Eastern Europe* (Syracuse: Syracuse University Press, 1996, orig. publ. 1967), 22–23. For a discussion of later, revisionist perspectives on Hasidism (and East European Jewish history in general), cf. Marci Shore, "The Jews in Eastern Europe: New Historiography," in *East European Politics and Societies and Cultures* 21 (2007): 505–06; Ada Rapoport-Albert, "Introduction," in *Hasidism Reappraised*, ed. Rapoport-Albert, (Oxford: Littman, 1998), xvii–xxiv; Moshe Rosman, *Founder of Hasidism: A Quest for the Historical Ba'al Shem Tov* (Berkeley: University of California Press,

motifs in Buber's religious philosophy and depiction of Hasidism. In his writings, Hasidism's Jewish character was associated with a sense of holiness, which was contrasted with the loss of comprehensive Jewishness that the advent of modernity brought. He described the Hasidic way of life as deeply spiritual and intense, humane and magical, communal and distinct. It gained its vitality from the fervor and exalted joy that Hasidim experienced in their everyday lives and through which they became whole and holy by their association with God.[48]

American Jewish thinkers demonstrated the relevance of Hasidism to American Jewry in the postwar decades by drawing parallels to the situation of East European Jewry in the aftermath of the attacks of 1648 and the rise and fall of the false messiah Shabetai Tsevi. "The conditions that contributed to the rise and spread of Hasidism in the eighteenth century reappeared in the twentieth century," Yeshiva University's Rabbi Joseph Lookstein argued, pointing to the "false messiahs" of democracy, equality, and reason. "They proved as futile and as frustrating as the Sabbati Zvis and Jacob Franks of an earlier day."[49] After national trauma and religious stagnation, Hasidism emerged as a force of spiritual renewal, which pushed back against the attacks of modernity on authentic Judaism. For this purpose, Buber and Heschel reconstructed an essence of Judaism from pre-Enlightenment folk spirituality, presenting Ashkenazic Jewry as inspirational for Western Jews.

To make it relevant and usable, however, its advocates first had to make it palatable to the political, religious, and aesthetic tastes of mid-twentieth-century American Jews. Buber achieved this largely by the way he presented Hasidism. His reconstructions made East European Judaism *kulturfaehig* (culturally

---

1996); Glenn Dynner, *Men of Silk: The Hasidic Conquest of Polish Society* (New York: Oxford University Press, 2016).
48 Cf. Buber's "Introduction" to *Tales: The Early Masters*, 1–3, and the tales themselves. In this notion, Buber's Hasidism is related to the dialogical philosophy of his *I and Thou* and, through it, to his critique of "religion" as a set of forms, beliefs, and institutions inimical to the encounter with God that reveals a living truth; cf. Arthur A. Cohen, "Martin Buber: The Bible and Hasidism [II]," *Jewish Frontier* XXIV (1957): 13; Ernst Simon, "From Dialogue to Peace: Martin Buber in Memoriam," *Conservative Judaism* 19 (1965): 28–29; Maurice Friedman, "Hasidism and the Contemporary Jew," *Judaism* 9 (1960): 201, 205. For other accounts of Hasidism emphasizing its holistic character, cf. Lucy S. Dawidowicz, "Yiddish: Past, Present, and Perfect," *Commentary* 33 (May 1962): 375–85; Gershon Kranzler, "Chasidism Can Point the Way," *Jewish Life* 26 (1959): 23–24; Fiedler, "Hasidism and the Modern Jew," 195.
49 Joseph H. Lookstein, "The Neo-Hasidism of Abraham J. Heschel," *Judaism* 5 (1956): 2; similarly, Samuel Levy, "The Future of Judaism," *Jewish Forum* 23 (1940): 175; Rosmarin, "Hassidism and Its Founder," 189. Textbooks also describe Hasidism as a reaction to the events of 1648, e.g. Pessin, *The Jewish People*, 99–112; Klaperman/Klaperman, vol. 3, 187–200.

legitimate), thus completing a supplementary act of emancipation, German-Jewish philosopher Ernst Simon remarked. It was no coincidence that in 1953 *Commentary* published Rosenzweig's report about his encounter with Hasidim in Warsaw, which reinforced the notion of Hasidic religious practice as aesthetically inspiring not despite, but because of, its quaint traditionalism.⁵⁰ Intellectual historian Paul Mendes-Flohr has traced the anti-modern impetus in the modern engagement with Hasidism to the fin-de-siècle disenchantment with modernity that was still prevalent when Buber originally presented East European Judaism to West European Jews in the early twentieth century. These highly-acculturated Jews, estranged from the tradition, welcomed Buber's presentation of Hasidism as an *"aesthetic* affirmation of Judaism."⁵¹ Two generations later, American Jews had a similar need for the re-legitimization of an authenticating reconstruction of their spiritual heritage, at least of the type presented by Buber. Thus, he was credited with reconnecting American Jews with their heritage. Journals as different as *Judaism* (rabbinic-religious) and *Jewish Currents* (Communist) hailed him as "the true mediator between the thinking, in our time, of the Eastern and Western worlds," as he "unlocked for Western Jewry a complex of thought and feeling which, through the years, contributed immensely toward bringing about profound changes in the inner substance of Jewish life and thought."⁵²

The praise from across the ideological spectrum reflected the appeal of a familiar trope: a spiritual essence, expressed through the newly appreciated aesthetics of Hasidism à la Buber, was sufficiently abstract as to be made usable for the widely divergent ideas of Judaism and Jewishness. Looking at the range of re-interpretations of Hasidism in postwar America, Orthodox thinker Charles Raddock, himself Hasidic, remarked that it had become "a kind of free-for-all, where every novice invades the sanctum to come up with another 'package' for the delectation of the unsuspecting reader." Writing with more detachment, but also critical of Buber's version in particular, scholar Rivkah Schatz-Uffenheimer noted: "There is nothing that you cannot link to Hasidism if you have enough diligence and yet greater boldness."⁵³

---

50 Ernst Simon, "Martin Buber: His Way Between Thought and Deed (On His 70th Anniversary)," *Jewish Frontier* XV (1948): 25; Franz Rosenzweig, "Discovery of the East European Jew: A Young Visitor in the Old Warsaw Ghetto," *Commentary* 15 (January 1953): 86–89.
51 Paul Mendes-Flohr, "Fin de Siecle Orientalism, the Ostjuden, and the Aesthetics of Self-Affirmation," in *Divided Passions: Jewish Intellectuals and the Experience of Modernity* (Detroit: Wayne State University Press, 1991), 100, emphasis in the original.
52 S. Eisenstadt, "Martin Buber at 80: Israeli Sage Fights for Arab-Jewish Unity," *Jewish Currents* 12 (1958): 21; Ernest M. Wolf, "Martin Buber and German Jewry," *Judaism* 1 (1952): 347.
53 Charles Raddock, "The Baal Shem, a Victim of Literary Fraud," *Jewish Forum* 43 (1960): 179; Raddock, "Unionism, Socialism and Orthodoxy: An Inquiry," *Jewish Life* 14 (1947): 43;

Hasidic Wholeness, Antinomianism, Ethical Judaism, and Proto-Socialism

Thinkers from highly different camps within American Jewry showed such boldness as they used different reconstructions of Hasidism for their respective agendas, making it a bellwether of the directions in which they wanted to take the community. The journal *Judaism* devoted an entire issue to Hasidism in 1960, in which religious thinker Steven Schwarzschild concluded: "The Besht is far from dead. Indeed he is more alive in America right now than he ever was, and it would seem that his vitality will continue to increase. He is reincarnated in the growing influence of and effectiveness of Hasidic Judaism in this country."[54] Particularly striking and illustrating Schwarzschild's argument was the fact that Norman Mailer was inspired to write highly imaginative, drug-infused responses to Buber's *Tales*, published in several installments in *Commentary* in 1962 and 1963.[55] On the left, the *Workmen's Circle Call's* anonymous reviewer of a biography of the Baal Shem Tov pointed to a widespread fascination with the Hasidic founder and the experience and philosophy associated with the movement. Other leftists pointed to Hasidism's redemptive potential for contemporary Jews, but also to its strangeness. The Communist *Jewish Currents* emphasized the ethical dimensions of Hasidism and appropriated Hasidic rabbis such as Levi-Yitshak of Berditchev as proto-Socialist champions of ordinary Jewish folk.[56] Reform Jewish writers exhibited a similar pattern of selective appropriation of

---

Rivkah Schatz-Uffenheimer, "Martin Buber: Master of Hasidic Teaching," review of *The Origin and Meaning of Hasidism*, by Martin Buber, *Judaism* 9 (1960, special issue on Hasidism): 279. A scholarly debate about the methodology and historical veracity of Buber's representation of Hasidism took place in several journals; cf. Michael Wyschogrod's introduction to Hayim Ben Isaac, "Man, the Master of All Created Worlds," *Commentary* 14 (December 1952): 595; Simon, "From Dialogue to Peace," 28–29; Schatz-Uffenheimer's critique; and Buber's response, "Interpreting Hasidism."

54 Steven S. Schwarzschild, "Survey of Current Theological Literature," *Judaism* 9 (1960): 269. In the introduction to the issue, the editors of *Judaism* point to "an implicit potential contribution [...] that Hasidism can make to the deepening and resurgence of one or another aspect of Jewish life in our day" ("This Issue:" n.p.).

55 Norman Mailer, "Responses & Reactions," *Commentary* 34 (December 1962): 504–506; five more installments followed under the same title in the February, April, June, August, and October issues of 1963. In the final piece, Mailer no longer engages Buber, but responds to Norman Podhoretz's controversial "My Negro Problem – And Ours," which had been published in the magazine in February 1963 (*Commentary* 35: 93–101).

56 "[Review of *Rabbi Israel Baal Shem Tov*, by Menashe Unger]," *Workmen's Circle Call* 35 (1964): 16; Mortimer J. Cohen, "When Saints Wage War," review of *For the Sake of Heaven*, by Martin

Hasidism, as they emphasized the role of the *tsaddik,* again Levi-Yitzhak in particular, as a model of spiritual-ethical leadership. The *CCAR Journal* printed a Hasidic tale that suggested the superiority of spirituality over ritual. Reform rabbi Herbert Weiner approached present-day Hasidism with sympathetic curiosity in two series of articles on Lubavitcher and Bratslaver Hasidism in Brooklyn.[57]

Orthodoxy's stance on the renewed interested in Hasidism as a reconstructed historical phenomenon was even more complex. Several writers offered hagiographic representations of historic Hasidism. Some acknowledged a decline from the pure origins of the movement and others claimed an uncorrupted continuity with the present.[58] Talmudist and sociologist Gershon Kranzler presented Hasidism as a guide for the revitalization of American Judaism, which, in "the age of supermachines [sic], but also of mass neuroses and supreme individual insecurity [needs] the strength that derives from faith."[59] Kranzler and other Orthodox commentators were careful, however, not to equate traditional Hasidism, on which they would model a Torah-true American Judaism, with the neo-Hasidism that they rejected. They saw it as an attempt to take the Torah out of Judaism and as an instant of legitimizing fashionable, but fatuous, appropriations of the tradition. Raddock was most forceful in emphasizing the fundamental differences. In an article entitled "Hasidism – and They Mean It!" he welcomed transplanted Hasidic groups in New York as a shot of Jewish religious commitment for American Jewry, extolling with proud particularism the uniqueness of Judaism that could be authentic only on its own terms.[60] On the other hand, he

---

Buber, *Workmen's Circle Call* 13 (1945): 14; Eisenstadt, "Buber at 80," 21; Abraham Bick, "Rabbi Levi-Itzhok of Berdichev," *Jewish Currents* 14 (1959): 26–27, 42.

57 Felix A. Levy, "A Survey of Current Books," *CCAR Journal,* January 1961: 63; Rabbi Levi Yitzhak of Berdichev, "Spirit in Matter and Faith in Works," *Judaism* 14 (1965): 220–23; Jacob J. Weinstein, "The Hasid Who Didn't Attend Services (A Hasidic Story Retold)," *CCAR Journal,* January 1956: 44–46; Herbert Weiner, "The Lubavitcher Movement I: Organized Mysticism," *Commentary* 23 (March 1957), 231–41; part II, "The Root and the Branches," *Commentary* 23 (April 1957): 316–27; Weiner, "Braslav in Brooklyn," *Judaism* 13 (1964): 351–60. For all his fascination with "real" Hasidism, Weiner juxtaposed its primitiveness with Buber's refined version.

58 Irvin Michlin, "Israel Ben Eliezer Baal Shem Tobh, 1700–1760," *Jewish Forum* 43 (1960): 117–21; Harry Rabinowicz, "The Fires of Hasidism," *Jewish Life* 32 (1964): 48–58; Meyer Waxman, "Israel Baal Shem," *Jewish Life* 27 (1960): 26–33.

59 Kranzler, "Chasidism Can Point the Way," 22.

60 Charles Raddock, "Hasidism – and They Mean It!" *Jewish Forum* 33 (1950), 232–34; Raddock, "Schneersohn, Heir to a Noble Tradition," *Jewish Forum* 34 (1951): 72–73; Raddock, "Hassidism: Upper Manhattan's Picturesque Newcomer," *Jewish Forum* 35 (1952): 79–81; Raddock, "The Invincible 'Dynasty' of Tsanz," *Jewish Forum* 37 (1954): 192–94; Raddock, "Imprint of a Unique Personality: Baruch Baer of Kaminetz," *Jewish Forum* 41 (1958): 58–61.

denounced the champions of "neo-Hasidism," from Buber on down, as seekers so misguided as to be on the road to apostasy:

> Thanks to Martin Buber and his fashionable parlor tales about the 'apostles' of Hassidism, this fashionable intelligentsia – some of them, at any rate – regard themselves as the true, legitimate heirs of the Baal Shem HaKadosh! [... We] must say to them, REFRAIN! It is they who [...] keep telling innocent readers that Hassidism is a 'revised' kind of Judaism salvaged from the 'straitjacket' of the Shulhan Arukh, that Hassidism is almost akin to the 'higher ethos' of Christianity, etc., etc.[61]

Raddock and fellow Orthodox polemicists aimed their criticism at the secular intellectuals infatuated with the "Buber mayses" in their attempts to find meaning in their Jewishness. These Orthodox thinkers feared that the intellectuals would use "neo-Hasidism" to universalize Judaism and reconstruct it on foreign terms. Raddock spelled out that a "surprising number of American intellectuals, brilliant, sensitive and searching, [who] want to come home to some kind of Judaism" would use Hasidism as an instrument to reconstruct Judaism as a broadly defined culture. Looking at the "lost intellectuals," "our Leslie Fiedlers, Irving Howes, Philip Rahvs, Alfred Kazins, and Clement Greenbergs," he warns that "the uninformed American Jewish intellectual starts out with a false perspective of 'Jewish culture.'"[62]

By this perspective, the thinkers he had in mind responded to what Podhoretz called "the discovery of many American Jewish intellectuals that they were as much products of Jewish culture as of Western civilization." These intellectuals explored Hasidism open-mindedly, as was reflected particularly, again, in *Commentary*. The journal re-printed historical sources about the dispute between the Hasidim and the Vilna Gaon and a story denouncing the Satmar Hasidim as extremist and intolerant, Weiner's inside research in the Lubavitch group, Buber's "Tales" and the critics of his methods as well as Mailer's responses, and reviews of books by and on Buber and others.[63] Like so many others, secular intellectuals

---

[61] Raddock, "The Baal Shem," 179, emphasis in the original.
[62] Charles Raddock, "Judaism and The Lost Intellectuals," *Jewish Forum* 41 (1952): 95–96, 98.
[63] "The Tanya and the Gaon: A Dispute," *Commentary* 21 (January 1956): 67–68; Ben-Isaac, "Man, the Master;" "From the Teachings of Habad Hasidism," *Commentary* 24 (July1957): 64–65; Harry Gersh and Sam Miller, "Satmar in Brooklyn: A Zealot Community," *Commentary* 28 (November 1959): 389–99; Kaufman, "The Stature of Buber;" Herberg, "How Can You Say 'God?'" The underlying assumption was that, following pure origins, Hasidism had degenerated and therefore needed to be rediscovered and translated into a contemporary idiom, in which it had great potential for modern Jews skeptical of established expressions of Jewishness. (Editors, "Introduction" to Buber's "Tales," 73) The motif of Hasidism's corruption appears frequently; cf.

Figure 20: The (seventh) Lubavitcher Rebbe, Menahem Mendel Schneersohn and a group of Hasidim carrying Torah scrolls, not dated. (American Jewish Archives)

were fascinated by the fervor and joy with which they equated the Hasidic experience of Judaism, in contrast to the bland, mundane reality of American Judaism. Alfred Kazin describes how he searched in vain for the qualities of the Hasidim, "great enthusiasts, dancers, walkers" before the Lord: "There were my people! But when you asked around, hoping there had been at least one Chassid somewhere among all your many praying grandfathers and great grandfathers and great-great-grandfathers [...] surely there was one still among these ancient bearded elders in our synagogue! – they shrugged their shoulders."[64]

Kazin's comment encapsulated the distance and dissatisfaction many intellectuals experienced vis-à-vis organized Jewish religious life. It stemmed from what they recognized as deficits of liberal Judaism: a rationalized religion which, as a mere part of a fragmented modern identity, seemed too atrophied and accommodationist to hold much promise of deeper meaning and salvation.

Arthur A. Cohen, "Martin Buber: The Bible and Hasidism [I]," *Jewish Frontier* XXIV (1957): 33–38; Kalman Marmor, "Excommunication of Hassidism," *Jewish Life [Morning Freiheit Association]* 9 (1956): 28–31; Simon, "From Dialogue to Peace," 30).
64 Alfred Kazin, *A Walker in the City* (Orlando: Harcourt, 1979; orig. publ. 1951), 104.

Hasidism, with its emphasis on experience and immediacy, but also with its anti-nomianism and the claim to give meaning to mundane activities and answers to existential questions, seemed like the perfect antidote.[65] Fiedler stated programmatically that "not reason but passion is the mode of redemption," and asserted "the need for the leap past rational scruples to belief, which alone can turn Judaism from a system of metaphors into a living faith." Judaism needed to be refashioned in order to counter its negative image and assert its unique way of thinking and life against a dominant Western modernity.[66] Mendes-Flohr found the alienated Jewish intellectuals' fascination with Hasidism to be driven by the urge to liberate themselves from the constricting images and expectations that were ascribed to them as Jews, from within the Jewish community and from without. "Buber's Hasidica seem to have held a specific attraction for Jews estranged from Judaism. They tended to view the Baal Shem and Rabbi Nachman, as portrayed by Buber, as adumbrating an alternative Jewish identity," based in a sensibility that "had little to do not only with bourgeois rationalism and materialism, but also with traditional Jewish law and religious practice."[67]

Distant as they were from traditional Judaism, these thinkers found in Hasidism a model of deeply-rooted Jewishness that allowed them to tap into the wellspring of its spiritual and creative potential. Many found the meaning they sought in Hasidism's venerable pastness, which they imbued with modern notions of spirituality and sacredness. Mailer took this imaginative engagement with Hasidism to a subjective and idiosyncratic extreme, writing that he first found consolation in Buber's tales as he was "riding the electric rail of long nights of marijuana." Finding that "these pieces were the first bits of Jewish devotional prose I read that were not deadening to me," he realized that "I had less connection to the past than anyone I knew." He professed his debt to Buber for helping him see that "I had at least a rudimentary sense of a clan across the centuries." With this realization, he may have spoken for other Jewish intellectuals in search of positive Jewishness, who, like him, were "granted the intoxication of a historic past."[68]

---

65 In this sense, the reconstruction of Hasidism parallels and overlaps with the emergence of the "new Jewish theology," for which Heschel was a key thinker. Cf. Robert G. Goldy, *The Emergence of Jewish Theology in America* (Bloomington: Indiana University Press, 1990).
66 Fiedler, "Hasidism and the Modern Jew," 195, 197; Simon, "Martin Buber," 25. Friedman similarly wrote off liberal Judaism: "The values of liberal Judaism have ceased to be demands placed upon us in the concrete life-situations in which we find ourselves;" cf. "Hasidism and the Contemporary Jew," 201–02, 205–06; Friedman, "[My Jewish Affirmation:] Biblical Dialogue, Covenant and Hasidic Fervor," *Judaism* 10 (Fall 1961): 300–03.
67 Mendes-Flohr, "Fin de Siecle Orientalism, " 100.
68 Mailer, "Responses and Reactions I," 505.

Secular intellectuals like Mailer used this intoxication to enhance their creativity in translating the Jewish past into a modern idiom – the only way to make it relevant and their way of appropriating it as meaningful. What Podhoretz wrote of the participants in a 1961 *Commentary* symposium may have been true not just for secular thinkers: "These intellectuals are aware that their kind of Jewishness provides little hope for the survival of even those Jewish traditions which they admire. Some pointed out that they are living off the religious and cultural capital of the past."[69] They sought to increase this cultural capital by reconstructing Hasidism and applying it to the contemporary situation of American Jewry. For religious thinkers like Heschel, it could serve as a model to expand the narrow concept of religion, while holding on to a religious core in a culturally conceived, comprehensively Jewish "way of life."[70] For secularists, Hasidic holism could mean imbuing a range of ideas and ideals with Jewish meaning: social progressivism for leftists, or preserving a secular Jewish spirit through social science, as Max Weinreich did. YIVO's research director compared the historical mission of the institute with that of the Hasidic *tsaddik:* "In it/him [YIVO/the *tsaddik*] the holy sparks [...] were gathered that were sprayed around everywhere."[71]

Weinreich's analogy inhabits a liminal space between secular and spiritual categories and thereby illustrates a larger phenomenon. Even thinkers not associated with formal Jewish religion sought in Hasidism paths to a new conceptual framework of Judaism or Jewishness: overcoming the constrictions of a liberal concept and reality of religion, emancipated from the ritual and behavioral demands of Orthodoxy, preserving the spiritual depth of the tradition and the grounding in a common past, while fully engaging with the modern world. The search for such a "third way" that would transcend the divisions in Jewish life engendered by modernity united religious and secular thinkers. If the challenge of Hasidism is met, "a new stage of modern Judaism may be reached," Friedman wrote: "a fusion of the fervor, community, and wholeness of Hasidism with the liberalism of the Western Jew and the communal and national consciousness of the Israeli."[72] Sounding almost imploring, Fiedler similarly articulated an ideal of spiritual wholeness for secular intellectuals:

---

69 Podhoretz, "Introduction: Jewishness and the Younger Intellectuals," 310.
70 Cf. Heschel, "The Two Great Traditions;" Friedman, "Hasidism and the Contemporary Jew," 200; Kranzler, "Chasidism Can Point the Way;" Weiner, "The Lubavitcher Movement II," 327.
71 Max Weinreich, "Jewish Scholarship Today" [Yiddish], speech at the 1941 Annual YIVO Conference, typescript, YIVO Archives, Max Weinreich Collection: RG 584.4, 7.
72 Friedman, "Hasidism and the Contemporary Jew," 206.

> Buber has made available for us the texts of a mode of belief for which we have been intellectually prepared, and to which we are pre-disposed by the fallen ritual pattern of our lives. It finds us at a moment when, disinclined to choose between available avenues of accommodation and alienation for its own sake, we are casting about for a new way.[73]

Many secular Jewish intellectuals expressed this "new way" to understand their Jewishness by engaging with literature and culture more generally: It was the place where they looked for elevation in the first place – and the place where they were to find out that they had lost the competition to shape a meaningful Jewishness out of the past for the American present.

---

[73] Fiedler, "Hasidism and the Modern Jew," 198.

9 Tevye in Kasrilevke, the *Fiddler* in America: East European Jewishness in Literature

In Isaac Rosenfeld's 1948 novel *Passage from Home*, Bernard Miller, the restless adolescent protagonist who flees from his home and its uncertain Jewishness, is urged by his stepmother to spend more time reading, so as to settle down: "'A Jewish book,' she exclaimed. [...] 'Ah, there are so many nice things – Sholem Aleichem, Peretz, Mendele. If that's too hard, your father could read them to you. You should take more of an interest in Jewish life.'"[1] At mid-century, American Jews collectively followed this advice and read these and other authors, taking more of an interest in Jewish life than before. But, like Bernard, most of them could not access their East European literary heritage in its original language and forms. Instead, they encountered it in translations, adaptations, anthologies, dramatizations, and other forms of cultural translation that made the texts accessible and relevant to them. The 1940s to 1960s were high points in American Jews' encounter with Eastern Europe in literature, which bridged the elite and popular discourses on the past. The motifs and motives of this encounter can be found not just in the works of fiction, but also in reviews and other forms of literary and cultural criticism. They served the ongoing cultural translation of the East European past into an American idiom.

Cultural translators, especially literary-minded intellectuals, such as Maurice Samuel, Isaac Rosenfeld, Irving Howe and others, played an important role in this process as critics, editors, and linguistic translators. They brought their own agendas to the reconstruction of the East European past as they explored their own sense of Jewishness. As such, these mostly secular intellectuals were themselves voices in the discourse that they had opened up in the mid-1940s. The publication in 1943 of Maurice Samuel's *The World of Sholom Aleichem* marked the beginning of a 20-year long intellectual battle over who in the English-language literary world would define the East European heritage.

Maurice Samuel Applies Sholem Aleichem to America

While Sholem Aleichem (1859–1916) and his work were already known to English-language American Jewish readers by mid-century, *The World of Sholom Aleichem*

---

[1] Isaac Rosenfeld, *Passage from Home* (New York: Markus Wiener, 1988; orig. publ. 1948), 79.

marked the beginning of a new outpouring of texts by and about the Yiddish writer.[2] Sholem Aleichem's stories were published in several journals, as were countless articles about him by literary, cultural, religious, and political thinkers.[3] In these secondary texts, Sholem Aleichem was claimed for divergent agendas: not just by Yiddishists, but also by rabbis calling for greater identification with Judaism, by leftists decrying poverty in capitalist society, and by secular intellectuals in support of literary modernism.[4] Cumulatively, the wide dissemination of his work lodged Sholem Aleichem firmly in the American Jewish consciousness. Several contemporary observers argued that the reason for first the lack and then the surge of interest in Sholem Aleichem was Westernized Jews' complicated attitude toward East European "others." Hebrew scholar Judah Goldin in 1950 attributed the growing preoccupation with East European Jewry to a sense of guilt and atonement for the very condescension that had previously prevented it. Yet, he also warned that the East European world was inaccessible to the American Jew. "It seems utterly irrelevant to his idiom. [...] If he is to take that world seriously, it needs to be made intelligible before it is held up as a model to him."[5]

This was the mission Samuel had taken up: to make the East European past intelligible and relevant to American Jews, translating it into their idiom so that they could see its character as a model for a community uncertain of itself. *The World of Sholom Aleichem* has been recognized as "an epochal moment in defining Sholem

---

2 The difference between the author Shalom Rabinovitz, his persona as the pseudonymous author Sholem Aleichem, and his eponymous narrator in many fictional or (pseudo-) autobiographical stories are outside the focus of this chapter, particularly as its protagonists tended to conflate the three.

3 A selection: Sholem Aleichem, "Wonders of America," *Jewish Life [Morning Freiheit Association]* 1 (1946): 15–16 (unless indicated otherwise, *Jewish Life* refers to the Communist journal, not the eponymous Orthodox one); "The Knife: A Story," *Commentary* 9 (January 1950): 151–58; "The Couple," *Jewish Frontier* XXI (1954): 16–21; "Toward My Biography: Notes on Becoming a Writer," *Commentary* 27 (April 1959): 338–40; "Coming to America: Letters on Board Ship from London to New York in 1906," *Jewish Currents* 13 (1958): 14–15. A selection of secondary texts: Ludwig Lewisohn, "Creative Nostalgia," review of *The World of Sholom Aleichem*, by Maurice Samuel, *Jewish Frontier* X (1943): 27; Irving Howe, "Sholem Aleichem and His People," review of *The Old Country*, by Sholem Aleichem, *Partisan Review* 13 (1946): 591–95; Lala Kaufman, "My Father, Sholem Aleichem: A Memoir," *Commentary* 24 (September 1957): 250–53; *Jewish Currents* 13 (1959; special issue on the Sholem Aleichem Centennial).

4 Ely E. Pilchik, "Of Books and Papers," *CCAR Journal*, June 1953: 49; Richard C. Hertz. "How to Be Happy as a Jew," in *Best Jewish Sermons of 5714*, ed. Saul I. Teplitz (New York: Jonathan David, 1954), 40–51; Aaron Gurstein, "The Work of Sholom Aleichem," *Jewish Life* 4 (1950): 12–15; Morris U. Schappes, "Sholem Aleichem Universal," *Jewish Currents* 13 (1959): 3–4.

5 Judah Goldin, "Remembrance of Things Past," review of *The Testament of the Lost Son*, by Soma Morgenstern, *Commentary* 10 (November 1950): 502–03.

Aleichem – and the East European Jewry he was increasingly identified with – for wartime and postwar American audiences." It not only kicked off the "nostalgia industry" for this past, but touched very early on the themes and concerns that would come to shape American Jewish identity: continuity in change, generational differences, holistic and fragmented identities, ethnicity and spirituality, ruptures through immigration and the Holocaust.[6]

From the very first pages, Samuel told his readers what they had been missing in their ancestral culture and pointed out unacknowledged continuities: "Sholom Aleichem is almost unknown to millions of Americans whose grandfathers made up his world. This is not simply a literary loss; it is a break – a very recent and disastrous one – in the continuity of a group history."[7] Writing in the middle of the Holocaust and World War II about East European Jewry, he presented a world that was being destroyed before his readers' eyes: a world in transition but still rooted in a tradition that made being Jewish both self-evident and self-conscious, complicated but beautiful and deeply meaningful, particularly in the face of the challenges posed by a bewildering modernity.[8] In Samuel's and other cultural translators' hands, Tevye would become the "universal grandfather of Jewish America."[9] Samuel urged his readers to realize what their own grandfathers, "a remarkable lot," had to offer for the big questions facing American Jews. "It is not a wholesome thing to believe that we and our posterity will find all the answers; for some of them were discovered in the very imperfect past."[10] The grandchildren had urgent reasons to turn to the past, given the rootlessness and shallowness that Samuel saw in their Jewishness. The only remnant of the East European *shtetl* he found was their saying the *Kaddish*, "that and perhaps the Day of Atonement, and a funny Yiddish word or two, and when it has not been changed, a name that keeps them out of certain jobs and country clubs." Modernity, immigration, and the nature of America had extinguished the religious intensity of Kasrilevke, Sholem Aleichem's fictional *shtetl*:

---

[6] Jeremy Dauber, *The Worlds of Sholem Aleichem: The Remarkable Life and Afterlife of the Man Who Created Tevye* (New York: Nextbook Schocken, 2013), 346–47.
[7] Maurice Samuel, *The World of Sholom Aleichem* (New York: Vintage, 1973; orig. publ. 1943), 7.
[8] Alisa Solomon calls the book "a literary call to arms," meant to raise support for the war effort (*Wonder of Wonders: A Cultural History of "Fiddler on the Roof"* (New York: Henry Holt, 2013), 52).
[9] Samuel, *World of Sholom Aleichem*, 168; Seth Wolitz, "The Americanization of Tevye or Boarding the Jewish 'Mayflower,'" *American Quarterly* 40 (1988): 530. The character's name is variously spelled "Tevyeh," "Tevye," and yet other ways in various primary and secondary sources; the same is true for the fictitious *shtetl* Kasrielevky (Kasrielevke, etc.) and other names of persons and places.
[10] Samuel, *World of Sholom Aleichem*, 7.

> Life and religion were indivisible for Kasrielevkites; they did not think of religion as of something tagged on to life, something separate, detachable, and optional. Their grandchildren and great-grandchildren in American cities have rabbis, synagogues, temples, Sunday schools, or even Yeshivas; they have activities, holy days, and high holy days; they have organizations and *landsmanshaften,* Zionist societies, B'nai B'riths, anti-defamation leagues, lodges, unions, cultural clubs, men's clubs: and all these things, including even the rabbis and synagogues, are additions and increments, in no way reproducing the folk wholeness of the Jewish life in Kasrielevky.[11]

Once again, a familiar motif colored the image of the East European past: the contrast between old country holism and New World fragmentation that shaped the image of America in Samuel's book. The penultimate chapter described America as alien to Sholom Aleichem's Jews: "a new land which shone from afar with the radiance of freedom and opportunity, but it was a land which, they forefelt [sic], would not understand them. – And did America understand them? Hardly."[12] Samuel's portrayal suggested that America and the old country differed not only on account of historical circumstances, but were essentially incompatible, divided by their respective spiritual qualities (or lack thereof). In this depiction, the political, cultural, and geographical setting for Tevye informed a mythical-spiritual essence of Jewishness that could hardly be reproduced elsewhere. Eminent critic Shmuel Niger made this notion explicit when he wrote that Sholem Aleichem was "expressing the innermost essence of the Jewish way of life and the Yiddish language." The stories revealed "the untapped treasures of Jewish folk life" and "present the substance of Jewish existence."[13]

As channeled by Samuel, Sholem Aleichem became a prime example of what Barbara Kirshenblatt-Gimblett has called "the popular arts of American Jewish ethnography," which provided material for the reconstruction of the past for present purposes.[14] She points out that *The World of Sholom Aleichem* (and Heschel's *The Earth Is the Lord's* and Bella Chagall's *Burning Lights*) served as models for the 1952 ethnography *Life is with People.*[15] Samuel, Niger, and many others suggested that Sholem Aleichem be read as an ethnographic source for

---

11 Samuel, *World of Sholom Aleichem*, 38, 53–54.
12 Samuel, *World of Sholom Aleichem*, 322.
13 S. Niger, "The Gift of Sholom Aleichem: He Brought Literature to a People," *Commentary* 2 (August 1946): 118.
14 Barbara Kirshenblatt-Gimblett, "Imagining Europe: The Popular Arts of American Jewish Ethnography," in *Divergent Centers: Shaping Jewish Cultures in Israel and America,* ed. Deborah Dash Moore and Ilan Troen (New Haven: Yale University Press, 2001), 167–84.
15 Kirshenblatt-Gimblett, "Imagining Europe," 156; Bella Chagall, *Burning Lights* (New York: Schocken, 1946).

the reconstruction of the vanished world of East European *shtetl* life. Erasing the creative grasp with which the author Shalom Rabinovitz crafted the persona of Sholem Aleichem, they presented "Sholem Aleichem" as an ethnographic recorder of authentic folk life. "He was a part of Russian Jewry; he was Russian Jewry itself," Samuel claimed in the opening pages of his book. "We could write a *Middletown* of the Russian-Jewish Pale basing ourselves solely on the novels and stories and sketches of Sholom Aleichem, and it would be as reliable a scientific document as any 'factual' study; more so, indeed."[16] Only a later critical

Figure 21: Sholem Aleichem (seated in the middle row, fourth from left, holding his hat) with prominent members of the Jewish community of Bedzin, a Polish *shtetl*, 1905–1913. The photo, taken during a visit of the author, illustrates his prominence and popularity. (United States Holocaust Memorial Museum)

---

16 Samuel, *World of Sholom Aleichem*, 6, 85; cf. Niger, "Gift of Sholom Aleichem," 119; Moshe Decter applied the same notion to Mendele: "the greatest 'anthropologist' of the shtetl." ("The 'Old Country' Way of Life: The Rediscovery of the Shtetl," review of *Life is with People*, by Mark Zborowski and Elizabeth Herzog, *Commentary* 13 (June 1952): 600–04) As mentioned in the previous chapter, *Life is with People* lists texts by Sholem Aleichem among its sources. Cf. also Dan Miron, *The Image of the Shtetl and Other Studies of Modern Jewish Literary Imagination* (Syracuse: Syracuse University Press, 2000), 6; Ruth R. Wisse, *Sholem Aleichem and the Art of Communication* (Syracuse: Syracuse University Press, 1980), 8. "Middletown" refers to eponymous studies by Robert S. and Helen M. Lynd of a typical small American city; the first one, *Middletown: A Study in American Culture*, was published in 1929 (New York: Harcourt Brace & World).

approach would start untangling the various threads that consciously went into the creation of "Sholem Aleichem" and his world.[17]

In Samuel's book and in many other cultural products of the period, history and memory, literature and scholarship were harnessed together to imaginatively reconstruct the essence of the East European Jewish past. Works like *The World of Sholom Aleichem* offered a notion of a folk-based cultural ethnicity that appealed to American Jews, as a foundation for identity beyond the reduction of Jewishness to Judaism. It was Jewish but also contained universal elements, was modern but grounded in continuity and thereby partook in the sacredness that was increasingly bestowed on the vanished world after the Holocaust. Such a firm, positive identity seemed missing among American Jews; the Workmen's Circle's Israel Knox wrote in 1950 that "it would be wonderful if we had a Sholem Aleichem in America," as a guide for Jews who saw themselves in a period of transition, in a no-man's land between the world that was and a world that was to be.[18]

Affirmation or Alienation: The Jewishness of Cultural Translators

As they refashioned quasi-canonical texts for their own needs, especially Yiddish classics, American Jews at mid-century continued a recurring pattern, which literary scholar David Roskies has called the "tactic of recycling the past to fertilize the present." He suggests that developments in postwar American Jewry were an incident of a larger pattern, as the translation of Yiddish classics into English was part of a cultural movement of renewal.[19] In his reading, the mid-century literary engagement with Eastern Europe was a particular example of the larger issue of contested Jewish memory. Roskies has argued that in the early nineteenth century, "the message of Jewish memory," previously the only approach to the past, went up for grabs, as competing "usable pasts" were employed by proponents of different responses to modernity in their fight for the soul of Judaism. He bestowed the title of authoritative explicator of the past upon the *engagé* writer, especially Sholem Aleichem. In the folk-speech of Tevye, creation, memory and historical reality worked in concert as they never had before. The career of Sholem Aleichem illustrates

---

[17] Cf. *Prooftexts* 6 (1986, no. 1: Special Issue, "Sholem Aleichem: The Critical Tradition").
[18] Israel Knox, "Wanted – An American Sholem Aleichem," *Workmen's Circle Call* 18 (1950): 6.
[19] David G. Roskies, "The Treasures of Howe and Greenberg," review of *A Treasury of Yiddish Stories,* ed. by Irving Howe and Eliezer Greenberg, et al., *Prooftexts* 3 (1983): 109, 110.

that "the institution of literature, and its ancillary branches of journalism, drama, criticism, and translation, brought multiple and competing pasthoods into every Jewish home." In claiming the role for the engagé writer, Roskies challenges other scholars' suggestions of who played that role, specifically the historian, as cast by Yosef Hayim Yerushalmi, and the rabbi-scholar, as presented by Ismar Schorsch.[20]

For literature to fulfill this function, it took authors, compilers, editors, reviewers, and critics to lead their community in the appropriation and interpretation of this past. These intellectuals had to rediscover this heritage for themselves first before translating it for others. Roskies' depiction of a larger pattern applies to American Jewish intellectuals at mid-century: they re-invented the past because they were themselves far from their people's cultural heritage. Re-inventing the past "prompts some kind of negotiated return, a reconciliation between the present and the forgotten past, the self and the folk."[21] This pattern of alienation and return applied not only to many of the secular New York Jewish intellectuals, but also to other cultural translators who returned to a different past. Maurice Samuel is a case in point for this pattern, particularly as the author of *The World of Sholom Aleichem*. Before he wrote such "tourists' guides through what for many readers are the uncharted regions of Jewish life," he himself had to physically return to Eastern Europe. Born in Romania, he had grown up in Paris and Manchester, estranged from Jewish tradition, before moving to the United States in 1914. Returning to Europe with the armed forces after World War I, he worked for a committee headed by Henry Morgenthau, Sr., which investigated pogroms in Poland, where he "discovered deep sources of affection and joy in his identification and integration with East European Jewry."[22] He "played a major role in the emergence of the American Jew's sense of Jewish identity and in the evolution of the American Jew's definition of Jewishness"; after the Holocaust in particular he contributed to the "re-Judaization" of American Jewry.[23]

---

[20] David G. Roskies, *The Jewish Search for a Usable Past* (Bloomington: Indiana University Press, 1999), 2, 9–12. Cf. Yosef Hayim Yerushalmi, *Zakhor: Jewish History and Jewish Memory* (New York: Schocken, 1989; orig. publ. 1982), 81; Ismar Schorsch, "Emancipation and the Crisis of Religious Authority: The Emergence of the Modern Rabbinate," in *From Text to Context: The Turn to History in Modern Judaism* (Waltham: Brandeis University Press/Hanover: University Press of New England, 1994), 9–50.
[21] David G. Roskies, *A Bridge of Longing: The Lost Art of Yiddish Storytelling* (Cambridge: Harvard University Press, 1995), 5, 9.
[22] Emanuel S. Goldsmith, "The Education of Maurice Samuel," in *The "Other" New York Jewish Intellectuals*, ed. Carole S. Kessner (New York: New York University Press, 1994), 228–29. Samuel himself described his return to Jewishness in the opening chapter of *Prince of the Ghetto: The Stories of Y. L. Peretz Retold* (New York: Schocken, 1959; orig. publ. 1948), 3–4.
[23] Goldsmith, "Education of Maurice Samuel," 230.

As the title suggests, *The World of Sholom Aleichem,* like other works of popular ethnography, projected an ethnic concept of Jewishness, once again balancing the breadth of a cultural notion with the spiritual essence at its core. Such ideas transcended the dichotomy of religion and ethnicity. The centrality of spirituality in the comprehensive, folk-based cultural ethnicity endowed otherwise profane dimensions of East European Jewish life with a new and distinct sacredness, a key aspect of the reconstruction of this past in the wake of the Holocaust.[24]

For Samuel, this sacralization was a key to the positive Jewishness he promoted in his career as a writer. In this, he differed from other cultural translators, specifically from the secular intellectuals around *Partisan Review* and *Commentary*. Few of these had a specific, conscious agenda to refashion "Jewishness" for American Jews; rather, by exploring the concept driven by their own agendas, they expanded the range of ideas, without actively advocating them. Samuel's affirmative stance vis-à-vis Jewishness made him a member of the group Carole Kessner has labeled "the 'other' New York Jewish intellectuals," a group of "men and women who were in no way ambivalent about their Jewishness." For Kessner, the key difference between these and the more celebrated writers was that "they never described themselves as alienated."[25] This was a key difference indeed. For the *Partisan Review* set, "alienation" was the guiding posture. From their point of view, the East European Jewish past looked very different than it did to Samuel, though both took Sholem Aleichem as a guide.

Isaac Rosenfeld: From Alienation to the Affirmation of a Cultural Jewishness

Isaac Rosenfeld (1918–1956) provides a contrasting example of cultural translation of the same material. Out of a different sensibility and ideology, Rosenfeld refashioned the past in a totally different way and in support of a very different discourse about Jewishness, past and present. Born in America to Yiddish-speaking Russian Jews, he saw his immigrant background as an obstacle to success as a writer. "That's my misfortune," he lamented in his journal in 1945–1946: "that I

---

[24] Cf. Anna P. Ronell, "Three American Jewish Writers Imagine Eastern Europe," in *Polin [vol. 19]: Polish-Jewish Relations in North America,* ed. Miecyzslaw B. Biskupski and Antony Polonsky (Oxford: Littman, 2007), 374–75.
[25] Carole S. Kessner, "Introduction," in *"The "Other" New York Jewish Intellectuals* (New York: New York University Press, 1994), 1, 10.

still have one ear in the old country.... My English isn't so good. It's correct."[26] This did not keep him from rising to the ranks of the "New York intellectuals," along with (and in the shadow of) his high school friend Saul Bellow.[27] If anything, his immigrant background afforded him a linguistic and cultural advantage, along with fellow intellectuals of a similar *milieu* and generation. In the assessment of literary scholar Hana Wirth-Nesher, Rosenfeld translated the two cultures into a new, in-between space that enriched American literature.[28] He translated Sholem Aleichem and other Yiddish authors for the *Treasury of Yiddish Stories* and other publications, and wrote stories, essays, and reviews for major intellectual journals of his time.[29] Literary scholar Jules Chametzky has credited Rosenfeld in particular for opening the door for a new generation of American Jewish writers to the aesthetic and creative potential of their own Yiddish-language immigrant cultural roots. Chametzky recognized a phrase in a *Partisan Review* text by Rosenfeld as being a translation from a Yiddish saying, and recalled his reaction: "One could do that! There was a whole world lying under one's skin, a veritable Atlantis, for some of us who had grown up in first- and second-generation Yiddish-speaking communities, which we had put behind us in our quest for a place in the 'real' America." Rosenfeld was "giving me and my generation permission to use our Jewish past."[30]

---

26 Quoted in S. A. Longstaff, "Ivy League Gentiles and Inner-City Jews: Class and Ethnicity Around *Partisan Review* in the Thirties and Forties," *American Jewish History* 80 (1991): 332, omission in the original.

27 For Rosenfeld's role within this group, cf. Benjamin Balint, *Running Commentary: The Contentious Magazine That Transformed the Jewish Left into the Neoconservative Right* (New York: Public Affairs, 2010, chap. 1; Nathan Glazer, "Commentary: The Early Years," in *Commentary in American Life*, ed. Murray Friedman (Philadelphia: Temple University Press, 2005), 40; Alfred Kazin, *New York Jew* (New York: Knopf, 1978), 40; Steven J. Zipperstein, "*Commentary* and American Jewish Culture in the 1940s and 1950s," *Jewish Social Studies* 3 (1997): 20–25.

28 Hana Wirth-Nesher, "Traces of the Past: Multilingual Jewish American Writing," in *The Cambridge Companion to Jewish American Literature*, ed. Hana Wirth-Nesher and Michael P. Kramer (Cambridge: Cambridge University Press, 2003), 115. For biographical information on Rosenfeld, cf. Steven J. Zipperstein, *Rosenfeld's Lives: Fame, Oblivion, and the Furies of Writing* (New Haven: Yale University Press, 2009); Mark Shechner, "Introduction," in *Preserving the Hunger: An Isaac Rosenfeld Reader*, ed. Shechner (Detroit: Wayne State University Press, 1988), 21–37.

29 Examples include the translation (with Eliezer Greenberg) of Sholom Aleichem, "The Knife: A Story," *Commentary* 9 (January 1950): 151–58, and stories and reviews: "The Hand That Fed Me," *Partisan Review* 11 (1944): 22; "Three Parables and a Dissertation," *Partisan Review* 15 (1948): 654–63; "America, Land of the Sad Millionaire," re-review of *The Rise of David Levinsky*, by Abraham Cahan, *Commentary* 14 (August 1952): 131–35; "Kreplach," review of *A Treasury of Jewish Folklore*, ed. by Nathan Ausubel, *Commentary* 6 (November 1948): 487–88.

30 Jules Chametzky, *Out of Brownsville: Encounters with Nobel Laureates and Other Jewish Writers: A Memoir* (Amherst: University of Massachusetts Press, 2012), 25, 27.

To Rosenfeld himself, this his positive engagement with the Jewish heritage did not come easily. Looking at Rosenfeld's work and life, his biographer has stated that alienation was Rosenfeld's personal leitmotif.[31] He applied this principle to his review of Samuel's *World of Sholom Aleichem,* within four pages of which he mentioned alienation nine times: Jews of the *shtetl* are alienated from modern culture, from nature, from the world of objects, and, because of their religion, from the world in a metaphysical sense. To him, the *shtetl* as portrayed by Sholem Aleichem represented the lost East European Jewish communities of the past. He pointed to the paradoxical role of religion in Sholem Aleichem's *shtetl,* but presented a very different picture of it than what affirmatively Jewish thinkers did. As Rosenfeld put it, "Kasrielevky was guarded but exhausted by an old religion, which had never learned to rationalize adaptation to the world." Traditional Judaism had the potential to transform itself into a source of meaning for modern Jews; after all, "it was fundamentally a secular religion, for it provided the only available basis for culture." Yet, to make the transition and redefine itself in cultural terms, traditional Judaism would have to give up its separation from the secular world: "while this religion embraced the world, it was also profoundly alienated from it."[32]

Rosenfeld was heralded by Daniel Bell as the voice of the alienated young Jew. Still, more (and earlier) than others in this cohort, Rosenfeld turned his roots in Yiddish-speaking immigrant culture into a source for his intellectual production.[33] A key passage from his autobiographical novel *Passage from Home* illustrates Rosenfeld's relationship to traditional Judaism and the potential it held to become meaningful as a spiritual culture. Protagonist Bernard Miller walks with his grandfather through their Jewish neighborhood, feeling vaguely ashamed to be seen with this immigrant from a far-away world. But, as he accompanies him to a Hasidic *shtibl,* Bernard encounters this exotic world sensuously. Judaism – sterile and stifling in his parents' version – is translated into a social and cultural experience that holds great meaning for those who embrace it:

> Feldman [the Rebbe] had finished speaking, but the men still sat motionless, watching him reverently, as if he had clarified a mystery before their eyes. The melody was heard again,

---

31 Mark Shechner, *After the Revolution: Studies in the Contemporary Jewish Imagination* (Bloomington: Indiana University Press, 1987), 107.
32 Isaac Rosenfeld, "The Humor of Exile," review of *The World of Sholom Aleichem,* by Maurice Samuel, *Partisan Review* 10 (1943): 294–95.
33 Daniel Bell, "A Parable of Alienation," *Jewish Frontier* XIII (1946): 16; Bell, "Reflections on Jewish Identity," *Commentary* 31 (June 1961): 476; David Twersky, "Left Right, Left Right: After Half a Century, *Commentary* Remains Defiantly Out of Step," *Moment* 20 (1995): 57.

coming softly from the corner, and it grew louder, sweeping across the room, and suddenly one of the chess players sprang up, clapped his hands and, followed by the other, began to dance. The men at the table also sprang up and joined the dance, holding their arms above their heads, clapping hands, turning and weaving on bent knees. Feldman lay back, his eyes half shut, a smile on his face, and he snapped out a rhythm with his ringed fingers.

Later, when we took our leave, I could see that my grandfather was transformed into a new person. A look of completeness lay on his face, an expression of gratitude as if for the ecstatic understanding to which Feldman had led him. Though unable to understand, I had shared the experience of that ecstasy, and I, too, felt grateful for it.[34]

One hears a distant echo of Rosenzweig's account of the powerful spiritual aesthetics he encountered on Yom Kippur in an Orthodox *shul* in Berlin in 1913.[35] Both experienced a connection that had previously been severed. Fictitious Bernard illustrates "Hansen's Law," as his search for such a connection involved his grandfather. Yet, when Bernard re-emerges from the experience, he feels that he cannot be part of this transplanted world. Like Rosenfeld, he finds himself facing "a Jewish world in crisis in which the conflicts of father and son [...] are symbols of a revolution in culture and belief that was changing American Jewry from a transplanted old world culture to something distinctly new and American."[36] In this sense, the novel was part of a larger project of "alienated" intellectuals using the East European past in their return to Jewishness.

On their way back to Jewishness, Rosenfeld and other secular thinkers found a helpful guide in Yitzhak Leib Peretz (1852–1915). The way Peretz was transmitted, culturally translated, and re-purposed for American Jews parallels the case of Sholem Aleichem. Peretz's fictional texts and essays were published widely in a variety of journals.[37] Texts about Peretz claimed him for various ideological perspectives, mostly for those on the left who latched onto his (ethnographic) focus on the folk and his early Socialism.[38] Again, it was Maurice Samuel who

---

34 Rosenfeld, *Passage from Home*, 94.
35 Cf. Nahum N. Glatzer, "Introduction," in *Franz Rosenzweig: His Life and Thought*, Presented by Nahum N. Glatzer (Indianapolis: Hackett, 1998), xvii.
36 Shechner, "Introduction," in *Passage from Home*, vi.
37 In 1947, YIVO sponsored a bilingual edition of Peretz texts; in 1952, the Workmen's Circle published a collection of his stories in English and, two years later, several of them were included in the *Treasury of Yiddish Stories*. A selection of other texts: Isaac Leib Peretz, "Bontshe Silent," *Jewish Life* 4 (1949): 20–22; "The Pious Cat," *Commentary* 9 (April 1950): 369–70; "The Interviewer at Work: Some Problems Posed by the Natives and the Terrain," *Commentary* 15 (February 1953): 195–99; "On History [adopted in dialogue form]," *Workmen's Circle Call* 29 (1960): 2–3; "The Victim," *Jewish Frontier* XXVII (1960): 16–17; "Our Platform [1894]," *Workmen's Circle Call* 34 (1963): 23; "The YIVO Bilingual Edition of Peretz," *News of the YIVO* 21 (June 1947): 1*.
38 A.A. Roback, "I. L. Peretz," *Jewish Frontier* VII (1940): 18–21; Frances Butwin, "A New Translation of Peretz," *Jewish Life* 2 (1948): 29–30; Israel Knox, "Peretz in English," *Workmen's*

was responsible for much of the writer's broad appeal. In 1948, he tried to popularize Peretz much the same way he had successfully popularized Sholem Aleichem five years before. He wrote *Prince of the Ghetto*, which provided the starting point for the critical reception of Peretz by secular intellectuals on a quest to overcome their alienation and re-connect to their Jewishness. Samuel's presentation of Peretz sounded like a program for American Jewish intellectuals at mid-century: "his conscious task was the intellectual improvement of his people," Samuel wrote. "It was Peretz's hope that Polish Jewry of tomorrow (that is, our today) would combine the strongest and most wholesome Jewish values with the highest achievements of the present."[39] While some critics sensed that Samuel was too quick to claim simplistic parallels with contemporaneous American Jewish thinkers and underestimated the ruptures that left them alienated, many other intellectuals picked up the programmatic message: Peretz could serve as a bridge to a modernizing Jewish world and the meaning it held for those trying to create a modern Jewishness in America.[40] In a *Commentary* review of *Prince of the Ghetto*, entitled "Mediator Between Past and Future," Leslie Fiedler paid tribute to the "real" Peretz, but recognized that Samuel's "pious and necessary misrepresentation, re-creation if you will," was helpful "to achieve the liaison with Europe which is indispensable to American spiritual life."[41] Fiedler's reading made clear why Peretz became "the intellectuals' intellectual," a vital link (particularly through Hasidism) to a past that appeared newly meaningful and usable:[42]

> For Samuel's fictive Prince there is a clear and urgent use: to act as a mediator between the American non-Yiddish-speaking Jew (particularly the intellectual) and what is valuable

---

Circle Call 17 (1949): 8; Zalman Yefroiken, "New Horizons for Our Children: The I. L. Peretz Schools of the Workmen's Circle," *Workmen's Circle Call* 19 (March 1951): 2–3; Yefroiken, "A Century Since the Birth of I. L. Peretz, Father of Yiddish Literature," *Workmen's Circle Call* 21 (1952): 3–4. In 1953, a Peretz Square was dedicated on the Lower East Side, with 15,000 people reportedly attending the ceremony; Joseph Mlotek, "Notes on Jewish Cultural Activities," *Workmen's Circle Call* 22 (1953): 14. In 1952, YIVO staged a Peretz exhibition; *News of the YIVO* 44 (March 1952): 5*.
39 Samuel, *Prince of the Ghetto*, 3–4, 6–7, 9–12.
40 Robert Alter voiced concerns that Samuel had claimed such continuities too easily: "Maurice Samuel & Jewish Letters," *Commentary* 37 (March 1964): 50–54. Ludwig Lewisohn defended Samuel, in "A Saga Is Continued," review of *Prince of the Ghetto*, by Maurice Samuel, *Jewish Frontier* XVI (1949): 35–37.
41 Leslie A. Fiedler, "Mediator Between Past and Future," *Commentary* 6 (December 1948): 582–83.
42 Cf. Howe/Greenberg, "Introduction," in *A Treasury of Yiddish Stories* (New York: Meridian, 1960; orig. publ. 1954), 56.

in his Yiddish past – that is to say, the East European, the ghetto past as opposed to the Hebrew past. It is true, for better or worse, that for such a Jew the ethos of his recent ancestors is most easily available as "literature," at a level where not belief but the suspension of disbelief is exacted.[43]

It was out of the modern impossibility of a unified Jewish experience of the past that Fiedler, Rosenfeld, and other intellectuals invoking Peretz, redirected the religious impulse into literature, or culture at large. "Secular equivalents had to be found for what was deserted in the sacred tradition, to preserve the cohesion of the original culture," Rosenfeld later emphasized.[44] The divisions and fragmentation of the modern Jewish experience could be made fruitful if Jews understood themselves as a community based on common cultural, even spiritual, values. The *Workmen's Circle Call* quoted Peretz's famous dictum that summed up what made his ideas attractive and usable for mid-century secular American Jewish thinkers on their "passages from home" into a new world: "He wrote, 'We should leave the ghetto, but with our own spiritual wealth.'"[45]

A Sacred Treasure: Anthologizing East European *Yiddishkayt* for American Jews

It is far from coincidental that Howe and Eliezer Greenberg included nine stories by Peretz in their *Treasury of Yiddish Stories*, more than by any of the other twenty-two authors represented in the collection. After all, the anthology, published in 1954, sought to portray a modern Jewish culture that tried to preserve coherence out of an identity that drew on, but was removed from, traditional Judaism – a project for which Peretz provided intellectual inspiration.[46] The editors of *The Treasury*

---

43 Howe/Greenberg, "Introduction," 582. "Suspension of disbelief" is an allusion to Soeren Kierkegaard. For the view of Peretz as a bridge, cf. also Anita Norich, *Discovering Exile: Yiddish and Jewish American Culture during the Holocaust* (Stanford: Stanford University Press, 2007), chap. 4.
44 "Symposium: Religion and the Intellectuals," *Partisan Review* 17 (1950): 246.
45 Zalman Yefroiken, "Peretz – The Father and Leader of Jewish Cultural Awakening," *Workmen's Circle Call* 21 (1952): 10. The original, longer quote is from Peretz's 1910 essay "What Our Literature Needs": "I am not proposing that we lock ourselves in a spiritual ghetto. We must leave it – but with our own soul, our own spiritual wealth." (in *Voices from the Yiddish*, ed. Irving Howe and Eliezer Greenberg (Ann Arbor: University of Michigan Press, 1976), 27)
46 "Ne'ilah in Gehenna," "Devotion without End," "The Dead Town," "Bontsha the Silent," "If Not Higher," "The Mad Talmudist," "Rabbi Yochanan the Warden," "The Golem," "Cabalists."

of *Yiddish Stories* were trying to achieve "the formidable task of preserving the national sense of identity and adapting it to the unfamiliar modes of the modern world." The *Treasury* was the first new anthology of Yiddish literature after the Holocaust, and Howe and Greenberg had reason to assume that their readers were not yet attuned to the ethnic culture they were about to encounter – nor did they live in a cultural climate that valued pre-modern Judaism as relevant, or the imagery of the *shtetl* as beautiful. Thus, the *Treasury* had to perform a major act of cultural translation in order to disseminate East European-born Yiddish culture to newly appreciative American Jewish readers.[47]

For this task, the editors recruited a group of literary intellectuals who, as translators for the anthology, and as writers, compilers, critics, and editors for other publications, were shaping how American Jewish readers in the mid-decades perceived their Yiddish heritage. Among them were Bellow, Milton Himmelfarb, Shlomo Katz, Alfred Kazin, Ludwig Lewisohn, Rosenfeld, Samuel, and Marie Syrkin.[48] The long introduction of 71 pages – plus another 20 pages of author biographies and a glossary – reflected and tried to bridge the gap between the subject and readers of the book. Those readers encountered over some 515 pages a wide range of authors, themes, and styles, from the three "classics" of modern Yiddish literature (Mendele, Sholem Aleichem, and Peretz) to later writers with markedly different perspectives on East European Jewry, among them Jacob Glatstein, Chaim Grade, Israel Joshua Singer, and Isaac Bashevis Singer.[49] The selection was subjective, revised the earlier canon, and reflected both the editors' individual tastes and the cultural moment, as Roskies analyzed: "what remained, by design and default, was a distillation of the modern Yiddish experience not unlike that portrayed in the second American-Jewish classic of the 1950s – *Life Is With People*."[50] Jeffrey Shandler has argued that the *Treasury* should be regarded as yet another example of the "popular arts of American Jewish ethnography," which made a past Jewish culture accessible to later audiences.[51]

The introduction to the *Treasury* suggested a commemorative perspective critical of Western liberalism, with its fragmented identities and reductive notion

---

47 Howe/Greenberg, "Introduction," in *Treasury of Yiddish Stories*, 1–2, 31.
48 The anthology as a genre was itself an instrument suited to introduce its audience to a foreign culture. Cf. David Stern, "Introduction," in *The Anthology in Jewish Literature* (New York: Oxford University Press, 2004), 2–11.
49 For a look at the subjective arrangement of the stories, cf. Jeffrey Shandler, "Anthologizing the Vernacular: Collections of Yiddish Literature in English Translation," in *The Anthology in Jewish Literature*, ed. David Stern (Oxford: Oxford University, 2004), 314–15
50 Roskies, "Treasures of Howe and Greenberg," 111.
51 Shandler, "Anthologizing," 314; Kirshenblatt-Gimblett, "Imagining Europe," 155–57.

of religion. The final sentence of the introduction showed that the anthology aimed to make the past, a vanished East European Yiddish culture, relevant to American readers. Whatever the future of these Yiddish writers, the editors wrote, "their past is certain. They wait for us, ready to speak, if we will only hear them."[52] The anthology focused on a supposed pre-modern moment in which Yiddish culture offered a major ideological, political, and social response to a rapidly advancing modernity. To Howe and Greenberg, this cultural moment, with its opportunities, had passed; after "a brief and tragic history" it had come to an end not through internal failures, but was destroyed from without. The book was dedicated "To the Six Million" who died when Western civilization collapsed. Authentic Jewishness was defined against this Western civilization, particularly against a moral weakness stemming from fragmented identities: "the world of the East European Jews, at least in its most serious and 'ideal' manifestations, did not accept the Western distinction between worldly and other-worldly, between that which is due to Caesar and that which is due to God." Rather, theirs was an experience that was unified and circumscribed mostly by a spiritual consensus. While they described how this spiritual consensus supported a rich and stable Jewish culture, Howe and Greenberg were far from extolling the virtue of pre-modern traditional Judaism, which supposedly relied upon the cultural isolation and intellectual dependency of its adherents. Instead, they pointed to modernizing forces from within Jewry that aimed to preserve Jewish distinctiveness, Hasidism and the Haskalah in particular.[53] Out of their dialectical interaction, a secular Yiddish culture was born for which the religious tradition was a constitutive point of reference.

The presentation of this culture places the *Treasury of Yiddish Stories* in the context of the sacralization, memorialization, and re-imagination that informed Samuel's reading of Sholem Aleichem's world, Rosenfeld's interpretation of Peretz, and Heschel's reconstruction of the world of Ashkenaz.[54] Literature proved to be a particularly congenial medium for the process of extending the concept of "Judaism" as a religion, of secularizing it to "Jewishness," or elevating Jewishness to a quasi-religious status.[55] Scholars have probed the notion that

---

52 Howe/Greenberg, "Introduction," in *Treasury of Yiddish Stories*, 71; cf. David G. Roskies, "Yiddish in the Twentieth Century: A Literature of Anger and Homecoming," in *Yiddish Language and Culture Then and Now*, ed. Leonard Jay Greenspoon (Omaha: Creighton University Press, 1998), 12.
53 Howe/Greenberg, "Introduction," in *Treasury of Yiddish Stories*, 1, 3, 7–8, 12, 19, 28.
54 Ronell, "Three American Jewish Writers," 374.
55 Cf. Edward Alexander, *Irving Howe and Secular Jewishness: An Elegy* (Cincinnati: Judaic Studies Program University of Cincinnati, 1995); Theodore Weinberger, "Yiddish Literature as

Howe, specifically, conceived of Yiddish literature as "sacred scripture" for his secular *Yiddishkayt*. This idea was part of the *zeitgeist*. The period in which the anthology was published was fraught with emotions and reflections that bestowed a sacred dimension onto American Jews' engagement with the East European past. Howe and Greenberg warned against romanticizing and sacralizing the past, but at the same time understood the impulse, as both Yiddish writers and their readers responded to the decline of the *shtetl* and its ultimate destruction in the Holocaust: "the romantic impulse became irresistible; it acquired a new and almost holy authenticity; for how could the Yiddish writers separate the sanctification of their martyrs from the celebration of the world that had given rise to them?"[56]

The Postwar *Shtetl:* Re-Invention of "the Greatest Invention of Yiddish Literature"

The *Treasury* placed particular emphasis on literature dealing with the *shtetl*, as it partook in post-Holocaust American Jews' reconstruction of a "sacred" past that could legitimize their underdetermined Jewishness. Thus, it added another aspect to the rich history of the *shtetl* as a literary *topos* with extra-literary functions.[57] Literary scholars have suggested parallels between the way Yiddish authors related to the *shtetl* and how their American Jewish readers did, particularly after the Holocaust. Dan Miron's analysis can be applied to both groups:

> [The *shtetl*] amounted to a tremendously potent myth that nourished and sustained an alienated, nostalgic, modern Jewish community (in essence, an emigrant community) that desperately needed to both remember an idealized "old home" (which had never existed in historical sense) and at the same time justify the modern Jew's "betrayal" of the old familial home he had left, hurtling himself into the cold, harsh, individualistic, and egotistic world

---

Secular Jewish Scripture: The World of Irving Howe," in *Yiddish Language and Culture: Then and Now*, ed. Leonard Jay Greenspoon (Omaha: Creighton University Press, 1998), 233–45.
56 Howe/Greenberg, "Introduction," in *Treasury of Yiddish Stories*, 4.
57 Howe/Greenberg, "Introduction," in *Treasury of Yiddish Stories*, 28; cf. Roskies, "Treasures of Howe and Greenberg," 111. The explicit statement (in the introduction) about the *shtetl* focus, which drove the selection of the texts, was visually supported by the illustrations by Ben Shahn, which depicted *shtetl* figures; they had been used previously in a book of translated stories by Sholem Aleichem (Shandler, "Anthologizing," 315).

of modernity. [...] Although its desertion was obligatory, it was also the source of a perpetual guilt.[58]

American Jews projected a range of sentiments onto the *shtetl* as the archetypal representation of the East European past: guilt over the desertion or even betrayal of the real or imagined place of origin; nostalgic longing and retrospective sacralization; needs for authenticating continuities or discontinuities, and for essentialist notions of Jewishness. The *shtetl* was, in Roskies' words, "arguably the greatest single invention of Yiddish literature," as it offered a key to modern Jewish self-understanding. As its image evolved in literary and other reconstructions, it served as the imaginary locus for different purposes: "as the ghetto-existence best left behind; as the Jewish body politic under siege; as the idealized *Heimat*, the local Old Country homeland, arrested in time; as paradise lost; and, finally, as the staging ground for Jewish mass martyrdom." Among these themes, two related aspects appear particularly relevant for the mid-century discourse about Jewishness in America: the "Judaization" of the *shtetl* and the spiritual nature of its world. With the secularizing pressure of modernity, the *shtetl* that American Jews encountered in Yiddish literature remained a "covenantal landscape," but did so by way of a translation of the traditional concept into modern terms of Jewishness: "The shtetl was reclaimed as the place of common origin (even when it wasn't), the source of a collective folk identity rooted in a particular historical past and, most importantly, as the locus of a new, secular, covenant. A new covenant was needed precisely because the old one was no longer viable."[59]

As the new covenant shifted the focus from "Judaism" to "Jewishness," it shaped the second aspect of the literary reconstructions of the *shtetl* that was particularly important to American Jewish readers: its Judaization. Following a literary tradition, Yiddish writers wrote non-Jewish inhabitants and institutions out of accounts that served functions of memory rather than history. "Unperturbed by any loyalty to historical truth, they created the 'classical' literary shtetl as a pure, unalloyed, and undiluted Jewish 'world,'" Miron wrote of Mendele and Sholem Aleichem.[60] The fact that in postwar America their fiction was seen as auto-ethnography gave additional authority to their presentations of the purely Jewish *shtetl* and to the folk-based, comprehensive, and sacralized cultural Jewishness of the new covenant.

---

58 Miron, *Image of the Shtetl*, xii.
59 Roskies, *Search for a Usable Past*, 41, 43–44, 57; cf. also Ben Cion Pinchuk, "Jewish Discourse and the *Shtetl*," *Jewish History* 15 (2001): 169–79.
60 Miron, *Image of the Shtetl*, xii, 4.

Figure 22: A postcard, issued in 1936 by the Y. L. Peretz Library, in honor of the centennial of the birth of Mendele Mokher Sforim (1835–1917). (United States Holocaust Memorial Museum)

Roskies has argued that the place of the *shtetl* in the self-understanding of millions of American Jews became fixed during the interwar years. As the example of Maurice Samuel's using Sholem Aleichem's world to "re-Judaize" American Jews indicates, however, that the need to reconstruct the *shtetl* was particularly pronounced among mid-century American Jews, intellectuals in particular.[61] Again, what Roskies wrote about Yiddish writers at the turn of the century holds true for American thinkers two generations later, as they repeated, revised, and replaced

---

[61] Cf. Asher Z. Milbauer, "Eastern Europe in American Jewish Writing," in *Handbook of American-Jewish Literature: An Analytical Guide to Topics, Themes, and Sources*, ed. Lewis Fried (Westport, CT: Greenwood Press, 1988), 357–60; Ronell, "Three American Jewish Writers," 373–74.

earlier reconstructions of the past: "the more estranged these Jews became, the more they were drawn back to the shtetl; even [...] to a shtetl they never knew," as in postwar America they sought places of origin to infuse their uncertain Jewishness with certainty and meaning.[62] Literary-minded intellectuals engaged the *shtetl* world of traditional Judaism in new ways to make it usable for their needs and tastes. As for many of them this meant seeing it through the lens of literary modernism, they re-invented the "greatest invention of Yiddish literature" and offered new images that challenged and competed with the traditional significance of *shtetl* Judaism and Jewishness for American Jews.

Isaac Bashevis Singer and the Subversive Spirituality of East European Judaism

Among the sheer number of literary treatments of the *shtetl* in post-1940 America, one author was particular influential, especially for how secular intellectuals used the *shtetl* to explore new ways of tapping into the creative and spiritual potential of their Jewishness: Isaac Bashevis Singer (1902–1991) intrigued American readers with his insider's perspective on the spiritual forces at work in this world. He was seen already by contemporaries as one of the last writers who could connect American Jews with their East European heritage, thanks to his biography as an immigrant and due to his deliberate turn to an English-language audience.[63] Singer was born the son of a Hasidic rabbi in Warsaw, where he began his literary career writing in Yiddish. He continued writing in Yiddish after he emigrated from Poland to the United States in 1935, where he wrote for the *Forverts,* but increasingly also wrote in English, serving, in effect, as his own translator. The relationship between the Yiddish and English versions of his works was controversial from the beginning. Singer significantly revised his Yiddish texts, making some of the English ones effectively "second

---

62 Roskies, *Search for a Usable Past*, 43.
63 Frank Cantor, "I. Bashevis Singer Revisited," *Jewish Currents* 20 (1965): 12. For a comprehensive analytical overview of such cultural products, cf. Jeffrey Shandler, *Shtetl: A Vernacular Intellectual History* (New Brunswick: Rutgers University Press, 2013), 72–82. Isaac Babel would be another choice for this role, particularly as literary intellectuals were so fascinated with this radical deconstruction of established ideas of Jewishness in the deliberate engagement with Cossack culture. Singer, however, is more relevant to the topic at hand not only because of his broader appeal to rank-and-file American Jewish readers, but also because he was himself a cultural translator with a conscious agenda for American Jewry.

originals," specifically tailored to a different audience, sometimes by sanitizing some of the more disturbing representations of the East European past for American Jewish readers.[64]

Through Singer's works, a very distinct imagery of this past was disseminated. Traversing a wide spectrum of themes and time periods, from seventeenth-century Sabbateanism to twentieth-century city life in Warsaw, his fiction depicted East European Jewish life as driven by demonic spirits manifested in dark energies and humanity's irresistible passions, from which resulted irrational behavior, religious superstition, and sexual transgressions. His world was filled with *dybbuks*, devils, thieves, false messiahs, and humans distinctly not conforming to idealized images of *shtetl* life, appearing crooked and cruel, ugly and lonely, suffering and poor and existentially beleaguered by vital forces beyond their control.[65] In his most famous story, "Gimpel the Fool," which first appeared in English translated by Bellow in *Partisan Review*, Gimpel is duped by the people of Frampol as he marries the town prostitute and believes, to the end, that the six children she bears are his.[66] The Workmen's Circle's Knox warned that the picture Singer painted of Jewish life in Poland "will trouble some of his readers and all those who have a feeling of reverence for the Jewish world that was and is now only of memory." To some, "it must seem at times like a view of the dark side of the moon," *Commentary* critic Dan Jacobson seconded.[67]

---

[64] Anita Norich, "Isaac Bashevis Singer in America: The Translation Problem," *Judaism* 44 (1995): 212, 215.

[65] A selection: Isaac Bashevis Singer, "Gimpel the Fool," *Partisan Review* 20 (1953): 300–13; "From the Diary of One Not Born," *Partisan Review* 21 (1954): 139–46; "The Wife Killer: A Folk Tale," *Midstream* 1 (1955): 60–71; "From My Father's Courtroom (The Will, Reb Moishe Ba-Ba-Ba)," *Commentary* 33 (April 1962): 299–305; "Yentl the Yeshiva Boy: A Story," *Commentary* 34 (September 1962): 213–24; "A Wedding in Brownsville," *Commentary* 37 (March 1964): 43–49. Major novels published in English included *Family Moskat* (1950), *Satan in Goray* (1955), *The Magician of Lublin* (1960), and *The Slave* (1962).

[66] In another story, "Taibeleh," a woman deserted by her husband, is visited night after night by the teacher's helper who poses as a *dybbuk* to sleep with her ("Taibele and Hurmizah," *Commentary* 35 (February 1963): 132–38). In "A Gentleman from Cracow," men and women engage in a public orgy in an apocalyptic scene, before the protagonist is revealed as the "Chief of the Devils," and "witches, werewolves, imps, demons, and hobgoblins plummeted from the sky." After Frampol is destroyed by a fire and then rebuilt, its inhabitants remain paupers. (*Commentary* 24 (September 1957): 231–39)

[67] Israel Knox, "[Review of *The Spinoza on Market Street, The Slave*, by Isaac Bashevis Singer]," *Workmen's Circle Call* 34 (1963): 15; Dan Jacobson, "The Problem of Isaac Bashevis Singer," *Commentary* 39 (February 1965): 49.

For all their deviation from established conventions of Yiddish and English-language literature on the East European past, these stories fascinated mid-century American Jews: "the demon-writer found a new pool of unsuspecting victims in the native born readers of America and still later – in their children," Roskies noted.[68] Contemporaneous literary critic Henry Goodman recorded with similar surprise that "a Singer Cult [...] has developed among intellectuals," with whom Singer's fiction resonated in particular.[69] Some explanations for the fascination with Singer's work sound familiar from the reception of Peretz: spiritual soul mates bravely facing the existential questions Western modernity posed to the thinking Jew, who mined the East European past and refashioned traditional ideas for answers. How could Judaism or Jewishness be meaningful in a culture that reduced them to a religion while at the same time questioning its spiritual force and supernatural assumptions? Some critics found Singer's work and persona convincing as a response: "Isaac Singer is an alienated Zaddik, a Hasid who has found Pascal's abyss in the Zohar," *Commentary* critic Kenneth Rexroth suggested in a review. Other critics claimed Singer for modern categories of thought, such as existentialism.[70] His work allowed different readers to project onto him different answers to questions of what meaning could be wrested from Jewishness for the American present.[71] Literary scholar Anita Norich suggests that it was such a longing for Jewish authenticity that linked the intellectuals and non-professional readers, as they found in Singer's depiction of the East European Jewish culture – as a vitally spiritual, creatively subversive, incessantly moving, alluringly different, yet distantly familiar culture – confirmation of their own quest for a meaningful Jewishness: "He speaks authoritatively to readers who are so far removed from the Eastern European world he describes that they have come to long for it, to reify it as the source of their own authenticity."[72]

Through literature, these intellectuals in their own quest for authentic Jewishness uncovered and explored the ambivalence of postwar American Jewry

---

68 David G. Roskies, "Introduction," *Prooftexts* 9 (1989): 3.
69 Henry Goodman, "The Dark World of Isaac Bashevis Singer," *Jewish Currents* 17 (1962): 3. Cf. also Judd Teller, "Unhistorical Novels," *Commentary* 21 (April 1956): 393–96.
70 Kenneth Rexroth, "Alienated: Indomitable," review of *Gimpel the Fool*, by Isaac Bashevis Singer, *Commentary* 26 (November 1958): 460; Irving Howe, "Demonic Fiction of a Yiddish 'Modernist,'" review of *The Magician of Lublin*, by Isaac Bashevis Singer, *Commentary* 30 (October 1960): 352–53; Eugene Goodheart, "Singer's Moral Novel," review of *The Slave*, by Isaac Bashevis Singer, *Midstream* 8 (1962): 102; Jacobson, "Problem of Singer," 50–51.
71 Roskies, "Introduction," 3.
72 Norich, "Singer in America," 211; cf. also Steven J. Zipperstein *Imagining Russian Jewry: Memory, History, Identity* (Seattle: University of Washington Press, 1999), 31.

Figure 23: Isaac Bashevis Singer, not dated. (American Jewish Archives)

about its acceptance in society at large and its relationship to its past. One literary text in particular, Philip Roth's story "Eli the Fanatic," illustrates how the more recent East European past in the form of refugees and Holocaust survivors complicated the American Jewish perspective. First published in *Commentary* in 1959, it suggests that beneath the seemingly stable sense of a liberal Judaism, expressed by conforming to white middle-class norms, lurked a suppressed ambivalence regarding alternative understandings of Jewishness that seemed to threaten the hard-won acceptance and respectability of the Jews in Woodenton. The "other," in this case, is embodied by a Holocaust survivor, Leo Tzuref, who plans to open a traditional *yeshivah* and bears all the trimmings of a Jewishness that combines illiberal traditionalism with ethnic particularism – precisely the dark past which the tradition-averse, inclusion-anxious Jews of the town thought they had overcome. In his encounters with Tzuref, an unresolved mixture of repulsion and attraction drives Eli, who represents of Woodenton's Jews, insane. He increasingly identifies with the "fanatic," trying on Tzuref`s clothes and thereby becoming a fanatic in the eyes of his neighbors. Lest they be disturbed by the ghosts of their past, they sedate Eli: "The drug calmed his soul, but it did not touch it down where the blackness had reached." The metaphor of blackness calls up the Holocaust and Tzuref's traditional Orthodoxy, both of which threaten to overwhelm Eli, who embodies a community larger than Woodenton. The story suggests that the darkness of the East European past and the Holocaust haunted postwar American

Jews, as it proved to be inassimilable into their world, much as their American Jewish lives seemed to be incompatible with the traditional East European Judaism that they had attempted to desert.[73]

In a general sense, American Jewish fiction engaging Jewishness and Judaism after the rupture of modernity, immigration, and the Holocaust was a radicalized continuation of another motif of modern Yiddish literature: the departure from the *shtetl* with the concomitant sense of guilt.[74] But, how long can one live with an unresolved mixture of attraction and rejection of one's past? Five years after Roth had unmasked their ambivalence and guilt, American Jews embraced a radically different perspective on the East European past. It illustrated their need for authenticity and affirmation.

Final Curtain: *Fiddler on the Roof*

On September 22, 1964 – some eighty years after the first Tevye story was published and fifty years after Sholem Aleichem came to America for good – a new Tevye announced, "Come, children. Let's go," taking his family from Anatevka to America. The simplicity of the statement highlighted the drama behind it, culminating in an individual decision that replayed events of historical proportion. Viewers may well have heard echoes of the biblical *Lekh Lekha* and the exodus motif at large, and may have felt spoken to. After all, Broadway ends near where their ancestors stepped ashore and where Tevye's fictitious journey was likely to take him. Some twenty-five years after Max Weinreich, the Lubavitcher Rebbe, and Abraham Joshua Heschel had arrived in the New York, yet another messenger brought the Old World heritage to the New.

American Jews responded with an enthusiastic welcome: the *Fiddler* got onto the Broadway stage 3,242 times.[75] But, the Tevye of the musical differed from earlier re-workings of the original, and his message responded to new American Jewish concerns. One of them was the Holocaust, which, from the early 1960s on, became more and more prominent in public and political activities.[76] Librettist Joseph Stein added a pogrom scene to *Fidder,* and anti-Semitism ran as a theme

---

[73] Philip Roth, "Eli, the Fanatic: A Story," *Commentary* 27 (April 1959): 309. Cf. also Zipperstein, *Imagining Russian Jewry*, 38–39; Wirth-Nesher, "Traces of the Past," 119.
[74] Miron, *Image of the Shtetl*, xii.
[75] Solomon, *Wonder of Wonders*, 5.
[76] This assessment is not questioned by Hasia Diner's recent demonstration of the issue's greater presence than previously assumed in American Jewish life in the immediate post-Holocaust

through the story.[77] Paired with the optimistic departure to America in the final scene, these motifs continued an associative sequence that linked Eastern Europe with negative images, and validated America as a polity beneficial and welcoming to Jewish life.[78]

More importantly, however, *Fiddler* spoke to another American-Jewish concern by idealizing the *shtetl* and, by extension, all of the East European Jewish past. In a familiar move, the two tropes were linked, as the negative imagery of the non-Jewish environment served to highlight the positive imagery of the clearly demarcated Jewishness of the East European experience. The *shtetl* embodied the positive essence of a past that was far removed from the present and elevated toward a sacred realm. Its destruction in the Holocaust had frozen it in memory and severed all direct connections and continuities with the present. The suppression of traditional Jewish life in the Soviet Union and the Cold War perspective on Eastern Europe further impeded any perception of continuity. Moreover, the spiritual elevation of the *shtetl* as the mythical space of authentic, vital Jewishness removed it from historical time.

In America, the *shtetl* past thus configured became a resource for the two related urges of affirming the Jews' Americanness as legitimate, and creating a sense of distinctiveness and difference, impulses related in the context of cultural pluralism. In order to affirm America as kosher, Tevye was, even more than in earlier versions of the Sholem Aleichem stories, re-created in the image of the "universal grandfather" of American Jews. Following "Hansen's Law," it was the grandfather to whom the third generation, coming of age in America, turned for a grounding in a meaningful past.[79] These grandchildren were adapting Tevye's timeless Jewish values to their new situation – with his approval, as he acknowledged the need for the adaptation. In this way, *Fiddler* developed motifs already

---

period: *We Remember with Reverence and Love: American Jews and the Myth of Silence after the Holocaust, 1945–1962* (New York: New York University Press, 2009).

[77] In the analysis of Jeremy Dauber, the pogrom scene echoed motifs from the Eichmann trial that had shaken the Jewish world just a few years before, such as the policeman insisting on his "following orders" in expelling the Jews from Anatevka; cf. Dauber, *The Worlds of Sholem Aleichem*, 365–66; cf. also Wolitz, "Americanization of Tevye," 527; Kirshenblatt-Gimblett, "Imagining Europe," 156.

[78] Pinchuk, "Jewish Discourse and the *Shtetl*," 169–70; Zipperstein, *Imagining Russian Jewry*: "Prologue."

[79] Marcus Lee Hansen, "The Third Generation in America," *Commentary* 14 (November 1952): 495.

present in the Sholem Aleichem stories, such as choice and individualism.[80] In the musical, their reconstruction in the service of postwar American social liberalism reached its climax. Tevye's response to his daughter Chava's plan to marry her gentile lover Fyedka was a case in point. Even though Tevye could not sanction the marriage, his agonizing and pondering reflected an individual, autonomous perspective on the changes that seemed to be the inevitable byproducts of modernization. In this modernization, the enlightened and wise Tevye could even sense, with great reluctance and fatalism, progress toward the betterment of Jews and humankind.

On the issue of intermarriage, the musical did not fully resolve the tensions between particularistic and universal values. In other instances, though, *Fiddler* presented Jewish and modern values as compatible or even congenial, if the former were adapted to the latter. "American ideals of individual rights, progress, and freedom of association are assimilated into the Judaic tradition, which is presented as a cultural tradition parallel to the American," literary scholar Seth Wolitz asserts. "The musical posits Jewish adaptability as the key to Jewish continuity."[81] In its message of openness to the surrounding non-Jewish society and culture, *Fiddler* validated the reality of American Jewry, whose abandonment of the *shtetl*, immigration to the United States, and accommodation to American culture constituted historically justified responses to the challenges and opportunities of modernization. It was "an engine of Jewish acculturation in America."[82]

Yet, the musical did not simply affirm mindless acceptance of American social and cultural norms. Rather, it probed a new balance of Americanness and Jewishness, universalism and particularism, accommodation and distinctiveness. The segment about Chava's marriage reflects the ambivalence of 1960s American Jews toward their adaptation and openness to American society: the issue of intermarriage tested their universalism, and many certainly identified with the

---

[80] Stephen J. Whitfield, "Fiddling with Sholem Aleichem: A History of Fiddler on the Roof," in *Key Texts in American Jewish Culture*, ed. Jack Kugelmass (New Brunswick: Rutgers University Press, 2003), 115.
[81] Wolitz, "Americanization of Tevye," 527. In this, the musical follows a long sequence of cultural products that showcase this tradition, often with the intention to legitimize Judaism and, by extension, the presence of Jews in America. Cf. Jonathan D. Sarna, "The Cult of Synthesis in American Jewish Culture," *Jewish Social Studies* 5 (1998/99): 52–79; Beth S. Wenger, *History Lessons: The Creation of American Jewish Heritage* (Princeton: Princeton University Press, 2010). Sylvia Barack Fishman in *Jewish Life and American Culture* (Albany: SUNY Press, 2000) has coined the concept "coalescence" for such mergers of American and Jewish ideas, which come to be seen as identical.
[82] Arnold J. Band, "Popular Fiction and the Shaping of Jewish Identity," in *Jewish Identity in America*, ed. David M. Gordis and Yoav Ben-Horin (Los Angeles: Wilstein Institute/University of Judaism, 1991, 224; Solomon, *Wonder of Wonders*, 355.

reservations Tevye expressed about Chava's decision to marry a non-Jew. But, did these reservations stem from a modern sense of peoplehood, or from pre-modern religious restrictions?[83] – Cue one of the most memorable songs from the musical: "Tradition." The notion of tradition connects religious Judaism and American Jewishness and thereby provides the legitimizing link that American Jews craved between the two parts of their identity, between the old country and the new. The musical employed "tradition" to give a stamp of authenticity to American Jewry's reconstruction of Jewishness. As cultural historian Alisa Solomon writes of the opening song,

> the theme performed an alchemical feat that would be the key to the show's success: by turning *toyre* (Torah) – Jewish law and religious practice – into "tradition," it handed over a legacy that could be fondly acclaimed without exacting any demands. Heritage, after all, is not something one does; it is something one has. Through *Fiddler*, Mostel and [director Jerome] Robbins – and millions of spectators in the decades to come – could cherish, honor, and admire a legacy in the safely secular, make-believe space of a theater.[84]

Fiddler redefined traditional religious norms, rituals, and practices in terms that supported a symbolic, cultural ethnicity. The audience experienced the authenticity of Anatevka vicariously, as "tradition" linked it to their own American Jewishness, which in the 1960s could be, and had to be, expressed consciously and visibly in terms of culture, the marker of ethnicity.[85] Re-defined as culture, tradition was potentially comprehensive, endowing mundane spheres of fragmented modern lives with Jewish meaning: "We have our traditions for everything: how to eat, how to sleep, how to work, even how to wear clothes," Tevye explained. Speaking in the first person plural, he suggested a coherent community which assigned every individual a place in a transcendental order. "Because of our traditions, everyone here knows who he is – and what God expects him to do." For American Jewish listeners, many of whom brought their uncertain Jewishness to the theater, the song endowed cultural traits, often symbolically expressed, with the shining patina of a venerable tradition and linked them to a religious origin. Tradition thus reconfigured became the key to the new, secular covenant that American Jews entered into with the God from their memories in a new promised land.[86]

---

83 For different interpretations of the musical's message on intermarriage, cf. Wolitz, "Americanization of Tevye," 528, and Ruth R. Wisse, "What's Wrong with *Fiddler on the Roof*," *Mosaic*, June 18, 2014.
84 Solomon, *Wonder of Wonders*, 155.
85 Band, "Popular Fiction," 222; Whitfield, "Fiddling with Sholem Aleichem," 120.
86 Roskies, *Search for a Usable Past*, 57. The long-lasting popularity of various musical pieces from the musical for bar/bat mitzvah ceremonies, weddings, and other religious and social oc-

Fiddler performed this task for American Jews with a liberating and exhilarating effect, as Solomon has reconstructed from audiences' reactions. "Today [...] it is hard to imagine just how thrilled audiences could have been to see men wearing *tzitzis* and women lighting Sabbath candles on a Broadway stage, and not as a joke." As an indigenous American cultural form, a Broadway musical bestowed the ultimate cultural legitimacy on the Jewish story, its characters, and aesthetics.[87] The joint American and Jewish legitimacy and the success of the production allowed *Fiddler* to define, with lasting effect and for Jewish and non-Jewish audiences, an imagery of East European Jewry: Tevye embodied how *the* East European Jew looked, dressed, talked, sang, danced, thought, prayed, and felt. For this image, the musical drew inspiration from paintings by Marc Chagall (for the title), photographs by Roman Vishniac and Alter Kacyzne, as well as from *Life is with People*.[88] Out of these variegated sources, it constructed a unified East European past. With no real-life place to check the imagination, the musical, like other cultural products of the time, was received as ethnography, as much as it was received as entertainment and memorialization of a vanished world.[89] In *Fiddler,* past and present were reconciled.

Despite, or rather because of, its success with audiences, critics, and with commentators of different stripes (including many from the Jewish left), *Fiddler* also had its detractors. Among others, the intellectuals around *Commentary* like Irving Howe, Cynthia Ozick, and Hillel Halkin were appalled.[90] At first sight, the critics' concerns were the one-dimensionality and cheap effects of the Broadway production, faults they had already observed with increasing alarm in other cultural products that, in their view, distorted or reified the East European past.[91] These intellectuals feared that sentimentality would erode the creative power of

---

casions testifies to the ongoing need for such validation and to the important traditionalizing function which the musical has served since the 1960s.

[87] Solomon, *Wonder of Wonders*, 2, 5, 214, 221–22. Jeremy Dauber also credits the musical for being "a vital part of the Judaizing of American culture." (*The Worlds of Sholem Aleichem*, 369)

[88] Wolitz, "Americanization of Tevye," 526; Solomon, *Wonder of Wonders*, 119.

[89] Solomon, *Wonder of Wonders*, 229.

[90] Wisse, "What's Wrong with *Fiddler;*" Solomon, *Wonder of Wonders*, 59–61, 229–33; an example of a positive review from the left is Robert Arnow, "Elegy for a Milkman," *Jewish Currents* 20 (1964): 34–37.

[91] Two reviews in *Commentary* can illustrate this point: Critic Isa Kapp entitled her assessment of Sholem Asch's *Tales of My People* (1949) "Pious Tearjerker" (*Commentary* 7 (January 1949): 99); four years later, Midge Decter called the theatrical adaptation *The World of Sholom Aleichem* a "folk falsification of the ghetto." ("Belittling Sholom Aleichem's Jews: Folk Falsification of the Ghetto," review of *The World of Sholom Aleichem*, by Arnold Perl, *Commentary* 17 (May 1954): 389–92)

the memory of the past, which they hoped to tap as a cultural resource. "The greatest risk of memory is sentimentality, and Jewish life has paid dearly for its sentimentality," Bell warned.[92]

Their concerns went even deeper, however. The thinkers who had opened up the discourse about the East European past and the American Jewish present saw *Fiddler* as the symbol of its failure, or, at best, its ending. In *Commentary,* Howe expressed his despair about the musical which presented "the cutest shtetl we never had." He found *Fiddler* to be too-easily digestible and simplified – a commodified consumer product that tempted American Jews to content themselves with a vicarious, symbolic, situational, and ultimately shallow sense of Jewishness, willfully forfeiting its deeper meaning and creative potential:

> American Jews suffer these days from a feeling of guilt because they have lost touch with the past from which they derive, and often they compound this guilt by indulging in an unearned nostalgia. The less [...] they know about East European Jewish life or even the immigrant Jewish experience in America, the more inclined they seem to celebrate it. As their own sense of Jewishness increasingly becomes fragile, more and more they feel [...] grateful for any public recognition of Jewishness.[93]

For Howe, *Fiddler* brought to the fore key problematic aspects of postwar American Jewishness: guilt over the desertion of the home culture, fragile Jewishness, and nostalgia— and the latter not out of concern for its object, but to prop up an otherwise sterile identity. His analysis of American Jews' relationship to their heritage anticipated Lederhendler's assessment of the role of "pastness," as American Jews fashioned America as a reference point for the future while fashioning Jewishness out of the past: "Self-validation in the American idiom turned toward the future, while self-validation in the Jewish idiom turned toward the past." In this context, "Fiddler was a parable of self-validation *at the expense of the past.*" This form of "mimicry" reflected the loss of the culture's creative power, as it was longer supported by a cohesive ethnic community or by cultural

---

92 Bell, "Reflections on Jewish Identity," 474.
93 Irving Howe, "Tevye on Broadway," *Commentary* 38 (November 1964): 75; cf. also Robert Alter, "Sentimentalizing the Jews," *Commentary* 40 (September 1965): 71–75. Cultural historian Michael Kammen has described the trajectory from the popularization to the commercialization of (folk) "heritage" in American society from the early decades of the twentieth century well into the post-1945 period. (Michael Kammen, *Mystic Chords of Memory: The Transformation of Tradition in American Culture* (New York: Knopf, 1991), 407–43, 535–46) The analogous Jewish process, symbolized by *Fiddler*, lagged behind the larger developments that Kammen analyzed.

producers like the "New York intellectuals," both of which were losing their power to sustain the vital and creative secular Jewishness of the interwar period.[94]

These intellectuals had added their voices to the discourse they had themselves created, often by trying to encounter the East European past through the medium of literature, which gave them wide berth in their attempts to reconstruct the past and make it usable. Yet, by the mid-1960s, some of these intellectuals sensed a sea change. "[It] may well be that 'Jewishness' as we have understood it is reaching an end," Howe concluded wearily in his review of *Fiddler*.[95] By that time, the recognizable collective of the "New York Jewish intellectuals" had disintegrated, as Norman Podhoretz chronicled.[96] They could no longer claim their self-appointed role as arbiters of the past in the service of their ideal of American Jewishness. Over twenty-five years, they had succeeded in expanding the field of options for how to conceive and express Jewishness. The boundaries of the discursive field were considerably wider in 1965 than they had been in 1940. But now, they sensed that the competition with the advocates of other ideals of Jewishness was largely over. Many American Jews had settled for a self-sufficiently placid notion of Jewishness that was corroborated by a usable East European past as enshrined in *Fiddler on the Roof*. As it reconstructed the traditional Jewish world of Eastern Europe in cultural terms, the musical appealed to impulses that had animated the intellectuals, too; it took these impulses farther, though, and to a conclusion fitting a new era. What the literary intellectuals had tried to keep open was now settled: Jewishness had a narrative with a beginning and tentative endings in defined places of reference, geographic or imaginary, in Anatevka, Israel, or suburban America. In the words of literary scholar Sidra DeKoven Ezrahi, "If exile is narrative, then to historicize the end of the narrative is to invite a form of epic closure that threatens the storytelling enterprise itself – an enterprise that remained alive, like Scheherazade, by suspending endings."[97] No matter how many encores *Fiddler* had: its success provided the final curtain for a discourse on the past that had begun with an open ending.

---

94 Eli Lederhendler, *New York Jews and the Decline of Urban Ethnicity, 1950–1970* (Syracuse: Syracuse University Press, 2001), 67–69, emphasis in the original.
95 Bell, "Reflections on Jewish Identity," 474; Howe, "Tevye on Broadway," 75.
96 Norman Podhoretz, *Making It* (New York: Random House, 1967), 109.
97 Sidra DeKoven Ezrahi, *Booking Passage: Exile and Homecoming in the Modern Jewish Imagination* (Berkeley: University of California Press, 2000), 14.

10 Conclusion: Re-Inventing Jewishness Out of Memory

In 1965, the broad American-Jewish discourse of the postwar decades was over. And yet, of course, it was not. It had begun much earlier than 1940 and continued beyond the smothering success of *Fiddler*. The discursive developing of a "usable past" that happened during these twenty-five years was part of an ongoing process of identity construction and re-construction, to which the absorption of the East European Jewish past into communal memory contributed in crucial ways. The postwar decades were a period of transition in how American Jews understood the nature of their group identity. The engagement both of elites from different camps and of a broader American Jewish public can be told as part of a larger process, in which changes in demography, ideology, political identification, language and, not least, scholarship converged and made for a broad cultural transformation.

As the native-born majority took over key roles in shaping the Jewish community, a new understanding of American Jewry had to be found. The mass immigration of their parents had created a community that needed to be Americanized. *Fiddler on the Roof*, the transfer of the East European heritage into an American idiom, most visibly symbolized the Americanization of the previous immigrant community. As the analysis of the musical demonstrated, Americanization was not simply assimilation to American social or cultural norms, but rather the re-construction of ethnicity, that is, group distinctiveness, within the American social, political, and cultural framework. (In this usage, the term "ethnicity" is neutral and does not connote a specifically *ethnic* as opposed to religious or other form of distinctiveness.) These processes were accompanied by conscious reflections on the part of intellectual elites, a segment that grew and differentiated as group ascent into a prospering middle class and broader access to higher education generated a growing class of professional thinkers dealing with the nature and future of American Jewry. This group included academics of various disciplines, notably from the growing social sciences. The communal engagement with the East European past took place in the context of a simultaneous shift in the way scholars conceived of (Jewish) ethnicity in America.[1]

---

[1] Crucial works on the question of American Jewish ethnicity include Jonathan Freedman, *Klezmer America: Jewishness, Ethnicity, Modernity* (New York: Columbia University Press, 2008); John Higham, *Send These to Me: Immigrants in Urban American* (orig. title: *Send These to Me: Jews and Other Immigrants in Urban America* (Baltimore: Johns Hopkins University Press, 1984; orig. publ. 1975)); Bethamie Horowitz, "Old Casks in New Times: The Reshaping of American Jewish Identity in the 21st Century," in *Ethnicity and Beyond: Theories and Dilemmas of Jewish Group Demarcation*, ed. Eli Lederhendler (New York: Oxford University Press, 2011), 79–90; Matthew Frye Jacobson, "Hyphen Nation:

It was the very persistence of Jewish group distinctiveness that in the mid-decades of the twentieth century challenged the scholarly paradigm of "assimilationism," which assumed a progressive decline of ethnicity due to the forces of Americanization. As scholars revised the concept, the validity of the underlying assimilation paradigm was undermined. This was already the case in Will Herberg's work *Protestant – Catholic – Jew*, which, while part of the assimilationist school, used "Hansen's Law" to explain circumscribed, yet persistent ethnicity as a periodic re-emergence tied to generational succession.[2] The assimilation paradigm was nuanced, as scholars clang to it in the face of the many challenges. Sociologist Herbert Gans, as late as 1979, stuck to a form of assimilationism, but acknowledged the persistence of ethnicity by extending his earlier concept of "symbolic Judaism" to the larger notion of a "symbolic ethnicity" which rested on the consumption of ethnic symbols and did not require any affiliation with ethnic groups or institutions.[3] Milton Gordon's *Assimilation in American Life*, published in 1964, the year *Fiddler on the Roof* premiered, differentiated between "acculturation" and "assimilation." Acculturation, the decline of cultural distinctiveness, does not necessarily lead to "assimilation," the dissolution of a group's distinctiveness. Jewish ethnicity in this analysis, based on behavioral distinctiveness and expressed in associational life, persists and defies the expectation of its disappearance assumed to result from Americanization.[4]

Ethnicity in American Intellectual and Political Life," in *A Companion to Post-1945 America*, ed. Jean-Christophe Agnew and Roy Rosenzweig (Malden: Blackwell, 2006), 175–91; Russell A. Kazal, "Revisiting Assimilation: The Rise, Fall, and Reappraisal of a Concept in American Ethnic History," *American Historical Review* 100 (1995): 437–71; Riv-Ellen Prell, "The Utility of the Concept of 'Ethnicity' for the Study of Jews," in *Ethnicity and Beyond*, 102–107; Jonathan D. Sarna, "Ethnicity and Beyond," in *Ethnicity and Beyond*, 108–12; Richard H. Thompson, *Theories of Ethnicity: A Critical Reappraisal* (New York: Greenwood Press, 1989).

2 Marcus Lee Hansen, "The Third Generation in America," *Commentary* 14 (November 1952): 492–500.

3 Herbert Gans, "Symbolic Ethnicity: The Future of Ethnic Groups and Cultures in America," *Ethnic and Racial Studies* 2 (1979): 1–20. Gans saw assimilation as ongoing (albeit in a "bumpy" rather than a straight line), and interpreted even the forms of symbolic ethnicity as signs of assimilation, as they draw on an Americanized repertoire of expressions ("Ethnic Invention and Acculturation: A Bumpy-Line Approach," *Journal of American Ethnic History* 12 (1992): 142–52). He subsequently extended the concept even further to include "symbolic religiosity" ("Symbolic Ethnicity and Symbolic Religiosity: Towards a Comparison of Ethnic and Religious Acculturation," *Ethnic and Racial Studies* 17 (1994): 577–92). For critiques of Gans' approach and his response, cf. Peter Kivisto and Ben Nefzger, "Symbolic Ethnicity and American Jews: The Relationship of Ethnic Identity to Behaviour and Group Affiliation," *Social Science Journal* 30 (1993): 1–12; Kathleen Neils Conzen, David A. Gerber, Ewa Morawska, George E. Pozzetta and Rudolph J. Vecoli, "The Invention of Ethnicity: A Perspective from the U.S.A.," *Journal of American Ethnic History* 12 (1992): 3–41.

4 Milton M. Gordon, *Assimilation in American Life: The Role of Race, Religion, and National Origins* (New York: Oxford University Press, 1964).

Gordon's book was situated within the transition toward the scholarly paradigm of "new ethnicity." This approach explained the increased salience of ethnic difference by the idea that ethnicity was primordial, hence "unmeltable."[5] It bolstered a new narrative of Americanization, as the "nation of immigrants" required that its members, groups and individuals, be "ethnic." The concept was based on the acceptance of ethnic difference and assent to an ideal of cultural pluralism or, later, even multiculturalism. The increased American Jewish nostalgic appreciation of the immigrant past, which bridged the gap between the East European past and the American present, was part of this new perspective, as it provided a founding myth which found tangible expression in the Lower East Side as a memory space and, on the other shore, in figures like Tevye, who would take his family to America.[6]

The culture reconstructed by the musical *Fiddler on the Roof* and embodied in Tevye served as the basis for the ethnic distinctiveness that American Jews sought in the 1960s. They were looking to both their Americanness and their Jewishness in the context of the new focus on cultural pluralism and the growing skepticism of the American mass culture around them. As American Jews of the 1960s reconstructed the past to serve as a resource, this "culture of retrieval was an overt response to disappointment in the present," in Lederhendler's words.[7] An ethnicity derived from the past was seen as an antidote to the homogenizing forces of American mass culture and suburbanization, which, in turn, were associated with the crisis of modernity and its destabilizing effects on society and the individual. "Because of our traditions we've kept our balance for many years," Tevye sang.[8] Thus, past-based ethnicity was

---

[5] Michael Novak, *The Rise of the Unmeltable Ethnics: The New Political Force of the Seventies* (New York: Macmillan, 1972); Nathan Glazer and Daniel P. Moynihan, *Beyond the Melting Pot: The Negroes, Puerto Ricans, Jews, Italians, and Irish of New York City* (Cambridge: M.I.T. Press, 1970, orig. publ. 1963). For the scholarly debate about this development, cf. Richard D. Alba, *Ethnic Identity: The Transformation of White America* (New Haven: Yale University Press, 1990); Joane Nagel, "Constructing Ethnicity: Creating and Recreating Ethnic Identity and Culture," in *New Tribalisms: The Resurgence of Race and Ethnicity*, ed. Michael W. Hughey (London: Macmillan, 1998), 237–72; Anthony D. Smith, *The Ethnic Revival* (Cambridge: Cambridge University Press, 1981); Mary C. Waters, *Ethnic Options: Choosing Identities in America* (Berkeley: University of California Press, 1990).

[6] Hasia R. Diner, *Lower East Side Memories: A Jewish Place in America* (Princeton: Princeton University Press, 2000). Cf. also *Remembering the Lower East Side: American Jewish Reflections*, ed. Hasia Diner, Jeffrey Shandler and Beth Wenger (Bloomington: Indiana University Press, 2000).

[7] Eli Lederhendler, *New York Jews and the Decline of Urban Ethnicity, 1950–1970* (Syracuse: Syracuse University Press, 2001), 90.

[8] Ethnicity scholar Matthew Frye Jacobson counts the musical among the cultural products that presented ethnicity as a form of self-expression and critical distance from American mainstream culture ("Hyphen Nation," 180–81).

re-validated within American culture as a marker of positive difference. American society was refashioned as a vibrant conglomeration of immigrants who were no longer defined against cultural standards set by a dominant group, such as WASPs. With some delay, society reproduced a shift in perspective that historians had seen before: Oscar Handlin related in 1951 how, in trying to write about the immigrants *in* American history, "I discovered that the immigrants *were* American history." It was only in the postwar decades that immigration achieved "iconic status" as a topic of American Jewish history.[9] For viewers of *Fiddler*, "Tevye is no longer merely a character; he has become an American type: the Old Country immigrant." With WASPs seen as just another ethnic group who happened to have landed on the American shore earlier than others, Wolitz put it succinctly: "Tevye, then, is the Jewish Pilgrim whose *Mayflower* has long since docked."[10]

The Tevye of the musical answered two needs that had become more urgent in a re-ethnicized American society which embraced cultural pluralism: ethnicity was best anchored in a past, and the cultural re-definition of distinctiveness called for a basis broader than religion. In doing so, the musical drew, wittingly or not, on scholarly shifts not just in the social sciences, but also in historiography that could add legitimacy to a specifically American, broad concept of Jewish identity. One such key development was the broadening of scholarly interests to include social history, as represented by the highly influential historians Jacob Katz and, with a different emphasis, Salo Baron; both continued an impulse given by Simon Dubnow in particular. Baron, in the first edition of his *Social and Religious History of the Jews* (1937), added religion to the social forces that gave the Jewish experience coherence over time.[11] Especially as social history preserved an openness to

---

[9] Oscar Handlin, *The Uprooted: The Epic Story of the Great Migrations that Made the American People* (New York: Grosset & Dunlap, 1951), 3, emphasis in the original; Paula E. Hyman, "The Normalization of American Jewish History," *American Jewish History* 91 (2003): 355.

[10] Seth Wolitz, "The Americanization of Tevye or Boarding the Jewish 'Mayflower,'" *American Quarterly* 40 (1988): 533; Jeremy Dauber, *The Worlds of Sholem Aleichem: The Remarkable Life and Afterlife of the Man Who Created Tevye* (New York: Nextbook Schocken, 2013), 368.

[11] Paula E. Hyman, "The Dynamics of Social History," in *Reshaping the Past: Jewish History and the Historians (Studies in Contemporary Jewry X)* ed. Jonathan Frankel (New York/Oxford: Oxford University Press, 1994), 93–111; Jonathan Frankel, "Assimilation and the Jews in Nineteenth-Century Europe: Towards a New Historiography," in *Assimilation and Community: The Jews in Nineteenth-Century Europe*, ed. Jonathan Frankel and Steven J. Zipperstein (Cambridge: Cambridge University Press, 1992), 17–18; Paula E. Hyman, "Jacob Katz as Social Historian," in *The Pride of Jacob: Essays on Jacob Katz and his Work*, ed. Jay Michael Harris (Cambridge: Harvard University Press, 2002), 86–89; Ismar Schorsch, "The Last Jewish Generalist [Obituary Salo W. Baron]" *AJS Review* 18 (1993): 46–49; Jacob Katz, *Tradition and Crisis: Jewish Society at the End of the Middle*

mutual influences among Jews and other groups (and when complemented by ethnographic works, like *Life is with People),* it painted a much broader picture of Jewish life than previous approaches. In the postwar period, YIVO and the work of Dubnow, who was received in America particularly the 1950s, brought both a commitment to social-scientific approaches to the Jewish experience and a focus on social history, framing how many younger American Jewish historians encountered the East European past.¹² This encounter took place during a time period when the previously dominant "nationalist" or "Jerusalem" school of Jewish history gradually lost influence, both among professional historians and in the construction of collective memory. In turn, the Jewish experience in the diaspora was increasingly rehabilitated, both in Europe and in the United States.¹³

For American Jewry, historians responded to the shifts in the concept of Jewish distinctiveness by applying the concept of an *ethnic* rather than national group to their subject. This conceptualization allowed for an understanding of the American Jewish experience as transcending extant categories that had characterized both academic historiography and popular perceptions of the past. American Jewish history could not be explained through the dichotomy of emancipation vs. nationalism, ideologically mutually exclusive models of Jewish modernization for which "Western" and "Eastern Europe" had come to stand.¹⁴ As a number of

---

Ages (New York: New York University Press, 1993, orig. publ. 1958, Hebr. 1957); Katz, *Out of the Ghetto: The Social Background of Jewish Emancipation, 1770–1870* (New York: Schocken, 1973); Salo W. Baron, *A Social and Religious History of the Jews* (New York: Columbia University Press, 1937). The postwar version of *Social and Religious History,* published 1952ff., de-emphasized the religious aspects and focused on the external dimension of the Jewish experience.

12 Paula E. Hyman, "The Ideological Transformation of Modern Jewish Historiography," in *The State of Jewish Studies,* ed. Shaye J. D. Cohen and Edward L. Greenstein (Detroit: Wayne State University Press, 1990), 145–47; Benjamin Nathans, "On Russian-Jewish Historiography," in *Historiography of Imperial Russia: The Profession and Writing of History in a Multinational State,* ed. Thomas Sanders (Armonk, NY: M. E. Sharpe, 1999), 412–17. The Jewish Publication Society published a selection of Dubnow's essays in 1958 *(Nationalism and History),* edited and introduced by Koppel Pinson (incl. the bulk of Dubnow's *Letters on Old and New Jewry).* The English edition of his world history began appearing in English in five volumes in 1967–73; cf. Frankel, Jonathan, "S. M. Dubnov: Historian and Ideologist," in Sophie Dubnov-Erlich, *The Life and Works of S. M. Dubnov: Diaspora Nationalism and Jewish History* (Bloomington: Indiana University Press, 1991), 2.

13 Hyman, "Ideological Transformation," 151–52; David N. Myers, *Re-Inventing the Jewish Past: European Jewish Intellectuals and the Zionist Return to History* (New York: Oxford University Press, 1995), 184.

14 This dichotomy has by now been thoroughly revised. A number of historians have contributed to the "rehabilitation" of the supposedly assimilationist West European Jewries, in response to the dominant negative image: Michael Graetz, *The Jews in Nineteenth-Century France: From the*

postwar American Jewish thinkers of different stripes already suggested, American Jewry could be seen as a product of both, synthesizing key elements such as Western liberal modernity and Eastern traditional peoplehood, enlightened progressiveness and spiritual traditionalism, shaped by social *and* religious forces.[15] While this narrative could serve as a foundation for an American and American-Jewish exceptionalism, the thrust in the postwar discourse was to link American Jewry in positive ways to two previously outstanding Jewish experiences, striving to assemble into a new whole what different models of modernization had fragmented. Thus inscribed into the continuum of Jewish history, American Jewry could claim legitimacy for its own type of Jewishness, a distinctly American one. Postwar American Jewry defined itself vis-à-vis both its parents, as it came of age and into its own.

A New Idea Out of Many Failing Ones

As the analysis of the discourse around the nature and meaning of Jewishness has shown, various groups of thinkers had very different advice for the adolescent searching for ways to understand himself out of the sources of the East European past. Immigrant intellectuals around YIVO brought their biographical and social-scientific impulse to the task in order to ground an unmoored community

---

French Revolution to the Alliance Israélite Universelle (Stanford: Stanford University Press, 1996); Marion Kaplan, *The Making of the Jewish Middle Class: Women, Family, and Identity in Imperial Germany* (New York: Oxford University Press, 1991); Jack Wertheimer, *Unwelcome Strangers: East European Jews in Imperial Germany* (New York: Oxford University Press, 1987); Ismar Schorsch, *Jewish Reactions to German Anti-Semitism* (New York: Columbia University Press, 1972). Cf. on this subject: Todd M. Endelman, "The Legitimization of the Diaspora Experience in Recent Jewish Historiography," *Modern Judaism* 11 (1991): 195–209; Endelman, "Response [to Hyman, "Ideological Transformation]," 160–61. The inversely one-sided accounts of the East European Jewish path to modernity have been similarly revised: Gershon D. Hundert, *Jews in Poland-Lithuania in the Eighteenth Century: A Genealogy of Modernity* (Berkeley: University of California Press, 2004); Eli Lederhendler, "Modernity Without Emancipation or Assimilation? The Case of Russian Jewry," in *Assimilation and Community: The Jews in Nineteenth-Century Europe*, ed. Jonathan Frankel and Steven J. Zipperstein (Cambridge: Cambridge University Press, 1992), 324–43; Benjamin Nathans, *Beyond the Pale: The Jewish Encounter with Late Imperial Russia* (Berkeley: University of California Press, 2002).

15 Cf. Robert Gordis, "American Jewry Faces Its Fourth Century," *Judaism* 3 (1954; Tercentenary issue): 298–99; Elliot E. Cohen, "Jewish Culture in America: Some Speculations by an Editor," *Commentary* 3 (May 1947): 414; S. Niger, "The Amalgam Which Is Jewish Life [Address at National Conference for Jewish Education, January 1951]," *Workmen's Circle Call* 19 (1951): 4.

in a positive, historical consciousness. The American-born intellectuals around *Commentary* provided cultural space for explorations that redefined traditional religious elements of Judaism in modern, cultural terms. Religious intellectuals similarly sought to modernize traditional Judaism by broadening its definition to include more Jewishness in Judaism as a spiritual culture, for which the East European past served as a model. The left advocated a Jewishness that would carry forward the cultural-progressive identity born in modernizing Eastern Europe.

By the mid-1960s, many of these ideas had failed in practice. Yiddish culture and political leftism turned out to be out of touch with the cultural and political realities of postwar American Jewry: Yiddish was powerless in the face of the linguistic assimilation of American-born Jews, and postwar liberalism and anti-Communism had pushed leftist ideologies to the margins of the spectrum. They spoke to a shrinking segment of American Jewry. Broader cultural reconstructions of Jewishness and Judaism by secular or religious intellectuals had wider appeal, but lacked the coherence, which imbued Yiddishism or ideological leftism with the promise of comprehensiveness and holism. Moreover, only a minority were ready to make the commitments that religious thinkers associated with the spiritual culture they advocated. Secular intellectuals, who tried to retain some of the social ferment, cultural subversiveness, and spiritual elevation they sensed in the East European heritage, faced what they felt was its cheap commodification for the uncritical affirmation of a parochial American Jewishness.

What, then, was the impact of a generation-long discourse around a community in search of a communal identity as both Americans and Jews? It lay in a common denominator that was hidden underneath the widely divergent prescriptions these groups offered for American Jewry. All groups tacitly agreed, given their otherwise widely divergent positions, that some form of Jewish spiritual essence could be derived from the East European experience. This essence could be expressed in various forms, ideas, and practices, and had been in the past. Collectively, these expressions formed a pluralistic culture of Jewishness. They had differed from each other in their different times and places, but were legitimate if they partook of the spiritual essence. If this essence was culturally and aesthetically translated into American terms, American Jewishness would be the latest incident of this timeless, culturally expressed Jewishness, which could inspire and legitimize a community by locating it in Jewish history.

This place in Jewish history required a conscious sense of continuity with the past. With different nuances, most participants in the great discourse on this past agreed on a common imperative. American Jews had to fulfill the *mitzvah* of consciously placing themselves in a spiritual continuity with their East European heritage. The contest over its role in communal memory derived its urgency from the sense of a powerful, sacred obligation which demanded to be channeled and integrated into their American lives. A story by Labor-Zionist writer Hayim Greenberg can illustrate how the complex forces working on American Jews let them feel both attracted and haunted by the East European past; its ominous title is, "The Dybbuk." Written in Yiddish in 1953, it was one of the last texts Greenberg wrote before his death. His *Jewish Frontier* published it in the following year, halfway through the period under consideration in this study and coinciding with the Tercentenary that let American Jewry take an inventory of itself. It relates how "Mr. X," East European-born and successful in America, worries his family because every day during his lunch break in Central Park he speaks Yiddish to himself in different voices. Confronted by his family, he rejects any suggestions of pathological behavior, but responds:

> Lately I have been deriving great pleasure – a pleasure, true, that is not unmixed with anguish and even physical pain – from becoming for one hour each day a small-town Jew, the type of small-town Jew of South Russia where, as you know, I hail from. Through some process unknown to me the small town, the *shtetl*, suddenly became resurrected with me. It is not I who am talking, it is the *shtetl* that talks through my mouth. Local Yiddish idioms and expressions that had lain dormant within me for many years suddenly reawakened. Images, gestures, and scenes that are no longer to be found in the *shtetl* of my early childhood have floated up to the surface of my memory. Indeed, how is one to find these scenes and images and gestures when the *shtetl* has been eradicated together with all its Jews? [...] My grandmother would probably define this as a Dybbuk. Call it a Dybbuk if you wish. I don't care. For, basically, what is a Dybbuk? It is someone or something that is no longer alive, according to our material concepts, but persists in wishing to live and seeks a "vessel" in which to continue living. He or it lives in this medium and talks through it. I do not care what specialists say about this. I consider it as entirely normal, and no one should get panicky over it.[16]

Mr. X then replicates several such theatrical scenes and dialogues for his audience of family members and friends: two *shtetl* dwellers talk about a calving, two others about an impending wedding, the seamstress hums a song at evening, the *melamed* from Lithuania is chased and mocked by students, a rich girl sneers at the offerings in a store, two men dispute the curriculum of a new girls' school, girlfriends chat on a Sabbath stroll. At the end of his performance, he asks his listeners for their judgment, and offers his own explanation: "I know that my *shtetl* is suspended in limbo and that it wants to live. It knows that it can never again be restored, that it is past, one hundred percent finished history – still it wants to live in somebody and through somebody." The Jews of the *shtetl* want to live in him, he feels, and in thousands of others. "You may say that others do not hear

---

[16] Hayim Greenberg, "The Dybbuk," *Jewish Frontier* XXI (1954): 31.

this appeal of the dead to live within us one hour a day, one hour a week, or even one hour a year. That only proves that the others are deaf. I am not deaf, nor am I blind. Therefore, I live in their stead."[17]

This little speech reflects the complicated mixture of impulses many American Jews felt as they thought of East European Jewry: mundane memories of individual people, relatives, and acquaintances; a sense of distant yet familiar places; vestiges of Yiddish and a religious tradition associated with these memories; a spiritual duty to remember East European Jewry and their destroyed world, as an abstraction and for the sake of Jewish identity; the pleasure and pain of remembering; and the need and the possibility to realize these impulses in the American present, by compartmentalizing them, without forfeiting the meaning they gave to their Jewishness.[18]

The *dybbuk* that brought forth these complex, fragmented, incoherent memories and urges may have urged American Jewish thinkers to do what Arthur Hertzberg advocated: "to come to terms with the last several centuries of Eastern European creativity, which recently ended so tragically before our eyes." These thinkers realized that "that world must be assimilated into the canon of the tradition and into the stream of Jewish history."[19] The torrent of texts about the East European past that were written, read, discussed, and performed in postwar America, from a scholarly paper presented at a YIVO conference to *Fiddler on the Roof* and from a Shabbat sermon to a flamboyant editorial in a Communist journal, in a textbook and in *Commentary*, was how American Jewry discursively assimilated this past into its group identity.

Community of Memory

This process was a crucial element in the fundamental transformation of American Jewry into a "community of memory" – a new paradigm of American Jewishness, shaped out of elements wrested from the reconstructed East European Jewish

---

17 Greenberg, "Dybbuk," 33.
18 The narrator relates that X's family got used to this odd behavior. He asks, but does not answer, the question of how X managed to discipline his *dybbuk* for twenty-three hours per day to be "normal," and limit being abnormal to one hour. "This is X's secret. I doubt very much whether he could explain it himself. I will never ask him." (Grenberg, "Dybbuk," 33)
19 Arthur Hertzberg, "The Worldly Jew," review of *Einems Yidishe Machshovos*, by Melech Ravitch, *Yidish un Yidishkeit*, by Yosef Opatoshu; *Kedushah un Gevurah bei Yidn*, by Y. Efroykin, *Commentary* 10 (July 1950): 87.

past.[20] The diversity and breadth of this past, reflected in the many competing images and narratives of the discourse that were worth remembering, made for a broad Jewish culture which gained coherence by means of an essence many thinkers called *Yiddishkayt*. It was employed as an antidote to modern, liberal religion's perceived lack of communal warmth, ethnic distinctiveness, or affirmative traditionalism. Bonds transcending narrowly religious commonalities, a positive sense of particularism, and an orientation toward a positive past offered meaning in a type of Jewishness that could not be generated in other ways. This type of Jewishness was based on reconstructed traditions that were inherently critical of modernity's presentness. They promised to be holistic in the face of modern, fragmented society's potential for crisis and instability, and redemptive for the wounded Jewish soul. The "relatedness" made of ethnic bonds and historical ties gained a modern form of sacredness, as traditional understandings of covenantal distinctiveness were re-articulated in modern terms, but retained a spiritual obligation of continuity, if only realized by a common consciousness of the past. "Group memory sanctifies what it chooses to retain by creating symbols and myths which become for it the true picture of the hallowed past," in Hertzberg's words.[21] Much as other originally religious precepts and concepts of Judaism, such as "chosenness," the "sacred relatedness" at the heart of the new paradigm of Jewishness was decoupled from narrowly religious frameworks and re-defined in ways that translated their religious core into a new idiom. It referred to relations across time and space that were realized vicariously and imaginatively, through individual and social forms of memory.[22]

It should be emphasized that the notion of Jewishness as a "community of memory" summarizes a conceptual exploration of Jewishness as it developed in this period in a realm hovering conceptually above the social reality of American Jewry. It offers a way to understand how the East European past was reconstructed and inscribed into the collective imagination and identity of American Jewry through cultural products. These products shaped the place of this past in American Jews' individual and communal identities.

This new paradigm of Jewishness, an intellectual construct reflecting the time and circumstances of its emergence, is relevant beyond the history of American

---

[20] Nathan Abrams makes the claim that *Commentary* was particularly instrumental in this regard ("'America Is Home:' *Commentary* Magazine and the Refocusing of the Community of Memory, 1945–1960," in *Commentary in American Life*, ed. Murray Friedman (Philadelphia: Temple University Press, 2005), 9–37.
[21] Hertzberg, "The Worldly Jew," 87.
[22] For an analysis of the transformation of the idea of "chosenness" in American Judaism, cf. Arnold M. Eisen, *The Chosen People in America: A Study in Jewish Religious Ideology* (Bloomington: Indiana University Press, 1983).

Jewry at a given point in time. It engages two crucial and related aspects of the thorny question of (Jewish) modernization, which translates into scholarly terms the "coming of age"-metaphor: the role and function of religion (Judaism) and the function of group memory in modern societies.

French sociologist of religion Danièle Hervieu-Léger has offered an approach to these issues that transcends existing theories of secularization and, objecting to the long-regnant Weberian antithesis of modernity and tradition, accounts for "new forms of religious belief." In her study *Religion as a Chain of Memory*, she defines religion by three elements: "the expression of believing, the memory of continuity, and the legitimizing reference to an authorized version of such memory, that is to say a tradition."[23] As such, her definition is broad enough to accommodate a broadly cultural Judaism in the concept of modern "religion," as it avoids a reduction to narrower definitions.[24] In her perspective on memory, Hervieu-Léger's reading is related to Yosef H. Yerushalmi's, whom she does not mention, as for both it is modernity's attack on memory that undermines traditional religion.[25] As in his argument, her approach provides a useful lens to look at the effects of modernity on traditional Judaism with its strong focus on the covenant and its ritual continuation. If modernity means that the preservation, renewal, and legitimacy of memory are undermined, traditional Judaism is undermined more than other religions by the advent of modernity. "One of the chief characteristics of modern societies is that they are no longer societies of memory, and as such ordered with a view to reproducing what is inherited," she writes. "Change, which is a function of modernity itself, has resulted in modern societies being less and less able to nurture the innate capacity of individuals and groups to assimilate or imaginatively to project a lineage of belief."[26] However, as modernity generates the need for the very type of groundedness in the past, which its constitutive orientation toward newness and change denies, modern societies generate "reconstructed forms of tradition," or invented traditions.

---

23 Danièle Hervieu-Léger, *Religion as a Chain of Memory* (New Brunswick: Rutgers University Press, 2000, orig. 1993 French), 97. For Jewish history, the Weberian narrative is the basis for the long-dominant view which suggests a delay in modernization between Western and Central Europe on the one hand, and Eastern Europe on the other.
24 Her broad definition is related to Thomas Luckmann's concept of a modern "invisible religion," articulated in *Invisible Religion: The Problem of Religion in Modern Society* (New York: Macmillan, 1967), and subject to the same criticism of dilution of the concept.
25 For another look at the effects of modernity on religion and an attempt at a "theology of memory" as a response, cf. Yehuda Kurtzer, *Shuva: The Future of the Jewish Past* (Waltham: Brandeis University Press/Hanover: University Press of New England, 2012).
26 Hervieu-Léger, *Religion as a Chain of Memory*, 124.

Hervieu-Léger's term for the process at hand is the "metaphorization" of religion. This concept has been used to explain specifically Jewish responses to modernity. Jewish studies scholar Andrew Bush takes Mordecai M. Kaplan's transformation of the *mitzvot* as a case in point, as they are a displacement of the sacred rather than a disenchantment. Kaplan's "folkways" were, metaphorically, commandments authored and authorized by the people. Bush points to the widespread broader cultural processes that combine displacement and retention of the sacred in the life practices and self-expression of Jews. Literary scholar Dan Miron analyzes the "metaphorization" of the *shtetl*, and David Roskies shows how the writer Ansky metaphorically identifies folklore with the Oral Torah. In these processes, the salient elements of Jewish distinctiveness are displaced from the divine commandments articulated in the Written and Oral Torah to the lived experience of Jewish people.[27] The transformation of Jewish religious knowledge into modern categories, resulting in a historical consciousness, has long been identified as a key process of Jewish modernization. The scholarly reconstructions of the heritage informed the more popular ways of engaging with the past that shaped communal "memory," a distinct way to relate to it.[28] Nevertheless, the same question that historian Michael Meyer asks of the function of Jewish history could be asked of Jewish memory: "Should the study of Jewish history principally serve to liberate the Jew from tradition by historicizing it or create a new attachment to the past by reconceiving it as a model or anchorage for the present?"[29] Postwar American Jews followed the second option in the face of an uncertain present.

For modern societies more generally, reconstructing traditions as memories becomes a way to tap into old-new sources of meaning, Hervieu-Léger writes: "Accelerated change, which is at the root of the characteristic instantaneousness of both individual and collective experience, paradoxically gives rise to appeals to memory. They underpin the need to recover the past in the imagination without which collective identity, just as individual identity, is unable to operate." Echoing Maurice Halbwachs' study on the function of cultural memory, Hervieu-Léger

---

27 Andrew Bush, *Jewish Studies: A Theoretical Introduction* (Piscataway: Rutgers University Press, 2011), 2–5; Dan Miron, "The Literary Image of the Shtetl," *Jewish Social Studies* 1 (1995): 12–14; David G. Roskies, "S. Ansky and the Paradigm of Return," in *The Uses of Tradition: Jewish Continuity in the Modern Era*, ed. Jack Wertheimer (New York: Jewish Theological Seminary, 1992), 258.
28 Ismar Schorsch, "The Ethos of Modern Jewish Scholarship," in *From Text to Context: The Turn to History in Modern Judaism* (Waltham: Brandeis University Press/Hanover: University Press of New England), 158–62.
29 Michael A. Meyer, "The Emergence of Jewish Historiography: Motives and Motifs," *History and Theory* 27 (1988): 160.

stresses how the process of inventing or reconstructing such memories becomes constitutive of the group's identity. It assumes a minimal sense of continuity as the fundament for a common future; this assumption is by no means certain, as a result society has "continually to reconstruct itself in new forms so as to ensure continuity for both the group and the individual. But without there being an organized and integrated social memory such reconstruction takes place in an entirely fragmentary way."[30]

The discourse and competition between various reconstructions of the East European past was a fragmentary way by which mid-century American Jewry refashioned its cultural memory to reconstitute itself under radically transformed circumstances. Cultural memory, in Hervieu-Léger's assessment, "incorporates – and constantly reactivates and reconstructs – the currents of thought which have outlasted past experiences and which are newly actualized in the present. In the interpretation given by Halbwachs, this inseparably creative and normative dynamic function of collective memory is engendered by society itself." The "authorized version" of group memory (one of the prerequisites of a modern religion) is produced by specialists. "The shifting and the shaping by means of which this heritage becomes a norm for the present and future are theoretically carried out by those in the group or society who are invested with the power to do so and/or dispose of the instruments of physical, ideological and symbolic coercion to have them carried out." In open societies without legally, socially, or morally binding authorities with power of coercion, the normativity of group memories is established discursively. Again in Hertzberg's words regarding the vanished world of East European Jewry: "That world must be assimilated into the canon of the tradition and into the stream of Jewish history."[31] The various versions of the past that compete to be assimilated into and define cultural memory are judged by the presentist criteria of how they fulfill the function of such a reconstructed past for the group at large: "Whether the past in question is relatively short or very long is only of secondary significance. The degree of ancientness confers an extra value on tradition, but it is not what initially established its social authority. What matters most is that the demonstration of continuity is capable of incorporating even the innovations and reinterpretations demanded by the present."[32]

---

30 Hervieu-Léger, *Religion as a Chain of Memory*, 142. Halbwachs' classical account is *The Collective Memory* (New York: Harper, 1980).
31 Hertzberg, "The Worldly Jew," 87.
32 Hervieu-Léger, *Religion as a Chain of Memory*, 87.

Re-Inventing the Past to Re-Invent Jewish Ethnicity

The constructed nature of memory, which preserves reconstructions of the past, places the idea of a "community of memory" into the context of another concept of ethnicity. One influential attempt to transcend the impasse between "assimilationism" and the pluralism of "unmeltable ethnics," the "invention paradigm" is particularly relevant as a framework in which to analyze reconstructions of the past. It applies larger insights about the constructedness of our world to the understanding of nations (Benedict Anderson), traditions (Eric Hobsbawm et al.), and ethnicity (Werner Sollors et al.).[33] These inventions respond to problems and deficits that modern societies or states cannot otherwise address. The invention of traditions has been seen as accompanying the most extreme stages of modernization, similar to how collective memory is re-asserted to compensate for experiences of discontinuity and rupture. The invention of ethnicity – bolstered by the re-invention of a common past – can similarly be explored as a theory to account for the persistence of ethnicity under specifically modern conditions.[34] For mid-century American Jews, who in their lifetime experienced or witnessed a series of ruptures – in Eastern Europe, as immigrants, through the Holocaust, reconstitution as an ethnic group in postwar America – the assertion of stable roots in the past compensated for rapid and painful modernization processes.[35] Their completion marked a coming of age.

---

[33] Benedict Anderson, *Imagined Communities: Reflections on the Origin and Spread of Nationalism* (London/New York: Verso, 2006; orig. publ. 1983); Eric Hobsbawm and Terence Ranger, eds., *The Invention of Tradition* (Cambridge: Cambridge University Press, 1983); Werner Sollors, ed. *The Invention of Ethnicity* (New York: Oxford University Press, 1989); cf. also Anthony D. Smith, "The Nation: Invented, Imagined, Reconstructed?" *Millennium – Journal of International Studies* 20 (1991): 353–68.

[34] Cf. Conzen et al., "The Invention of Ethnicity;" Lawrence H. Fuchs et al. "'The Invention of Ethnicity:' The Amen Corner [with response]," *Journal of American Ethnic History* 12 (1992): 53–63; Ewa Morawska, "In Defense of the Assimilation Model," *Journal of American Ethnic History* 13 (1994): 76–87; Michael Roth, *The Ironist's Cage: Memory, Trauma, and the Construction of History* (New York: Columbia University Press, 1995), 181.

[35] Lederhendler points to the processes of religious modernization going on in Eastern Europe during the time of mass immigration, and stresses the discontinuity experienced by the immigrants in this regard: "In their own lives, Judaism had to be constructed anew, drawing in some ways upon traditional values and practices, but no longer rooted in the familiar milieu of home." The reconstruction took place in the framework of the separation of religion into a private sphere, differentiated from other aspects of individual and communal life so

The notion of "invented ethnicities" rejects earlier essentializing conceptualizations of ethnic groups and ethnicity as stable, static, and natural, and emphasizes in contrast the fluidity of these concepts and the agency of ethnics. According to Sollors' approach, the invention of ethnicity is a way to metaphorically-symbolically naturalize relationships that are no longer based on descent, but on assent to ethnic pluralism as the ideal guiding American society; again, to be American requires being (and remaining) ethnic. In the context of invented ethnicity, "generations," as in Hansen's Law, also serve as a metaphor invoking fictive organic community and kinship, in order to construct community and continuity.[36]

However, these very premises make the concept of invented communities profoundly problematic for the question of *Jewish* community and continuity. It would imply that the notion of a Jewish community, or people, across time and space is a mere postulate, or construct, as well. Models that suggest the objective existence of such a group, based on religious or national characteristics, would then just be attempts to shore up ideals which, at least under modern conditions, no longer have any objective basis or historic legitimacy. Zionism, for example, deprived of the centuries-long religious orientation around the land of Israel, would lose much legitimacy beyond its role as a modern nationalist movement. Kaplan's spiritual elevation of Jewish peoplehood and the "sacred relatedness" with other Jews that post-Holocaust American Jews may have sensed at the core of their Jewishness was based on a belief in actual transhistorical ties to a Jewish people and its fate through time.

Could "memory" break the impasse, due to its double nature as a modern social and cultural construct and as a pre-modern religious imperative reflecting the origins of Judaism and the Jewish people in a historical event, the making of a covenant at Sinai? If so, it could ground an understanding of Jewish peoplehood

---

characteristic of modernity. While in the immigrant experience, Judaism remained a collective experience (albeit in a fundamentally changed form); future generations had to contend with the effects the newly privatized role of religion had on Judaism as a source of meaning and identity (Lederhendler, *New York Jews and the Decline of Urban Ethnicity,* 97–101).

36 Werner Sollors, "First Generation, Second Generation, Third Generation ... : The Cultural Construction of Descent," in *Beyond Ethnicity: Consent and Descent in American Culture* ed. Sollors (New York: Oxford University Press, 1986), 208–36. Gans (in "Symbolic Ethnicity and Symbolic Religiosity") accepts the constructedness of ethnicity, but objects that the constraints on people's agency and the shrinking ethnic repertoire result in increasingly acculturated forms of invented ethnicity; he suggests that new constructions of ethnicity are even potential evidence of continuing acculturation.

in transhistorical bonds that are rooted in the covenant as has been confirmed by ritual re-enactment and other social practices over centuries.

Thus, the invention paradigm and the notion of Jews as a "community of memory" ask in a fundamental way about the role of the past and how it has been preserved, transmitted, reconstructed, and reconfigured to fit modern needs. These questions touch on a central nerve of Jewish modernity. Yerushalmi, in *Zakhor*, meditated about the erosion of Jewish group memory and the inability of historiography, as the faith of "fallen" Jews, to restore the pre-modern providential and holistic view of the Jewish experience that was preserved in group memory and thereby preserved the group.[37] The historian as the "physician of memory" cannot heal the wounds modernity inflicted on the Jewish soul, let alone redeem it.[38]

While in Yerushalmi's reading the rupture of modernity means that there is no way back to the holism of pre-modern times, American Jewish reconstructions and invocations of the East European past may be an attempt at just that: at the experience of a comprehensive, unbroken, enchanted Jewishness – by engaging with the past, through memory enshrined in cultural products. It is an attempt to compensate for the stress of modernity, by which Yerushalmi and his interpreters explain the new role of historiography, but which shapes the Jewish engagement with the past more generally. "The use of history writing to shore up the collective identities or memories of groups under enormous economic, social, and cultural pressure signals the fragility of their solidarity," intellectual historian Michael Roth writes of modern Jewish communities.[39] Because all modern Jews are "fallen," after tradition can no longer hold them or hold the pressures of modernity in check, they have a need to be grounded in the past: "hardly any Jew today is without any past," Yerushalmi writes. "The choice for Jews as for non-Jews is not whether or not to have a past, but rather – what kind of past shall one have," – crucially, whether it be "history" or "memory."[40]

---

[37] Yosef Hayim Yerushalmi, *Zakhor: Jewish History and Jewish Memory* (New York: Schocken, 1989; orig. publ. 1982), 86–103.
[38] Eugen Rosenstock-Huessy, *Out of Revolution: Autobiography of Western Man* (New York: Four Wells, 1964; orig. publ. 1938), 696.
[39] Roth, *The Ironist's Cage*, 181.
[40] Yerushalmi, *Zakhor*, 99. This dichotomy and the notion that modernity brought the secularization of Jewish history have been challenged by various scholars from several perspectives. Cf. Amos Funkenstein, "Collective Memory and Historical Consciousness," *History & Memory* 1 (1989): 5–26. Among the many articles, cf. the contributions by Sidra DeKoven Ezrahi, Moshe

The dichotomy of history and memory has been challenged by various scholars from several perspectives. Intellectual historian David N. Myers sees a "dialectical mediation between Jewish memory and history in the modern age."[41] Fellow historian Moshe Rosman has argued for the importance of "metahistory" as a source of meaning and guidance for societies: "It is metahistory, not history, that is inscribed in society and culture; but it is historiography, portraying history, that does the inscribing." Their depiction of the past is among the fundaments of how people, Jews in this case, live their lives and understand themselves.[42] In Yerushalmi's reading, memory trumped history as a source of a meaningful, broad, and deep Jewishness – an ideal out of reach for modern Jews. To Yerushalmi at least, modern Jews could no longer relate to a past that was passed on in the category of *Heilsgeschichte* (salvific history), after its traditional vessel, "memory," had been broken.

Whether postwar American Jews constructed "memory" or "metahistory" as the basis for a group identity, the question remained whether this was strong enough a fundament to build on, or merely a vicarious, symbolic, or imaginative *ersatz* of the pre-modern experience of a Jewish identity in the literal sense of "sameness." Undeniably, there was the urge to relate to the past, tap it for the meaning it might preserve, understand how it shaped the present and future. This urge had driven American Jews' engagement with the East European heritage in a period of transition that entered a new stage in the mid-1960s. It had started out of a sense of deep uncertainty about the meaning of Jewishness. At the end of this generation-long quest, memory of this past had gained greater conscious importance as the common denominator of a culturally conceived Jewishness. Still, a sense of wonderment about the past remained, as an essay in *Judaism* by poet Richard Fein illustrated; published in 1967, it sounds like a retrospective of the past twenty-five years:

> Yet again we stand at an unmarked and crucial crossroad, it is this inevitable separation from the old community, and from the reliable ancient heritage that is even strange to one's parents, that results in a compelling drive for the special community of secular ideas,

---

Idel, David N. Myers, Amnon Raz-Krakotzkin, and Gavriel Rosenfeld in *Jewish Quarterly Review* 97 (2007); Kerwin L. Klein, "On the Emergence of Memory in Historical Discourse," *Representations* 69 (2000): 127–50.
41 Myers, *Re-Inventing the Jewish Past*, 183.
42 Moshe Rosman, *How Jewish Is Jewish History?* (Oxford/Portland, OR: Littman, 2007), 54–55. Rosman builds on Hayden White's classical conceptualization, in *Metahistory: The Historical Imagination in Nineteenth-Century Europe* (Baltimore: Johns Hopkins University Press, 1973).

that promotes in the Jew almost a Platonic love of ideas for themselves. As if in the rush to the world of ideas the Jew creates his version of experience which at the same time disengages him from the past of his people and illuminates the past community of belief and suffering that remains as pure and as vital in his imagination as only the unattainable, the pure idea can be. He wishes to retain the image of past Jewish life, and keep holy his sense of that suffering community, because of his admiration of its possibility to survive all the tricks of time.

Tellingly, Fein's essay was entitled, "Jewishness – the Felt Ambiguity."[43]

Epilogue

What remains of the conversation of many voices and of the memories that were constructed in the postwar decades as a basis for a changing American Jewish community? How has the East European past figured in American Jewish life and its communal memory in the periods that followed? As this past has been reconstructed again and again by a community refashioning itself again and again, a few threads and examples of larger developments can be discerned.

Historian Steven Zipperstein has pointed to a "surplus of memory" of the East European experience that has shaped the contemporary American Jewish imagination, as reflected by the presence of terms and concepts derived from it. "Pogrom" and *shtetl* are obvious cases which also represent extremes of the spectrum between highly negative and nostalgic perspectives on this past.[44] In the postwar decades, this surplus was organized, inventorized, and prioritized. Through the process, the East European Jewish story became an American story, not just in the form of *Fiddler on the Roof*. Nor did the musical and the year 1964 mark the end point of the processes through which the surplus was re-organized and inventorized in different ways and according to new priorities.

In the mid-1960s, a broader development began, in which American Jews harvested what had been sown and cultivated over previous decades. Ethnic differences became newly legitimate and important in the period after *Fiddler*, when American Jewry, in line with larger societal developments, shifted from a mode of integration to particularism. During the re-ethnicization of American society and culture in the 1960s and 1970s, a country or culture of origin was a prerequisite for a full ethnic identity. The East European Jewish past served as

---

[43] Richard J. Fein, "Jewishness – The Felt Ambiguity," *Judaism* 16 (1967): 137.
[44] Steven J. Zipperstein, *Imagining Russian Jewry: Memory, History, Identity* (Seattle: University of Washington Press, 1999), 3–4.

a basis for a proud distinctiveness in ethno-national terms. Historian Gershon Hundert has described this sense of Jewish pride as an inheritance that American Jewry received from Eastern Europe. His approach to Jewish modernization points to a *mentalité* which East European Jews developed in response to the various forces that together constitute "modernization."[45] A central element of this *mentalité* is a positive sense of Jewish identity: self-affirmation, a sense of superiority, solidarity, group loyalty, and separateness are its key ingredients. As immigrants brought this *mentalité* to America, it was translated and transformed into new terms, by which it became usable in the new context.

Much of the new, particularistic, positive Jewishness that has developed in America since the mid-1960s has been expressed in cultural terms, especially if one subsumes religious behavior under this category. The renewed interest in the Yiddish language and culture is one such expression of a broadly-experienced sense of positive distinctiveness, and not just the resumption of a strand that vied for hegemony (and lost) in the postwar decades. The *Jewish Catalogs* of the 1970s expressed an anti-modern disappointment with established Jewish religious life in America by a fascination with more traditional, folk-derived practices and rituals. These envisioned a broad, communal Jewish identity, for which Eastern Europe could serve as a distant model.[46] East European sounds, music, particularly Hasidic, *niggunim* and, in Orthodox communities, Yiddish or Ashkenazic-pronounced Hebrew, also echo a past that is preserved for its aesthetic value or for reasons of traditionalism, but also partakes in the import of cultural categories that expand the concept of Judaism as a "religion."

In the political realm, the Soviet Jewry movement that began in the 1960s overcame the perceptual separation of pre-Communist or at least pre-Cold War Jewish life in the Soviet Union from its earlier stages. Whereas in the 1950s many depictions of Soviet Jewry emphasized the discontinuities with the pre-Soviet past, the differences from American Jewry, and the forced dissolution of Jewish distinctiveness, the Soviet Jewry movement was borne of a sense of solidarity and the recognition of a persistent ethno-national Jewish identity that recalled earlier expressions of East European Jewishness.

With the fall of the Berlin wall and the opening up of the former East bloc, the renewed interest in the fate of East European Judaism and Jewry after the

---

45 Hundert, *Jews in Poland-Lithuania in the Eighteenth Century*, 3–4, 233–40.
46 Richard Siegel, Michael Strassfeld and Sharon Strassfeld, *The (First) Jewish Catalog: A Do-It-Yourself Kit* (Philadelphia: Jewish Publication Society, 1973); Sharon Strassfeld and Michael Strassfeld, *The Second Jewish Catalog: Sources and Resources* (Philadelphia: Jewish Publication Society, 1976).

Holocaust and Communism could be expressed in real rather than imagined encounters. The growing number or more visible presence of native-born Jews in the countries of the former East bloc and the attraction of old-new centers of Jewish life, such as in Kracow and other cities, testify to a renewed interest in the East European past as a source for a meaningful Jewishness.

These developments relate the past in new ways to the American present. Yet, many of them draw not just on a repertoire of images, lessons, narratives, and terms that was created two generations earlier by thinkers in a lively, controversial debate in the mid-decades of the twentieth century. More fundamentally, they continue the perception that united the different participants in this debate: American Jews recognize the East European Jewish experience as a crucial cultural resource that can be engaged for the sake of their ever-changing present.

Bibliography

Primary Sources (created before 1966)
Periodicals

CCAR Journal [Central Conference of American Rabbis; Reform]
Commentary
Conservative Judaism
Dos Yiddishe Vort [Yiddish, Orthodox]
Jewish Currents [Communist, succeeding *Jewish Life*]
Jewish Forum [Orthodox]
Jewish Frontier [Labor- Zionist]
Jewish Life [Orthodox, succeeding *Orthodox Union*]
Jewish Life [*Morning Freiheit Association;* Communist, renamed *Jewish Currents*]
Judaism
News of the YIVO[1]
Partisan Review
Workmen's Circle Call [WCC]
YIVO Annual of Jewish Social Science

Individual published sources (selection)[2]

Alter, Robert. "Maurice Samuel & Jewish Letters." *Commentary* 37 (March 1964): 50–54.
Alter, Robert. "Sentimentalizing the Jews." *Commentary* 40 (September 1965): 71–75.
American Jewish Congress. "Statement of Sponsorship." *Judaism* 1 (1952): 2.
American Jewish Tercentenary Committee. *The American Jewish Tercentenary, 1654–1954: "Man's Opportunities and Responsibilities Under Freedom."* New York: American Jewish Tercentenary Committee, 1953.
"A New YIVO Exhibition: The Jewish Township in Eastern Europe, 1900–1939." *News of the YIVO* 70 (April 1959): 3*, 4*.
An Expert on Soviet Affairs. "Anti-Semitism in the Soviet Union." *CCAR Journal*, October 1956: 28–39, 54.
"Archive of the American Jewish Tercentenary Committee at YIVO." *News of the YIVO* 58 (September 1955): 4*.
Arnow, Robert. "Elegy for a Milkman." *Jewish Currents* 20 (1964): 34–37.
Babel, Isaac. *Red Cavalry.* New York: Norton, 2002 (orig. publ. 1926, Engl. 1929).
Bamberger, Bernard J. "Charting the Future of Reform Judaism." *CCAR Journal*, January 1958: 10–16.
Baritz, Loren. "A Jew's American Dilemma." *Commentary* 33 (June 1962): 523–26.
Baskin, Joseph. "Fifty Years of the 'Bund.'" *Workmen's Circle Call* 16 (1948): 4, 14.
Bell, Daniel. "A Parable of Alienation." *Jewish Frontier* XIII (1946): 12–19.

---

[1] The bilingual newsletter, which over time appeared under different titles, distinguishes its English-language pages by an asterisk (*) from the Yiddish ones; articles were not signed.
[2] This bibliography lists the most important primary sources; additional sources are given in the footnotes.

Bell, Daniel. "Parables from Jewish Existence." Review of *The Eternal Light,* by Morton Wishengrad. *Commentary* 4 (November 1947): 495–97.
Bell, Daniel. "Reflections on Jewish Identity." *Commentary* 31 (June 1961): 471–78.
Bellow, Saul. *The Adventures of Augie March.* New York: Viking, 1953.
Bergman, Maius. "Return to Poland: Pages From a Diary." *Commentary* 27 (May 1959): 395–404.
Bernstein, David. "The American Jewish Tercentenary." In *American Jewish Yearbook 1956,* edited by Morris Fine, 101–118. New York: American Jewish Committee, 1956.
Blanton, Smiley and Norman Vincent Peale. *Faith Is the Answer: A Psychiatrist and a Pastor Discuss Your Problems.* New York: Abingdon-Cokebury, 1940.
Boorstin, Daniel J. "A Dialogue of Two Histories: 'Jewish Contributions to America' in a New Light." *Commentary* 8 (October 1949): 311–16.
Buber, Martin. "Tales of the Hasidim." *Commentary* 3 (January 1947): 73–78.
Buber, Martin. "More Tales of the Hasidim." *Commentary* 3 (February 1947): 175–180.
Buber, Martin. *Tales of the Hasidim: The Early Masters.* London: Thames & Hudson, 1956; orig. publ. 1947.
Buber, Martin. *Hasidism.* New York: Philosophical Library, 1948.
Buber, Martin. *The Legend of the Baal-Shem.* London: Routledge, 2002; orig. publ. 1955.
Buber, Martin. "Interpreting Hasidism." *Commentary* 36 (September 1963): 218–23.
Cahan, Abraham. *The Rise of David Levinsky.* New York: Harper, 1960; orig. publ. 1917.
Cohen, Elliot. "An Act of Affirmation: Editorial Statement." *Commentary* 1 (November 1945): 1–3.
Cohen, Elliot. "Jewish Culture in America: Some Speculations by an Editor." *Commentary* 3 (May 1947): 412–20.
Commentary. "Jewishness and Younger Intellectuals [Symposium]." *Commentary* 31 (April 1961): 311–59.
"Declaration of the 19th Annual Conference of the Yiddish Scientific Institute – YIVO." *Newsletter of the YIVO* 7 (February 1945): 3*.
Decter, Moshe. "The 'Old Country' Way of Life: The Rediscovery of the Shtetl." Review of *Life is with People,* by Mark Zborowski and Elizabeth Herzog. *Commentary* 13 (June 1952): 600–04.
Decter, Midge. "Belittling Sholom Aleichem's Jews: Folk Falsification of the Ghetto." *Commentary* 17 (May 1954): 389–92.
"Dr. M. Weinreich Has Arrived in America" [Yiddish]. *Forverts,* March 20, 1947: 1.
Efron, Zalman [Yefroiken]. "Our Approach to Jewish Life." *Workmen's Circle Call* 22 (1953): 6–8.
Elberg, Simcha. "Winter Night [Yiddish]." *Dos Yiddishe Vort* 39 (1957): 8–10.
Elberg, Simcha. "Back to Historical Rabbanut [Yiddish]." *Dos Yiddishe Vort* 49 (1958): 17–19.
Elberg, Simcha. "City and Shtetl [Yiddish]." *Dos Yiddishe Vort* 55 (1959): 12–13.
Elberg, Simha. "Jewishness in America [Yiddish]." *Dos Yiddishe Vort* 79 (1962): 7–9, 33.
Elberg, Simcha. "A New Era of Jewishness in America [Yiddish]." *Dos Yiddishe Vort* 59 (1959): 11–13.
Engel, Gerold. "An Appraisal of the Rabbis' Visit to Moscow." *Jewish Forum* 40 (1957): 162–63.
Faierstein, Morris M., Abraham Joshua Heschel, and Gershon Jacobson. "Abraham Joshua Heschel and the Holocaust." *Modern Judaism* 19 (1999): 255–75.
Fiedler, Leslie A. "Mediator Between Past and Future." Review of *Prince of the Ghetto,* by Maurice Samuel. *Commentary* 6 (December 1948): 582–84.
Fiedler, Leslie A. "Hasidism and the Modern Jew." *Commentary* 7 (January 1949): 195–98.
Fineberg, S. Andhil. "Religion Behind the Iron Curtain." *CCAR Journal,* June 1962: 12–16, 37.
Finkelstein, Louis, ed. *The Jews: Their History, Culture, and Religion,* 3rd ed. New York: Harper & Row, 1960.

Fishman, S. "The YIVO and the Purposeful Jewish Life in America." *Workmen's Circle Call* 17 (1949): 5–6.
Fiszman, Joseph R. "One Benefit Above All." *Workmen's Circle Call* 23 (1954): 6, 16.
Frank, Gerold. "Visit to the Old Country: The Lodz That Was." *Commentary* 14 (October 1952): 345–51.
Friedlaender, Israel. "Judaism in America: A Prophecy." *Conservative Judaism* 1 (1945): 25–26.
Friedman, Maurice. "Martin Buber and Judaism." *CCAR Journal*, October 1955: 13–18.
Friedman, Maurice. "Hasidism and the Contemporary Jew." *Judaism* 9 (1960): 197–206.
Gamoran, Mamie, *The New Jewish History, Book 3: From the Discovery of America to Our Own Day*. Cincinnati: Union of American Hebrew Congregations, 1957.
Gaster, Theodor. "Yizkor: The Living and the Dead: The Community as Woven by Memory." *Commentary* 15 (March 1953): 236–43.
Gay, Ruth, *Jews in America: A Short History*. New York: Basic Books, 1965.
Gersh, Harry. "The New Suburbanites of the 50's: Jewish Division." *Commentary* 17 (March 1954): 209–21.
Glazer, Nathan and Daniel P. Moynihan. *Beyond the Melting Pot: The Negroes, Puerto Ricans, Jews, Italians, and Irish of New York City*. 2nd ed. Cambridge: M.I.T. Press, 1970; orig. publ. 1963.
Gold, Michael. *Jews Without Money*. New York: Carroll & Graf, 1984; orig. publ. 1930.
Goldberg, I[tche]. "Our Yiddish Literary Heritage: Its Meaning and Value for the English-Speaking Jew." *Jewish Currents* 15 (1960): 14–18.
Goldstein, Israel. *American Jewry Comes of Age*. New York: Bloch, 1955.
Goodman, Saul. "Jewish Secularism in America – Permanence and Change." *Judaism* 9 (1960): 319–30.
Goodman, Saul. "Simon Dubnow: A Revaluation." *Commentary* 30 (December 1960): 511–15.
Gordis, Robert. "The Task Before Us: A Preface to Our Journal." *Conservative Judaism* 1 (1945): 1–8.
Gordis, Robert. "Toward a Renascence of Judaism." *Judaism* 1 (1952): 3–10.
Gordis, Robert. "American Jewry Faces Its Fourth Century." *Judaism* 3 (1954; Tercentenary issue): 293–301.
Gordon, Albert I. *Jews in Suburbia*. Boston: Beacon, 1959.
Gordon, Milton M. *Assimilation in American Life: The Role of Race, Religion, and National Origins*. New York: Oxford University Press, 1964.
Greenberg, Clement. "Self-Hatred and Jewish Chauvinism: Some Reflections on 'Positive Jewishness.'" *Commentary* 10 (November 1950): 426–33.
Greenberg, Hayim. "What Is Happening to Soviet Jewry? An Open Letter to the Soviet Ambassador to the U.S." *Jewish Frontier* XVIII (1951): 5–8.
Greenberg, Hayim. "Zionism and Diaspora." *Jewish Frontier* XVIII (1951): 7–9.
Greenberg, Hayim. "The Dybbuk." *Jewish Frontier* XXI (1954): 31–33.
Halpern, Ben. *The American Jew: A Zionist Analysis*. New York: Theodor Herzl Foundation, 1956.
Handlin, Oscar. *The Uprooted: The Epic Story of the Great Migrations That Made the American People*. New York: Grosset & Dunlap, 1951.
Handlin, Oscar. *Adventure in Freedom: Three Hundred Years of Jewish Life in America*. New York: McGraw-Hill, 1954.
Handlin, Oscar. "The American Jewish Pattern, After 300 Years: The Recent Decades – The Prospect Ahead." *Commentary* 18 (October 1954): 296–307.

Hansen, Marcus Lee. "The Third Generation in America." *Commentary* 14 (November 1952): 492–500.

Harap, Louis. "Anti-Semitism and the Rosenbergs." *Jewish Life [Morning Freiheit Association]* 6 (1952): 24–26.

Harap, Louis. "Stalin and the Jewish People." *Jewish Life [Morning Freiheit Association]* 7 (1953): 3–4.

Harap, Louis. "Literary Breakthrough – To What?" *Jewish Currents* 19 (1964): 16–22.

Held, Adolph. "Jewish Culture and the American Jewish Community." *Workmen's Circle Call* 28 (1959): 2–3.

Herberg, Will. *Judaism and Modern Man: An Interpretation of Jewish Religion*. Philadelphia: Jewish Publication Society, 1951.

Herberg, Will. "How Can You Say 'God?'" Review of *Eclipse of God* and *At the Turning*, by Martin Buber. *Commentary* 14 (December 1952): 615–20.

Herberg, Will. *Protestant – Catholic – Jew: An Essay in American Religious Sociology*. Chicago: University of Chicago Press, 1983; orig. publ. 1955.

Hertzberg, Arthur. "The Worldly Jew." Review of *Einems Yidishe Machshovos*, by Melech Ravitch; *Yidish un Yidishkeit*, by Yosef Opatoshu; *Kedushah un Gevurah bei Yidn*, by Y. Efroykin. *Commentary* 10 (July 1950): 87–90.

Heschel, Abraham Joshua. "The Eastern European Era in Jewish History." *YIVO Annual of Jewish Social Science* 1 (1946): 86–105.

Heschel, Abraham Joshua. "The Two Great Traditions: The Sephardim and the Ashkenazim." *Commentary* 5 (May 1948): 416–22.

Heschel, Abraham Joshua. *The Earth Is the Lord's: The Inner World of the Jew in Eastern Europe*. Woodstock, VT: Jewish Lights, 1995; orig. publ. 1949; republ. as paperback 1963.

Heschel, Abraham Joshua. "Architecture of Time." *Judaism* 1 (1952): 44–51.

Heschel, Abraham Joshua. "YIVO's Task Now." *News of the YIVO* 64 (March 1957): 2*–3*.

Howe, Irving. "Sholom Aleichem and His People." Review of *The Old Country*, by Sholom Aleichem. *Partisan Review* 13 (1946), 591–95.

Howe, Irving. "Of Fathers and Sons." Review of *Passage from Home*, by Isaac Rosenfeld. *Commentary* 2 (August 1946): 190–92.

Howe, Irving. "The Lost Young Intellectual: A Marginal Man, Twice Alienated." *Commentary* 2 (October 1946): 361–67.

Howe, Irving. "[Untitled contribution to symposium: Judaism and the 'Lost' Intellectuals]." *Jewish Forum* 35 (1952): 130–31.

Howe, Irving and Eliezer Greenberg, eds. *A Treasury of Yiddish Stories*. New York: Meridian, 1960; orig. publ. 1954.

Howe, Irving. "Peretz Off-Broadway." *Commentary* 37 (January 1964): 71–73.

Howe, Irving. "Tevye on Broadway." *Commentary* 38 (November 1964): 73–75.

Jewish Forum. "Judaism and the 'Lost' Intellectuals: A Symposium." *Jewish Forum* 35 (1952): 128–35.

Kahn, Sholom J. "Cultural Activities." In *American Jewish Year Book 1948–1949*, edited by Harry Schneiderman and Morris Fine, 178–210. New York: American Jewish Committee, 1949.

Kallen, Horace M. "Democracy versus the Melting-Pot." In *Culture and Democracy in the United States*, 67–125. New York: Boni & Loveright, 1924; orig. publ. 1915. Katz, Jacob. *Tradition and Crisis*. New York: Schocken, 1958.

Katz, Jacob. *Tradition and Crisis*. New York: Schocken, 1958.

Kazin, Alfred. *A Walker in the City*. Orlando: Harcourt, 1979; orig. publ. 1951.

Klaperman, Gilbert and Libby Klaperman. *The Story of the Jewish People, vol. 3: From the Golden Age in Spain Through the European Emancipation.* New York: Behrman House [for the Rabbinical Council of America], 1958.

Klaperman, Gilbert and Libby Klaperman. *The Story of the Jewish People, vol. 4: From the Settlement of America Through Israel Today.* New York: Behrman House [for the Rabbinical Council of America], 1961.

Kligsberg, Moses. "Socio-Psychological Problems Reflected in the YIVO Autobiography Contest." *YIVO Annual of Jewish Social Science* 1 (1946): 241–49.

Kligsberg, Moses. "YIVO Preserves Jewish Culture." *Workmen's Circle Call* 16 (1948): 15–16.

Kligsberg, Moses. "The Golden Land: The Jewish Immigrant in America: Self-Portrait." *Commentary* 5 (May 1948): 467–72.

Knox, Israel. "Books: The World of Sholem Aleichem, by Maurice Samuel." *Workmen's Circle Call* 11 (1943): 17.

Knox, Israel. "A World to Remember." Review of *The World of Sholem Aleichem*, by Sholom Aleichem. *Workmen's Circle Call* 13 (1944): 14–16.

Knox, Israel. "Is America Exile or Home? We Must Begin to Build for Permanence." *Commentary* 2 (November 1946): 401–08.

Knox, Israel. "Wanted: Another 'The Rise of David Levinsky.'" *Workmen's Circle Call* 15 (1947): 7.

Knox, Israel. "Wanted – An American Sholem Aleichem." *Workmen's Circle Call* 18 (1950): 6.

Knox, Israel. "300 and 70." *Workmen's Circle Call* 24 (1955): 6–7, 18.

Knox, Israel. "A Memorable Year." *Workmen's Circle Call* 26 (1957): 6–7.

Konvitz, Milton R. "Yivo Comes to Morningside." *Commentary* 3 (January 1947): 48–54.

Kugelmass, J. Alvin. "Name-Changing – And What It Gets You: Twenty-five Who Did It." *Commentary* 14 (August 1952): 145–50.

Lakritz, William B. "Congregational School Curricula – An Evaluation." *The Synagogue School* 13 (1955): 3–14.

Lestshinsky, Jacob. "New Conditions of Jewish Survival." *Jewish Frontier* XIV (1947): 40–48.

Lewisohn, Ludwig. *The American Jew: Character and Destiny.* New York: Knopf, 1950.

Lewisohn, Ludwig. "Reflections on the Jewish Situation, Part I: Re-Examination." *Jewish Frontier* XVII (1950): 5–8.

Lewisohn, Ludwig. "To the Young Jewish Intellectuals." *Jewish Frontier* XIX (1952): 5–8.

Leyeles, A. "To Thee America." *Workmen's Circle Call* 14 (1944): 8–9.

Liebman, Joshua Loth. *Peace of Mind.* New York: Simon & Schuster, 1946.

Lookstein, Joseph H. "The Neo-Hasidism of Abraham J. Heschel." *Judaism* 5 (1956): 248–55.

Mailer, Norman. "Responses & Reactions." *Commentary* 34 (December 1962): 504–06 (and five more installments, publ. through October 1963).

Mark, Yudel. "Changes in the Yiddish Schools." In *Jewish Education in the United States: A Documentary History*, edited by Lloyd P. Gartner, 188–97. New York: Teachers College Press, 1969; orig. publ. 1949.

Mark, Yudel. "The Shtetl in Retrospect: Pseudo-Science." Review of *Life is with People*, by Mark Zborowski and Elizabeth Herzog. *Jewish Frontier* XIX (1952): 25–27.

Neuburger, Gottfried. "Moscow Revisited." *Jewish Life* 24 (1957): 9–13.

Niger, Shmuel. "The Gift of Sholom Aleichem: He Brought Literature to a People." *Commentary* 2 (August 1946): 116–23.

Niger, Shmuel. "The Amalgam Which Is Jewish Life." *Workmen's Circle Call* 19 (1951): 4–5.

Niger, Shmuel. "An Appreciation of I.L. Peretz." *Commentary* 27 (June 1959): 523–26.

Parzen, Herbert. "When Secularism Came to Russian Jewry." *Commentary* 13 (April 1952): 355–62.

Parzen, Herbert. "The Passing of Jewish Secularism in the United States." *Judaism* 8 (1959): 195–205.
Peretz, Yitzhak/Isaac Leib. "The Pious Cat: A Story." *Commentary* 9 (April 1950): 369–70.
Peretz, Yitzhak/Isaac Leib. "The Interviewer at Work: Some Problems Posed by the Natives and the Terrain." *Commentary* 15 (February 1953): 195–99.
Peretz, Yitzhak/Isaac Leib. "Bontsha the Silent." In *A Treasury of Yiddish Stories*, edited by Irving Howe and Eliezer Greenberg, 223–30. New York: Meridian, 1960; orig. publ. 1954.
Peretz, Yitzhak/Isaac Leib. "If Not Higher." In *A Treasury of Yiddish Stories*, edited by Irving Howe and Eliezer Greenberg. New York: Meridian, 1960; orig. publ. 1954.
Peretz, Yitzhak/Isaac Leib. "Our Platform [1894]." *Workmen's Circle Call* 34 (1963): 23.
Pessin, Deborah. *The Jewish People, Book III*. New York: United Synagogue of America, 1953.
Petuchowski, Jakob J. "The Grip of the Past: A Study in the Dynamics of Religion." *Judaism* 8 (1959): 132–41.
Podhoretz, Norman. "Jewish Culture and the Intellectuals: The Process of Rediscovery." *Commentary* 13 (May 1955): 451–57.
Podhoretz, Norman. "Introduction - Jewishness and the Younger Intellectuals: A Symposium." *Commentary* 31 (April 1961): 306–10.
Poll, Solomon. "The Role of Yiddish in American Ultra-Orthodox and Hassidic Communities." *YIVO Annual of Jewish Social Science* 13 (1955): 125–52.
Raddock, Charles. "Hasidism - and They Mean It!" *Jewish Forum* 33 (1950): 232–34.
Raddock, Charles. "Schneersohn, Heir to a Noble Tradition." *Jewish Forum* 34 (1951): 72–73.
Raddock, Charles. "Judaism and the Lost Intellectuals." *Jewish Forum* 41 (July 1952): 95–98.
Raddock, Charles. "The Baal Shem, a Victim of Literary Fraud." *Jewish Forum* 43 (1960): 179.
Riesman, David. *The Lonely Crowd: A Study of the Changing American Character*. New Haven: Yale University Press, 1950.
Rosenblatt, Sidney. "Mendele Mocher Sforim." *Jewish Life [Morning Freiheit Association]* 3 (1949): 10–13.
Rosenfeld, Isaac. "The Humor of Exile." Review of *The World of Sholom Aleichem*, by Maurice Samuel. *Partisan Review* 10 (1943): 294–97.
Rosenfeld, Isaac. "The Ghetto and the World." Review of *Prince of the Ghetto*, by Maurice Samuel. *Partisan Review* 16 (1948): 206–11.
Rosenfeld, Isaac. *Passage from Home*. New York: Markus Wiener, 1988; orig. publ. 1948.
Rosenfeld, Isaac. "Images of a Lost World." Review of *Polish Jews*, by Roman Vishniac and *The Vanished World*, by Raphael Abramovitch. *Commentary* 7 (February 1949): 201–02.
Rosenfeld, Isaac. "America, Land of the Sad Millionaire." *Commentary* 14 (August 1952): 131–35.
Rosenfeld, Max. "Philosopher of Jewish Secularism: Zhitlovsky's Pioneering Ideas Continue to Stimulate Progressive Jewish Life." *Jewish Currents* 19 (June 1965): 6–11, 31–33.
Rosenzweig, Franz. "Discovery of the East European Jew: A Young Visitor in the Old Warsaw Ghetto." *Commentary* 15 (January 1953): 86–89.
Rossman, Evelyn N. [pseud.]. "The Community and I: Belonging: Its Satisfactions and Dissatisfactions." *Commentary* 18 (November 1954): 393–405.
Rossman, Evelyn N. [pseud.]. "The Community and I: Two Years Later – The Wine, or the Blessing?" *Commentary* 21 (March 1956): 230–38.
Roth, Philip. "Eli, the Fanatic: A Story." *Commentary* 27 (April 1959): 292–309.
Roth, Philip. *Goodbye, Columbus, and Five Short Stories*. Cleveland: World Pub., 1963.

Rubenstein, Richard L. "The Intellectual and Contemporary Jewish Life." *Conservative Judaism* 14 (1960): 40–46.
Samuel, Maurice. *The World of Sholom Aleichem*. New York: Vintage, 1973; orig. publ. 1943.
Samuel, Maurice. *Prince of the Ghetto: The Stories of Y. L. Peretz Retold*. New York: Schocken, 1959; orig. publ. 1948.
Samuel, Maurice. "The Story That Must Build Itself: On Jewish History and John Hersey's 'The Wall.'" *Jewish Frontier* XVII (1950): 11–20.
Samuel, Maurice. "Monument to European Jewry." Review of *The Earth is the Lord's*, by Abraham Joshua Heschel. *Congress Weekly*, 27 March 1950: 7–9.
Schachter, Zalman. "Hasidism and Neo-Hasidism." *Judaism* 9 (1960): 216–21.
Schatz-Uffenheimer, Rivkah. "Martin Buber: Master of Hasidic Teaching." *Judaism* 9 (1960): 277–81.
Schwarzschild, Steven S. "Survey of Current Theological Literature." *Judaism* 9 (1960): 269–76.
Seligman, Lester G. "A Second Look at the Tercentenary." *Judaism* 4 (1955): 110–15.
Sherman, C. Bezalel. "Reflections on the Tercentenary." *Jewish Frontier* XX (1953): 8–12.
Sherman, C. Bezalel. "In the American Jewish Community: American Jewry at the Crossroads." *Jewish Frontier* XXXI (1964): 7–11.
Sherman, C. Bezalel. "What American Jewish Youth Ask." *Jewish Frontier* XXXII (1965): 7–9.
Sholem Aleichem. "The Trial of Shomer: A Critical Essay." *Jewish Life [Morning Freiheit Association]* 3 (1949): 21–23
Sholem Aleichem. *Adventures of Mottel, the Cantor's Son*. New York: Schuman, 1953.
Sholem Aleichem. "Hodel." In *A Treasury of Yiddish Stories*, edited by Irving Howe and Eliezer Greenberg, 168–82. New York: Meridian, 1960; orig. publ. 1954.
Sholem Aleichem. "The Couple." *Jewish Frontier* XXI (1954): 16–21.
Sholem Aleichem. "Toward My Biography: Notes on Becoming a Writer." *Commentary* 27 (April 1959): 338–40.
Shuchat, Wilfred. "How to Face a New Age." In *Best Jewish Sermons of 5715–5716*, edited by Saul I. Teplitz, 177–83. New York: Jonathan David, 1956.
Sillen, Samuel. "A Visit With Polish Jewry." *Jewish Life [Morning Freiheit Association]* 4 (1950): 21–24.
Silver, Harold. "'An Oy for an Eye or an Eye for an Eye': Some Reactions Towards the Trend Away from Ashkenazic Pronunciation." *CCAR Journal*, June 1962: 41–49.
Singer, Isaac Bashevis. "Problems of Yiddish Prose in America." *Prooftexts* 9 (1989; Yidd. orig. publ. 1943): 5–12.
Singer, Isaac Bashevis. "Gimpel the Fool." *Partisan Review* 20 (1953): 300–13.
Singer, Isaac Bashevis. "The Little Shoemakers." In *A Treasury of Yiddish Stories*, edited by Irving Howe and Eliezer Greenberg, 523–44. New York: Meridian, 1960; orig. publ. 1954.
Singer, Isaac Bashevis. *Satan in Goray*. New York: Noonday, 1955.
Singer, Isaac Bashevis. *Gimpel the Fool, and Other Stories*. New York: Noonday, 1957.
Singer, Isaac Bashevis. *The Magician of Lublin*. New York: Fawcett Crest, 1982; orig. publ. 1960.
Sklare, Marshall, *Conservative Judaism: An American Religious Movement*. Glencoe, IL: Free Press, 1955.
Sklare, Marshall. "The Values of Eastern European Jewry and of American Society." *Jewish Frontier* XVIII (1961): 7–11.
Soloff, Mordecai I. *How the Jewish People Lives Today*. Cincinnati: Union of American Hebrew Congregations, 1952; orig. publ. 1940.

Soloveitchik, Joseph B., *Halakhic Man*. Philadelphia: Jewish Publication Society, 1983; Hebrew orig. published 1944.
Soloveitchik, Joseph B. "Confrontation." *Tradition* 6 (1964): 5–29.
Sontag, Susan. "Demons and Dreams." *Partisan Review* 29 (1962): 460–63.
Steindletz, E. "Hasidism and Psychoanalysis." *Judaism* 9 (1960): 222–28.
Stein, Joseph. *Fiddler on the Roof: Based on Sholem Aleichem's Stories*. New York: Crown, 1964.
Stern, William. "What Are the Positive Factors for Jewish Survival in America?" *Workmen's Circle Call* 27 (1958): 5–6.
Teplitz, Saul I., ed. *Best Jewish Sermons of 5714*. New York: Jonathan David, 1954.
Teplitz, Saul I., ed. *Best Jewish Sermons of 5715–5716*. New York: Jonathan David, 1956.
Teplitz, Saul I., ed. *Best Jewish Sermons of 5719–20*. New York: Jonathan David, 1960.
Trunk, Isaiah. "The Cultural Dimension of the American Jewish Labor Movement." *YIVO Annual of Jewish Social Science* XVI: (1976): 342–93.
Tumin, Melvin M. "Conservative Trends in American Jewish Life." *Judaism* 13 (1964): 131–42.
Vishniac, Roman, *Polish Jews: A Pictorial Record*. New York: Schocken, 1947.
Weiner, Herbert. "The Lubavitcher Movement I: Organized Mysticism." *Commentary* 23 (March 1957): 231–41.
Weiner, Herbert. "The Lubavitcher Movement II: 'The Root and the Branches.'" *Commentary* 23 (April 1957): 316–27.
Weinreich, Max. "The YIVO Faces the Post-War World." *Newsletter of the YIVO* 7 (February 1945): 7*.
Wishengrad, Morton. *Eternal Light*. New York: Crown, 1947.
Wouk, Herman. *Marjorie Morningstar*. London: Hodder, 2008; orig. publ. 1955.
Workmen's Circle National Convention. "Resolution on Jewish Affairs." *Workmen's Circle Call* 16 (1948): 17–18.
Yefroiken [Efron], Zalman. "New Horizons for Our Children: The I. L. Peretz Schools of the Workmen's Circle." *Workmen's Circle Call* 19 (1951): 2–3.
Yefroiken [Efron], Zalman. *Dos lebediḳe yorṭ leyenbukh far dem driṭn lernyor*. New York: Workmen's Circle, 1954.
Yefroiken [Efron], Zalman and Hyman B. Bass. *Dos lebendike Vort [for third year]*. New York: Workmen's Circle, 1954/1959.
Yefroiken [Efron], Zalman. "Our Schools: Meeting the Challenge of Change." *Workmen's Circle Call* 35 (1964): 9.
YIVO. "[Mission Statement]." *Newsletter of the YIVO* 1 (1943): 1*.
"YIVO Announces Essay Contest on Jewish Life in America." *News of the YIVO* 32 (1949): 2*.
"YIVO to Establish Central Archives on Jews in America." *News of the YIVO* 38 (1950): 1*–2*.
Zborowski, Mark and Elizabeth Herzog. *Life is with People: The Jewish Little-Town of Eastern Europe*, 3rd ed. New York: International Universities Press, 1952.
Zeligs, Dorothy F. *A History of Jewish Life in Modern Times*. New York: Bloch, 1938.
Zukerman, Jacob T. "What's on the Horizon for our Arbeter Ring?" *Workmen's Circle Call* 26 (1957): 4–5, 15.

Archival sources

American Jewish Tercentenary Committee, *The American Jewish Tercentenary Community Manual*. New York: American Jewish Tercentenary Committee, 1954. (printed brochure, American Jewish Archives (AJA), Horace Kallen papers (MS-1), box 46, folder 6)
Anon. [Solomon Grayzel?]. "The Publication Committee of the JPS: Agenda for The Meeting on October 15, 1961." (typescript, AJA, JPS records (MS-388), folder 3)

Belth, Norman, *Everyman's Guide: The American Jewish Tercentenary, 1654–1954*. New York: American Jewish Tercentenary, December 1953. (printed brochure, AJA, Horace Kallen papers (MS-1), box 46, folder 6)
Div. *The Eternal Light*. New York: JTS Communications Dept. (typescripts of radio program, 1944ff.)
Div. "Excerpts from letters received by Eternal Light program [1946]." (typescript, JTS Archive, RG 11-C, box 26, folder 39)
Div. [Oscar Handlin, ed.]. "Report on a Conference on the Jewish Experience in America [sponsored by *Commentary*]," May 1948. (typescript, YIVO Archives, Max Weinreich Collection, RG 584 folder 225A)
Grayzel, Solomon. "Minutes of the Publication Committee." April 30, 1961. (typescript, AJA, JPS records (MS-388), folder 3)
Rabinowitz, Olga [Mrs. Sholom Aleichem] "[Letter to Maurice Samuel]." May 28, 1942. (typescript, AJA, Maurice Samuel papers (MS-89), box 36, folder 25)
Samuel, Edith [Mrs. Maurice Samuel]. "[Letter to William Koshland of Alfred E. Knopf]." December 26, 1972. (typescript, AJA Maurice Samuel papers (MS-89), box 36, folder 20)
Samuel, Maurice. "[Letter to Alfred A. Knopf]." November 16, 1947. (typescript, AJA, Maurice Samuel papers (MS-89), box 36, folder 20)
Samuel, Maurice. "[Letter to Joseph C. Lesser of Alfred E. Knopf]." December 30, 1951. (typescript, AJA, Maurice Samuel papers (MS-89), box 36, folder 25)
Steinberg, Milton. "Commentary Magazine - Benefit or Detriment to American Judaism?" November 18, 1949. (typescript, AJA, Julian Morgenstern papers (MS-30), box 10, folder 30)
Weinreich, Max. "[Jewish Scholarship Today; speech at 1941 Annual YIVO Conference, Yiddish]." 1941. (typescript, YIVO Archives, RG 584.4)
Weinreich, Max. "Jewish Culture in America – To-Day and To-Morrow [Speech at Commencement of Baltimore Hebrew College]." June 10, 1945. (typescript, YIVO Archives, *RG 584.9*, 1–7)

Secondary Literature (created since 1966)

Abrams, Nathan. "'America Is Home': *Commentary* Magazine and the Refocusing of the Community of Memory, 1945–1960." In *Commentary in American Life*, edited by Murray Friedman, 9–37. Philadelphia: Temple University Press.
Ackerman, Walter. "Let Us Now Praise Famous Men and Their Fathers in the Generations: History Books for Jewish Children in America." *Dor Ledor: Studies in the History of Jewish Education in Israel and the Diaspora*, II (1984): 1–35.
Alba, Richard D. *Ethnic Identity: The Transformation of White America*. New Haven: Yale University Press, 1990.
Alexander, Edward. *Irving Howe and Secular Jewishness: An Elegy*. Cincinnati: Judaic Studies Program University of Cincinnati, 1995.
Altman, Richard and Mervyn Kaufman. *The Making of a Musical: Fiddler on the Roof*. New York: Crown, 1971.
Anderson, Benedict. *Imagined Communities: Reflections on the Origin and Spread of Nationalism*. Rev. ed. London/New York: Verso, 2006; orig. publ. 1983.
Aschheim, Steven E. *Brothers and Strangers: The East European Jew in German and German Jewish Consciousness, 1800–1923*. Madison: University of Wisconsin Press, 1982.
Ausmus, Harry J. *Will Herberg: From Right to Right*. Chapel Hill, 1987.
Balint, Benjamin. *Running Commentary: The Contentious Magazine That Transformed the Jewish Left into the Neoconservative Right*. New York: Public Affairs, 2010.

Band, Arnold J. "Popular Fiction and the Shaping of Jewish Identity." In *Jewish Identity in America,* edited by David M. Gordis and Yoav Ben-Horin, 215–225. Los Angeles: Wilstein Institute/University of Judaism, 1991.
Baron, Salo W. *History and Jewish Historians: Essays and Addresses.* Philadelphia: Jewish Publication Society, 1964.
Baron, Salo W. *The Russian Jews Under Tsars and Soviets.* New York: Macmillan, 1976.
Batnitzky, Leora. *How Judaism Became a Religion: An Introduction to Modern Jewish Thought.* Princeton: Princeton University Press, 2011.
Berger, Bennet M. "The New York Intellectuals." *American Jewish History* 80 (1991): 382–89.
Berman, Lila Corwin. "American Jews and the Ambivalence of Middle-Classness." *American Jewish History* 93 (2007): 409–34.
Berman, Lila Corwin. *Speaking of Jews: Rabbis, Intellectuals, and the Creation of an American Public Identity.* Berkeley: University of California, 2009.
Berman, Lila Corwin. "Blame, Boundaries, and Birthrights: Jewish Intermarriage in Midcentury America." In *Boundaries of Jewish Identity,* edited by Susan A. Glenn and Naomi B. Sokoloff, 91–109. Seattle: University of Washington Press, 2010.
Berman, Lila Corwin. "Jewish Urban Politics in the City and Beyond." *Journal of American History* 99 (2012): 492–519.
Biale, David. "Modern Jewish Ideologies and the Historiography of Jewish Politics." In *Reshaping the Past: Jewish History and the Historians (Studies in Contemporary Jewry X),* edited by Jonathan Frankel, 3–16. New York/Oxford: Oxford University Press, 1994.
Blidstein, Gerald J. "On the Jewish People in the Writings of Rabbi Joseph B. Soloveitchik." *Tradition* 24 (1989): 21–43.
Bloom, Alexander. *Prodigal Sons: The New York Intellectuals and Their World.* New York: Oxford University Press, 1986.
Bodian, Miriam. *Hebrews of the Portuguese Nation: Conversos and Community in Early Modern Amsterdam.* Bloomington: Indiana University Press, 1999.
Bourdieu, Pierre. *The Field of Cultural Production: Essays on Art and Literature.* New York: Columbia University Press, 1993.
Boyarin, Jonathan. *Storm From Paradise: The Politics of Jewish Memory.* Minneapolis: University of Minnesota Press, 1992.
Brenner, Michael. *The Renaissance of Jewish Culture in Weimar Germany.* New Haven: Yale University Press, 1996.
Breslauer, S. Daniel. "Abraham J. Heschel's Politics of Nostalgia." *Journal of Church and State* 22 (1980): 307–13.
Buhle, Mari Jo, Paul Buhle, and Dan Georgakas, eds. *Encyclopedia of the American Left.* 2nd ed. New York: Oxford University Press, 1998.
Buhle, Paul. *From the Lower East Side to Hollywood: Jews in American Popular Culture.* New York/London, 2004.
Bush, Andrew. *Jewish Studies: A Theoretical Introduction.* Piscataway: Rutgers University Press, 2011.
Butler, Jon. "Jack-in-the-Box Faith? The Religion Problem in Modern American History." *Journal of American History* 90 (2004): 1357–78.
Caputi, Mary. *A Kinder, Gentler America: Melancholia and the Mythical 1950s.* Minneapolis: University of Minnesota Press, 2005.
Chametzky, Jules. *Out of Brownsville: Encounters With Nobel Laureates and Other Jewish Writers: A Memoir.* Amherst: University of Massachusetts Press, 2012.

Cohen, Michael R. *The Birth of Conservative Judaism: Solomon Schechter's Disciples and the Creation of an American Religious Movement.* New York: Columbia University Press, 2012.
Cohen, Naomi W. *Not Free to Desist: The American Jewish Committee 1906–1966.* Philadelphia: Jewish Publication Society, 1972.
Cohen, Shaye J. D. and Edward L. Greenstein, eds. *The State of Jewish Studies.* Detroit: Wayne State University Press, 1990.
Conzen, Kathleen Neils, David A. Gerber, Ewa Morawska, George E. Pozzetta, and Rudolph J. Vecoli. "The Invention of Ethnicity: A Perspective from the U.S.A." *Journal of American Ethnic History* 12 (1992): 3–41.
Cooney, Terry A. *The Rise of the New York Intellectuals: "Partisan Review" and Its Circle.* Madison: University of Wisconsin Press, 1986.
Cooney, Terry A. "New York Intellectuals and the Question of Jewish Identity." *American Jewish History* 80 (1991): 344–60.
Dauber, Jeremy. *The Worlds of Sholem Aleichem: The Remarkable Life and Afterlife of the Man Who Created Tevye.* New York: Nextbook Schocken, 2013.
Dawidowicz, Lucy S. *The Golden Tradition: Jewish Life and Thought in Eastern Europe.* Syracuse: Syracuse University Press, 1996; orig. publ. 1967.
Dekel-Chen, Jonathan. "East European Jewish Migration: Inside and Outside." *East European Jewish Affairs* 44 (2014): 154–70.
Diner, Hasia, Jeffrey Shandler, and Beth Wenger, eds. *Remembering the Lower East Side: American Jewish Reflections.* Bloomington: Indiana University Press, 2000.
Diner, Hasia R. *Lower East Side Memories: A Jewish Place in America.* Princeton: Princeton University Press, 2000.
Diner, Hasia. *The Jews of the United States, 1654 to 2000.* Berkeley: University of California Press, 2004.
Diner, Hasia R. *We Remember With Reverence and Love: American Jews and the Myth of Silence After the Holocaust, 1945–1962.* New York: New York University Press, 2009.
Dinnerstein, Leonard. *Antisemitism in America.* New York: Oxford University Press, 1994.
Dobroszycki, Lucjan and Barbara Kirshenblatt-Gimblett. *Image Before My Eyes: A Photographic History of Jewish Life in Poland.* New York: Schocken, 1977.
Dobroszycki, Lucjan. "YIVO in Interwar Poland: Work in the Historical Sciences." In *The Jews of Poland Between Two World Wars,* edited by Yisrael Gutman, Ezra Mendelsohn, Jehuda Reinharz, and Chone Shmeruk, 494–518. Waltham: Brandeis University Press/Hanover: University Press of New England, 1989.
Dunner, Pini and David N. Myers. "A Haredi Attack on Rabbi Joseph Ber Soloveitchik: A Battle Over the Brisker Legacy From 1984." *Jewish Quarterly Review* 105 (2015): 131–38.
Eisen, Arnold M. "Theology, Sociology, Ideology: Jewish Thought in America, 1925–1955." *Modern Judaism* 2 (1982): 91–103.
Eisen, Arnold M. *The Chosen People in America: A Study in Jewish Religious Ideology.* Bloomington: Indiana University Press, 1983.
Elazar, Daniel J. and Rela Mintz Geffen. *The Conservative Movement in Judaism: Dilemmas and Opportunities.* Albany: SUNY Press, 2000.
Englund, Steven. "The Ghost of the Nation Past." Review of *Lieux de mémoire,* by Pierre Nora. *Journal of Modern History* 64 (1992): 299–320.
Estraikh, Gennady. "Metamorphoses of *Morgn-frayhayt.*" In *Yiddish and the Left,* edited by Gennady Estraikh and Mikhail Krutikov, 144–66. Oxford: Legenda, 2000.
Ezrahi, Sidra DeKoven. *Booking Passage: Exile and Homecoming in the Modern Jewish Imagination.* Berkeley: University of California Press, 2000.

Ezrahi, Sidra DeKoven. "Fiction and Memory: *Zakhor* Revisited." *Jewish Quarterly Review* 97 (2007): 521–29.
Fein, Richard J. "Jewishness - The Felt Ambiguity." *Judaism* 16 (1967): 131–40.
Finkelman, Yoel. "Nostalgia, Inspiration, Ambivalence: Eastern Europe, Immigration, and the Construction of Collective Memory in Contemporary American Haredi Historiography." *Jewish History* 23 (2009): 57–82.
Fishman, David E. "The Bund and Modern Yiddish Culture." In *The Emergence of Modern Jewish Politics*, edited by Zvi Gitelman, 107–19. Pittsburgh: Pittsburgh University Press, 2003.
Fishman, David E. *The Rise of Modern Yiddish Culture*. Pittsburgh: University of Pittsburgh Press, 2005.
Fishman, David E. "Yiddish Schools in America and the Problem of Secular Jewish Identity." In *Religion or Ethnicity*, edited by Zvi Gitelman, 69–89. New Brunswick: Rutgers University Press, 2009.
Fishman, Sylvia Barack. *Jewish Life and American Culture*. Albany: SUNY Press, 2000.
Fox, Frank. "Mark Zborowski: The Spy Who Came Out of the 'Shtetl.'" *East European Jewish Affairs* 29 (1999): 119–28.
Frankel, Jonathan. *Prophecy and Politics: Socialism, Nationalism, and the Russian Jews, 1862–1917*. Cambridge: Cambridge University Press, 1981.
Frankel, Jonathan. "The Crisis of 1881–82 as a Turning Point in Modern Jewish History." In *The Legacy of Jewish Migration, 1881 and Its Impact*, edited David Berger, 9–22. New York: Brooklyn College Press, 1983.
Frankel, Jonathan and Steven J. Zipperstein, eds. *Assimilation and Community: The Jews in Nineteenth-Century Europe*. Cambridge: Cambridge University Press, 1992.
Frankel, Jonathan, ed. *Crisis, Revolution, and Russian Jews*. Cambridge: Cambridge University Press, 2009.
Freedman, Jonathan. *Klezmer America: Jewishness, Ethnicity, Modernity*. New York: Columbia University Press, 2008.
Friedman, Murray, ed. *"Commentary" in American Life*. Philadelphia: Temple University Press, 2005.
Funkenstein, Amos. "Collective Memory and Historical Consciousness." *History & Memory* 1 (1989): 5–26.
Gallagher, Catherine and Stephen Greenblatt. *Practicing New Historicism*. Chicago: University of Chicago Press, 2000.
Gans, Herbert. "Symbolic Ethnicity: The Future of Ethnic Groups and Cultures in America." *Ethnic and Racial Studies* 2 (1979): 1–20.
Gans, Herbert. "Ethnic Invention and Acculturation: A Bumpy-Line Approach." *Journal of American Ethnic History* 12 (1992): 142–52.
Gans, Herbert. "Symbolic Ethnicity and Symbolic Religiosity: Towards a Comparison of Ethnic and Religious Acculturation." *Ethnic and Racial Studies* 17 (1994): 577–92.
Gans, Herbert. "Toward a Reconciliation of 'Assimilation' and 'Pluralism:' The Interplay of Acculturation and Ethnic Retention." *International Migration Review* 31 (1997): 875–93.
Geertz, Clifford. *The Interpretation of Cultures: Selected Essays*. New York: Basic Books, 1973.
Genack, Menachem D., ed. *Rabbi Joseph B. Soloveitchik: Man of Halacha, Man of Faith*. Hoboken, NJ: Ktav, 1998.
Gillman, Neil. *Conservative Judaism: The New Century*. New York: Behrrman, 1993.
Gitelman, Zvi, ed. *The Emergence of Modern Jewish Politics: Bundism and Zionism in Eastern Europe*. Pittsburgh: University of Pittsburgh Press, 2003.

Gittleman, Sol, *From Shtetl to Suburbia: The Family in Jewish Literary Imagination*. Boston: Beacon Press, 1978.

Glasser, Paul. "Max Weinreich." In *YIVO Encyclopedia of Jews in Eastern Europe,* edited by Gershon D. Hundert, 2014–16. New Haven: Yale University Press, 2008.

Glazer, Nathan. "Hansen's Hypothesis and the Historical Experience of Generations." In *American Immigrants and Their Generations: Studies and Commentaries on the Hansen Thesis after Fifty Years,* edited by Peter Kivisto and Dag Blanck, 104–12. Urbana/Chicago: University of Illinois Press, 1990.

Glenn, Susan A. *The Jewish Cold War: Anxiety and Identity in the Aftermath of the Holocaust*. Ann Arbor: Frankel Center of Judaic Studies, University of Michigan, 2015.

Goffman, Ethan and Daniel Morris, eds. *The New York Public Intellectuals and Beyond: Exploring Liberal Humanism, Jewish Identity, and the American Protest Tradition*. West Lafayette, IN: Purdue University Press, 2009.

Goldsmith, Emanuel S. *Architects of Yiddishism at the Beginning of the Twentieth Century: A Study in Jewish Cultural History*. Rutherford, NJ: Farleigh Dickinson University Press, 1976.

Goldstein, Eric L. *The Price of Whiteness: Jews, Race, and American Identity*. Princeton: Princeton University Press, 2006.

Goldy, Robert G. *The Emergence of Jewish Theology in America*. Bloomington: Indiana University Press, 1990.

Goodheart, Eugene. "The Abandoned Legacy of the New York Intellectuals." *American Jewish History* 80 (1991): 361–76.

Gordis, Robert. "The Genesis of *Judaism:* A Chapter in Jewish Cultural History." *Judaism* 30 (1981): 390–95.

Gordon, Peter Eli. "Franz Rosenzweig and the Philosphy of Jewish Existence." In *The Cambridge Companion to Modern Jewish Philosophy,* edited by Michael L. Morgan and Peter Eli Gordon, 122–46. Cambridge: Cambridge University Press, 2007.

Goren, Arthur. "A Golden Decade for American Jews, 1945–1955." In *A New Jewry? America Since the Second World War (Studies in Contemporary Jewry VIII),* edited by Peter Y. Medding, 3–20. New York: Oxford University Press, 1997.

Grainge, Paul. *Monochrome Memories: Nostalgia and Style in Retro America*. Westport, CT: Praeger, 2002.

Greene, Daniel. *The Jewish Origins of Cultural Pluralism: The Menorah Society Association and American Diversity*. Bloomington: Indiana University Press, 2011.

Greenspoon, Leonard Jay, Ronald Simkins, and Brian Horowitz, eds. *The Jews of Eastern Europe*. Omaha: Creighton University Press, 2005.

Gurock, Jeffrey S. *The Men and Women of Yeshiva: Higher Education, Orthodoxy, and American Judaism*. New York: Columbia University Press, 1988.

Gurock, Jeffrey S. *American Jewish Orthodoxy in Historical Perspective*. Hoboken, NJ: Ktav, 1996.

Gurock, Jeffrey S. *From Fluidity to Rigidity: The Religious Worlds of Conservative and Orthodox Jews in Twentieth Century America*. Ann Arbor: Frankel Center of Judaic Studies, University of Michigan, 1998.

Gurock, Jeffrey S. "American Judaism Between the Two World Wars." In *The Columbia History of Jews and Judaism in America,* edited by Marc Lee Raphael, 93–113. New York: Columbia University Press, 2008.

Halbwachs, Maurice. *The Collective Memory*. New York: Harper, 1980.

Hale, Grace Elizabeth. *A Nation of Outsiders: How the White Middle Class Fell in Love With Rebellion in Postwar America*. New York: Oxford University Press, 2011.

Hart, Mitchell. "The Historian's Past in Three Recent Jewish Autobiographies." *Jewish Social Studies* 5 (1999): 132–60.
Hartman, David. "The Halakhic Hero: Rabbi Joseph B. Soloveitchik, Halakhic Man." *Modern Judaism* 9 (1989): 249–73.
Heilman, Samuel C. *Sliding to the Right: The Contest for the Future of American Jewish Orthodoxy.* Berkeley: University of California Press, 2006.
Heinze, Andrew R. *Jews and the American Soul: Human Nature in the Twentieth Century.* Princeton: Princeton University Press, 2004.
Hervieu-Léger, Danièle. *Religion as a Chain of Memory.* New Brunswick: Rutgers University Press, 2000.
Heschel, Susannah. "Imagining Judaism in America." In *The Cambridge Companion to Jewish American Literature,* edited by Hana Wirth-Nesher and Michael P. Kramer, 31–49. Cambridge: Cambridge University Press, 2003.
Higham, John. *Send These to Me: Immigrants in Urban American [orig. title: Send These to Me: Jews and Other Immigrants in Urban America]* Rev. ed. Baltimore: Johns Hopkins University Press, 1984, orig. publ. 1975.
Hilmes, Michele, ed. *NBC: America's Network.* Berkeley: University of California Press, 2007.
Hobsbawm, Eric. "Introduction: Inventing Traditions." In *The Invention of Tradition,* edited by Eric Hobsbawm and T. Ranger, 1–14. Cambridge: Cambridge University Press, 1983.
Hollander, Paul. *Political Pilgrims: Travels of Western Intellectuals to the Soviet Union, China, and Cuba, 1928–1978.* New York: Oxford University Press, 1981.
Hoover, Stewart M. and Douglas K. Wagner. "History and Policy in American Broadcast Treatment of Religion." *Media, Culture and Society* 19 (1997): 7–27.
Horowitz, Bethamie. "Old Casks in New Times: The Reshaping of American Jewish Identity in the 21st Century." In *Ethnicity and Beyond: Theories and Dilemmas of Jewish Group Demarcation (Studies in Contemporary Jewry XXV),* edited by Eli Lederhendler, 79–90. New York: Oxford University Press, 2011.
Howe, Irving. "The New York Intellectuals: A Chronicle and a Critique." *Commentary* 46 (October 1968): 29–50.
Howe, Irving. *Selected Writings, 1950–1990.* New York: Harcourt Brace Jovanovich, 1990; orig. publ. 1969.
Howe, Irving. *World of Our Fathers: The Journey of the East European Jews to America and the Life They Found and Made.* 2nd ed. New York: Schocken, 1990; orig. publ. 1976.
Howe, Irving, *The End of Jewish Secularism.* New York: Hunter College, 1995.
Hundert, Gershon D. *Jews in Poland-Lithuania in the Eighteenth Century: A Genealogy of Modernity.* Berkeley: University of California Press, 2004.
Hutchison, William R. *Religious Pluralism in America: The Contentious History of a Founding Ideal.* New Haven: Yale University Press, 2003.
Hutton, Patrick H. "Collective Memory and Collective Mentalities: The Halbwachs-Ariès Connection." *Historical Reflections/Réflexions historiques* 15 (1988): 311–22.
Hyman, Paula E. "The Dynamics of Social History." In *Reshaping the Past: Jewish History and the Historians (Studies in Contemporary Jewry X),* edited by Jonathan Frankel, 93–111. New York/Oxford: Oxford University Press, 1994.
Hyman, Paula E. "Jacob Katz as Social Historian." In *The Pride of Jacob: Essays on Jacob Katz and his Work,* edited by Jay Michael Harris, 85–96. Cambridge: Harvard University Press, 2002.
Hyman, Paula E. "The Normalization of American Jewish History." *American Jewish History* 91 (2003): 353–59.

Hyman, Paula E. "Recent Trends in European Jewish Historiography." *The Journal of Modern History* 77 (2005): 345–56.
Idel, Moshe. "Yosef H. Yerushalmi's *Zakhor* – Some Observations." *Jewish Quarterly Review* 97 (2007): 491–501.
Jacobson, Matthew Frye. "Hyphen Nation: Ethnicity in American Intellectual and Political Life." In *A Companion to Post-1945 America*, edited by Jean-Christophe Agnew and Roy Rosenzweig, 175–91. Malden: Blackwell, 2006.
Jacobson, Matthew Frye. *Roots Too: White Ethnic Revival in Post-Civil Rights America*. Cambridge: Harvard University Press, 2006.
Jacoby, Russell. *The Last Intellectuals: American Culture in the Age of Academe*. New York, 1987.
Jeffers, Thomas L. *Norman Podhoretz: A Biography*. Cambridge: Cambridge University Press, 2012.
Jick, Leon. "The Reform Synagogue." In *The American Synagogue: A Sanctuary Transformed*, edited by Jack Wertheimer, 85–110. Cambridge: Cambridge University Press, 1987.
Joselit, Jenna Weissman. *New York's Jewish Jews: The Orthodox Community in the Interwar Years*. Bloomington: Indiana University Press, 1994.
Jumonville, Neil, *Critical Crossings: The New York Intellectuals in Postwar America*. Berkeley: University of California Press, 1991.
Kammen, Michael. *Mystic Chords of Memory: The Transformation of Tradition in American Culture*. New York: Knopf, 1991.
Kaplan, Cimmy. "The Ever-Dying Denomination: American Jewish Orthodoxy, 1824–1965." In *The Columbia History of Jews and Judaism in America*, edited by Marc Lee Raphael, 167–88. New York: Columbia University Press, 2008.
Kaplan, Edward K. "The American Mission of Abraham Joshua Heschel." In *The Americanization of the Jews*, edited by Robert M. Seltzer and Norman J. Cohen, 355–74. New York: New York University Press, 1995.
Kaplan, Edward K. and Samuel Dresner. *Abraham Joshua Heschel: Prophetic Witness*. New Haven: Yale University Press, 1998.
Kaplan, Edward K. *Spiritual Radical: Abraham Joshua Heschel in America, 1940–1972*. New Haven: Yale University Press, 2007.
Kaplan, Lawrence. "Revisionism and the Rav: The Struggle for the Soul of Modern Orthodoxy." *Judaism* 48 (1999): 290–311.
Karper, Altie. "A History of Schocken Books in America, 1945–2013." In *Konsum und Gestalt: Leben und Werk von Salman Schocken und Erich Mendelsohn vor 1933 und im Exil*, edited by Antje Borrmann, Doreen Mölders, and Sabine Wolfram, 271–81. Berlin: Hentrich & Hentrich, 2016.
Kassow, Samuel D. "The Shtetl in Interwar Poland." In *The Shtetl: New Evaluations*, edited by Steven T. Katz, 121–39. New York: New York University Press, 2006.
Kassow, Samuel D. *Who Will Write Our History? Emanuel Ringelblum, the Warsaw Ghetto, and the Oyneg Shabes Archive*. Bloomington: Indiana University Press, 2007.
Katz, Daniel. *All Together Different: Yiddish Socialists, Garment Workers, and the Labor Roots of Multiculturalism*. New York: New York University Press, 2011.
Kaufman, Matthew. "The Menorah Journal and Shaping American Jewish Identity: Culture and Evolutionary Sociology." *Shofar* 30 (2012): 61–79.
Kazal, Russell A. "Revisiting Assimilation: The Rise, Fall, and Reappraisal of a Concept in American Ethnic History." *American Historical Review* 100 (1995): 437–71.
Kazin, Alfred, *New York Jew*. New York: Knopf, 1978.

Kessner, Carole S., ed. *The "Other" New York Jewish Intellectuals*. New York: New York University Press, 1994.

Kirshenblatt-Gimblett, Barbara. Introduction to *Life Is With People: The Culture of the Shtetl*, edited by Mark Zborowski and Elizabeth Herzog, 2nd ed., ix–xlviii. New York: Schocken, 1995.

Kirshenblatt-Gimblett, Barbara. "Coming of Age in the Thirties: Max Weinreich, Eduard Sapir, and Jewish Social Science." *YIVO Annual of Jewish Social Science* 23 (1996): 1–103.

Kirshenblatt-Gimblett, Barbara. "Imagining Europe: The Popular Arts of American Jewish Ethnography." In *Divergent Centers: Shaping Jewish Cultures in Israel and America*, edited by Deborah Dash Moore and Ilan Troen, 155–91. New Haven: Yale University Press, 2001.

Kivisto, Peter and Dag Blanck, eds. *American Immigrants and Their Generations: Studies and Commentaries on the Hansen Thesis After Fifty Years*. Urbana/Chicago: University of Illinois Press, 1990.

Kivisto, Peter and Ben Nefzger. "Symbolic Ethnicity and American Jews: The Relationship of Ethnic Identity to Behaviour and Group Affiliation." *Social Science Journal* 30 (1993): 1–12.

Klein, Kerwin L. "On the Emergence of Memory in Historical Discourse." *Representations* 69 (2000): 127–50.

Knapp, Steven. "Collective Memory and the Actual Past." *Representations* 26 (1989): 123–49.

Kobrin, Rebecca. *Jewish Bialystok and Its Diaspora*. Bloomington: Indiana University Press, 2010.

Konvitz, Milton R., ed. *The Legacy of Horace M. Kallen*. Rutherford, NJ: Fairleigh Dickinson University Press, 1987.

Krah, Markus. "Role Models of Foils for American Jews? *The Eternal Light*, Displaced Persons, and the Construction of Jewishness in Mid-Twentieth-Century America." *American Jewish History* 96 (2010; publ. 2012): 265–86.

Krasner, Jonathan. "'New Jews' in an Old-New Land: Images in American Jewish Textbooks Prior to 1948." *Journal of Jewish Education* 69 (2003): 7–22.

Krasner, Jonathan. "Constructing Collective Memory: The Re-Envisioning of Eastern Europe as Seen Through American Jewish Textbooks." in *Polin [vol. 19]: Polish-Jewish Relations in North America*, edited by Miecyzslaw B. Biskupski and Antony Polonsky, 229–55. Oxford: Littman, 2007.

Kugelmass, Jack, ed. *Key Texts in American Jewish Culture*. New Brunswick: Rutgers University Press, 2003.

Kurtzer, Yehuda. *Shuva: The Future of the Jewish Past*. Waltham: Brandeis University Press/ Hanover: University Press of New England, 2012.

Kuznitz, Cecile Esther. "YIVO." In *YIVO Encyclopedia of Jews in Eastern Europe*, edited by Gershon D. Hundert, 2090–96. New Haven: Yale University Press, 2008.

Kuznitz, Cecile Esther. *YIVO and the Making of Modern Jewish Culture: Scholarship for the Yiddish Nation*. New York: Cambridge University Press, 2014.

Lederhendler, Eli. *New York Jews and the Decline of Urban Ethnicity, 1950–1970*. Syracuse: Syracuse University Press, 2001.

Leventman, Seymour. "From Shtetl to Suburb." In *The Ghetto and Beyond*, edited by Peter Rose, 33–56. New York: Random House, 1969.

Liebman, Charles S. *The Ambivalent American Jew: Politics, Religion, and Family in American Jewish Life*. Philadelphia: Jewish Publication Society, 1973.

Liebman, Charles. "Diaspora Influence on Israel: The Ben Gurion-Blaustein 'Exchange' and Its Aftermath." *Jewish Social Studies* 36 (1974): 271–80.

Longstaff, S. A. "Ivy League Gentiles and Inner-City Jews: Class and Ethnicity Around *Partisan Review* in the Thirties and Forties." *American Jewish History* 80 (1991): 325–43.

Luckmann, Thomas. *The Invisible Religion*. New York: Macmillan, 1967.
Marty, Martin E. *Modern American Religion [vol. II]: The Noise of Conflict, 1919–1941*. Chicago: University of Chicago Press, 1991.
Marty, Martin E. *Modern American Religion [vol. III]: Under God Indivisible, 1941–1960*. Chicago: University of Chicago Press, 1996.
Megill, Allan. "History, Memory, and Identity." *History and the Human Sciences* 11 (1998): 37–62.
Mendelsohn, Ezra. *Class Struggle in the Pale: The Formative Years of the Jewish Workers' Movement in Tsarist Russia*. Cambridge: Cambridge University Press, 1970.
Mendes-Flohr, Paul. "Fin de Siecle Orientalism, the Ostjuden, and the Aesthetics of Self-Affirmation." In *Divided Passions: Jewish Intellectuals and the Experience of Modernity*, 77–132. Detroit: Wayne State University Press, 1991.
Meyer, Michael A. *The Origins of the Modern Jew: Jewish Identity and European Culture in Germany, 1749–1824*. Detroit: Wayne State University Press, 1967.
Meyer, Michael A. "The Emergence of Jewish Historiography: Motives and Motifs." *History and Theory* 27 (1988): 160–75.
Meyer, Michael A. *Response to Modernity: A History of the Reform Movement in Judaism*. Detroit: Wayne State University Press, 1995; orig. publ. 1988.
Michels, Tony. *A Fire in Their Hearts: Yiddish Socialists in New York*. Cambridge: Harvard University Press, 2005.
Michels, Tony. "Exporting Yiddish Socialism: New York's Role in the Russian Jewish Workers' Movement." *Jewish Social Studies* 16 (2009): 1–26.
Michels, Tony. "Is America Different? A Critique of American Jewish Exceptionalism." *American Jewish History* 96 (2010): 201–24.
Michels, Tony, ed. *Jewish Radicals: A Documentary History*. New York: New York University Press, 2012.
Milbauer, Asher Z. "Eastern Europe in American Jewish Writing." In *Handbook of American-Jewish Literature: An Analytical Guide to Topics, Themes, and Sources*, edited by Lewis Fried, 357–90. Westport, CT: Greenwood Press, 1988.
Miron, Dan. "Between Science and Faith: Sixty Years of the YIVO Institute." *YIVO Annual of Jewish Social Science* 19 (1990): 1–15.
Miron, Dan. "The Literary Image of the Shtetl." *Jewish Social Studies* 1 (1995): 1–44.
Miron, Dan. *The Image of the Shtetl and Other Studies of Modern Jewish Literary Imagination*. Syracuse: Syracuse University Press, 2000.
Moore, Deborah Dash. *At Home in America: Second Generation New York Jews*. New York: Columbia University Press, 1981.
Moore, Deborah Dash. "At Home in America? Revisiting the Second Generation." *Journal of American Ethnic History* 25 (2006): 156–68.
Morawska, Ewa. "Changing Images of the Old Country in the Development of Ethnic Identity among East European Immigrants, 1880–1930s: A Comparison of Jewish and Slavic Representations." *YIVO Annual of Jewish Social Science* 21 (1993): 273–341.
Morawska, Ewa. "In Defense of the Assimilation Model." *Journal of American Ethnic History* 13 (1994): 76–87.
Morawska, Ewa. "Becoming Ethnic, Becoming American: Different Patterns and Configurations of the Assimilation of Eastern European Jews, 1880–1940." in *Divergent Jewish Cultures, Israel and America*, edited by Deborah Dash Moore and Ilan Troen, 277–303. New Haven: Yale University Press, 2001.

Morawska, Ewa. "Immigrants, Transnationalism, and Ethnicization: A Comparison of This Great Wave and the Last." In *E Pluribus Unum: Contemporary and Historical Perspectives on Immigrant Political Incorporation,* edited by Gary Gerstle and John Mollenkopf, 175–212. New York: Russell Sage Foundation, 2001.

Morawska, Ewa. "Polish-Jewish Relations in America, 1880–1940." In *Polin [vol. 19]: Polish-Jewish Relations in North America,* edited by Miecyzslaw B. Biskupski and Antony Polonsky, 71–86. Oxford: Littman, 2007.

Morawska, Ewa. "Ethnicity as a Primordial-Situational-Constructed Experience: Different Times, Different Places, Different Constellations." In *Ethnicity and Beyond: Theories and Dilemmas of Jewish Group Demarcation (Studies in Contemporary Jewry XXV),* edited by Eli Lederhendler, 3–25. New York: Oxford University Press, 2011.

Moss, Kenneth B. "At Home in Late Imperial Russian Modernity - Except When They Weren't: New Histories of Russian and East European Jews, 1881–1914." *Journal of Modern History* 84 (2012): 401–52.

Munk, Reinier, *The Rationale of Halakhic Man: Joseph B. Soloveitchik's Conception of Jewish Thought.* Amsterdam: Gieben, 1996.

Myers, David N., *Re-Inventing the Jewish Past: European Jewish Intellectuals and the Zionist Return to History.* New York: Oxford University Press, 1995.

Myers, David N. "Recalling *Zakhor*: A Quarter-Century's Perspective." *Jewish Quarterly Review* 97 (2007): 487–90.

Nadell, Pamela S. "Jews and Judaism in the United States." In *The Cambridge Guide to Jewish History, Religion, and Culture,* edited by Judith R. Baskin and Kenneth Seeskin, 208–32. Cambridge/New York: Cambridge University Press, 2010.

Nadler, Allan. "Soloveitchik's Halakhic Man: Not a 'Mithnagged.'" *Modern Judaism* 19 (1993): 119–47.

Nagel, Joane. "Constructing Ethnicity: Creating and Recreating Ethnic Identity and Culture." In *New Tribalisms: The Resurgence of Race and Ethnicity,* edited by Michael W. Hughey, 237–72. London: Macmillan, 1998.

Nora, Pierre. "Between Memory and History: *Les Lieux de Mémoire*." *Representations* 26 (1989): 7–24.

Norich, Anita. "Isaac Bashevis Singer in America: The Translation Problem." *Judaism* 44 (1995): 208–18.

Norich, Anita. *Discovering Exile: Yiddish and Jewish American Culture During the Holocaust.* Stanford: Stanford University Press, 2007.

Novak, Michael. *The Rise of the Unmeltable Ethnics: The New Political Force of the Seventies.* New York: Macmillan, 1972.

Patai, Raphael. "Memory in Religion." *Midstream* 29 (1983): 48–51.

Phillips, Nelson and Cynthia Hardy. *Discourse Analysis: Investigating Processes of Social Construction.* Thousand Oaks, CA: Sage Publications, 2002.

Pierpoint, Claudia Roth. "The Book of Laughter: Philip Roth and His Friends." *The New Yorker,* October 7, 2013.

Pinchuk, Ben Cion. "Jewish Discourse and the *Shtetl*." *Jewish History* 15 (2001): 169–79.

Podhoretz, Norman, *Making It.* New York: Random House, 1967.

Prell, Riv-Ellen. "Community and the Discourse of Elegy: The Postwar Suburban Debate." in *Imagining the American Jewish Community,* edited by Jack Wertheimer, 67–90. Waltham: Brandeis University Press/Hanover: University Press of New England, 2007.

Prell, Riv-Ellen. "Triumph, Accommodation, and Resistance: American Jewish Life from the End of World War II to the Six-Day War." In *The Columbia History of Jews and Judaism in America*, edited by Marc Lee Raphael, 114–42. New York: Columbia University Press, 2008.

Prell, Riv-Ellen. "The Utility of the Concept of 'Ethnicity' for the Study of Jews." In *Ethnicity and Beyond: Theories and Dilemmas of Jewish Group Demarcation (Studies in Contemporary Jewry XXV)*, edited by Eli Lederhendler, 102–07. New York: Oxford University Press, 2011.

Rakeffet-Rothkoff, Aaron. "Rabbi Joseph B. Soloveitchik: The Early Years." *Tradition* 30 (1996): 193–209.

Raz-Krakotzkin, Amnon. "Jewish Memory Between Exile and History." *Jewish Quarterly Review* 97 (2007): 530–43.

Redlich, Shimon, *War, Holocaust and Stalinism: A Documented History of the Jewish Anti-Fascist Committee in the USSR*. Luxembourg: Harwood Academic Publishers, 1995.

Redlich, Shimon. "Returning to the Shtetl: Differing Perceptions." In *Polin [vol. 17]: The Shtetl: Myth and Reality*, edited by Miecyzslaw B. Biskupski and Antony Polonsky, 267–75. Oxford: Littman, 2004.

Robinson, Ira and Maxine Jacobson. "'When Orthodoxy Was Not as Chic as It Is Today:' *The Jewish Forum* and American Modern Orthodoxy." *Modern Judaism* 31 (2011): 285–313.

Ronell, Anna P. "Three American Jewish Writers Imagine Eastern Europe." In *Polin [vol. 19]: Polish-Jewish Relations in North America*, edited by Miecyzslaw B. Biskupski and Antony Polonsky, 373–91. Oxford: Littman, 2007.

Rosenfeld, Gavriel David. "A Flawed Prophecy? *Zakhor*, the Memory Boom, and the Holocaust." *Jewish Quarterly Review* 97 (2007): 508–20.

Roskies, David G. and Diane K. Roskies. *The Shtetl Book*. New York: Ktav, 1975.

Roskies, David G. "The Treasures of Howe and Greenberg." *Prooftexts* 3 (1983): 109–14.

Roskies, David G. "Introduction." *Prooftexts* 6 (1986): 1–5.

Roskies, David G. "Introduction." *Prooftexts* 9 (1989): 1–4.

Roskies, David G. *A Bridge of Longing: The Lost Art of Yiddish Storytelling*. Cambridge: Harvard University Press, 1995.

Roskies, David G. "Yiddish in the Twentieth Century: A Literature of Anger and Homecoming." In *Yiddish Language and Culture Then and Now*, edited by Leonard Jay Greenspoon, 1–16. Omaha: Creighton University Press, 1998.

Roskies, David G. *The Jewish Search for a Usable Past*. Bloomington: Indiana University Press, 1999.

Roskies, David G. "The Shtetl as Imagined Community." In *The Shtetl: Image and Reality*, edited by Gennady Estraikh and Mikhail Krutikov, 4–22. Oxford: Legenda, 2000.

Roskies, David G. "Pilgrimage, 2003." In *Bounded Mind and Soul: Russia and Israel, 1880–2010*, edited by Brian Horowitz and Shai Ginsburg, 189–203. Bloomington: Slavica Publishers, 2013.

Rosman, Moshe. *How Jewish Is Jewish History?* Oxford/Portland, OR: Littman, 2007.

Roth, Michael. *The Ironist's Cage: Memory, Trauma, and the Construction of History*. New York: Columbia University Press, 1995.

Saks, Jeffrey. "An Index to Rabbi Joseph B. Soloveitchik's 'Halakhic Man.'" *Torah U-Madda Journal* 11 (2002–2003): 107–22.

Sapoznik, Henry. "Broadcast Ghetto: The Image of Jews on Mainstream American Radio." *Jewish Folklore and Ethnology Review* 16 (1994): 37–39.

Sarna, Jonathan D. *JPS: The Americanization of Jewish Culture, 1889–1989: A Centennial History of the Jewish Publication Society*. Philadelphia: JPS, 1989.

Sarna, Jonathan D. "American Jewish Education in Historical Perspective." *Journal of Jewish Education* 64 (1998): 8–21.

Sarna, Jonathan D. "The Cult of Synthesis in American Jewish Culture." *Jewish Social Studies* 5 (1998/99): 52–79.
Sarna, Jonathan D. *American Judaism: A History.* New Haven: Yale University Press, 2004.
Sarna, Jonathan D. "Ethnicity and Beyond." In *Ethnicity and Beyond: Theories and Dilemmas of Jewish Group Demarcation (Studies in Contemporary Jewry XXV)*, edited by Eli Lederhendler, 108–12. New York: Oxford University Press, 2011.
Scholem, Gershom G. "Martin Buber's Interpretation of Hasidism." In *The Jewish Expression*, edited by Judah Goldin, 397–418. New Haven: Yale University Press, 1976; orig. publ. 1971.
Schorsch, Ismar. "The Last Jewish Generalist [Obituary Salo W. Baron]." *AJS Review* 18 (1993): 39–50.
Schorsch, Ismar. *From Text to Context: The Turn to History in Modern Judaism.* Waltham: Brandeis University Press/Hanover: University Press of New England, 1994.
Segal, Eli, *The Eternal Light: The Unauthorized Guide to the Superb NBC Broadcast Series.* Newtown, CT: Yesteryear Press, 2005.
Shandler, Jeffrey. "Heschel and Yiddish: A Struggle With Signification." *Journal of Jewish Thought and Philosophy* 2 (1993): 245–99.
Shandler, Jeffrey. *While America Watches: Televising the Holocaust.* Oxford: Oxford University Press, 2000.
Shandler, Jeffrey. "'The Time of Vishniac:' Photographs of Prewar East European Jewry in Postwar Contexts." *Polin* [vol. 16]: Focusing on Jewish Popular Culture, edited by Michael Steinlauf and Antony Polonsky, 313–33. Oxford: Littman, 2003.
Shandler, Jeffrey. "Anthologizing the Vernacular: Collections of Yiddish Literature in English Translation." In *The Anthology in Jewish Literature*, edited by David Stern, 304–23. Oxford: Oxford University Press, 2004.
Shandler, Jeffrey. *Adventures in Yiddishland: Postvernacular Language and Culture.* Berkeley: University of California Press, 2006.
Shandler, Jeffrey. *Jews, God, and Videotape: Religion and Media in America.* New York: New York University Press, 2009.
Shandler, Jeffrey. *Shtetl: A Vernacular Intellectual History.* New Brunswick: Rutgers University Press, 2013.
Shapiro, Edward S. "World War II and American Jewish Identity." *Modern Judaism* 10 (1990): 65–84.
Shapiro, Edward S. "The Search of American Jewish Identity." In *What Is American About the American Jewish Experience?*, edited by Marc Lee Raphael, 108–22. Williamsburg, VA: College of William and Mary, 1993.
Shapiro, Edward S. *We Are Many: Reflections on American Jewish History and Identity.* Syracuse, NY: Syracuse University Press, 2005.
Shapiro, Edward S., ed. *Yiddish in America: Essays on Yiddish Culture in the Golden Land.* Scranton: University of Pennsylvania Press, 2008.
Shechner, Mark. *After the Revolution: Studies in the Contemporary Jewish Imagination.* Bloomington: Indiana University Press, 1987.
Shechner, Mark, ed. *Preserving the Hunger: An Isaac Rosenfeld Reader.* Detroit: Wayne State University Press, 1988.
Shore, Marci. "The Jews in Eastern Europe: New Historiography." *East European Politics and Societies and Cultures* 21 (2007): 503–19.
Siegel, David S. and Susan Siegel. *Radio and the Jews: The Untold Story of How Radio Influenced America's Image of Jews, 1920s–1950s.* Yorktown Heights: Book Hunter Press, 2007.

Siegel, Richard, Michael Strassfeld, and Sharon Strassfeld, eds. *The (First) Jewish Catalog*. Philadelphia: Jewish Publication Society, 1973.

Singer, David and Moshe Sokol. "Joseph Soloveitchik: Lonely Man of Faith." *Modern Judaism* 2 (1982): 227–72.

Sklare, Marshall and Joseph Greenblum. *Jewish Identity on the Suburban Frontier: A Study of Group Survival in the Open Society*, 2nd ed. Chicago: University of Chicago Press, 1979; orig. publ. 1967.

Smith, Anthony D. *The Ethnic Revival*. Cambridge: Cambridge University Press, 1981.

Sokol, Moshe. "'Ger ve-Toshav Anokhi:' Modernity and Traditionalism in the Life and Thought of Rabbi Joseph B. Soloveitchik." *Tradition* 29 (1994): 32–47.

Sollors, Werner. "First Generation, Second Generation, Third Generation …: The Cultural Construction of Descent." In *Beyond Ethnicity: Consent and Descent in American Culture*, edited by Sollors, 208–36. New York: Oxford University Press, 1986.

Sollors, Werner, ed. *The Invention of Ethnicity*. New York: Oxford University Press, 1989.

Sollors, Werner, ed. *Theories of Ethnicity*. New York: New York University Press, 1996.

Solomon, Alisa. *Wonder of Wonders: A Cultural History of "Fiddler on the Roof."* New York: Henry Holt, 2013.

Soloveitchik, Haym. "Rupture and Reconstruction: The Transformation of Contemporary Orthodoxy." *Tradition* 28 (1994): 64–130.

Soyer, Daniel. "Between Two Worlds: The Jewish Landsmanshaftn and Questions of Immigrant Identity." *American Jewish History* 76 (1986): 5–25.

Soyer, Daniel. *Jewish Immigrant Associations and American Identity in New York, 1880–1939*. Cambridge: Harvard University Press, 1997.

Soyer, Daniel. "Documenting Immigrant Lives at an Immigrant Institution: The YIVO Autobiographical Contest of 1942." *Jewish Social Studies* 5 (1999): 218–43.

Soyer, Daniel. "Back to the Future: American Jews Visit the Soviet Union in the 1920s and 1930s." *Jewish Social Studies* 6 (2000): 124–59.

Soyer, Daniel. "Revisiting the Old World: American-Jewish Tourists in Inter-War Eastern Europe." In *Forging Modern Jewish Identities: Public and Private Struggles*, edited by Michael Berkowitz, Susan L. Tananbaum, and Sam W. Bloom, 16–38. London: Valentine Mitchell, 2003.

Soyer, Daniel. "Yiddish Scholars Meet the Yiddish-Speaking Masses: Language, the Americanization of YIVO, and the Autobiography Contest of 1942." In *Yiddish in America: Essays on Yiddish Culture in the Golden Land*, edited by Edward S. Shapiro, 55–79. Scranton: University of Scranton Press, 2008.

Soyer, Daniel. "Transnationalism and Mutual Influence: American and East European Jewries in the 1920s and 1930s." In *Rethinking European Jewish History*, edited by Jeremy Cohen and Moshe Rosman, 201–20. Oxford: Littman, 2009.

Staub, Michael. *Torn at the Roots: The Crisis of Jewish Liberalism in Postwar America*. New York: Columbia University Press, 2002.

Stier, Oren Baruch. "Memory Matters: Reading Collective Memory in Contemporary Jewish Culture." *Prooftexts* 18 (1998): 67–82.

Strassfeld, Sharon and Michael Strassfeld. *The Second Jewish Catalog: Sources and Resources*. Philadelphia: Jewish Publication Society, 1976.

Svonkin, Stuart. *Jews Against Prejudice: American Jews and the Fight for Civil Liberties*. New York: Columbia University Press, 1997.

Tobias, Henry J. *The Jewish Bund in Russia From Its Origins to 1905*. Stanford: Stanford University Press, 1972.

Trunk, Isaiah. "The Cultural Dimension of the American Jewish Labor Movement." *YIVO Annual of Jewish Social Science* XVI (1976): 342–93.
Twersky, David. "Left Right, Left Right: After Half a Century, *Commentary* Remains Defiantly Out of Step." *Moment* 20 (1995): 40–45, 57–59.
Veidlinger, Jeffrey. *Jewish Public Culture in the Late Russian Empire*. Bloomington: Indiana University Press, 2009.
Vromen, Suzanne. "Maurice Halbwachs and the Concept of Nostalgia." *Knowledge and Society* 6 (1986): 55–66.
Vromen, Suzanne. "The Ambiguity of Nostalgia." *YIVO Annual of Jewish Social Science* 21 (1993): 69–86.
Wald, Alan M. *The New York Intellectuals: The Rise and Decline of the Anti-Stalinist Left From the 1930s to the 1980s*. Chapel Hill, NC: University of North Carolina Press, 1987.
Wall, Wendy. *Inventing the "American Way:" The Politics of Consensus from the New Deal to the Civil Rights Movement*. Oxford: Oxford University Press, 2008.
Waters, Mary C. *Ethnic Options: Choosing Identities in America*. Berkeley: University of California Press, 1990.
Weinberg, David H. *Between Tradition and Modernity: Haim Zhitlovsky, Simon Dubnow, Ahad Ha'am, and the Shaping of Modern Jewish Identity*. New York: Holmes & Meier, 1996.
Weinberger, Theodore. "Yiddish Literature as Secular Jewish Scripture: The World of Irving Howe." In *Yiddish Language and Culture: Then and Now,* edited by Leonard Jay Greenspoon, 233–45. Omaha: Creighton University Press, 1998.
Wenger, Beth S. *New York Jews and the Great Depression: Uncertain Promise*. New Haven: Yale University Press, 1996.
Wenger, Beth S. *History Lessons: The Creation of American Jewish Heritage*. Princeton: Princeton University Press, 2010.
Wertheimer, Jack. *Unwelcome Strangers: East European Jews in Imperial Germany*. New York: Oxford University Press, 1991.
Wertheimer, Jack, ed. *The Uses of Tradition: Jewish Continuity in the Modern Era*. New York: Jewish Theological Seminary, 1992.
Wertheimer, Jack. *A People Divided: Judaism in Contemporary America*. New York: Basic, 1993.
Wertheimer, Jack, ed. *Tradition Renewed: A History of the Jewish Theological Seminary of America [2 vols]*. New York: Jewish Theological Seminary, 1997.
Wertheimer, Jack, ed. *Imagining the American Jewish Community*. Waltham: Brandeis University Press/Hanover: University Press of New England, 2007.
White, Hayden. *Metahistory: The Historical Imagination in Nineteenth-Century Europe*. Baltimore: Johns Hopkins University Press, 1973.
Whitfield, Stephen J. "The Ethnicity of the New York Intellectuals." *Revue LISA/LISA e-journal* 1 (2003): 179–89.
Whitfield, Stephen J. "Fiddling with Sholem Aleichem: A History of Fiddler on the Roof." In *Key Texts in American Jewish Culture,* edited by Jack Kugelmass, 105–25. New Brunswick: Rutgers University Press, 2003.
Wirth-Nesher, Hana and Michael P. Kramer, eds. *The Cambridge Companion to Jewish American Literature*. Cambridge: Cambridge University Press, 2003.
Wisse, Ruth R. "Ups and Downs of Yiddish in America." In *Yiddish in America: Essays on Yiddish Culture in the Golden Land,* edited by Edward S. Shapiro, 1–21. Scranton: University of Scranton Press, 2008.

Wodak, Ruth, Rudolf de Cillia, Martin Reisigl, and Karin Liebhart. *The Discursive Construction of National Identity*. Edinburgh: Edinburgh University Press, 1999.

Wolff, Larry. *Inventing Eastern Europe: The Map of Civilization on the Mind of the Enlightenment*. Stanford: Stanford University Press, 1994.

Wolitz, Seth. "The Americanization of Tevye or Boarding the Jewish 'Mayflower,'" *American Quarterly* 40 (1988): 514–36.

Wurzburger, Walter. "Rav Joseph B. Soloveitchik as Posek of Post-Modern Orthodoxy." *Tradition* 29 (1994): 5–20.

Wyler, Marjorie G. "The Eternal Light: Judaism on the Airwaves." *Conservative Judaism* 39 (1986/87): 18–22.

Yerushalmi, Yosef Hayim. *Zakhor: Jewish History and Jewish Memory*. New York: Schocken, 1989; orig. publ. 1982.

Yerushalmi, Yosef Hayim. "Exile and Expulsion in Jewish History." In *Crisis and Creativity in the Sephardic World, 1391–1648*, edited by Benjamin R. Gampel, 3–22. New York: Columbia University Press, 1997.

Zerubavel, Yael. *Recovered Roots: Collective Memory and the Making of Israeli National Tradition*. Chicago: University of Chicago Press, 1995.

Zipperstein, Steven J. "*Commentary* and American Jewish Culture in the 1940s and 1950s." *Jewish Social Studies* 3 (1997): 18–28.

Zipperstein, Steven J. *Imagining Russian Jewry: Memory, History, Identity*. Seattle: University of Washington Press, 1999.

Zipperstein, Steven J. "American Jews and the European Gaze." *American Jewish History* 91 (2003): 379–86.

Zipperstein, Steven J. *Rosenfeld's Lives: Fame, Oblivion, and the Furies of Writing*. New Haven: Yale University Press, 2009.

Index

Affiliation 24, 38, 40, 42, 44, 132, 242
Ahad Ha'am (Asher Ginzberg) 83, 91, 99, 101
Americanization 16, 21, 25, 29, 31, 48, 66, 87, 91, 97, 132, 133, 135, 136, 146, 148, 176, 241–243
American Jewish Committee (AJC) 29, 38, 81, 87, 183
American Jewish Congress 38, 59, 98
American Jewish Tercentenary (1954) 45, 46, 52, 77, 89, 101, 122, 162, 200, 248
Anderson, Benedict 254
Anti-Semitism 22, 27, 31, 32, 37, 38, 96, 148, 149, 155, 234
A Social and Religious History of the Jews (Baron) 244
Assimilation 42, 58, 67, 79, 80, 101, 140, 152, 241, 242, 247, 254
Assimilation in American Life (M. Gordon) 242
A Treasury of Yiddish Stories (Howe/Greenberg) 220, 224–226

Ba'al Shem Tov (Israel Ben Eliezer) 115, 141, 172, 200, 202, 205
Bamberger, Bernard 125
Baron, Salo W. 244
Baskin, Joseph 146, 155
Bell, Daniel 92, 221, 239
Bellow, Saul 32, 78, 220, 225, 231
Ben Gurion, David 29
Berkovits, Eliezer 100
Blanton, Smiley 31
Blaustein, Jacob 29
Bokser, Ben-Zion 99
Borowitz, Eugene 124
Bourdieu, Pierre 15
Buber, Martin 1, 71, 89, 90, 93, 101, 200, 201–205, 207, 209, 211
Bund 75, 90, 145, 146, 148, 151
Burning Lights (B. Chagall) 215

Cahan, Abraham 33, 155
Central Conference of American Rabbis (CCAR, Reform) 52, 121

Cohen, Elliot 71–72, 74, 77–80, 82–84, 86–87, 90, 94
Cold War 9, 14, 18, 21, 26, 30, 38, 78, 147, 165, 194, 235, 259
Commentary (journal) 4, 7, 10, 16, 17, 21, 22, 35, 48, 57, 60, 71–79, 81, 82, 84–86, 88–90, 92–94, 96, 102, 107, 125, 184, 185, 200, 201, 204, 205, 207, 210, 219, 223, 231–233, 238, 239, 247, 249
Communism 1, 17, 25, 26, 27, 30, 38, 75, 121, 122, 144, 147–149, 151, 160, 194, 198, 204, 205, 247, 249, 259, 260
Conservative Judaism 4, 119, 124, 126–32, 140, 189
Coughlin, Father Charles 37
Czarism 58, 121, 145, 149, 154, 165, 175, 195

Dawidowicz, Lucy S. 182, 202
Decter, Midge 92
Decter, Moshe 185
Diaspora 11, 29, 30, 58, 60, 150, 245
Diaspora nationalism 245
Discourse analysis 14–15
Distinctiveness, Jewish 5, 6, 22, 38, 79, 83, 85, 101, 123, 127, 146, 147, 176, 178, 226, 245, 252, 259
Dos Lebendike Vort (Yefroiken/Bass) 198, 199
Dos Yiddishe Vort 133, 135, 138, 141
Dresner, Samuel 128
Dubnow, Shimon 49, 50, 60, 91, 151, 202, 244, 245

Efron, Zalman *see* Yefroiken, Zalman
Eichmann, Adolf (trial) 13
Elberg, Simcha 139, 140
"Eli the Fanatic" (Roth) 11, 233
Ethnicity 6–8, 10, 12, 16–18, 21, 23, 37, 38, 40, 42, 58, 59, 68, 82, 92, 120, 124, 125, 127, 129, 132, 141, 146, 147, 156, 157, 176, 183, 185, 214, 217, 219, 225, 233, 237, 239, 241–244, 250, 254, 255, 258
Ethnography 167, 179, 181, 182, 184, 185–88, 215, 216, 219, 222, 225, 228, 238, 245

Exile 11, 76, 196, 240
Exodus (Uris) 30

Fackenheim, Emil 97, 123
Faith is the Answer (Blanton/Peale) 31
Fein, Richard 102, 257, 258
Fiddler on the Roof (musical) 5, 11, 16, 17, 157, 168, 188, 212, 234–244, 249, 258
Fiedler, Leslie 201, 207, 209, 210, 223, 224
Finkelstein, Louis 39, 170–71, 175
Forverts (newspaper) 1, 2, 149, 151, 155, 230
Frank, Anne 27
Freehof, Solomon B. 29
Freud, Sigmund 31, 44, 53, 57
Friedlaender, Israel 129

Gamoran, Emanuel 195
Gamoran, Mamie 189, 191
Gans, Herbert 242
Geertz, Clifford 13
Gentleman's Agreement (movie) 32
Gersh, Harry 10, 22, 23, 24, 35, 36, 39, 40, 44
"Gimpel the Fool" (I. B. Singer) 231
Gittelsohn, Roland 125
Glatzer, Nahum N. 92
Glazer, Nathan 81
Goldberg, Itche 156
Goldin, Judah 88, 213
Gold, Michael 33
Goodbye Columbus (Roth) 33
Goodman, Henry 155, 232
Goodman, Saul 91, 99
Gordis, Robert 28, 98, 100–02
Gordon, Albert 22
Gordon, Milton 242
Goren, Arthur 8
Grayzel, Solomon 48, 168
Greenberg, Clement 92, 207
Greenberg, Eliezer 224–25
Greenberg, Hayim 148, 248–49

Halakhah 115–118, 120, 141
Halakhic Man (Soloveitchik) 110, 113–17
Halbwachs, Maurice 252, 253
Halpern, Ben 43
Handlin, Oscar 23, 34, 46, 71, 244

Hansen, Marcus Lee 7, 187, 222, 235, 242, 255
Harap, Louis 148
Haredi Orthodoxy 25, 66, 113
Hasidism 1, 3, 4, 13, 17, 19, 20, 71, 85, 89, 90, 99, 104, 109, 110, 114, 115, 117, 118, 130, 131, 142, 155, 169, 172, 176–78, 189, 200–10, 221, 223, 226, 230, 259
Haskalah 108, 113, 181, 196, 202, 226
Hebrew 29, 32, 40, 55, 65, 67, 90, 99, 114, 119, 124, 155, 191, 192, 213, 224, 259
Herberg, Will 42, 43, 97, 201, 242
Hertzberg, Arthur 73, 74, 76, 89, 91, 249, 250, 253
Hervieu-Léger, Danièle 251–53
Herzog, Elizabeth 180
Heschel, Abraham Joshua 1, 3, 4, 19, 26, 28, 50, 52, 71, 74, 75, 84, 90, 92, 93, 97, 101, 103–111, 116, 118, 119, 122, 130, 131, 143, 159, 164, 201, 203, 210, 215, 226
Historiography 197, 244–46, 256, 257
Hobsbawm, Eric 254
Holocaust 5, 12, 13, 19–21, 25–30, 37, 48–51, 62, 63, 73, 74, 78, 86, 88, 104, 121, 132, 139, 140, 145, 153, 155, 159, 164, 182, 187, 191, 194, 195, 198, 199, 214, 216–19, 225, 227, 229, 233–35, 254, 255
Howe, Irving 76, 80, 82, 212, 224–27, 238–40

Identity, Jewish 6, 8, 10, 12, 13, 15–17, 19, 21, 24, 27, 29, 32, 34, 40, 42, 44, 47, 48, 53, 55, 57–60, 63, 66, 68, 71–73, 76–79, 82, 83, 87, 88, 90, 94, 98, 115, 116, 125–28, 132, 146, 150, 154, 156, 157, 168, 172, 177, 184, 188, 189, 190–92, 196, 201, 202, 208, 209, 214, 217, 218, 224–26, 228, 237, 239, 241, 244, 247, 249, 250, 252, 253, 256–59
Immigration 6, 18, 22, 25, 26, 29, 35, 47, 56, 57, 120, 126, 139, 140, 143, 145, 151, 155, 173, 186, 187, 214, 234, 236, 241, 244
Interfaith relations 38, 39, 85, 112, 171, 175
Interwar years (U.S.) 3, 8, 10, 11, 12, 20, 22, 23, 24, 38, 44, 144, 146, 190, 191, 229, 240
Israel *see* State of Israel

Jewish Currents (journal, successor of [Communist] *Jewish Life*) 148, 149, 157, 183, 204, 205
Jewish Forum (journal) 133, 136–38
Jewish Frontier (journal) 148, 150, 152, 153, 155, 159, 185, 186, 248
Jewish Identity on the Suburban Frontier (Sklare/Greenblum) 34
Jewish left 24, 26, 78, 144–47, 153, 154, 156, 157, 160, 162–64, 166, 183, 198, 205, 210, 213, 247
Jewish Life (journal, *Morning Freiheit Association*, Communist; succeeded by *Jewish Currents*) 148–58, 161–63
Jewish Life (journal, Orthodox; successor of *Orthodox Union*) 133–37, 148
Jewishness 5–11, 15–18, 21–25, 30, 31, 33–40, 42–44, 47, 48, 52–58, 60, 61, 64, 65, 67, 69–71, 73–94, 96, 98, 99, 101, 102, 105, 107, 108, 116, 120, 122, 124–31, 140–44, 146, 147, 150, 152–54, 156, 158–60, 162–66, 169, 172, 176–79, 183–92, 194, 196–200, 203, 204, 207, 209–12, 214, 215, 217–19, 222, 223, 226–28, 230, 232–37, 239, 240, 241, 243, 246, 247, 249, 250, 255–60
Jewish Publication Society (JPS) 167, 168
Jewish Theological Seminary (Conservative) 4, 39, 104, 126, 129, 170, 171, 174
Jews in Suburbia (A. Gordon) 22
Jews Without Money (Gold) 33
Judaism (journal) 97–103, 108, 118, 119, 125, 143, 164, 178, 187, 204, 205, 257–58
Judaism as a Civilization (Kaplan) 196
Judeo-Christian tradition 42, 175, 176

Kahn, Benjamin 130, 183
Kallen, Horace 52, 59, 79, 102
Kaplan, Mordecai Menahem 83, 108, 190
Katz, Jacob 202, 244
Kazan, Elia 32
Kazin, Alfred 207, 208, 225
Keeping Posted (journal) 191
Kieval, Herman 129
Klaperman, Gilbert and Libby 189, 191, 193, 194, 196, 197

Kligsberg, Moses 56, 63–65
Knopf, Alfred E. (publisher) 169
Knox, Israel 78, 147, 151, 152, 158–65, 217, 231
Kranzler, Gershon 206
Kristol, Irving 90
Kurzweil, Baruch 99–101

Landsmanshaftn 24, 25, 26, 35, 57, 63, 215
Lestshinsky, Jacob 153
Levi-Yitshak of Berditchev 172, 176, 205, 206
Liebman, Joshua Loth 31, 44, 172
Life is with People (Zborowski/Herzog) 11, 17, 27, 44, 130, 131, 162, 167, 179, 181–88, 215, 225, 238, 245
Lindbergh, Charles 37
Lithuania 62, 110, 111, 114–16, 248
Lower East Side (New York) 243

Mahler, Raphael 52
Mailer, Norman 71, 205, 207, 209, 210
Marjorie Morningstar (Wouk) 33
Mark, Yudel 66, 185, 198, 199
Mead, Margaret 179, 180, 182, 184
Memory 5, 6, 7, 15–18, 49, 73–75, 82, 89, 94, 106, 107, 115, 117, 119, 121, 143, 152, 158, 161–67, 182, 189, 199, 202, 217, 231, 235, 237, 239, 241, 243, 245, 247–58
Mendele Mocher Sforim (Sholem Yankev Abramovitz) 75, 130, 131, 150, 151, 155, 157, 163, 212, 225, 228, 229
Menorah Journal 79
Mitnagdim 110, 116, 117
Monroe, Marilyn 27
Morawska, Ewa 6, 10, 15
"Morning Freiheit" (organization) 25
Moscow 26, 27, 121, 149
Mostel, Zero 30, 237
Musar movement 117, 123, 172
Myerson, Bess (Miss America 1945) 32

National Community Relations Advisory Council (NCRAC) 38
Nazi Germany 1, 26, 37
New Jewish History (Gamoran) 189
Newman, Paul 30

New York 1, 2, 11, 23, 25, 32, 47, 48, 50, 51, 62, 66, 68, 71, 75, 78, 88–99, 111, 133, 139, 170, 191, 200, 206, 218, 219, 220, 234, 240
Niger, Shmuel 83, 86, 101, 215

Orthodox Judaism 13, 26, 28, 64, 65, 100, 110–13, 115, 116, 118, 119, 121, 126, 127, 131–38, 140–42, 174, 187, 189, 204, 206, 207, 210, 222, 233, 259
Orthodox Union (journal, succeeded by *Jewish Life*) 135, 141

Palestine 28, 65
Partisan Review (journal) 78, 84, 85, 219, 220, 231
Parzen, Herbert 4, 71, 74, 92, 98, 99
Passage from Home (Rosenfeld) 212, 221
Peace of Mind (Liebman) 31, 44, 172
Peale, Norman Vincent 31
Peck, Gregory 32
Peoplehood, Jewish 11, 120, 124–127, 151, 164, 196, 237, 246, 255
Peretz, Yitzhak/Isaac Leib 50, 58, 85, 125, 142, 150, 157, 163, 172, 179, 187, 212, 222–226, 229, 232
Pessin, Deborah 189, 191, 193, 195–197
Petuchowski, Jakob 84
Pilchik, Ely 123
Playboy (magazine) 27
Podhoretz, Norman 78, 82, 89, 90, 183, 200, 207, 210, 240
Poland 1, 4, 11, 14, 19, 20, 27, 49, 56, 85, 92, 110, 136, 152, 159, 173, 193, 194, 145, 218, 223, 230, 231
Presley, Elvis 27
Prince of the Ghetto (Samuel) 85, 169, 223
Protestant – Catholic – Jew (Herberg) 42, 242
Psychology 30, 31, 35, 44, 48, 53–58, 69, 76, 114, 141, 143, 159

Rabbinical Assembly (Conservative) 52
Raddock, Charles 133, 140–42, 204, 206, 207
Rahv, Philip 207
Reform Judaism 29, 52, 84, 110, 119–25, 127, 131, 133, 136, 140, 189, 196, 205, 206
Reich, Nathan 58, 59, 60, 66

Religious revival 39, 40, 91, 133
Riesman, David 76
Roosevelt, Franklin D. 37
Rosenberg case 27, 147
Rosenfeld, Isaac 71, 85, 212, 219
Rosenzweig, Franz 7, 71, 90, 92, 204, 222
Roth, Philip 11, 33, 69, 76, 83, 233
Russia 14, 27, 58, 106, 121, 122, 144, 152, 155, 156, 165

Salanter, Israel 123, 172, 174–76
Samuel, Maurice 85, 153, 154, 159, 162, 168, 169, 177, 212, 218, 222, 229
Schappes, Morris 148, 149
Schocken Books (New York) 168, 187
Schor, Ilya 131
Schorsch, Ismar 218
Schwarzschild, Steven 205
Secularism 24, 40, 65, 96, 98, 99, 141, 144, 155, 159, 165, 198, 210
Shankman, Jacob 122
Sherman, C. Bezalel 100, 150, 152, 162
Shneerson, Yosef Yitshak 1, 2, 3, 19, 26, 208, 234
Sholom Aleichem *see* Sholem Aleichem
Sholem Aleichem (Shalom Rabinovitz) 30, 90, 99, 101, 123, 136, 150, 155, 157, 162, 163, 169, 172, 175, 177–79, 187, 212–17, 219–23, 225, 226, 228, 229, 234, 236
Shtetl 3, 10, 11, 17, 20, 25, 27, 35, 44, 50, 75, 92, 130, 137, 139, 160, 162, 173, 174, 177, 179, 180–182, 184–86, 188, 214, 216, 221, 225, 227–31, 234–36, 239, 248, 252, 258
Shuchat, Wilfred 30, 44, 130, 183
Shulman, Charles 122, 125
Sinclair, Jo 152
Singer, Isaac Bashevis 85, 172, 225, 230, 233
Sitarski, Marian Jerzy (cover image) 19, 20
Six Day War (1967) 28
Sklare, Marshall 33, 34, 41, 42
Socialism 17, 65, 76, 144, 148, 155, 156, 160, 165, 181, 190, 198, 205, 145
"sociological Jewishness" (Berman) 43
Social sciences 5, 10, 32, 43, 47, 52, 53, 56, 61, 63, 72, 76, 183, 184, 197, 202, 241, 245

Sollors, Werner 254, 255
Soloveitchik, Joseph B. 97, 110–19, 133
Sontag, Susan 85
Soviet Union 1, 11, 14, 27, 38, 122, 144, 148, 149, 151, 172, 182, 198, 235, 259
Stanislawow (Poland) 19
State of Israel 21, 28–30, 40, 49, 78, 100, 113, 122–24, 129, 131, 133, 138, 147, 151, 155, 165, 172, 174, 176, 200, 210, 217, 225, 240, 255
Steinberg, Milton 96, 97, 102
Suburbanization 21, 24, 31, 33–36, 39–42, 44, 58, 81, 119, 124, 132, 133, 190, 240, 243
"symbolic ethnicity" (Gans) 242, 255
Synagogue 9, 13, 15, 24, 29, 34, 39–44, 96, 107, 115, 118, 119, 121, 124, 132, 133, 135, 179, 194, 208, 215

Tales of the Hasidim (Buber) 201
"Tevye" (Sholem Aleichem/*Fiddler on the Roof*) 30, 136, 157, 177, 212, 214, 215, 217, 234–38, 243, 244
Textbooks 13, 17, 167, 188, 189–92, 195–99, 249
The Adventures of Augie March (Bellow) 32, 78
The Earth is the Lord's (Heschel) 90, 105, 159, 215
"The East European Era in Jewish History" (Heschel) 105
The Golden Tradition (Dawidowicz) 182
The Jewish People (Pessin) 189
The Rise of David Levinsky (Cahan) 33
The Rise of the Unmeltable Ethnics (Novak) 43
The Story of the Jewish People (Klaperman/ Klaperman) 189
The World of Sholom Aleichem (Samuel) 13, 168, 169, 183, 212, 213, 215, 217–19

Vilna 1, 25, 50, 62, 66, 104, 110, 114, 115, 117, 161, 172, 207
Vilna Gaon 110, 114, 115, 172, 207
Vishniac, Roman 13, 49, 238
Volozhin Yeshivah 90, 110, 117, 172

Warsaw 51, 66, 75, 92, 104, 111, 155, 204, 230, 231
Wasteland (Sinclair) 152, 159, 160
Weiner, Herbert 206, 207
Weinreich, Max 1–3, 16, 19, 47, 48, 50, 53–60, 63, 65–69, 71, 76, 91, 92, 210, 234
Weinreich, Uriel 27
White, Hayden 257
Wishengrad, Morton 171
Workmen's Circle 13, 24, 25, 33, 42, 146, 147, 149, 151–59, 162–65, 190, 217
Workmen's Circle Call (journal) 152, 153, 155, 158, 159, 161, 165, 205, 224
World Over (journal) 190
Wouk, Herman 33

Yefroiken [Efron], Zalman 161, 190, 198
Yerushalmi, Yosef Hayim 218, 251, 256, 257
Yeshivah 35, 110, 111, 114, 116, 122, 133, 138, 140, 215
Yeshiva University (Orthodox) 112, 203
Yiddish 1–4, 11–13, 16, 19, 20, 25, 27, 29, 30, 32, 39, 47, 48, 50–53, 55, 60, 61, 63, 65–70, 73, 75, 81, 82, 87, 89, 91, 92, 94, 104, 105, 133, 136, 138, 140–42, 148, 154–57, 159–62, 165, 169, 177, 178, 189, 190, 197–200, 213–215, 217, 219–21, 223–30, 232, 234, 247–49, 259
Yiddishism 52, 61, 65, 67, 79, 82, 94, 101, 141, 142, 144, 153, 155, 156, 158, 159, 161, 166, 185, 198, 199, 213, 247
Yiddishkayt 7, 22, 36, 61, 65, 87, 101, 108, 119, 126, 129, 132, 141, 142, 144, 147, 159, 165, 199, 224, 227, 250
YIVO (Institute for Jewish Research) 1, 2, 4, 13, 16, 25, 47–73, 75, 81, 82, 91, 93, 94, 105, 107, 141, 144, 159–61, 165, 172, 175, 185, 210, 245, 246, 249

Zakhor (Yerushalmi) 256
Zborowski, Mark 180–85, 187, 188
Zhitlosvski, Khayim 163
Zionism 11, 29, 43, 51, 65, 148, 150, 151, 155, 161, 181, 182, 215, 255
Zukerman, Jacob 33

www.ingramcontent.com/pod-product-compliance
Lightning Source LLC
Chambersburg PA
CBHW030609230426
43661CB00053B/1912